BASIC ELECTRONICS TECHNOLOGY

Alvis J. Evans, BS, MS
Assistant Professor
Tarrant County Junior College

Jerry D. Mullen, BS, MEd.
Associate Professor
Tarrant County Junior College

Danny H. Smith, BS
Instructor
Tarrant County Junior College

WITH CONTRIBUTIONS BY:

Editors:

   Gerald Luecke, MSEE
   Mgr. Product Development
   Kenneth M. Krone

Editorial Staff:

   Charles W. Battle
   Leslie E. Mansir

Texas Instruments Information Publishing Center

TEXAS INSTRUMENTS

P.O. Box 225474, MS-8218 • Dallas, Texas 75265

THIS BOOK WAS DEVELOPED BY:

The Staff of the Texas Instruments Information Publishing Center
P.O. Box 225474,MS8218
Dallas, Texas 75265

FOR MARKETING AND DISTRIBUTION INQUIRE TO:

Orm F. Henning
Marketing Manager
P.O. Box 225474,MS8218
Dallas, Texas 75265

ACKNOWLEDGEMENTS:

Appreciation is expressed to Hewlett-Packard Company for
supplying equipment photographs, to Don Falk for his comments,
and Darlene Evans for her review and contributions during her
word processing.

WORD PROCESSING:

Betty Brown

DESIGN AND ARTWORK BY:

Plunk Design

ISBN 0-89512-179-4
Library of Congress Catalog Number: 85-50218

TABLE OF CONTENTS

PREFACE

This book is an overview of electronic technology. Its contents are based upon semiconductor devices and integrated circuits. It centers on the application of semiconductor electronic circuits in systems.

But it is more than a circuits application book, it is also a systems application book. It explains the basic concepts for accomplishing a particular function electronically, supports the circuit and system discussions with added theory as necessary for understanding the circuit or system principles, and enhances the discussion with practical worked-out examples. It is divided into two major parts — analog and digital. The mathematics used are restricted to simple arithmetic and simple algebra. Scientific notation is used to simplify the calculations, and electron current flow is used throughout the book to avoid the conflicting discussion of conventional current.

Since semiconductor devices are used throughout the book, the book begins with a discussion of how diodes, transistors, and the different types of semiconductor devices operate.

A discussion of the use of such active devices in basic amplifier and oscillator circuits is followed by a description of the operation of audio circuits, AM/FM radio circuits, and TV with its full spectrum of video circuits, including VCR's (video cassette recorders).

Every electronic system needs a power supply, therefore, a chapter is devoted to discussing voltage regulated and current regulated power supplies, both continuous and switching.

In like fashion, a chapter is devoted to test equipment, and a chapter on troubleshooting audio, radio, and TV circuits completes the analog part of the book.

The digital part of the book begins with a chapter that contains a general discussion of digital circuits explaining and reviewing combinational and sequential digital circuits. A second chapter develops microprocessor system concepts and a third explains solid-state memories used in microcomputer systems.

Since computers must talk with each other, with other digital equipment, and with humans, all the types of interface circuits used for communicating are discussed, showing standards for signals and hardware interconnections.

The book concludes with a chapter on detecting problems in and maintaining microcomputer systems.

Even with such a broad scope coverage, we have attempted to give an in-depth look at the basic circuits and functions that make up the electronic systems of yesterday, today, and in the future, so that one volume would provide a quick reference for the engineer, technician, beginning student or technically interested consumer. We hope we have succeeded.

A.E., J.M., D.S.

BASIC SEMICONDUCTOR COMPONENTS

INTRODUCTION

The main purpose of any semiconductor device is to control the flow of electrons. It accomplishes this because of its valve-like effect on a circuit. The semiconductor becomes the so-called "active" part of the circuit, whereas the other components, such as resistors, capacitors, and coils are the so-called passive components. We shall see how components like diodes, transistors and integrated circuits have been developed to perform some pretty sophisticated tricks to make electrons do just what we want them to do.

In this chapter, we will cover the basic concepts of semiconductor (solid-state) devices, how they operate, and what they do in a circuit. This is an important chapter because it provides the foundation for many of the concepts covered in subsequent chapters.

First, we will cover the fundamentals of semiconductor technology which are common to all solid-state components. This is followed by information on diodes and bipolar signal transistors. Next, the different types of field-effect transistors, which represent a significant evolvement in solid-state technology, are described. Then, the area of power semiconductors is covered. The chapter ends with a discussion about one of the most sophisticated applications of solid-state technology to date — that of integrated circuits.

BASIC SEMICONDUCTOR THEORY

Atomic Structure and Semiconductors

The atom is made up of a nucleus orbited by tiny negatively-charged particles called electrons, as illustrated in *Figure 1.1a*. The electron orbits are arranged in shells (or rings) surrounding the nucleus, as illustrated in *Figure 1.1b*. The nucleus is made up of protons and neutrons. A proton has a positive charge equal in magnitude, but opposite in polarity to that of an electron. A neutron has no charge.

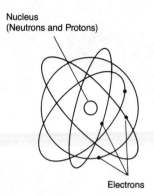

a. Electrons Orbiting the Nucleus

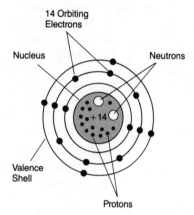

b. A Silicon Atom

Figure 1.1   The Structure of an Atom

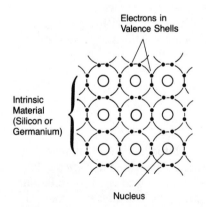

Figure 1.2   Crystal Structure Held Together by Covalent Bonding

The outermost shell, called the valence shell, contains a maximum of eight electrons. Elements with five or more electrons in the outer shell are electrical insulators, elements with four electrons in the outer shell are semiconductors, and elements with one to three electrons in the outer shell are electrical conductors. Although all three types of elements have a place in electronics, it is semiconductor materials that have made possible the sophistication of today's technology.

Silicon (Si) and germanium (Ge) are the two most common semiconductor elements used as semiconductor devices. The atoms of the elements are joined together by what is called covalent bonding to form a crystalline structure. Each atom has four electrons in its outer shell. When they form a crystalline structure, as in *Figure 1.2*, each atom shares its four electrons with the adjoining atoms. This sharing of electrons causes the atoms to act as if each had eight electrons in its outer shell. As a result the crystalline substrate becomes very electrically stable, acting like an insulator.

Silicon and germanium, in their pure form are referred to as intrinsic materials. To make these materials useful for semiconductors, impurities must be added so that the material can conduct electricity. The process of adding impurities is called doping. The two types of impurities used for doping are called trivalent and pentavalent; trivalent, meaning three electrons in the valence shell and pentavalent, meaning five electrons in the valence shell.

Figure 1.3a is an example of a semiconductor crystalline structure with a pentavalent impurity. The common pentavalent impurities are arsenic, antimony, bismuth, and phosphorous. Four of the five electrons of the pentavalent material are shared with the other surrounding atoms, and the fifth electron is a free electron. Since pentavalent doping allows the material to contribute free electrons, it then becomes what is called a donor. Because the charged carrier is the electron (electrons have a negative charge), the crystalline structure is referred to as N-type semiconductor material. When a voltage is applied to N-type material, the free electrons in this material will flow from the negative potential toward the positive potential.

Figure 1.3b is an example of trivalent doping. The common trivalent impurities are aluminum, indium, gallium, and boron. Because the trivalent material has only three electrons in its outer shell, a vacancy or a hole is left. Since the impurity has created a hole which can accept an electron, it is called an acceptor. The charged carrier in this type of material is the hole, which is a positive charged carrier, and this material is referred to as P-type semiconductor material. When a voltage is applied to P-type material, the holes are said to flow from the positive potential toward the negative potential. This phenomenon, known as hole flow, is possible only in P-type material.

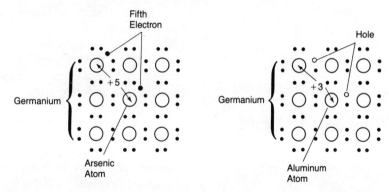

a. N-Type Semiconductor Crystal Created by Pentavalent Doping

b. P-Type Semiconductor Crystal Created by Trivalent Doping

Figure 1.3 Doping Semiconductor Materials

When a voltage is applied to P-type material, as in *Figure 1.4*, an electron will move to the closest hole between it and the positive potential. Consider each section of *Figure 1.4* as one frame of a movie film. When the electron in frame A jumps to the hole, a new hole is created in the electron's place, indicated by the hole in frame B. When the electron in frame B jumps toward the positive potential and into the hole, a new hole is created by its vacancy in frame C. This process continues as long as there are holes available, and new holes are continually created as electrons leave the P-type material to go to the positive terminal of the applied potential.

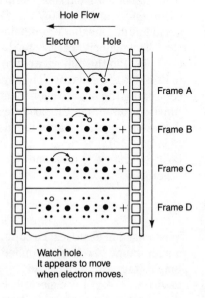

Watch hole.
It appears to move
when electron moves.

Figure 1.4 Hole Flow in P-Type Semiconductor Material

As you look at the frames A through D, it appears the hole has moved from positive to negative. A common misconception is that hole flow and conventional current flow (positive to negative) are the same. Hole flow occurs only in P-type semiconductor material, whereas electron flow occurs in N-type semiconductor materials and in conductors.

Semiconductor Diodes

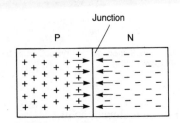

a. Electrons and Holes Drifting Together at Junction

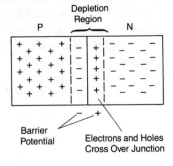

b. Electron and Hole Accumulation in Area of Junction

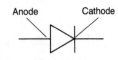

c. Symbol

Figure 1.5 P-N Junction Showing Electron and Hole Flow

A semiconductor diode is made up of both N-type and P-type materials physically formed together. The N material forms the cathode of the diode, and the P material forms the anode. Where the two types of materials meet each other during their manufacture is called the P-N junction (*Figure 1.5a*).

The holes in the P material are attracted to the electrons in the N material, and likewise the electrons in the N material are attracted to the holes in the P material. The electrons along the edge of the junction drift across the junction and fill the holes along the P side, leaving vacancies or holes on the N side, as illustrated in *Figure 1.5b*.

This process of drifting, or diffusion, will stop after a few electrons have crossed the junction to the P material. The electrons on the P side create a negative potential which repels any additional electrons that might try to cross the junction. Likewise, the holes on the N side create a positive potential which repels any other holes that might attempt to cross the junction. This potential across the P-N junction is referred to as a potential hill or a barrier potential. Typical barrier potentials at room temperature are 0.7 volt for silicon and 0.3 volt for germanium. The diode symbol is shown in *Figure 1.5c*.

The majority carrier for P-type semiconductor material is the hole, and the majority carrier for N-type semiconductor material is the electron. The region on the P side of the junction containing the negative ions, and the region on the N side of the junction containing the positive ions, are jointly referred to as the depletion region, because it is depleted of the majority carrier (*Figure 1.5b*). The depletion region has an equal number of positive-charge ions on one side and negative-charge ions on the other side.

Diode Biasing

When used in electrical circuits, semiconductor devices will have a wide range of voltages applied. These voltages, referred to as bias voltages, and the resulting currents determine how the device will react in an electrical circuit. In this section, we will discuss the effects these voltages have on the junction diode.

Reverse-Biased Diode

If an external bias voltage is applied to the P-N junction of the diode, as shown in *Figure 1.6a*, the bias voltage is negative on the P side and positive on the N side. The electrons (majority carriers) in the N material will be drawn away from the P-N junction and toward the positive terminal of the bias voltage. Likewise, the holes (majority carriers) of the P side will be drawn away from the P-N junction toward the negative terminal of the bias voltage. This action results in a very wide depletion region and an increase in the barrier potential, equal to that of the applied bias voltage. With this widened depletion region and increased barrier potential, there is no majority carrier current across the junction and the diode is said to be reverse biased.

Any electrons that might be found on the P side and any holes found on the N side are considered to be minority-charged carriers. Although no majority-charged carriers will cross the widened depletion region of the reverse-biased diode, minority-charged carriers will flow freely. Minority carriers cause what is called leakage current to flow. Generally, the higher the quality of the semiconductor device, the less leakage current it has.

Figure 1.6b illustrates a graph of the reverse-biased diode characteristics. Vertically, in the negative direction, is reverse current, and horizontally, in the negative direction, is reverse bias voltage. The reverse current is referred to as reverse saturation current (I_S) and is very small. Typically this current is 1 microampere for silicon-type diodes and approximately 10 microamperes for germanium-type diodes.

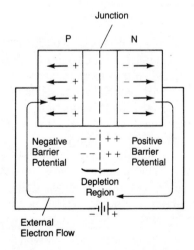

a. Electron and Hole Flow in a Reverse-Biased Diode

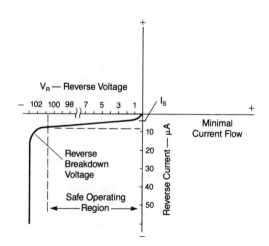

b. Characteristic Curve of a Reverse-Biased Diode

Figure 1.6   P-N Diode with Reverse Bias Applies

Very little reverse voltage is required to initiate reverse current. Once the current has reached its saturation level, the current will increase only slightly as voltage increases. This is shown by the nearly-level slope of the curve.

There is a limit to the amount of reverse voltage that can be applied to a diode. This limit is referred to as reverse breakdown voltage and can range from just a few volts to several hundred volts for different diode types. Once reverse breakdown voltage is reached (also called the avalanche voltage), current will increase greatly with only a very small increase in reverse voltage, as indicated by the almost vertical portion of the curves. Usually the diode is destroyed.

A reverse-biased diode operating inside the reverse breakdown voltage has a very large reverse resistance. It can be calculated at a given point by dividing the reverse voltage by the reverse saturation current. Usually, reverse saturation current is given as a specification, but not the reverse resistance.

Example 1-1: Determine the reverse resistance if a reverse voltage of 8 volts causes 1 microampere to flow.

$$R_R = \frac{V_R}{I_R} \qquad (1\text{-}1)$$

Substituting into equation *1-1*,

$$R_R = \frac{8V}{1\mu A}$$

or

$$R_R = 8M\Omega$$

The reverse resistance of this diode is 8 megohms.

Forward-Biased Diode

When a diode's bias voltage is applied with positive to the P material and negative to the N material, as shown in *Figure 1.7a*, it is forward biased. As the applied voltage increases from 0 volts, the positively charged holes in the P material are repelled by the positive voltage and forced toward the P-N junction. Similarly, the negatively charged electrons in the N material are repelled by the negative voltage and forced toward the junction. This action reduces the width of the depletion region, as well as decreasing the barrier potential. This action continues until the applied voltage reaches the barrier potential level. Once the applied voltage exceeds the barrier potential level, the depletion region will disappear completely and the majority current will flow.

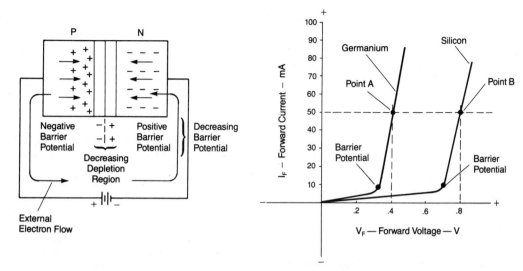

a. Electron and Hole Flow in a Forward-Biased Diode

b. Characteristic Curves of Two Forward-Biased Diodes

Figure 1.7   P-N Diode with Forward Bias Applied

The graph in *Figure 1.7b* illustrates the forward bias characteristics of a germanium diode compared to a silicon diode. This graph illustrates the plot of forward current (I_F) in a positive vertical direction against forward voltage (V_F) in a positive horizontal direction. In both examples, very little forward current flows until the applied bias voltage (V_F) exceeds the barrier potential (0.3 volt for germanium and 0.7 volt for silicon). Once the barrier potential has been overcome, forward current increases almost linearly as the applied voltage (V_F) is increased because the forward-biased diode is behaving as a low-resistance resistor. The forward resistance of a diode can be calculated at any point on the forward characteristic curve.

Example 1-2: The forward resistance of the germanium diode at point A is calculated as follows:

$$R_F = \frac{V_F}{I_F} \qquad\qquad (1\text{-}2)$$

Substituting into equation *1-2*,

$$R_F = \frac{0.4A}{50mA}$$

or

$$R_F = 8\Omega$$

The forward resistance of this germanium diode is 8 ohms.

In a like manner, the forward resistance for the silicon diode at point B can be calculated as follows:

Substituting into equation *1-2*,

$$R_F = \frac{0.8V}{50mA} \qquad (1\text{-}3)$$

or

$$R_F = 16\Omega$$

The forward resistance of this silicon diode is 16 ohms.

Dynamic resistance or ac resistance is calculated as the change in forward voltage divided by the change in forward current of the diode.

Effects of Temperature

So far we have discussed forward and reverse bias characteristics for the diode only at room temperature. As temperature is increased, both holes and electrons are generated in semiconductor material due to the thermal agitation of the atoms, thereby increasing the conductivity of the material. An increase in temperature increases forward or reverse current for a particular bias voltage. *Figure 1.8* illustrates the comparative effects of temperature on silicon and germanium diode characteristics.

Since germanium is a better conductor than silicon, the effects of temperature are more prominent on the germanium diode. The reverse saturation current of both silicon and germanium about doubles for every 10 degrees increase in temperature. The reverse saturation current for germanium would increase from 10 microamperes at 25°C to 40 microamperes at 45°C as shown in *Figure 1.8a*. If the reverse saturation current for a silicon diode is 1 microampere at 25°C, then at 45°C reverse saturation current should be 4 microamperes as shown in *Figure 1.8b*. *Figure 1.8b* illustrates the change in forward current for a fixed forward voltage of 0.7 volt when temperature is increased from 25°C to 45°C. Also, if we observe *Figure 1.8b* for a fixed forward current of 1 milliampere, we can see that the forward voltage is reduced to maintain the same current as a result of an increase in temperature. Therefore, diode voltage is said to have a negative temperature coefficient.

This negative temperature coefficient can have a destructive effect on a semiconductor. As its temperature increases due to its internal current, its current increases, which heats it further, and so on, until its maximum forward current rating is exceeded. This problem is called thermal runaway. Transistors are more susceptive to this effect than diodes.

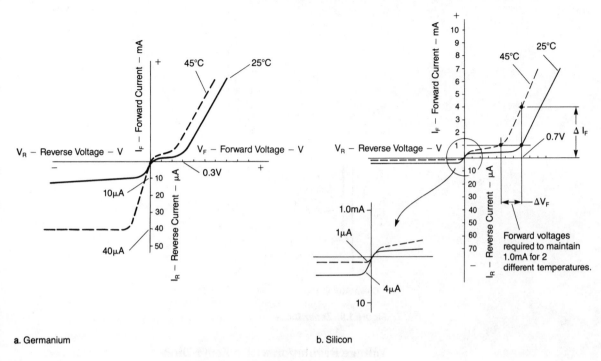

a. Germanium

b. Silicon

Figure 1.8   Effect of Temperature on Diode Characteristic Curves

SPECIAL DIODES

Zener Diode

The zener diode looks and operates like the basic junction diode, but is designed to function at breakdown voltage when reverse-biased. This breakdown voltage is called the zener voltage or avalanche voltage. *Figure 1.9a* illustrates the reverse characteristics of the zener diode along with its electrical symbol shown in *1.9b*.

When the reverse-biased voltage of a zener diode is reached, the diode breaks down and zener current (I_Z) increases very rapidly. Like the junction diode, the zener diode will be destroyed by excessive current, unless the zener current is limited by a current limiting resistor. Zener diodes are operated in this breakdown region between the zener knee current (I_{ZK}) and the maximum zener current (I_{ZM}) which is limited only by the power dissipation in the device. *Figure 1.9a* shows the normal operation region for I_Z.

Notice that the change in reverse voltage from I_{ZK} to I_{ZM} is very small. This is indicated by the nearly perfectly vertical portion of the reverse current curve. Because of this very small change in voltage with a large change in current, the zener diode is an excellent voltage regulation device.

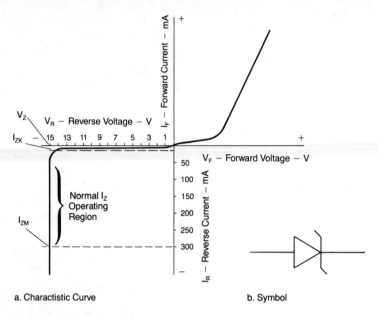

a. Charactistic Curve   b. Symbol

Figure 1.9   Zener Diode

Voltage Regulation with a Zener Diode

Figure 1.10a shows a source applied to a load. As the load resistance decreases, the line current increases as would be expected. This increase in line current will increase the voltage drop across the internal resistance of the source (R_i). Kirchoff's voltage law, as shown in equation *1-3*, states that, "the sum of the voltage dropped around a closed loop must equal the source voltage." Equation *1-4* indicates that an increase in V_{Ri} will result in a decrease in the voltage applied to the load (V_{OUT}).

$$V_{EMF} = V_{Ri} + V_{OUT} \qquad\qquad (1\text{-}3)$$

By rearranging the terms,

$$V_{OUT} = V_{EMF} - V_{Ri} \qquad\qquad (1\text{-}4)$$

If a very high load resistance value is applied to the source, there is no problem maintaining the proper supply voltage. If the load resistance is decreased significantly, a voltage regulator is required. In designing a zener voltage regulator, precautions must be taken to keep I_Z between I_{ZK} (minimum) and I_{ZM} (maximum). If I_Z falls below I_{ZK}, regulation will be lost. If I_Z exceeds I_{ZM}, the diode will be damaged.

Example 1-3: *Figure 1.10b* illustrates a simple zener diode voltage regulator circuit. R_1 limits the maximum zener current (I_{ZM}). Refering to *Figure 1.9*, we can see that the zener voltage for this particular diode is 15 volts, $I_{ZK} = 10$ milliamperes, and $I_{ZM} = 300$ milliamperes. If the desired output voltage is 15 volts, a higher supply voltage is required to supply the zener. In the example of *Figure 1.10b*, 20 volts is used as the supply voltage.

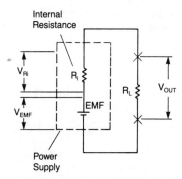

a. Power Supply Internal Resistance

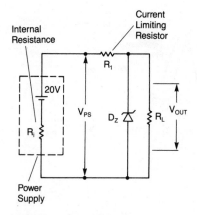

b. Zener Diode Regulator Circuit

Figure 1.10 Compensating for Internal Voltage Drops

Refering to the circuit in *Figure 1.10b*, consider the two load current extremes: R_L equal to 0 ohms (shorted load) and R_L equal to infinity (open load). If R_L is open, all the current will flow through R_1 and D_Z, and it must be limited to 300 milliamperes. To find the value of R_1 to limit the zener current to 300 milliamperes, divide the voltage drop across R_1 (5 volts) by the maximum allowable zener current. R_i is ignored because its voltage drop would reduce I_{ZM}.

$$R_1 = \frac{V_{R1}}{I_{ZM}} \quad (1\text{-}5)$$

Substituting into equation *1-5*,

$$R_1 = \frac{5V}{300mA}$$

or

$$R_1 = 16.7\Omega$$

If R_L is shorted, all of the circuit voltage (20 volts) will be dropped across R_1. The current through D_Z will be zero.

After determining the value of R_1, the minimum value of R_L must be determined. In order to maintain the zener voltage, I_Z cannot be less than I_{ZK}, which is 10 milliamperes, and all the remaining current must flow through the load resistor, R_L. As a result, the maximum load current must be the maximum allowable zener current, I_{ZM}, less I_{ZK}. The load voltage (15V) divided by the maximum load current (290 milliamperes) should produce the minimum load resistance.

$$R_{LMIN} = \frac{V_Z}{I_{ZM} - I_{ZK}} \quad (1\text{-}6)$$

Substituting into equation *1-6*,

$$R_{LMIN} = \frac{15V}{300 - 10mA}$$

or

$$R_{LMIN} = 51.7\Omega$$

Tunnel Diode

In a tunnel diode, the depletion region is very narrow because of extremely heavy doping, and charged carriers are said to tunnel through the depletion region with the slightest forward bias applied.

Figure 1.11a compares a tunnel diode to a P-N junction diode. The extremely heavy doping of the tunnel diode affects both the forward and reverse characteristics. The diode will conduct in either direction with very little applied voltage. The region between point B and point C is called the negative resistance region. In this region, current is inversely proportional to voltage. An increase in voltage results in a decrease in current.

The tunneling effect increases the switching speed of the diode, thus making it very attractive for high-speed computer and oscillator applications from 300MHz upwards into the GHz range. The symbol for the tunnel diode is shown in *Figure 1.11b*.

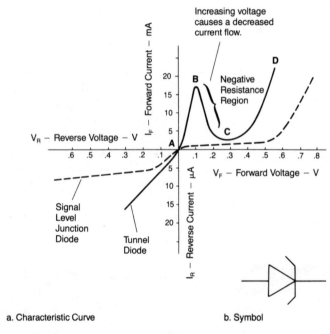

a. Characteristic Curve   b. Symbol

Figure 1.11   Characteristics of a Tunnel and Junction Diode Compared

Four-Layer Diode

The four-layer diode, was named after its inventor, William Shockley, and is constructed of four doped substrate layers. *Figure 1.12a* shows how the four layers are arranged alternately with P-type and N-type material. The terminal attached to the P-type material is the anode and the terminal attached to N-type material is the cathode. The four layers create three P-N junctions: J_1, J_2, and J_3. When the diode is forward-biased as shown, junctions one and three are forward biased while junction two is reverse-biased. The reverse bias junction limits forward current flow to minority-charged carriers.

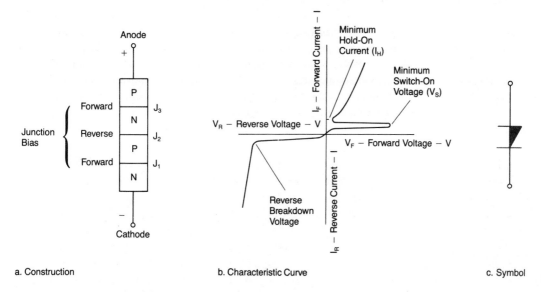

a. Construction   b. Characteristic Curve   c. Symbol

Figure 1.12   Characteristics of the Four-Layer Diode

As indicated in *Figure 1.12b*, the forward current does not increase much as the forward voltage is increased up to the switch-on voltage. Once the diode's forward voltage (junction two reverse voltage) is increased to the reverse breakdown voltage of J_2, the diode switches on. This voltage is called the forward switch-on voltage (V_S). I_S is the minimum switch-on current, while I_H is the minimum hold-on current. Once the diode switches on, the diode resistance is decreased from several thousand ohms to a few hundred ohms, and the voltage across the device is reduced to the knee voltage of two junction diodes in series.

The four-layer diode is commonly used in relaxation oscillators and as a trigger device for silicon control rectifiers. Its symbol is illustrated in *Figure 1.12c*.

Light-Emitting Diodes

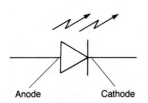

Figure 1.13   Light-Emitting Diode Symbol

The light-emitting diode (LED) is made from gallium phosphide (GaP), gallium arsenide (GaAs), or gallium arsenide phosphide (GaAsP).

When electrons from the N-type material cross the junction of a forward-biased LED, they combine with the holes in the P-type material. This recombination of charged carriers (electrons and holes) gives off energy in the form of light. If the semiconductor material is translucent, the light can be seen. *Figure 1.13* illustrates the LED. The wavy arrows represent light emission.

Varactor Diode

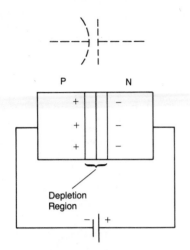

a. Reverse Bias Decreases Capacitance

b. Symbol

Figure 1.14　Varactor Diode

The varactor diode, sometimes called a voltage-variable capacitor (VVC), is a diode in which the reverse junction capacitance varies with reverse voltage. When voltage of a reverse-biased diode is increased, as shown in *Figure 1.14a*, the depletion region is increased, and when the voltage is decreased, the depletion region is decreased. The depletion region is depleted of majority-charged particles which make it a very poor conductor so it acts as a dielectric. The capacitance of the P-N junction is shown by the following equation:

$$C = \frac{\epsilon A}{d} \qquad (1\text{-}7)$$

Where ϵ is the dielectric constant, A is the area of the plates (in this instance, the area of the P-material and the N-material), and d is the distance between the plates (width of the depletion region). The depletion width is proportional to the applied voltage, thus, capacitance of a varactor is approximately inversely proportional to the applied voltage.

All P-N diodes have junction capacitance when the diode is reverse-biased and the capacitance varies as a function of reverse voltage. The junction capacitance of a normal diode varies by a factor of four, but that of a varactor diode varies by a factor of ten, because the varactor diode is designed to enhance the capacitive effect. The varactor is often used as a voltage controlled tuning device to control the frequency of an oscillator. *Figure 1.14b* shows the electrical symbol for the varactor.

BIPOLAR JUNCTION TRANSISTOR

The junction transistor is constructed of one type semiconductor material sandwiched between material of another type, as illustrated by *Figure 1.15a* and *1.15c*. This construction can be P-type between two N-type slabs, creating an NPN transistor, or vice-versa, creating a PNP transistor. *Figures 1.15b* and *1.15d* show the electrical symbol for each type. Just as in the diode, the arrow points to the N-type material. So if the arrow is pointing out, the symbol is for an NPN transistor, and if the arrow is pointing in, the symbol is for a PNP transistor. The arrow also indicates the emitter of the transistor.

The three sections of a transistor are:
1. Emitter
2. Base
3. Collector

The emitter discharges either electrons or holes (depending upon whether it is a N or P-type material), through the base section to the collector section, where these charged carriers are collected.

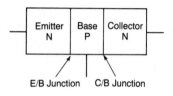

a. NPN Type

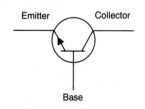

b. NPN Symbol

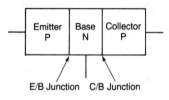

c. PNP Type

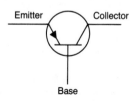

d. PNP Symbol

Figure 1.15   NPN/PNP Junction Transistor Construction

This explains the names emitter and collector. Since the base is a different type material than the emitter and collector, two P-N junctions are created; these are referred to as the emitter-base junction and the collector-base junction.

Figure 1.16 illustrates the proper biasing for an NPN transistor in the active mode. Battery B₁ is used to forward bias the emitter-base (E-B) junction, and battery B₂ is used to reverse bias the collector-base (C-B) junction. The E-B junction, being forward-biased, has the narrower depletion region, whereas the C-B junction, being reversed-biased, has a wider depletion region. Once battery B₁ exceeds the barrier potential of the E-B junction, majority-charged carriers will flow freely across the E-B junction into the base area. Because the base area is more lightly-doped than the collector, the reverse-biased depletion region extends deeply into the base area. When the majority-charged carriers (electrons) from the N-type emitter are emitted into the very narrow P-type base, they become minority-charged carriers. (In P-type material the hole is the majority charge carrier.) Reverse-biased junctions enhance the flow of minority-charged carriers. The reverse-biased C-B junction carries the minority carriers (electrons) into the collector. A large majority of the minority carriers (electrons) are swept from the base to the collector. The more that come into the base, the more that go to the collector. A very small number of the electrons in the base will flow out the base lead and become base current. This is the very essence of what is called transistor action: A small base current controls a much larger collector current. If the barrier potential of the base emitter junction is not exceeded, no current will flow from emitter to collector except for leakage current.

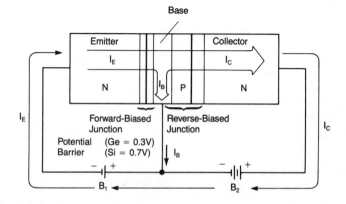

Figure 1.16   Transistor Biasing in the Active Mode

Transistors are considered current-amplifying devices, whereas the electron tubes they replaced were voltage-amplifying devices. The emitter current is equal to the sum of the base current and the collector current. Thus:

$$I_E = I_B + I_C \qquad\qquad (1\text{-}8)$$

Basic Transistor Circuit Configurations

When a device has three terminals, one of the terminals must be connected so that it is common to both the input of the circuit and the output. A transistor is a three-terminal device, thus it is connected so that any one of the three terminals is common to both input and output.

If the base is common to both input and output, as shown in *Figure 1.17a*, it is a common-base circuit. If the collector is common to both the input and the output, as shown in *Figure 1.17b*, it is a common-collector circuit. The third, and most common configuration, is the common-emitter circuit. Once again the common terminal (emitter) is connected to both input and output as shown in *Figure 1.17c*.

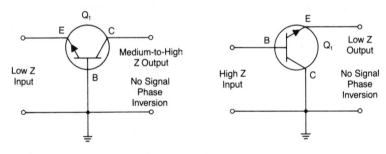

a. Common Base   b. Common Collector

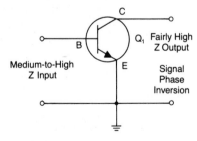

c. Common Emitter

Figure 1.17   Three Basic Transistor Circuit Configurations

Notice, in all three circuit configurations, that the collector is never the input and the base is never the output. The main differences between the circuits are their input and output impedances, and whether or not they invert the signal. Therefore, it is these characteristics that determine which configuration is best for a particular application. Our discussion on transistors will be limited to the common-emitter circuit, because it is the most widely-used configuration.

Family of Characteristic Curves for Common-Emitter Amplifier

The operational performance of a transistor amplifier will be evaluated using the output characteristics curve of a common-emitter circuit. Starting with both power supplies of *Figure 1.18* set at 0 volts, PS_1 will be increased until I_B equals the first base current step of 20 microamperes. Once the first I_B step is set, PS_2 is incremented in steps of 2 volts, and the corresponding values of I_C are recorded. This procedure will generate the graph shown in *Figure 1.19a*. Next, PS_1 is increased until I_B equals the next step — 40 microamperes. The procedure of incrementing the collector-emitter voltage and recording the corresponding collector currents is repeated. The graph of *Figure 1.19b* is the result. The above procedure is repeated for I_B of 60 microamperes and 80 microamperes with the results shown in *Figure 1.19c* and *1.19d*. The individual graphs of *Figures 1.19a* thru *d* are superimposed on one graph to create what is called a family of curves, as shown in *Figure 1.19e*.

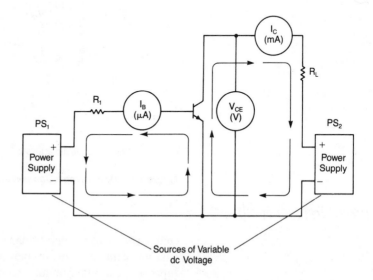

Figure 1.18   Circuit Used to Plot Output Characteristic Curves for a Junction Transistor

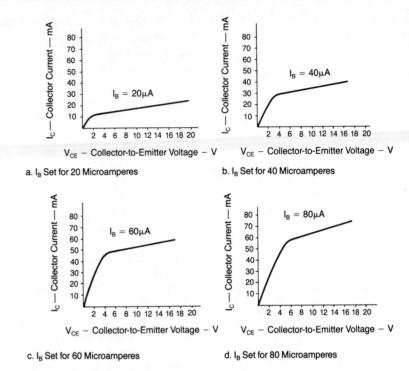

a. I_B Set for 20 Microamperes

b. I_B Set for 40 Microamperes

c. I_B Set for 60 Microamperes

d. I_B Set for 80 Microamperes

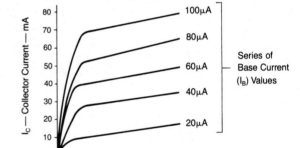

e. Common-Emitter Output Characteristic Family of Curves

Figure 1.19 *Developing a Complete Family of Characteristic Curves*

Current Transfer Ratio

One of the most important parameters of a transistor is the current transfer ratio, or current gain. The symbol used to represent current gain for a common emitter circuit is the Greek letter, beta. Beta (β) is the ratio of collector current to base current, and current gain is always the ratio of the output current to input current.

The equation for beta, sometimes called the h_{fe} of a transistor, is as follows:

$$\beta = h_{fe} = \frac{\Delta I_C}{\Delta I_B} \qquad\qquad (1\text{-}9)$$

The h-parameters (h_{fe}) are used only for ac circuit analysis. However, a version of it is used for dc current gain as shown in equation *1-10*.

$$\beta = h_{FE} = \frac{I_C}{I_B} \qquad\qquad (1\text{-}10)$$

The difference is that the ac current gain computation requires a change in collector current divided by a change in base current, while the dc gain is the total collector current divided by the total base current.

Example 1-4: Find the dc current gain at point Q using the output characteristic curves in *Figure 1.20*.

To find the dc beta at point Q in *Figure 1.20*, first find the base current closest to the Q point, and record it (60 microamperes). Next, find the collector current by drawing a horizontal line from point Q to the I_C scale on the graph (25 milliamperes). Divide the collector current by the base current, and the result is beta. Beta is a ratio so there are no units.

Substituting into equation *1-10*,

$$\beta = h_{FE} = \frac{25\text{mA}}{60\mu\text{A}}$$

$$\beta = h_{FE} = 417$$

Example 1-5: Find the ac gain using the output characteristic curves in *Figure 1.20*.

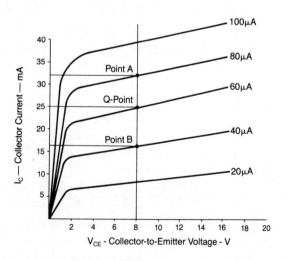

Figure 1.20 Typical Output Characteristic for a NPN Transistor

The current gain requires a change (Δ) in collector current divided by a change (Δ) in base current. Using the Q point as the starting point, pick a convenient point above the Q point (point A) and a point below the Q point (point B). Points A and B are usually the same distance above and below the Q point on a straight vertical line, or a fixed V_{CE}.

In our solution, illustrated in *Figure 1.20*, point A is 80 microamperes and point B is 40 microamperes. The change in I_B is equal to point A minus point B, or 40 microamperes. The corresponding collector currents for points A and B are 32.5 milliamperes and 17.5 milliamperes, respectively.

Substituting into equation *1-9*,

$$h_{fe} = \frac{(32.5 - 17.5)\text{mA}}{(80 - 40)\mu\text{A}}$$

or

$$h_{fe} = 375$$

Common-Emitter Transistor Amplifier

The simple amplifier circuit in *Figure 1.21a* is a common-emitter fixed-bias amplifier. R_L is the load resistor used to limit the collector current to a predetermined value when the transistor is in saturation. R_B is the base resistor which determines the base current when no input signal is applied. This base current is called the quiescent current, and is usually abbreviated as the Q-point.

Example 1-6: Design a simple fixed-biased transistor amplifier using the circuit configuration shown in *Figure 1.21a*, and using the output characteristic curves of *Figure 1.21b*.

Parameters: $I_{CMAX} = 7\text{mA}$

$V_{CC} = 15\text{V}$

Step 1: Find the value of R_L. The load resistance is determined by dividing the applied voltage (V_{CC}) by the maximum allowable collector current.

$$R_L = \frac{V_{CC}}{I_C}$$

$$R_L = \frac{15\text{V}}{7.0\text{mA}}$$

$$R_L = 2.14\text{k}\Omega$$

Choosing the closest standard value,

$$R_L = 2.2\text{k}\Omega$$

Step 2: Draw the dc load line on the graph, from V_{CC} to I_{CMAX}. For maximum signal voltage output, find the point on the load line at one half V_{CC}. This point will be the Q-point.

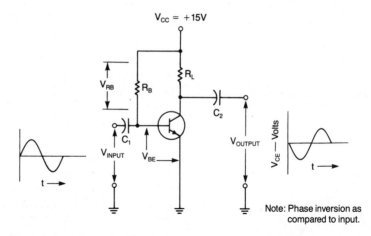

a. Simple Common-Emitter Amplifier Circuit

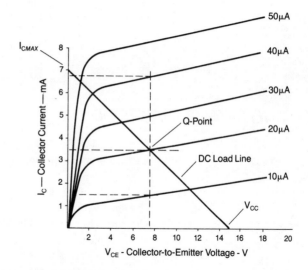

b. Characteristic Curves for Circuit

Figure 1.21   Simple Common-Emitter Amplifier

Step 3: To find the value of R_B, divide the voltage across R_B by the current that will flow through R_B. The base-emitter voltage (V_{BE}) is 0.7 volts for silicon and 0.3 volts for germanium (barrier potential). Assuming a silicon transistor, the voltage across R_B (V_{RB}) is the applied voltage V_{CC} minus the base emitter voltage V_{BE}. The current flowing through R_B is the base current I_B at the Q-point. I_{BQ} is equal to 20 microamperes.

$$R_B = \frac{V_{CC} - V_{BE}}{I_{BQ}}$$

$$R_B = \frac{(15 - 0.7)V}{20\mu A}$$

$$R_B = 715k\Omega$$

BASIC ELECTRONICS TECHNOLOGY

Choosing the closest standard value,

$$R_B = 720k\Omega$$

The amplifier is now designed for a static condition of 20 microamperes input and 3.5 milliamperes output (*Figure 1.21b*). When an input signal is applied, I_B varies as the applied signal varies. I_C varies as I_B varies. If I_B in *Figure 1.21b* is increased to 40 microamperes, I_C will increase to 6.8 milliamperes. Similarly, as the input signal decreases I_B to 10 microamperes, I_C will decrease to 1.5 milliamperes.

To show the ac amplification of the transistor, increasing I_B to 40 microamperes causes I_C to increase to 6.8 milliamperes. Decreasing I_B to 10 microamperes causes I_C to decrease to 1.5 milliamperes. Substituting into equation *1-9*:

$$h_{fe} = \frac{(6.8 - 1.5)mA}{(0.04 - 0.01)mA}$$

$$h_{fe} = \frac{5.3mA}{.03mA}$$

or

$$h_{fe} = 176$$

JUNCTION FIELD-EFFECT TRANSISTOR

The junction field-effect transistor (JFET) is constructed of a section of one type semiconductor material sandwiched between two sections of the other type material, as illustrated in *Figures 1.22a* and *1.22b*. The center section is called the channel, and if the channel is made of N-type material, it is an N-channel JFET. Current should flow through the channel only, and not through the P-N junction formed by the gates.

One end of the channel is called the source and the other end is called the drain. The third terminal, called the gate, is made up of two sections of like semiconductor material, but are usually connected internally to create one gate lead. If the gates are not connected internally and the JFET has four leads, it is referred to as a tetrode-connected JFET.

Theory of Operation

The N-channel JFET is biased with a positive drain voltage ($+V_{DD}$), and the P-channel JFET is biased with a negative drain voltage ($-V_{DD}$). If a positive drain voltage is applied to an N-channel JFET and the gate is left disconnected, drain current (I_D) will flow as if it were flowing through a resistor.

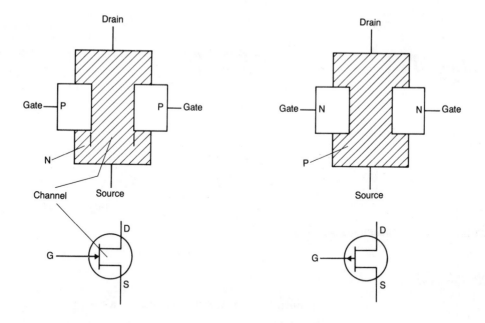

a. N-Channel JFET and Symbol

b. P-Channel JFET and Symbol

Figure 1.22 *Construction of the Junction Field-Effect Transistor*

In *Figure 1.23a*, the gate is connected to the source, which is at ground potential, assuring a gate to source voltage of zero volts ($V_{GS} = 0V$). As current begins to flow through the resistive channel, voltage is dropped linearly along the channel. Close to the drain, the channel voltage is a large positive voltage; close to the source the channel voltage is a small positive voltage. All along the channel, the P-N junction is reverse-biased, with the N-channel being positive with respect to the P-gate. Because the channel is more lightly doped than the gate, the depletion region extends deeply into the channel, and more so closer to the drain. The depletion region is void of majority charged carriers (electrons in N-material), thus acting as an insulator. The depletion regions extend into the channel from both sides, reducing the flow of drain current. If the gate-source voltage (V_{GS}) is increased negatively as indicated in *Figure 1.23b*, the depletion region will reduce I_D even more. If V_{GS} is further increased (*Figure 1.23c*), the depletion region will meet at the center of the channel, cutting off I_D completely.

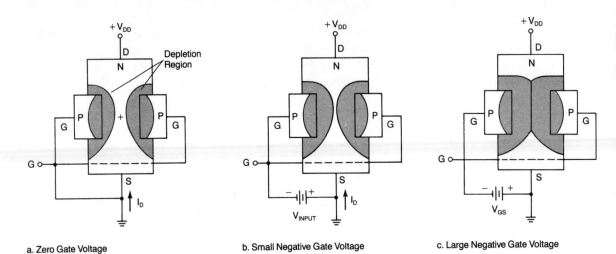

a. Zero Gate Voltage   b. Small Negative Gate Voltage   c. Large Negative Gate Voltage

Figure 1.23   Junction Field-Effect Transistor Biasing

Characteristic Curves

The output characteristics curves for a common source JFET are illustrated in *Figure 1.24*. The curves are obtained by maintaining a constant gate-to-source voltage (V_{GS}) and increasing the drain-source voltage (V_{DS}) in steps. Drain current is then recorded for each step of V_{DS}; each curve being plotted in *Figure 1.24* at a different V_{GS}, starting with V_{GS} = 0V.

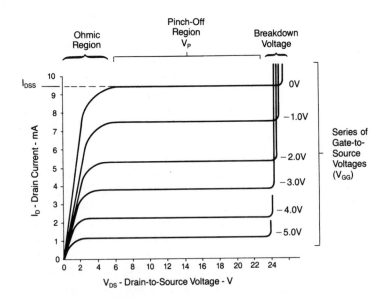

Figure 1.24   Output Characteristics for N-Channel Junction Field-Effect Transistor

With a V_{GS} of 0 as illustrated in *Figure 1.24a*, the drain-source voltage is increased slightly. The increase of V_{DS} generates a corresponding increase in drain current (I_D), which in turn causes the reverse bias of the channel-gate junction, extending the depletion region slightly into the channel. At this point, the depletion region does not extend far enough to affect I_D. The drain current behaves as if it were flowing through a resistor and increases at a nearly linear rate with each increase of V_{DS}. This is referred to as the ohmic region of the curves. At some point, as V_{DS} continues to increase, the depletion region will penetrate far enough into the channel to start affecting I_D. The depletion region will eventually reach a point at which the channel is saturated with little or no increase in I_D with increased V_{DS}. This point is called the pinch-off voltage (V_P). The region between the pinch-off voltage and breakdown voltage is called the pinch-off region for the JFET. The current value at which I_D becomes saturated is called drain-source saturation current (I_{DSS}). There should be a reverse bias on the channel-gate junction so that the gate will never draw current.

Amplification is made possible by increasing and decreasing the gate voltage around a fixed gate value (the Q-point) in the pinch-off region. A corresponding drain current will vary accordingly to produce an amplified representation of the input signal.

METAL OXIDE SEMICONDUCTOR FIELD-EFFECT TRANSISTOR

Theory of Operation

The Metal Oxide Semiconductor Field-Effect Transistor (MOSFET), like the JFET, is a low-power, high-input impedance device with a source, gate, and drain. Unlike the JFET, the MOSFET has no gate-channel P-N junction. The gate and channel of the MOSFET are insulated from one another by a thin layer of silicon dioxide. The presence of the silicon dioxide means that the gate does not always have to be reversed-biased as does the JFET.

The MOSFET can be operated in two different modes, enhancement mode and depletion mode. The enhancement mode widens the channel by applying the proper bias voltage. The depletion mode is much like the JFET in that the channel is narrowed by depleting it of charged carriers. The MOSFET is also occasionally referred to as an insulated-gate FET (IGFET).

E-MOS

The enhancement metal oxide semiconductor (E-MOSFET) construction is shown in *Figure 1.25a*. Starting with a lightly doped (high resistive) P-type substrate, two areas of heavily doped (low resistive) N-type material are diffused into the substrate. The two areas of N-type material create the source and drain. The entire block surface is covered with a thin layer of silicon dioxide which is an insulator. Contact is made to the N-type source and drain through holes, which are cut through the silicon dioxide layer. The gate is a metal plate which is deposited on the surface of the silicon dioxide thus, the silicon dioxide acts as an insulator between the metal gate and the semiconductor substrate. This construction forms three layers: metal, oxide, and semiconductor; hence the name metal oxide semiconductor (MOS).

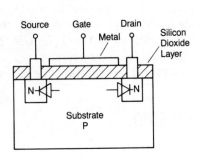

a. Construction

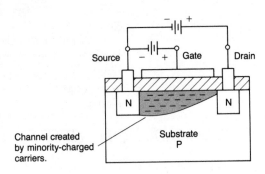

b. Effect of Biasing

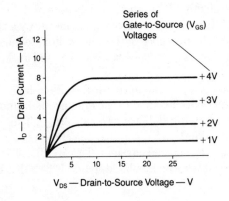

c. Family of Characteristic Curves

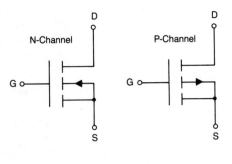

d. Symbols

Figure 1.25   N-Channel E-MOS FET

If a positive potential is applied to the drain and a negative potential is applied to the source, very little current will flow between the source and drain, provided no potential is applied to the gate. The two P-N junctions between source, substrate, and drain form two back-to-back diodes, as illustrated in *Figure 1.25a*. The source diode is forward-biased, the drain diode is reverse-biased. The substrate potential is about the same as the source.

When a positive potential is applied to the gate, as shown in *Figure 1.25b*, the minority-charged carriers (electrons) in the P-type substrate are attracted toward the positive voltage on the metal gate. The insulating property of the silicon dioxide prevents the electrons from flowing into the gate so they build up under the gate.

The electrons provide an N-type bridge or channel between the source and the drain so that the drain current (I_D) can flow through the channel to the drain. As the positive charge on the gate is increased, the channel is enhanced (widened) so more drain current can flow.

Figure 1.25c shows the drain characteristic curves. The drain characteristics indicate that drain current is not present without a positive potential applied between the gate and source. As V_{GS} increases positively, I_D increases. *Figure 1.25d* depicts the electrical symbols for the E-MOSFETs. The symbols show the channel as three dashes indicating that the channel is not present without the gate potential.

D-MOS (Depletion)

The depletion MOSFET is constructed similarly to the E-MOSFET with one major difference. *Figure 1.26a* illustrates that the D-MOSFET has a physical N-type material channel between the source and drain areas. When a positive potential is applied to the drain and a negative potential is applied to the source, with no potential applied to the gate ($V_{GS} = 0V$), drain current will flow, just as it did with the JFET.

As illustrated in *Figure 1.26b*, the drain current decreases as the potential on the gate is made more negative. The negative charge on the gate attracts majority-charged carriers (holes) which deplete the N-channel of electrons and increase the resistance of the channel. Thus, with a negative potential on the gate, the D-MOSFET acts like its cousin, the JFET.

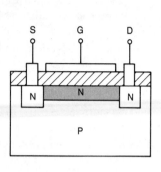

a. Construction

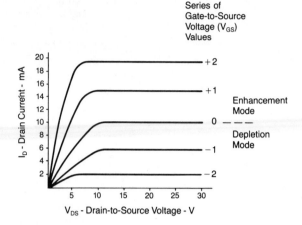

Series of Gate-to-Source Voltage (V_{GS}) Values

b. Drain Characteristics for N-Channel D-MOSFET

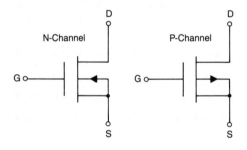

c. Symbols

Figure 1.26 D-MOSFET

However, the D-MOSFET offers another mode of operating because, as a result of the insulating properties of the silicon dioxide layer, the gate potential can be made positive without gate current flowing. As the gate potential is increased positively, the D-MOSFET will begin operating in the enhancement mode and drain current (I_D) will increase. Because the D-MOSFET can operate in both depletion and enhancement modes, it is sometimes called the depletion-enhancement MOSFET (DE-MOSFET). *Figure 1.26c* shows the symbols for the D-MOSFETs.

CMOS

CMOS (Complementary Metal Oxide Semiconductor), as shown in *Figure 1.27*, is a combination of P-channel and N-channel enhancement MOSFETs used in a complementary circuit arrangement that is useful in digital logic circuitry. Among its advantages are: extremely low power dissipation, requires only one dc power supply, operates over a wide range of supply voltages, and can drive as many as 50 gate inputs. CMOS logic gates can be designed to use only MOSFETs.

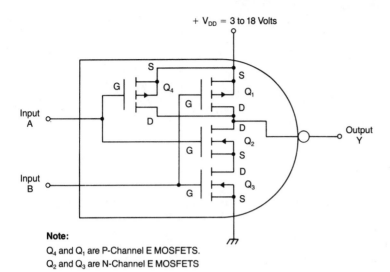

+ V_{DD} = 3 to 18 Volts

Input A

Input B

Output Y

Note:
Q_4 and Q_1 are P-Channel E MOSFETS.
Q_2 and Q_3 are N-Channel E MOSFETS

A	B	Y
0	0	1
0	1	1
1	0	1
1	1	0

a. IC Schematic

b. Truth Table

Figure 1.27 Two Input CMOS NAND Gate

Figure 1.27a shows a CMOS two-input NAND gate, and *Figure 1.27b* illustrates the truth table for the gate. If inputs A and B are both low, the gate on the P-channel transistors Q_4 and Q_1 are both negative in relation to their sources, causing them to conduct at saturation. The gates of N-channel transistors Q_2 and Q_3 are at the same potential as their sources, causing them to be cut off. Thus, the output will be high (one).

Consider the condition when input A is low and input B is high. Transistor Q_4 will conduct, and transistor Q_2 will be off. The high on input B will cause transistor Q_1 to be off and transistor Q_3 to be conducting. Because transistors Q_2 and Q_3 are in series, as long as one of the two is off (Q_2 in this example), the output will be high. A similar condition is present when input A is high and input B is low. Since Q_3 is off, the output will be high.

Consider the last possible input combination, where inputs A and B are both high. This results in transistors Q_2 and Q_3 conducting at the same time, causing the output to be grounded through the series pair. Thus, the output will be low (zero). Chapter 8 will cover this topic of logic gates in greater detail.

POWER DEVICES

Silicon Controlled Rectifier

The silicon controlled rectifier (SCR) works like a diode with a control gate. The SCR is constructed like the four-layer diode of *Figure 1.12a* with a lead, called the gate, connected to the P-section nearest the cathode, as in *Figure 1.28a. Figure 1.28b* shows the symbol.

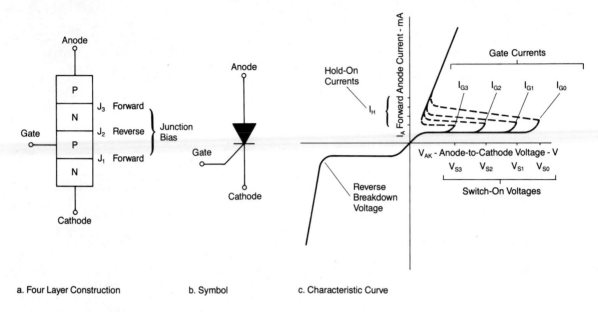

a. Four Layer Construction   b. Symbol   c. Characteristic Curve

Figure 1.28   Silicon-Controlled Rectifier

With gate current I_G equal to 0, the SCR characteristic curve (*Figure 1.28c*) looks the same as the four-layer diode curve (*Figure 1.12b*). By increasing the gate current (I_G), the anode-cathode voltage (V_{AK}) at which the SCR will switch on (V_S) is decreased. Once the SCR is switched on, it behaves like a forward-biased diode, and will remain switched on as long as the forward anode current (I_A) remains above the hold-on current (I_H). The larger I_G is, the less hold-on current is required.

Figure 1.29a illustrates a phase controller, which is a common application of an SCR. The SCR can conduct in only one direction, like any other diode, so the negative portion of the ac voltage is clipped off as illustrated in *Figure 1.29b*. But with the control gate, the SCR can be switched on at any positive input voltage, from zero volts to peak volts of the ac input voltage. *Figure 1.29b* shows that the SCR switches on at a phase angle of 90 degrees with R_V at a high value. If R_V of the circuit in *Figure 1.29a* is decreased, allowing more gate current to flow, the SCR will switch on at a lower applied voltage, as indicated in *Figure 1.29b*. This is an effective way of controlling the power to a load; that is, by varying the average output current (duty cycle).

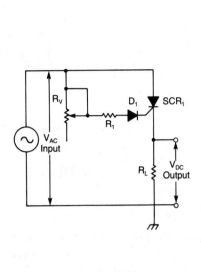

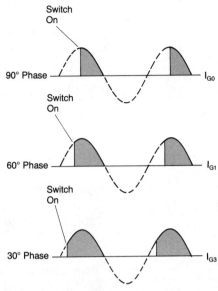

Note: Shadowed area indicates conduction

a. Schematic

b. Output Waveforms for a Series of Gate Current Values

Figure 1.29   SCR Phase Controller

Triac

The triac, which is also called a bidirectional triode thyristor, is essentially two SCRs in parallel with the anode of one tied to the cathode of the other, as illustrated in *Figure 1.30a*. The triac behaves just as the SCR, except the triac can conduct easily in either direction, making it very useful in controlling ac loads in which rectification is not desired. *Figure 1.30b* shows a full-wave power (phase) controller, a very common circuit for the triac. In this circuit, a diac is used to fire (trigger) the triac. A diac is a triac without the gate, and behaves just as the triac with gate current equal to zero. The diac could be compared to two parallel four-layer diodes connected with opposite polarity.

Power Transistors

Power transistors are usually defined as transistors that will output at least 1 watt of power, and are used in applications requiring large currents for sustained periods. The power rating of a transistor is based on:

1. Its ability to operate effectively at high voltages and current without excessive non-linearity or thermal or voltage breakdown.
2. Its ability to dissipate internally-generated heat.

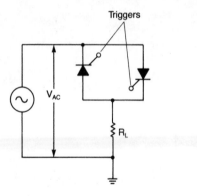

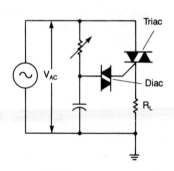

a. Two SCRs Used as a Triac   b. Full Wave Phase Controller

Figure 1.30   Two Triac Circuits

The power rating is the maximum allowable power dissipation of the transistor that does not exceed the maximum junction temperature, while still maintaining thermal stability.

The maximum junction temperature is the temperature that, if exceeded, results in permanent damage to the transistor. Thermal instability is a result of increased collector current generating an increase in collector junction temperature, which in turn increases the collector leakage current and results in an increase in junction temperature, etc. This regenerative action, called thermal runaway, may permanently damage the transistor.

The maximum collector current that can be carried by the transistor without damage is the current rating. Exceeding the current rating of the transistor may result in a large decrease in current gain. The power rating of the transistor may be exceeded at maximum collector voltage if the current rating is not exceeded. Under these conditions, there is also an increased risk of melting an internal component lead.

Power transistors are often constructed so that the collector semiconductor material is bonded to the transistor case itself. This construction allows the case to carry the heat away from the collector junction. In addition, the transistor case can be mounted to a heat sink, which conducts the heat away from the transistor case and dissipates it into the air.

SEMICONDUCTOR FABRICATION TECHNIQUES

We will discuss only three of the many methods of fabrication:
1. Grown method
2. Alloyed method
3. Diffusion method

In the grown method, a P-N junction is formed during a crystal pulling process. A spinning rod is dipped into a crucible of molten silicon and slowly pulled out. The silicon attaches itself to the rod, and as it is pulled out of the crucible, it cools and hardens. As it is pulled, the crystal silicon is first doped with N-type impurities and then later doped with P-type impurities, creating a P-N junction. The large silicon rod produced can be sliced into small P-N junction diodes.

In the alloy method, an alloy P-N junction is formed by placing a P-type impurity pellet on an N-type substrate, or placing an N pellet on a P-type substrate, and heating the two until the are liquefied. Once they have cooled, a P-N junction is formed.

The diffusion method of P-N diode fabrication employs a heating chamber containing an impurity vapor, either trivalent or pentavalent. With this method the substrate is heated, but not melted, to increase the activity of the elements involved. The vapor is then diffused into the substrate creating a P-N junction when cooled.

Integrated Circuits

An integrated circuit (IC) is an electrical circuit consisting of many components in one package, which may not be any larger than one discrete transistor. ICs provide many advantages over the same circuit in discrete form, including smaller packaging, increased reliability, reduced power consumption, and economy.

Monolithic Fabrication

The monolithic process is the most efficient method for mass production of integrated circuits. In a monolithic integrated circuit, all components are fabricated by placing a very thin, highly-polished silicon wafer in an oven at a high temperature and exposing it to an atmosphere of semiconductor atoms. The process of introducing the wafer to a heated atmosphere is called the diffusion method. Usually, the semiconductor wafer is P-type substrate and the atmosphere of semiconductor atoms is N-type impurities. Next, oxygen is introduced into the oven chamber and a thin coating of silicon dioxide, which acts as an insulator, is formed on the wafer. Finally, the wafer looks like the cut-away in *Figure 1.31a.*

After a pretested circuit is selected for IC fabrication, a mask is made to diffuse the collectors of all the transistors at once. The other components are also designed into the mask, which at this point is many times larger than the actual IC. It is then photographed and reduced to about eight to ten times the size of the desired IC, and that photo is then reproduced for each IC to be produced.

These photographs are laid side-by-side and the entire arrangement is photographed and reduced to actual IC size. Approximately 250 tiny photos will fit on one wafer about 3.5 inches across. The surface of the wafer (see *Figure 1.31a*) is coated with a photosensitive emulsion and the mask is placed on the wafer. Once the mask is in place, the wafer is exposed to ultra-violet light. The wafer then goes through a developing process which hardens the areas not exposed to light and allows the exposed areas of silicon dioxide to be etched away by hydrofluoric acid. The end result is a wafer resembling the cut-away of *Figure 1.31b*.

The islands of silicon dioxide represent the locations of transistor collectors and other components of the integrated circuit. The layer of N-material not covered by the silicon dioxide is then exposed by the diffusion process to P-type impurities, which change the uncovered N-type material into P-type material, creating the isolated N-type collectors of *Figure 1.31b*.

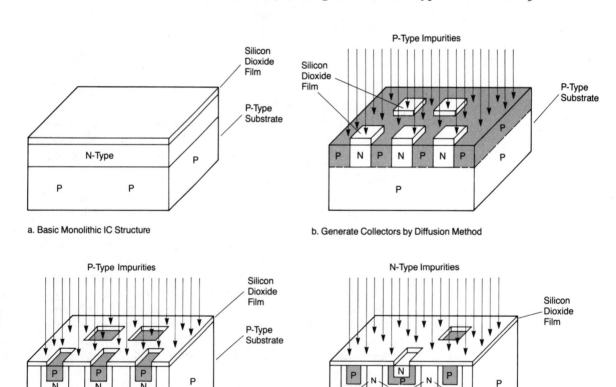

a. Basic Monolithic IC Structure

b. Generate Collectors by Diffusion Method

c. Generate Base, Diode Anode, and Resistors by the Diffusion Method

d. Generate Emitter by Diffusion Method

Figure 1.31   Monolithic Integrated Circuit Fabrication Techniques

A new silicon dioxide film is formed on the surface of the wafer. The process of photoemulsion, masking, and diffusion is repeated, but this time with another mask designed to create the base area of the transistors, the anodes of diodes, and a p-type resistor, as illustrated by *Figure 1.31c*.

The process is repeated a third time with a mask to form the emitter section of the transistors by diffusion with N-type impurities, as illustrated in *Figure 1.31d*. Notice that the resistor and diode do not receive exposure to the impurities in this step.

Finally, holes are etched through the final silicon dioxide layer to form connections to the component parts, and a thin film of aluminum is patterned to form point-to-point contacts for the circuit components. *Figure 1.32a* shows the final integrated circuit, with an equivalent schematic drawing of the circuit in *Figure 1.32b*. The wafer is cut, and each IC is tested and packaged. This is an extremely simplified example. One piece integrated circuits with from 10,000 to 100,000 components are presently in production to make complete microcomputers on one chip or semiconductor memories with 256K bits. This is not the end; the trend to higher complexity will continue as the technology develops to meet the challenge.

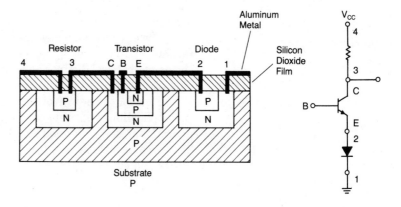

a. Cross Section of Completed IC

b. Equivalent Schematic

Figure 1.32 *Monolithic Bipolar Integrated Circuit*

SUMMARY

In this chapter, we have learned about semiconductor atomic structure and how it can serve as a valve for electrons. The availability of free electrons in N-type materials and holes in P-type materials is determined by the addition of the impurity material. Free electrons and holes are necessary for current to flow. The interaction of these electrons and holes at the P-N junction provides the medium of overall control of current flow, and hence, the phenomena of amplification and rectification.

Although all types of diodes work on the same theories and principles, differences in construction emphasize certain desirable characteristics. For example, the zener diode uses the breakdown voltage to achieve circuit voltage regulation; the varactor diode uses variable junction capacitance to tune oscillator circuits.

The bipolar junction transistor is a current-controlled device. It provides current gain by using the base current to control the flow of collector current, gain being defined as the ratio of output to input current.

Field-effect transistor technology, which followed junction technology, actually has a similarity to vacuum-tube technology, because the FET is a voltage-controlled device. A small voltage change on the FET gate controls a large current (or voltage change) at the drain.

Power control devices are an application of the junction technology to control higher voltages and currents. Therefore, the chief practical distinction is thermal considerations. Heat sinks are often used to help dissipate heat from the device.

Finally, the next evolvement of solid-state technology was the application of discrete component design to the production of operational, self-contained circuitry on a single chip of material. This became a whole new branch of semiconductors, known as integrated circuits.

CHAPTER 1 QUIZ

1. The atom is made of:
   a. electrons and protons surrounded by neutrons.
   b. neutrons and protons surrounded by electrons.
   c. electrons and neutrons surrounded by protons.
   d. none of the above.

2. Hole flow is a phenomenon in which:
   a. a hole moves from a positive potential toward a negative potential.
   b. a hole moves from a negative potential toward a positive potential.
   c. electrons flow from a positive potential to a negative potential.
   d. electrons flow backward.

3. Semiconductor atoms are held together by:
   a. ionic bonding.
   b. covalent bonding.
   c. metallic bonding.
   d. intrinsic bonding.

4. Semiconductor material is made more conductive by a process called:
   a. dropping.
   b. emitting.
   c. bonding.
   d. doping.

5. At a P-N junction, electrons drift across the junction to the P side and holes drift across to the N side to form a voltage called the:
   a. bias voltage.
   b. applied voltage.
   c. barrier potential.
   d. collector voltage.

6. The collector of a PNP transistor is made up of:
   a. P-type material.
   b. N-type material.
   c. intrinsic material.
   d. all of the above.

7. The center section of a PNP transistor is the:
   a. collector.
   b. acceptor.
   c. emitter.
   d. base.

8. The emitter current, as compared to the base and collector currents, is always:
   a. equal, because the emitter, base, and collector are in series.
   b. the largest of the three currents.
   c. the smallest of the three currents.
   d. smaller than the collector, but larger than the base current.

$I_E = I_B + I_C$

9. Beta is the current gain of a:
   a. common-base circuit.
   b. common-collector circiut.
   c. common-emitter circuit.
   d. none of the above.

10. The zener diode is normally:
    a. forward-biased.
    b. emitter-biased.
    c. cathode-biased.
    d. reverse-biased.

11. The field-effect transistor is sometimes referred to as a:
    a. unijunction device.
    b. bipolar device.
    c. unipolar device.
    d. bijunction device.

12. The three leads of an FET are:
    a. emitter, source, and drain.
    b. source, gate, and drain.
    c. cathode, gate, and anode.
    d. cathode, drain, and anode.

13. The field-effect transistor amplifier is normally operated in the:
    a. ohmic region.
    b. triode region.
    c. breakdown region.
    d. pinch-off region.

14. The zener diode is normally
    operated in the:
    a. breakdown region.
    b. ohmic region.
    c. non-linear portion of the
       forward-biased
       characteristic curve.
    d. b and c above.

15. The drain of the N-channel
    field-effect transistor is
    normally connected to:
    a. the most negative terminal.
    b. the most positive terminal.
    c. the gate.
    d. ground.

16. The gate of an N-channel
    JFET is normally biased with:
    a. a positive voltage of 1 to 5
       volts.
    b. a negative voltage of 1 to 5
       volts.
    c. an input diode for clamping.
    d. b and c above.

17. Pinch-off voltage is:
    a. the drain-source voltage at
       which I_D no longer increases
       with V_{DS}.
    b. the dividing point between
       the ohmic region and the
       pinch-off region.
    c. both of the above.
    d. none of the above.

18. An E-MOS field-effect
    transistor:
    a. has no channel until gate
       voltage is applied.
    b. has a physical channel
       between drain and source.
    c. must have gate current to
       operate properly.
    d. none of the above.

19. When using the monolithic
    method of integrated circuit
    fabrication:
    a. the emitter is formed first.
    b. the collector is formed first.
    c. the base is formed first.
    d. it makes no difference which
       is formed first.

20. The silicon controlled rectifier
    is:
    a. used to control the power of
       ac devices.
    b. used to trigger a diac.
    c. used for voltage regulation.
    d. used to control the power of
       dc devices.

AMPLIFIER AND OSCILLATOR CIRCUITS

INTRODUCTION

Amplifiers and oscillators have several important similarities; for this reason they have both been incorporated into this chapter. At the heart of both circuit types is a semiconductor device which provides amplification within the circuit. Circuit components surround the device and establish the required operating conditions for the device to function.

Amplifiers are introduced first. The chapter covers basic amplifier parameters and characteristics, how circuits are designed to establish the required operating voltages, and common circuits for small signal amplifiers, power amplifiers, and operational amplifiers.

A section on the principles of oscillation introduces oscillators. This is followed by a detailed explanation of various discrete component types of oscillators, and common IC versions of these oscillators. UHF and microwave oscillators are treated separately because of their unique design considerations.

AMPLIFIER CHARACTERISTICS AND COMPONENTS

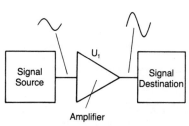

Represents anything from a discrete component to a complete multistage IC package.

Figure 2.1   Amplifier as a System Component

When semiconductor devices operate in a switching mode, the circuits are digital circuits; when the devices operate linearly, the circuits are analog circuits.

The most commonly used analog circuit is called an amplifier. It is represented by the triangular symbol shown in *Figure 2.1*. This symbol may represent a single discrete transistor and its associated bias and coupling network, or a multistage integrated circuit amplifier. Between these two extremes are many different amplifier circuit configurations.

The operational characteristics of all amplifiers may be described in terms of a few basic parameters: gain, impedance and distortion. Amplifiers are used to transform a small input signal into a large output signal, and are powered by a battery or electronic power supply.

Gain

Gain of a circuit is the measurable increase in signal level from input to output. The gain of any amplifier is calculated as the ratio of the circuit's output signal level to the input signal level as shown in equation 2-1. The input and output signal levels may be measured in terms of current, voltage, or power, but gain is often specified in decibel (dB) units.

$$\text{In General,} \quad \text{Gain} = \frac{\text{Output}}{\text{Input}} \tag{2-1}$$

When expressed in decibels, the equations require the use of logarithms to the base 10.

$$\text{For Voltages,} \quad \text{Gain}_{dB} = 20 \log_{10} \frac{V_{OUT}}{V_{IN}} \tag{2-2}$$

$$\text{For Currents,} \quad \text{Gain}_{dB} = 20 \log_{10} \frac{I_{OUT}}{I_{IN}} \tag{2-3}$$

$$\text{For Power,} \quad \text{Gain}_{dB} = 10 \log_{10} \frac{P_{OUT}}{P_{IN}} \tag{2-4}$$

In general, gain (amplification factor) is symbolized by the letter A. The equation for voltage gain is written as follows:

$$A_v = \frac{V_{OUT}}{V_{IN}} \tag{2-5}$$

Because gain is only a ratio of two like quantities, it has no absolute units. The decibel (dB) is the relative unit used, indicating the relative difference in the two electrical measurements.

Example 2-1: An amplifier outputs an ac signal of 360 milliwatts when its input is 40 milliwatts. Using equation 2-1, the amplifier's power gain is determined as follows:

$$\text{Power Gain} = \frac{360\text{mW}}{40\text{mW}}$$

$$\text{Power Gain} = 9$$

To express the power gain in decibels (equation 2-4):

$$\text{Power Gain} = 10 \log_{10} \frac{360\text{mW}}{40\text{mW}}$$

$$\text{Power Gain} = 9.5\text{dB}$$

Thus, the power gain in this case may be expressed as a pure number 9, or in decibels as 9.5dB.

Impedance

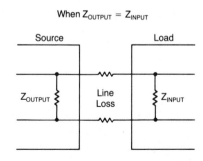

When $Z_{OUTPUT} = Z_{INPUT}$

Figure 2.2   Maximum Power Transfer

An amplifier's input and output impedances define another important circuit characteristic. As a part of an electronic system, an amplifier receives its input signal from a prior circuit, called a stage, or an external input device; and delivers its output to a succeeding stage or a load device as shown in *Figure 2.1.* At its input, the amplifier must not present too great a load to the signal source, which may be another amplifier's output (see *Figure 2.2*), or the signal source will be unable to provide enough signal power to drive the amplifier input. An ideal amplifier has infinite input impedance, requiring no current from the signal source. The amplifier delivers its output signal to a load which may be another amplifier stage, or a transducer — a loudspeaker, for example. The greatest power transfer and lowest distortion is achieved when the amplifier's output impedance equals the input impedance of the circuit or transducer being driven.

Distortion

The third parameter by which an amplifier circuit may be characterized is called distortion. Recall that an amplifier is designed to increase the amplitude of its input signal by its gain factor. Since there are no perfect components nor circuits, all amplifiers distort the input signal. Any of the three parameters of the input signal — frequency, phase, or amplitude — may be distorted by an amplifier as shown in *Figure 2.3.*

Frequency distortion occurs when a certain range of frequencies is amplified more or less than others. This distortion results from the capacitance and inductance values distributed throughout the circuit. The degree of frequency distortion in an amplifier is described by its frequency response specification, which indicates the relative output over a certain frequency spectrum.

Phase distortion occurs when certain groups of frequencies require different amounts of time to pass through an amplifier. Although a sine wave consists of a single frequency, other waveforms, called complex waves, can be shown to consist of combinations of sinusoids of different frequencies. For an amplifier to faithfully reproduce this complex waveform, it must not delay any frequency component, or the complex waveform will be distorted.

Amplitude distortion is sometimes called non-linear distortion, because the output signal is not a faithful reproduction of the input signal waveshape. There are three types of amplitude distortion: harmonic, intermodulation, and transient intermodulation.

Distortion Parameter	Result	Example or Observable Effect
Frequency	Different gain values for different groups of frequencies.	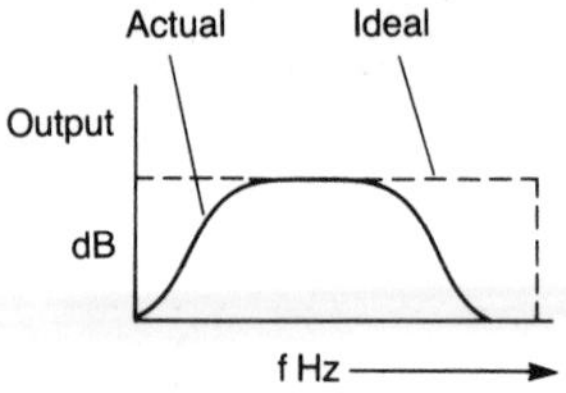
Phase	Variations in the transit time from input to output for certain frequencies.	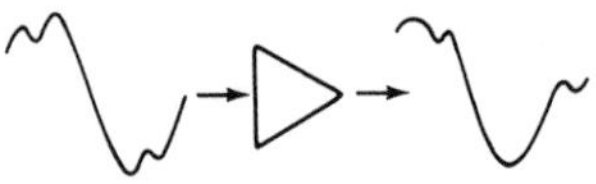
Amplitude A. Harmonic	Unwanted frequencies are added during the process of amplification.	
B. Intermodulation	One sine wave modulates another.	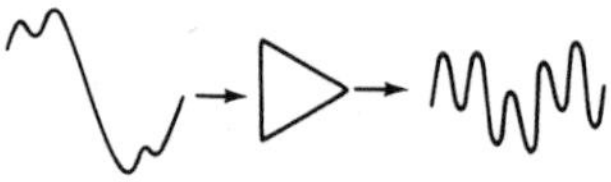
C. Transient Intermodulation	Input signal changes in amplitude too rapidly for amplifier to respond accurately.	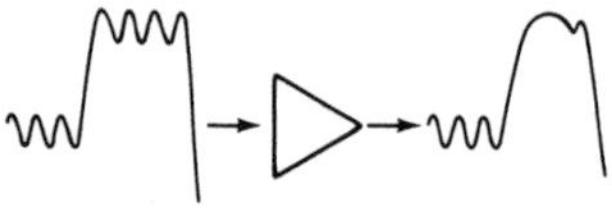

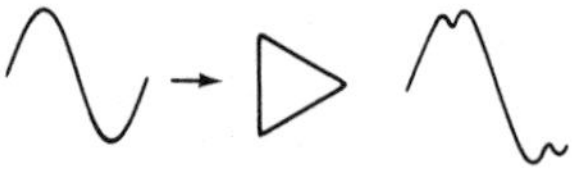

Figure 2.3 Amplifier Distortion Characteristics

Harmonic distortion occurs when unwanted frequencies are generated in the amplifying device and added to the desired signal. It is impossible to completely eliminate in practical amplifying devices. The degree of this type of distortion is measured in terms of the magnitude of the unwanted frequencies. In amplifier specifications, harmonic distortion is usually called total harmonic distortion (THD) and is given as a percentage of the output signal.

Intermodulation distortion causes one sinusoidal component to modulate another. New frequencies are produced which become part of the output signal.

Transient intermodulation distortion occurs when input signals change so rapidly that the amplifier cannot track them. Therefore, severe intermodulation distortion occurs until the amplifier recovers, catching up with the input signal.

Voltage and Power Amplifiers

The ability of an amplifier to deliver a signal must be matched to the requirements of the load being supplied. The load may be a tiny radio speaker, requiring less than a watt, or perhaps a transmitter antenna requiring megawatts. The circuit coupling the power to the load is called a power amplifier or power output stage. The voltage amplifier stages preceding the power stage increase the feeble input signal to a level sufficient to drive the power output stage. Voltage and power amplifiers have significant differences from one another; therefore, they will be examined separately.

Amplifying Devices

In order to amplify, a device must be capable of producing a relatively large change in its output voltage and/or current in response to a small change at its input. This is illustrated symbolically in *Figure 2.1*. The sine wave at the input controls the device so that it produces a larger sine wave at the output. The earliest electronic amplifying devices were triode vacuum tubes. As shown in the schematic of *Figure 2.4a*, an input signal applied between the grid and the cathode controls the current in the cathode-plate circuit. The large plate current flowing through the load resistor, R_L, produces a voltage drop across the resistor which is much larger than the input signal voltage. Improvements in vacuum tubes eventually led to the development of the tetrode and the pentode tubes. Today, most general purpose amplifiers use semiconductor devices to provide amplification. The bipolar transistor, as shown in *Figure 2.4b* performs the same function as the triode tube of *Figure 2.4a*, but it does it more efficiently (i.e., it consumes far less energy from the power supply). Another popular semiconductor amplifying device is the field-effect transistor (FET) shown in *Figure 2.4c*. Each of the devices in *Figure 2.4* is shown in simplified amplifier circuit configurations, merely for the sake of comparison.

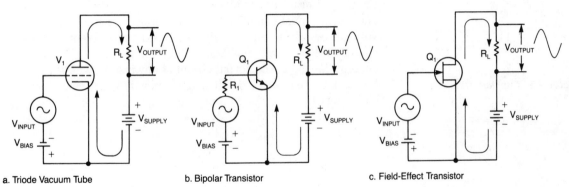

a. Triode Vacuum Tube   b. Bipolar Transistor   c. Field-Effect Transistor

Figure 2.4   Typical Amplifying Devices and Their Circuits

The devices used in power amplifiers differ from those used in voltage amplifiers physically and electronically. Power amplifying devices are physically larger and are designed to operate with higher voltage and current levels than their voltage amplifying counterparts. But otherwise, the basic concepts of both types of amplifier circuits are similar.

AMPLIFIER BIASING AND DC CIRCUITS

Each of the three amplifier schematics in *Figure 2.4* includes two dc power supplies in the form of battery cells. In most practical amplifier circuits, a single dc supply is used to supply all the required power. In any amplifier, the dc supply must satisfy three requirements of the circuit:

1. It provides the energy the amplifier uses to convert a small input signal to a larger output signal.
2. It sets the operating point of (biases) the amplifying device in the proper operating range.
3. It combines with a load device to set the electrical operating conditions of the amplifier.

The dc circuit used to achieve these requirements is called the bias circuit. The bias circuit should prevent changes in the optimum operating conditions even if the amplifying device's characteristics change during operation. While no bias circuit meets this ideal perfectly, a well-designed circuit provides the operational stability required.

Graphic Analysis

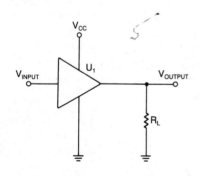

Figure 2.5 Amplifier with Load

A load R_L is shown attached to the output of an amplifier in *Figure 2.5*. This load, along with the power supply, is used to set the operating output power limitations of the amplifier. Output signal current cannot exceed V_{CC}/R_L. This is somewhat more obvious in the bipolar transistor circuit of *Figure 2.6*. The maximum current in the emitter-collector circuit is limited again by the load resistor to V_{CC}/R_L. When the collector current is zero, the transistor is not conducting and the voltage between collector and emitter must equal V_{CC} (in order to satisfy Kirchhoff's voltage law). Between these limits of maximum current and zero current are an infinite number of other current levels. The actual current flowing in the output circuit at any instant will be between these limits and will be determined by the transistor's characteristics, commonly represented as a resistance.

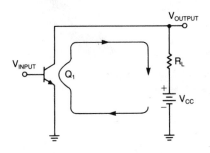

Figure 2.6 DC Output Circuit for a Bipolar Junction Transistor Amplifier

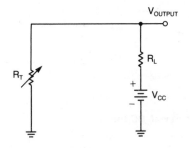

Figure 2.7 Equivalent DC Output Circuit for Bipolar Junction Transistor Amplifier

Observe the equivalent dc circuit in *Figure 2.7*. The transistor is represented as a variable resistance whose value is governed by the current in the base circuit. This is best demonstrated by observing a family of output characteristic curves for the transistor. In *Figure 2.8*, each individual curve represents the conductance characteristic of the collector-to-emitter circuit for a specific base current. The conductance, which is the reciprocal of resistance, is expressed as follows:

$$G = \frac{I}{V} \qquad (2\text{-}6)$$

Example 2-1: The transistor's conductance at point A is 4mA/13V (equation *2-6*), or 308 microsiemens (micromhos). Since resistance is the reciprocal of conductance, the emitter-to-collector resistance at point A is 3.2 kilohms. When V_{CE} is held constant but base current is increased, as point B indicates, the collector current increases. Thus the transistor's emitter-to-collector resistance was decreased by the increased base current.

When this characteristic information is combined with the effects of the load resistor, operation of the circuit in *Figures 2.6* and *2.7* is completely described, as is shown in *Figure 2.9*. The straight line with the negative slope, called the load line, is the locus of possible operating points for the circuit as the base current varies.

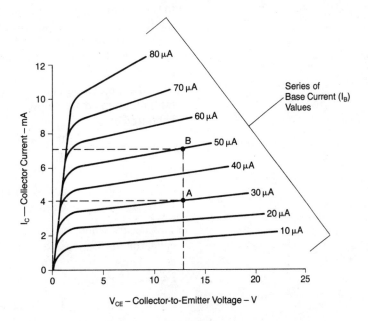

Figure 2.8 Typical Common-Emitter Family of Characteristic Curves (NPN Transistor)

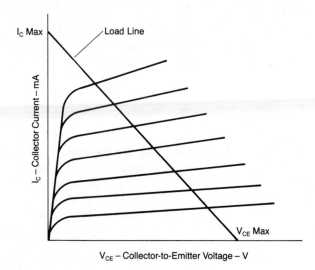

Figure 2.9   Family of Characteristic Curves with DC Load Line

Example 2-2: Given a specific transistor and the load resistance, a load line can be drawn. This is one of the first steps in the design of a bias circuit. It is also useful in analyzing circuit malfunctions. The output circuit is shown for a simple bipolar transistor amplifier in *Figure 2.10a*. The input circuitry is not shown, but it completes the common emitter configuration for the amplifier. There are two operating extremes: when the transistor saturates, maximum current flows, and when the transistor is cut off, minimum current flows. In the ideal case, maximum current is limited only by R_L, so:

$$I_{MAX} = \frac{V_{CC}}{R_L} \qquad (2\text{-}7)$$

$$I_{MAX} = \frac{12V}{2.5 \times 10^3 \Omega}$$

$$I_{MAX} = 4.8mA$$

This occurs when the transistor is saturated. Its emitter-to-collector resistance is zero, so the voltage across it must also be zero. These conditions are represented by point Y of the graph in *Figure 2.10b*.

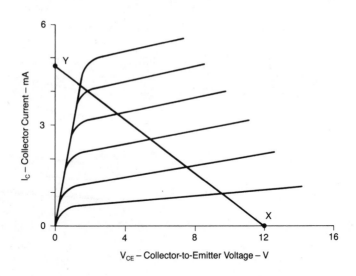

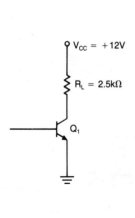

a. Circuit for Load Line

b. Characteristic Curves

Figure 2.10 Drawing the Load Line

At the other extreme, minimum current is achieved when the transistor's emitter-to-collector resistance is infinite. Zero current flows, and the voltage across the transistor equals V_{CC}, or 12 volts. These conditions are represented at point X. Since the circuit is resistive, it has a linear characteristic, and points X and Y are its extremes, or end points. Typical amplifier operation is at a condition somewhere between X and Y, but always along the dc load line between the two extremes.

Without an input signal applied, the circuit's operating conditions are fixed at a specific point on the load line called the quiescent operating point, or Q-point. As illustrated in *Figure 2.11*, the Q-point is completely specified by three parameters: collector-to-emitter voltage, collector current, and base current. When an input signal causes base current to change, both the other two parameters change in response, and the operating point shifts along the load line. For increased base currents the shift is up the load line, and for decreased base currents the shift is down the load line.

For voltage amplifiers, the primary goal is to increase signal voltage amplitude. To allow for the widest amplitude variation in input signals, the Q-point should be located at the mid-point of the load line. This permits the operating point to fluctuate the maximum amount between the two extremes. If the input signal is not too great, the circuit operates linearly, introducing negligible amplitude distortion. This is termed Class A operation.

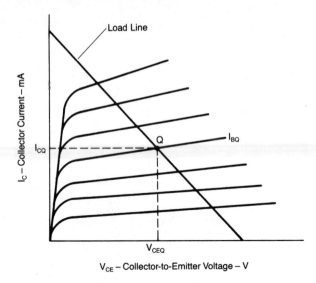

Figure 2.11 Locating the Q-Point

For some applications, it may be desired to amplify only increases (not decreases) in base current caused by the input signal. This can be accomplished by locating the Q-point at the cutoff point (lower extreme) of the load line. The transistor conducts linearly when the operating point shifts upward, but it remains cut off when the operating point attempts to shift downward. Amplifying in this manner is called Class B operation.

A third possibility is to locate the Q-point below the cutoff point. The transistor will conduct only if the signal driven increase in base current is greater than some minimum amount. Although this obviously introduces significant amplitude distortion, this mode of operation does have its applications. It is called Class C operation.

Another intermediate class of amplifier operation is Class AB operation. In this case, the Q-point is placed along the lower half of the dc load line, but above the cutoff point. The transistor conducts for all increases in base current, and for small decreases. It cuts off for the larger decreases in base current, however.

Figure 2.12a shows the Q-point location for the classes of operation described here. *Figure 2.12b* shows how the same sine wave input will be amplified by each of the amplifier classes of operation. The bias circuits for voltage amplifiers provide Class A operation. Classes B, C, and AB are used primarily for power amplifier circuits. Some of these circuits are described in the following sections.

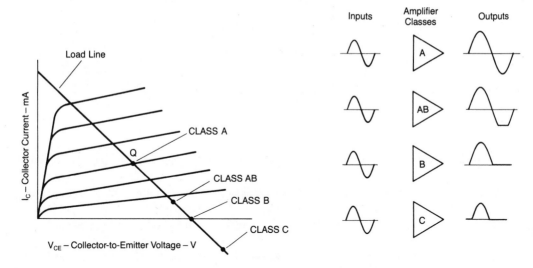

a. Family of Characteristic Curves   b. Amplification of a Sine Input

Figure 2.12 Q-Points for Various Operating Conditions

Fixed Current Bias

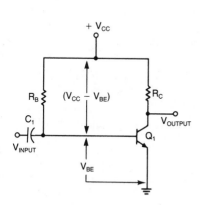

Figure 2.13 Fixed Current Bias Circuit

The Q operating point is set by a bias circuit. A simple bias arrangement, known as fixed current bias, is illustrated in *Figure 2.13*. Assuming that leakage current is negligible, the base current is determined by V_{CC} and R_B. Because these two are constant, the current is also constant. The base current value is given by the equation:

$$I_B = \frac{(V_{CC} - V_{BE})}{R_B} \qquad (2\text{-}8)$$

Example 2-3: In *Figure 2.13*, if V_{CC} equals 15V and R_B is 220 kilohms, base current equals (equation *2-8*):

$$I_B = \frac{(15V - 0.7V)}{220 \times 10^3 \Omega}$$

Note: The value 0.7V is used as the typical V_{BE} for a silicon transistor.

or

$$I_B = 65\mu A$$

The fixed current bias circuit is quite simple, requiring a minimum number of components. However, the bias it provides is inflexible, causing difficulties if the original transistor in the circuit must be replaced or if the circuit's operating conditions change. For example, changes in the ambient temperature can change the biasing requirement of the transistor.

A family of characteristic curves represents a transistor's operation. Two transistors, though they are the same part number, may have slightly different operating characteristics. These differences are illustrated in *Figure 2.14*.

Figure 2.14a shows the output characteristics for one transistor of a given type, while *Figure 2.14b* is a set for another transistor of the same type. In both *a* and *b*, point X is marked at V_{CE} = 9 volts and I_B = 40 microamperes. In *a*, the corresponding collector current is 4.5 milliamperes, while in *b*, it is 6 milliamperes. In a fixed current bias circuit, if the transistor in *a*, is replaced by the transistor in *b*, the operating conditions will be different. For the same base current, different amounts of collector current flow, hence, the transistor in *b* can be saturated by a smaller increase in base current than the one in *a*. As a result, fixed bias circuits should be restricted in use to circuits that have small collector voltage changes.

Characteristic differences like those illustrated in *Figure 2.14* may also occur for the same transistor at different temperatures. Increased temperature tends to cause more collector current to flow, even when base current is fixed, because gain increases with temperature. A fixed current bias circuit has no way to compensate for such characteristic changes, and some other bias arrangement is generally preferred.

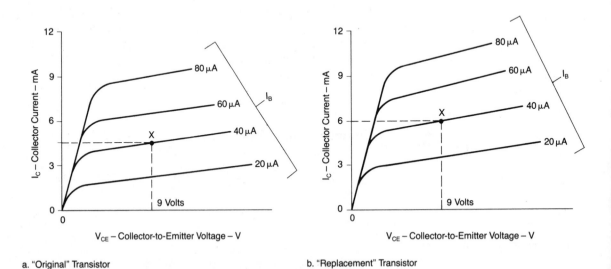

a. "Original" Transistor

b. "Replacement" Transistor

Figure 2.14 *Typical Characteristic Curve Differences of Two Transistors of the Same Type*

Collector Feedback Bias

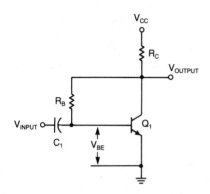

Figure 2.15 Collector Feedback Bias Circuit

The bias arrangement shown in *Figure 2.15* provides some improvement over the fixed bias circuit. It uses collector feedback bias to allow the base current to react to changes in collector current. As the figure shows, the base resistor is attached to the collector and not to V_{CC}. If collector current should increase for any reason, the collector voltage decreases, reducing the voltage across R_B, which reduces base current. Since collector current is directly proportional to base current, a reduction in base current causes a corresponding reduction in collector current.

By allowing base current to be changed, the collector feedback bias circuit avoids some of the difficulties associated with the fixed bias circuit previously described. However, some of the circuit's ac output signal is also fed back to the input during operation, reducing the amplifier's gain. Even though the gain loss may be a disadvantage, the collector feedback bias circuit is widely used because of its simplicity.

Voltage Divider Bias

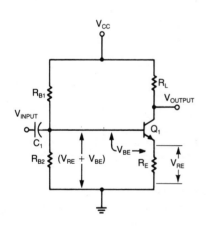

Figure 2.16 Voltage Divider Bias Circuit

The circuit in *Figure 2.16*, a sophisticated version of collector feedback bias, is probably the most commonly used common emitter bias circuit. The two resistors R_{B1} and R_{B2} form a voltage divider from V_{CC}, placing a fixed voltage at the base of the transistor. This voltage divider not only fixes the base voltage, but also the voltage across the emitter resistor, R_E, which fixes the emitter current. Because collector and emitter currents are almost equal in a common emitter circuit, a constant current in the emitter circuit assures a constant collector current.

With reference to *Figure 2.16*, the voltage developed across R_{B2} equals the sum of V_{BE} and the voltage across R_E. Since V_{BE} is typically 0.7 volt, the voltage across R_E is 0.7 volt less than that across R_{B2}.

Limitations on the values of R_{B1} and R_{B2} are necessary to ensure that changes in the transistor's base current do not significantly affect the dc bias at the base. Base current flows in R_{B1} along with the voltage divider current. When the circuit amplifies an input signal, the base current is subject to constant change. Base current, therefore, must be negligible as compared to the voltage divider current in order to prevent significant shifts in the voltage across R_{B2}. This can be accomplished by choosing R_{B1} and R_{B2} so that the voltage divider current approximately equals the collector current at the Q-point.

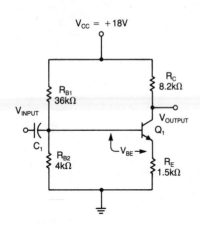

$V_{CC} = +18V$

R_{B1}
$36k\Omega$

R_C
$8.2k\Omega$

V_{INPUT}

C_1

V_{OUTPUT}
Q_1

V_{BE}

R_{B2}
$4k\Omega$

R_E
$1.5k\Omega$

Figure 2.17 Voltage Divider Bias Circuit (Example 2-4)

Since the dc current gain (h_{FE}) of most small signal amplifier transistors is 20 or more, base current will be 1/20 or less of the collector current; therefore, its effect on base voltage is negligible. The stable bias arrangement provided by the voltage divider bias circuit can best be appreciated by analyzing an example circuit.

Example 2-4: Refer to the circuit of *Figure 2.17*. The equation for the voltage across R_{B2} in the voltage divider of R_{B1} and R_{B2} from 18 volts is:

$$V_{RB2} = \frac{R_{B2}}{R_{B2} + R_{B1}} \times 18V \qquad (2\text{-}9)$$

Substituting values gives

$$V_{RB2} = \frac{4k\Omega}{36k\Omega + 4k\Omega} \times 18V$$

or

$$V_{RB2} = 1.8V$$

The emitter resistor voltage is the difference between 1.8 volts and 0.7 volts

$$V_{RE} = 1.8V - 0.7V$$
$$V_{RE} = 1.1V$$

The emitter current is calculated by Ohm's law (equation *2-10*) using the R_E value of 1.5 kilohms and the value of V_{RE} of 1.1 volts.

$$I = \frac{V}{R} \qquad (2\text{-}10)$$

$$I = \frac{1.1V}{1.5k\Omega}$$

$$I = 0.73mA$$

The collector current is approximately the same. Changes in the transistor's characteristics have little effect on the dc operating point.

Differences in operating temperatures or differences in transistor output characteristics both are evidenced by differences in the transistor's dc current gain (h_{FE} or beta). Example *2-4* illustrates the stability in operating conditions afforded by the voltage divider bias circuit. Variations in h_{FE} have little effect on Q-point location. This kind of stability makes the voltage divider bias circuit a very popular design for amplifier biasing.

SMALL SIGNAL AMPLIFIER AC ANALYSIS

Small signal amplifiers are typically used as the first several stages of amplifier systems. Variations of the voltage divider bias circuit are used here to illustrate the characteristics of such stages.

Coupling Methods

Coupling networks are used between stages of an amplifier to transmit the ac signal from one stage to the next without upsetting the bias arrangement provided by the bias networks. In its simplest form, a coupling network may be a series capacitor whose reactance is low enough to pass the signal without objectionable attenuation, while blocking the dc bias levels between stages. This type coupling is shown in *Figure 2.18*. A capacitor at the input passes the signal to the base of the transistor, and an output capacitor transmits the amplified signal to the succeeding stage. Because of the two capacitors, the bias voltages of the stage have no effect on either the signal source or the load circuits.

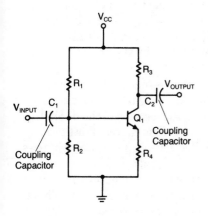

Figure 2.18 RC Coupling

Another way to isolate stages is to use transformers to couple the signal. In *Figure 2.19* the collector resistor of the bias circuit has been replaced by a transformer for coupling purposes. Changes in the collector current are electromagnetically coupled to the secondary of the transformer. The secondary is connected to the input of the next amplifier stage. Again, the dc collector voltage of the first stage is isolated from the base voltage of the second stage.

Both capacitor coupling and transformer coupling can be used for amplifying ac signal voltages. If dc voltage levels are to be amplified, special integrated circuit designs incorporating directly coupled devices are used.

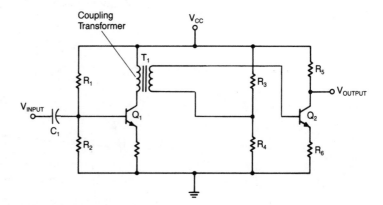

Figure 2.19 Transformer Coupling

AC Load Line

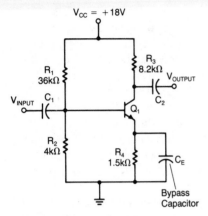

For the voltage divider bias circuit, output current flows through both the collector resistor and the emitter resistor. Thus, although the emitter resistor is used mainly because of its stabilizing effect in the bias circuit, it has some of the signal voltage developed across it which reduces the amount of output voltage dropped at the collector. The result is that gain is decreased.

In small signal amplifiers, the emitter resistor is almost always bypassed by a large capacitor C_E as shown in *Figure 2.20*. This provides a low impedance path for the ac output signal current, eliminating the emitter signal voltage feedback. The stability offered by the voltage divider bias circuit is still available, but the reduction in gain caused by the emitter resistor is avoided.

Two different output circuits exist — one for the dc of the bias arrangement, and another for the ac signal. Recall that the output circuit resistance determines the location of the dc load line on the transistor's output characteristic curves. For the ac signal, the impedance is different because of C_E, the large bypass capacitor, so the load line for the ac circuit also is different. *Figure 2.21* shows both the dc and the ac load lines for the amplifier stage circuit in *Figure 2.20*. Note that the ac load line's slope is greater than for the dc load line, because the ac impedance is smaller than the dc resistance. Note also that the two lines intersect at the Q-point, the point at which the transistor operates when no signal is applied. When a signal is applied, the ac operating point shifts up and down along the ac load line.

Figure 2.20　Amplifier Stage with Bypassed Emitter Resistor

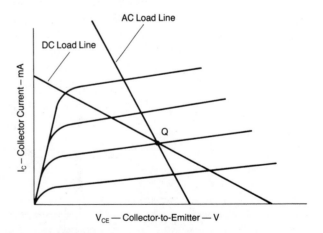

Figure 2.21　AC and DC Load Lines Compared

Voltage Gain

Input signal voltages increase and decrease the base voltage, thereby varying the base current above and below the dc bias level. At the amplifier output, collector voltage increases and decreases because of the transistor's response to the changing base current. All this activity can be observed by plotting the changes on the ac load line. The following example illustrates such an analysis.

Example 2-5: The graph in *Figure 2.22* shows the output characteristics for the circuit of *Figure 2.20*. Assume that an input signal voltage of 0.1 volt peak-to-peak is applied to the stage. Therefore, the Q-point base voltage, 1.8 volts, is increased to 1.85 volts and decreased to 1.75 volts by this signal. Base current varies directly as the voltage, changing from the Q-point value of 20 microamperes to a maximum of 24 microamperes and to a minimum of 16 microamperes. *Figure 2.22* indicates these base current limits on the load line. The corresponding collector currents are also marked on the vertical axis. The minimum collector current, 560 microamperes, causes 4.6 volts to be dropped across R_C, leaving 13.4 volts from the collector to ground. Maximum collector current of 840 microamperes drops 6.9 volts across R_C, leaving 11.1 volts from the collector to ground.

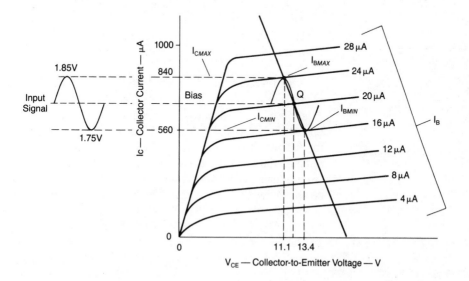

Figure 2.22 Small Signal Amplifier Analysis

Thus, the signal at the collector varies from 11.1 volts to 13.4 volts, or 2.3 volts peak to peak. Voltage gain, from equation *2-1*, is:

$$A_V = \frac{V_{OUT}}{V_{IN}}$$

$$A_V = \frac{2.3V}{0.1V}$$

$$A_V = 23$$

In the example, maximum collector voltage occurred when the base current reached its minimum. This is called phase shift, and it always equals 180 degrees for a common emitter amplifier like the one of *Figure 2.20*.

Frequency Response

Ideally, the voltage gain of a small-signal amplifier should remain constant for all input signal frequencies within the linear operating range of the amplifier. Of course, this ideal condition can never be completely realized. At extremely low frequencies, the input coupling capacitor may appreciably attenuate the input signal. Gain will be reduced if the input signal frequency is so low that the coupling capacitor's reactance exceeds about one-tenth of the circuit input resistance. The output coupling capacitor and the emitter bypass capacitor will also limit the gain at low frequencies. Higher capacitive reactances in both cases reduce the available output signal.

At very high frequencies, the interelement capacitances of the transistor itself cause its characteristics to be altered. The current gain of a transistor is smaller at very high frequencies than at low frequencies, again resulting in a reduction in amplifier gain.

Figure 2.23 is a frequency response curve for an amplifier. It is a plot of voltage gain versus frequency. Voltage gain is relatively constant in the middle part of the response curve. At both ends, however, the gain drops off for the reasons previously mentioned. The frequencies at which the gain has fallen to approximately 0.707 of the mid-range gain are called the cutoff frequencies. The lower and upper cutoff frequencies are marked on the curve in *Figure 2.23*. The range of frequencies between these two cutoff points is called the passband.

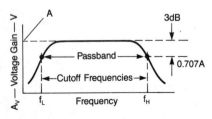

Figure 2.23 Frequency Response Curve

The cutoff points are sometimes called the half-power points or the 3dB points. If the mid-range voltage is considered to be 1 volt, then the cutoff point voltage is 0.707 volt. The power developed across a 50 ohm load at the mid-range is expressed as:

$$P = \frac{V^2}{R} \tag{2-11}$$

$$P = \frac{(1V)^2}{50\Omega}$$

$$P = 0.02W$$

At the cutoff points, the load power would be

$$P = \frac{(0.707V)^2}{50\Omega}$$

$$P = \frac{0.5V^2}{50\Omega}$$

or

$$P = 0.01W$$

At the cutoff points, only one-half the power is available. In decibel units, the relative power is calculated by equation *2-4*:

$$P_{dB} = 10 \log_{10} \frac{P_{OUT}}{P_{IN}}$$

$$P_{dB} = 10 \log_{10} \frac{0.02W}{0.01W}$$

$$P_{dB} = 10 \times 0.3$$

or

$$P_{dB} = -3dB$$

The power gain in this case is negative because of the reduction in power of the half-power points.

Input and Output Impedance

Ideally, an amplifier should have infinite input impedance and zero output impedance causing no drain on the previous stage, and an unlimited ability to drive the next stage. Common emitter amplifiers, unfortunately, rate poorly on both of these parameters. Their input impedance typically is only a few thousand ohms, while typical output impedance may be tens of thousands of ohms. For small-signal amplifier applications, these shortcomings can often be overcome by careful attention to system design. The high output impedance usually causes no real difficulties because small-signal amplifiers do not usually have to drive load devices requiring large currents.

For high input impedance, modern small-signal amplifiers are usually designed with field-effect transistors (FETs). The input circuit (gate-to-source) of FET amplifiers is reverse biased, which makes the input impedance dependent only upon the bias circuit. The bias circuit can be designed to match the amplifier to the source's impedance.

POWER AMPLIFIERS

An amplifier capable of delivering large amounts of power to a load must be capable of dissipating significant power in its own circuitry. Its transistor(s) typically must operate over a wide range of collector voltages and currents (large dynamic range) and usually dissipate more than one watt. The resistors in its bias network are usually low resistance, high wattage devices. In addition to these physical characteristics, power amplifiers usually operate as Class B or Class AB circuits, as opposed to the Class A operation of the small signal amplifiers investigated previously.

Class A

Class A amplifiers provide linear operation as long as the input signal does not overdrive the transistor. Refer again to *Figure 2.12a* and *12b*. For a power amplifier, Class A operation requires that the Q-point be located as nearly as possible at the center of the ac load line for low distortion output. Except for the typical values of the resistors, the bias circuit is the same as that used for small-signal amplifiers.

A significant disadvantage of Class A operation is that the transistor must dissipate appreciable power even when no input signal is applied, because its bias point is the no signal condition at the center of its signal swing. The exact amount of power may be calculated by multiplying collector current by collector-to-emitter voltage at the Q-point. The circuit is not very efficient because at no signal condition the circuit dissipates power but is delivering no signal (no power) to its load. Although the same situation is true for small-signal amplifiers, it is not a significant problem because the Q-point power is relatively low. One solution to the problem is to select another class of operation.

Class B and AB

Recall that Class B operation is achieved by biasing the amplifier transistor at its cutoff point, permitting the transistor to conduct for only one-half cycle of the input signal. This, of course, does not result in linear operation, but it does prevent the transistor from dissipating power when no input signal is applied.

The non-linearity problem can be partially overcome by connecting two Class B amplifiers so that one conducts for the positive portion of the input signal while the other conducts for the negative portion. This is called push-pull operation and the basic circuit is shown in *Figure 2.24*. Two equal amplitude but out-of-phase input signals are required, as shown. These can be provided by coupling the input signal to the amplifier with a center-tapped transformer or by using some other type of phase splitter circuit. The output signals from the two transistors are transformer coupled to the load, shown here as R_L.

If the two transistors are biased exactly at cutoff, the characteristic of Class B operation as previously explained, they will not begin to conduct until the input signal voltage forward biases the base-emitter junction. Until this occurs, no output signal is produced. Crossover distortion is inherent in the circuit operation, but this distortion can be prevented by biasing the transistors slightly above cutoff, in AB operation.

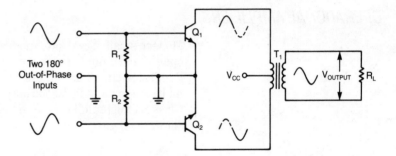

Figure 2.24   Two Class B Amplifiers in Push-Pull Configuration

Transformerless Power Amplifiers

The weight, size, and expense of the output transformers used in the Class B and AB amplifiers previously described can be eliminated by the use of two complementary transistors. *Figure 2.25a* shows one such design. The amplifier is an emitter follower (common collector) push-pull amplifier designed for Class B operation. Only one input signal is required because the NPN transistor (Q_1) is forward biased by the positive excursion and the PNP Q_2 transistor responds to the negative excursion. The output signal is capacitively coupled to the load.

Figure 2.25b shows essentially the same circuit designed with the Darlington transistor configuration. The advantage of this circuit is a much higher input impedance as compared to other designs.

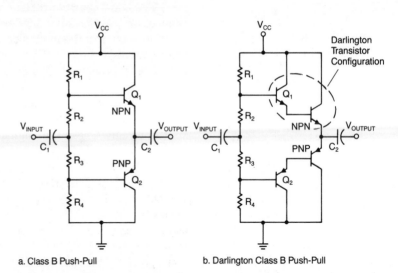

a. Class B Push-Pull　　　　　　　　b. Darlington Class B Push-Pull

Figure 2.25　*Transformerless Emitter-Follower Power Amplifiers*

OPERATIONAL AMPLIFIERS

Modern small-signal amplifiers are often designed using operational amplifiers (op amps). Op amps are direct-coupled integrated circuit amplifiers having differential inputs. They are multi-stage amplifiers, the output stage of which is usually a Class B emitter follower. Symbolically they are represented as shown in *Figure 2.26*.

Characteristics

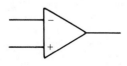

a. Symbol

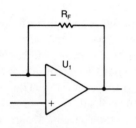

b. Typical Degenerative Feedback Circuit

Figure 2.26　*Operational Amplifiers*

The input marked "+" in *Figure 2.26* is called the non-inverting input, and the "−" input is called the inverting input. For most amplifier circuits, some type of feedback is used to set the gain to the desired level. (Feedback means that a portion of the output signal is channeled back to the input by means of an electronic circuit, as shown in *Figure 2.26b*.) If the feedback signal is in-phase with the input signal it is called regenerative feedback; out-of-phase feedback is called degenerative feedback. Regenerative feedback is used for oscillators, whereas degenerative feedback is generally used for amplifier circuits. The gain of an operational amplifier without feedback is called open-loop gain. When feedback is used, the gain figure is called closed-loop gain.

Feedback also controls the frequency response of an op amp circuit. Although op amps will amplify frequencies from dc to more than 1MHz, such bandwidth is not usually required in practical applications, and feedback is employed to adjust the trade-off between voltage gain and bandwidth.

The input impedance of op amps may be extremely high, usually more than a megohm, while the output impedance is relatively low, often less than 100 ohms. These impedances also depend partly on the feedback networks used. High input impedance, low output impedance, high gain, and wide bandwidth make the operational amplifier more nearly like the ideal amplifier than any other circuit examined so far.

Differential Amplifiers

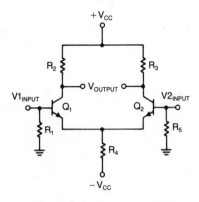

Figure 2.27   Differential Amplifier

The input stage of most op amps is a differential amplifier. A typical differential amplifier is diagrammed in *Figure 2.27*. The two transistors and their associated bias resistors are matched so that the two halves of the circuit conduct equal currents when no signal is applied at either input (the base leads of the transistors). The output signal, measured between the two collectors, is zero when no signal is applied. When a signal is applied to either input, the balance condition is upset and a difference voltage can be measured between the collectors. Inputs may be applied to either input or to both inputs simultaneously. In either case, the output is the amplified difference between the two inputs. In an op amp package, the differential output voltage is applied to several more stages of amplification before it is coupled to the op amp output.

Example 2-6: A differential amplifier's gain is 150. If the signal at one input is 30 millivolts and the other input signal is 28 millivolts, find the output voltage. Given the equation *2-5*:

$$A_V = \frac{V_{OUT}}{V_{IN}}$$

By rearranging the equation

$$V_{OUT} = V_{IN} \times A_V$$
$$V_{OUT} = (30 - 28)mV \times 150$$

or

$$V_{OUT} = 300mV$$

Direct-Coupled Amplifiers

Figure 2.28 is a typical op amp schematic showing how the amplifier stages are dc coupled. Notice that no coupling capacitors are used between stages, requiring the output transistor of one stage to be a part of the input bias of the succeeding stage. Because of this feature, input signals as dc levels, ac signals, and ac signals with dc levels may be amplified.

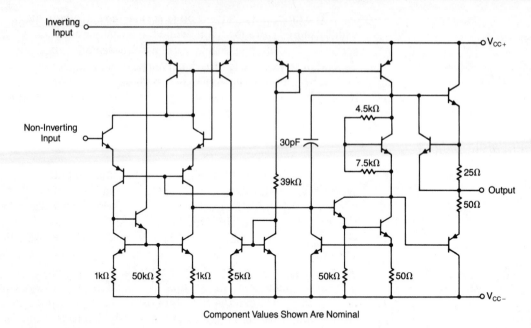

Figure 2.28 Production Op Amp Schematic

Basic Amplifier Circuits

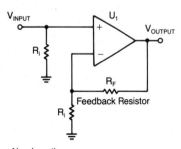

a. Non-Inverting

Two operational amplifier circuits are shown in *Figure 2.29*. A non-inverting amplifier is diagrammed in *a*, while *b* shows an inverting amplifier. Note that in both circuits a resistor is used to feed some of the output signal back to the input. For both circuits, the gain is controlled by the ratio of the two resistors, R_F and R_i. Precision resistors may be used to set the gain value, allowing for superb gain control and stability over a wide range of ambient temperatures. This feature makes the op amp ideal for use in precision measurement instrumentation.

For the non-inverting amplifier, the input signal is applied to the non-inverting input. The gain is determined by the following expression:

$$A_V = \frac{R_F}{R_i} + 1. \qquad (2\text{-}12)$$

The gain of the inverting amplifier is determined by this expression:

$$A_V = -\frac{R_F}{R_i} \qquad (2\text{-}13)$$

where the minus sign indicates that the output signal is 180 degrees out of phase with the input. The input signal is applied through R_i to the inverting input.

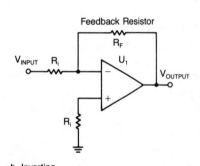

b. Inverting

Figure 2.29 Operational Amplifiers

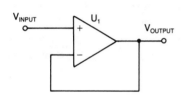

a. Voltage Follower

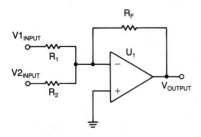

b. Summing Amplifier

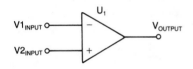

c. Comparator

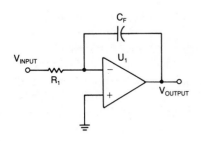

d. Integrator

Figure 2.30   Other Op Amp Applications

It was mentioned previously that the bandwidth of an op amp circuit depends partly on the feedback used. Op amps do not have a lower cutoff frequency because they are dc coupled. The upper cutoff frequency is determined from the equation:

$$f_C = f_o \frac{A_O}{A_C} \qquad (2\text{-}14)$$

where f_C is the closed-loop cutoff frequency, f_o is the open-loop cutoff frequency, A_O is the open-loop gain, and A_C is the closed loop gain.

Example 2-7: The specifications for the SN72741 op amp give A_O as 200,000 (typical value) and f_o as approximately 10 Hz. If feedback is used to set the closed loop gain to 40, find the upper cutoff frequency. Substituting into equation 2-14:

$$f_C = 10\text{Hz} \frac{2 \times 10^5}{4 \times 10^1}$$

$$f_C = 50\text{kHz}$$

One other important op amp specification is slew rate. Slew rate, which is the maximum rate at which the output signal can change, limits the bandwidth for large signals. According to the specification sheet, the slew rate of the SN72741 is 0.5 volt/microsecond. If an input signal should cause the output to attempt to change at a rate greater than the slew rate, the output signal would be distorted.

The usefulness of the operational amplifier is demonstrated by the circuits in *Figure 2.30*. As the figure illustrates, the same op amp can be used for a number of different purposes just by changing the support circuitry. In *Figure 2.30a*, the op amp is used as a voltage follower, an op amp version of the emitter follower circuit. It is just a special case of the non-inverting amplifier in which R_F is 0 and $A_V = 1$.

A summing amplifier like the one in *Figure 2.30b* can be used to combine two or more input signals. The output voltage from input V_1 is determined as follows by using equation 2-13:

$$V_O = -\frac{R_F}{R_1}V_1 \qquad (2\text{-}15)$$

A similar equation determines the output voltage due to input V_2. If R_1 and R_2 are equal, the combined output voltage is the gain times the sum of the input voltages, V_1 and V_2. The expression is:

$$V_O = -\frac{R_F}{R_1}(V_1 + V_2) \qquad (2\text{-}16)$$

The minus sign indicates inversion. Any number of inputs can be combined by this circuit.

Without any feedback the op amp can be used as a comparator, as in *Figure 2.30c*. The output voltage level will be either a low level or a high level. If the signal at the inverting input is greater than the signal at the non-inverting input, the output saturates in its most negative voltage direction. Reversing the two signals causes the output to saturate in the most positive voltage direction.

The operational amplifier got its name because it was originally designed to perform mathematical operations. The summing amplifier, for example, acts as an adder when the feedback resistor equals the input resistors. The calculus operation of integration is performed by the integrator circuit of *Figure 2.30d*. Operational amplifiers are used for many other purposes such as active filters, current sources, and precision rectifiers.

OSCILLATOR CONCEPTS

An oscillator is an electronic circuit which produces an output signal that varies periodically. The output signal may be sinusoidal or non-sinusoidal. Most oscillators are constructed by providing regenerative feedback to an amplifier. Recall that regenerative feedback means that a portion of the output signal is fed back in phase with the amplifier's input, reinforcing the input.

Principles of Oscillation

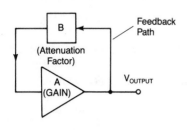

If certain conditions are met, an amplifier becomes an oscillator circuit and will produce an output signal without an external input signal applied. The required condition for oscillation is called the Barkhausen Criterion. *Figure 2.31* helps explain the oscillation requirement. The A inside the amplifier symbol represents the gain of the amplifier. The block labelled B is the feedback network. B represents the network's attenuation factor. If B equals 0.1 for example, the feedback to the amplifier input is one-tenth the level of the amplifier output. The feedback network must also make sure that the feedback signal at the amplifier input is of the proper phase. For example, if the amplifier is an inverting amplifier, the feedback network must also invert the portion of the output it returns to the input so the feedback will be regenerative. The Barkhausen Criterion states that a circuit like the one in *Figure 2.31* will oscillate if the product A × B is equal to or greater than 1 when the phase of the feedback signal is regenerative.

Figure 2.31 Basic Oscillator Structure

Oscillators are often classified according to the type of feedback network employed. In the sections that follow, some common oscillator circuits are described. Although the general amplifier symbol is used throughout, the actual amplifier circuit may be a discrete transistor amplifier or an integrated circuit amplifier. In most cases, however, an inverting type amplifier is used.

Phase Shift Oscillator

One way to reinvert the output of an inverting amplifier is to use an RC network for feedback. The circuit in *Figure 2.32* uses three RC circuits to provide a total phase shift of 180 degrees by designing the RC circuits so that each provides 60 degrees phase shift. The oscillation frequency is calculated by:

$$f = \frac{1}{2\pi RC\sqrt{6}}$$

(2-17)

When R_1C_1, R_2C_2 and R_3C_3 are equal.

Colpitts and Hartley Oscillators

The feedback networks in the circuits of *Figure 2.33* are LC circuits. In both oscillators, the feedback circuit acts like a filter to couple the desired oscillator frequency to the amplifier input while blocking all others. The oscillator frequency equals the resonant frequency of the tank circuit formed by the capacitance and inductance.

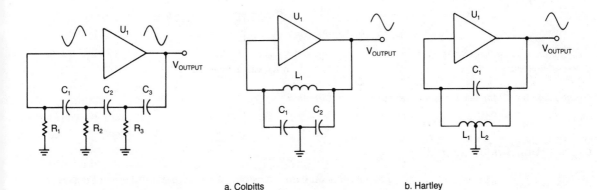

a. Colpitts   b. Hartley

Figure 2.32 Phase Shift Oscillator   **Figure 2.33 Two LC Oscillators**

Wien Bridge Oscillator

A popular low frequency oscillator is the Wien Bridge oscillator of *Figure 2.34*. The circuit uses a non-inverting amplifier and an ac bridge to meet the Barkhausen Criterion. The bridge circuit is most easily seen in *Figure 2.34a*. It is balanced only at the oscillation frequency. In *Figure 2.34b*, the non-inverting amplifier is more easily distinguished.

If the bridge is designed so that $R_1 = R_2$, let the symbol R represent either value. If $C_1 = C_2$, let the symbol C represent either value. Then the frequency of oscillation is determined by the expression:

$$f = \frac{1}{2\pi RC} \qquad\qquad (2\text{-}18)$$

The Barkhausen Criterion is met only if R_4 is equal to or greater than twice the value of R_3.

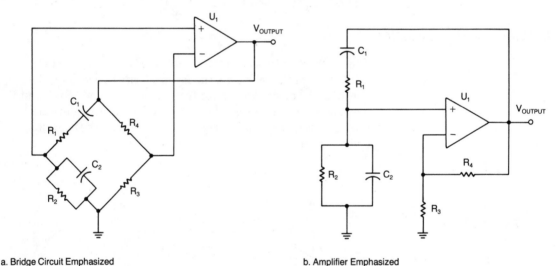

a. Bridge Circuit Emphasized   b. Amplifier Emphasized

Figure 2.34   Two Examples of a Wien Bridge Oscillator Circuit

Crystal-Controlled Oscillator

The oscillation frequency of the circuits examined so far has been determined by the resistors, capacitors, or inductors in the feedback network. Because the values of R, C, and L may vary slightly when the temperature changes, the oscillation frequency will also vary. In some situations, the variation may be so great that it is intolerable. When a high priority is placed on frequency stability, crystal-controlled oscillators are commonly used.

The crystals of certain materials, such as quartz, have natural oscillation frequencies just like a resonant LC circuit. This phenomenon is called the piezoelectric effect. Because the crystal's resonant frequency is relatively independent of temperature changes, they may be used to control the frequency of an oscillator, keeping the frequency amazingly stable despite changes in the ambient temperature.

Crystals may be operated at their series resonant frequency, their parallel resonant frequency, or, for very high frequency oscillators, in multiples (harmonics). *Figure 2.35* shows a crystal-controlled oscillator circuit in which the crystal is used in its series resonant mode. The crystal effectively locks the circuit into oscillating at the crystal's resonant frequency. There are many other variations of the crystal-controlled oscillator, but in all cases the oscillating frequency is controlled by a resonant frequency of the crystal.

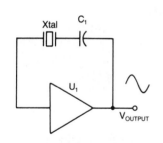

Figure 2.35   Crystal Oscillator

Negative Resistance Oscillators

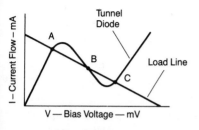

a. Typical Circuit

b. Operating Characteristics

Figure 2.36   Tunnel Diode Oscillator

The tunnel diode is a device that has a negative resistance region, i.e., at one point in its operation an increase in applied voltage causes a decrease in current. While the tunnel diode is not the only device which exhibits a negative resistance characteristic, it will be used here to demonstrate the design of negative resistance oscillators.

Tunnel diodes have a frequency limit which may extend into the gigahertz range. This makes them particularly useful for extremely high frequency oscillators like the one in *Figure 2.36a*. Resistors R_1 and R_2 bias the tunnel diode to establish the load line shown in *Figure 2.36b*. R_P represents the coil resistance of the LC tank circuit. Normally, R_P would dampen the oscillations, but in the tunnel diode oscillator, the negative resistance of the tunnel diode counteracts the attenuating effects of resistance, thus sustaining oscillations.

The three points A, B, and C marked on the load line illustrate the oscillation effect. Operation is stable at points A and C because the resistance is positive there, but operation is unstable at point B, in the negative resistance region. The operating point of the tunnel diode can be made to switch rapidly through the negative resistance region by varying the bias voltage. The variation in bias voltage is provided by the tank circuit's flywheel effect.

Other Types of Non-Sinusoidal Oscillators

Figure 2.37 shows two other oscillator circuits, each of which produces a non-sinusoidal output. In *Figure 2.37a*, two transistors use RC coupling to create an astable multivibrator. The transistors alternate between saturation and cutoff. When one is in saturation the other is in cutoff, so that the signal at either collector is approximately a square wave. The frequency of the square wave depends on the values of the RC coupling network.

The circuit in *Figure 2.37b* is a unijunction oscillator. It is a form of relaxation oscillator which uses an RC circuit to determine the frequency of oscillation. The RC time constant is the primary determinant of the output frequency. This circuit provides three different output signals. The voltage across the capacitor can be made to vary in a sawtooth fashion, while negative and positive pulses are available at the two base leads of the unijunction, as shown in the figure. Both the circuits in *Figure 2.37* are used for low frequency oscillators in applications where stability is not critical.

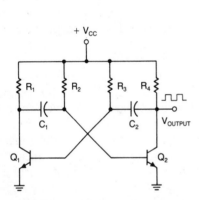

a. Astable Multivibrator

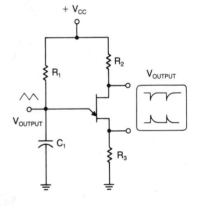

b. Unijunction Oscillator

Figure 2.37   Two Non-Sinusoidal Oscillators

UHF AND MICROWAVE OSCILLATORS

The oscillator circuits presented so far, except for the tunnel diode, are intended for operation at frequencies no more than a few megahertz. The components used in these oscillators have physical limitations which prevent them from operating properly at higher frequencies. A few of the more common types of microwave oscillators which use specially-designed vacuum-tube amplifier tubes will be described here.

Reflex Klystron Oscillator

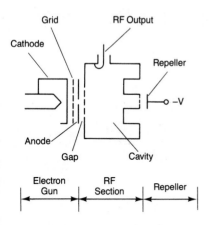

Figure 2.38   Reflex Klystron Tube

A cutaway view of a klystron tube is shown in *Figure 2.38*. This tube, which is used as the amplifying element in many microwave oscillators, has three major parts: the electron gun, the RF section, and the repeller. The electron gun emits a focused beam of high velocity electrons. The velocity is achieved by accelerating the electrons toward a positively charged anode. Focusing is accomplished by either electromagnetic or electrostatic means.

The oscillation in the klystron occurs in its RF section. In it, a metal chamber called a cavity resonator acts as an LC resonant circuit. The gaps in the cavity (as shown in *Figure 2.38*) provide the capacitive element, while the cavity walls themselves react to the magnetic field surrounding the moving electrons to produce self-inductance. The values of the capacitance and inductance depend on the physical dimensions of the cavity, which can be made to resonate at a desired microwave frequency by mechanically adjusting its size.

A low-level RF input excites the cavity so that it resonates. The electron beam is alternately accelerated and retarded, causing the electrons to collect in clusters as they pass through the cavity. A repeller electrode reflects the clusters back into the cavity and through a catcher gap, where they induce an RF sine current. Power is coupled from the cavity to the load via the RF output terminal.

Magnetron Oscillator

Magnetrons are vacuum tubes which, like klystrons, produce high frequency oscillations by accelerating electron clusters past resonant cavities. Magnetrons, however, use an external magnet to produce a field which determines the path followed by the electrons as they proceed from cathode to anode. The three main types of magnetrons are pulsed, continuous wave (CW), and frequency modulated (FM). Pulsed magnetrons are widely used for radar applications, CW magnetrons are used for industrial heating and Doppler-effect radar and FM magnetrons are used for microwave communication systems.

A typical magnetron is shown in *Figure 2.39a*. The cathode emits electrons into the region surrounded by the anode. This entire region is encased by the external magnet. In *Figure 2.39b* one type of magnetron anode, the vane type, is shown in greater detail. The cathode is shown at the center of the circular anode.

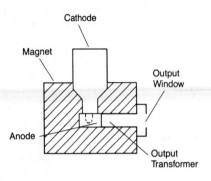

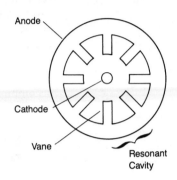

a. Typical Magnetron   b. Vane Type Magnetron

Figure 2.39   Magnetron Structure

The anode is divided into a number of resonating cavities by vanes which extend toward the cathode. When electrons are emitted from the cathode they are drawn toward the anode, but their path is distorted by the magnetic field so that they travel past the ends of the anode vanes. In the process, they induce currents in the vanes which sustain oscillations in the resonant cavities. The frequency is determined by the physical dimensions of the resonant cavity.

Backward-Wave Oscillator

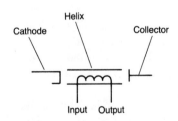

Figure 2.40   Traveling Wave Tube

The backward-wave oscillator uses the interaction between an RF signal and an electron beam to stimulate oscillations. To achieve oscillation over a wide band of frequencies, the backward-wave oscillator uses the principle of the traveling-wave tube, diagrammed in *Figure 2.40*. An electron beam is accelerated through the center of a helical coil while an RF signal is injected into the coil. In some areas, the RF field will accelerate the electrons, but in other areas it retards them. Retarded electrons lose energy to the RF field, thereby amplifying it.

The backward-wave oscillator is designed so that a severe mismatch exists at the collector end of the tube, and reflections are produced. The reflected wave travels toward the cathode and is in phase with the input wave. This regenerative feedback sustains oscillations. Backward-wave oscillators are tunable by varying the RF input voltage.

SUMMARY

In this chapter we have examined the basic concepts of amplifiers and oscillators. We learned that all amplifiers have three major parameters in common — gain, impedance, and distortion.

Gain is the relative increase in signal strength, usually indicated in dB units; impedance is the net ac circuit resistance of the input and output points, and distortion is the relative fidelity of the output waveforms as compared to the input.

The power supply, through the dc baising network, supplies the electrical energy and the biasing levels, permitting the amplifier to increase the level of the input signal. The quiescent dc level maintained by the input biasing network determines whether the entire signal will be amplified or part of it will be in the cut-off region. Class A bias sets the operation at the midpoint of the amplifier load line, whereas Class C bias pushes it beyond cutoff, allowing only signal peaks to be amplified. Intermediate classes bias between these extremes.

Each active semiconductor device has its own family of curves which graphically show the relationships between input and output for a range of transistor bias voltages and currents. A load line value superimposed on the curves is used to design the bias network.

The operational characteristics of a given semiconductor are partially determined by the bias voltages developed. The circuitry to develop transistor bias includes fixed bias, collector feedback bias, and voltage divider bias. The latter is the most desirable because of its stability.

There are two basic types of amplifiers — small signal and power. The small signal type is usually a voltage or low current gain device. Power amplifiers convert a low level voltage signal into a power output signal which is used to drive an audio speaker, a printer, a display or some other electromechanical device.

All oscillators are basically amplifier circuits with positive feedback and sometimes a tuned circuit. There is a wide variety of oscillator circuits, but their frequency of oscillation is determined by the component values chosen for the feedback path. Important oscillator parameters include frequency of operation, output waveform and frequency stability.

Oscillators designed for the UHF and microwave region do not utilize discrete electronic component layout conventions, but are really mechanical assemblies. This is because the frequencies involved are so high that the stray and distributed reactances resulting from "low frequency" assembly methods would far exceed the acceptable limits, and the circuits would not function properly.

71

QUIZ

120 MV TO 3V

3000 = 3VOLTS

MILLIVOLTS = 1000

120 MILLIVOLTS

1. An amplifier outputs 3 volts rms when its input is 120 millivolts. Its voltage gain is:
   a. 4.
   b. 15.
   c. 25.
   d. 40.

2. An amplifier delivers the maximum power to its load when the amplifier's output impedance:

   Pg 41
   ?

   a. equals its input impedance.
   b. equals the load impedance.
   c. is zero.
   d. is infinite.

3. For Class A operation, an amplifier's Q-point should be located:
   a. near the center of the load line.
   b. near the saturation point.
   c. near the cutoff point.
   d. below the cutoff point.

4. A circuit which produces bias not affected by variations in transistor dc gain characteristics is called:
   a. fixed current bias.
   b. voltage divider bias.
   c. collector feedback bias.
   d. power supply bias.

5. At an amplifier's lower cutoff frequency, voltage gain is:
   a. one-half the gain at the center frequency.
   b. one-half the gain at the high-frequency cutoff.
   c. equal to the gain at the high-frequency cutoff.
   d. equal to the power gain.

6. A primary disadvantage of Class A power amplifiers is that they:
   a. require a phase splitter at the input.
   b. dissipate appreciable power with no input signal.
   c. operate linearly if not overdriven.
   d. operate non-linearly.

7. A signal fed back in phase with an input signal is called:
   a. closed-loop feedback.
   b. degenerative feedback.
   c. regenerative feedback.
   d. resonant feedback.

8. When used for amplifiers, op amps usually employ:
   a. non-inverting feedback.
   b. differential feedback.
   c. open-loop feedback.
   d. degenerative feedback.

9. An op amp used as an inverting amplifier has an input resistor of $47k\Omega$ and a feedback resistor of $560k\Omega$. The amplifier voltage gain is about:
   a. 8.
   b. 12.
   c. 47.
   d. 560.

   $\frac{560}{47} = 12$

10. The primary advantage of the crystal-controlled oscillator over LC or phase shift oscillators is:
    a. power dissipating capability.
    b. frequency stability.
    c. frequency range.
    d. tuning capability.

RADIO CIRCUITS

INTRODUCTION

Modern radio systems, equipment and circuits are the product of many scientific and technological developments. Since the invention of the telegraph and telephone in the Nineteenth Century, rapid progress has been made in the development of the electronic technologies necessary for the advancement of wireless communications techniques.

In this chapter, some of the fundamentals of modulation, transmission, reception and antennas are covered. These basic communications concepts are then given more in-depth analysis, covering common AM and FM transmission and reception practices.

Then, special communications techniques such as single-sideband, pulsed-type multiplexing, stereocasting, pulse-code modulation, and digital transmission techniques are covered. Each method has its unique characteristics which may reduce bandwidth, improve signal-to-noise ratio, or in some way improve transmission efficiency and quality.

Next, two-way communications systems are addressed. Commercial radio, citizens band, and amateur radio are the major systems in this field.

Finally, antennas and transmission lines, which are the receiver's and transmitter's interface with each other, are described in terms of their concepts and parameters.

COMMUNICATIONS SYSTEMS

Principles of Radio Communications

Perhaps the simplest of all radio communications systems is illustrated in the block diagram of *Figure 3.1*. Audio signals from the microphone, which are amplified by audio amplifiers, are used to modulate the RF carrier in the transmitter. (The modulating information could be a video signal, digital data, or any other similar source). The modulated RF is amplified to drive the antenna elements, so the RF energy is radiated into the space around it. At the receiver, another antenna intercepts a small portion of this radiated energy and supplies it to the receiver. The receiver selects the RF signal with tuning circuits, amplifies the signal to a usable level, detects (demodulates) the information superimposed on the radio frequency carrier, amplifies this information to drive an output device such as a loudspeaker to reproduce the voice signals as sound. For other systems output transducers such as picture tubes or digital computer terminals convert input information, into a form that can be perceived by human senses.

Methods of Modulation

Modulation is the process by which some property of the radio frequency signal radiated from the transmitting antennna is varied in accordance with the intelligence to be transmitted. Efficient transmission is not practical at the relatively low frequencies which make up the intelligence, because of the enormous wavelengths involved.

Three forms of modulation of an RF carrier wave are possible. All vary a property of the carrier at the modulating information rate:

1. Amplitude modulation (AM) varies the amplitude of the carrier.
2. Frequency modulation (FM) varies the frequency of the carrier.
3. Phase modulation (PM) is similar to FM except that the phase of the carrier is varied.

Figure 3.2a shows a waveform comparison of the three methods of modulation. Notice the similarity between frequency and phase modulation as depicted in the resultant waveform. *Figure 3.2b* shows simplified modulation circuits using microphone signals as the modulation information.

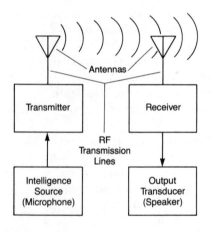

Figure 3.1　Basic Radio Communication System

Antennas

Antennas come in a tremendous variety of designs to give the appropriate radiation (transmitting) or reception (receiving) patterns, gain, frequency response, and impedance. The transmission line, which carries the signal to or from the antenna, must have the same characteristic impedance as the antenna for maximum transfer of energy to occur.

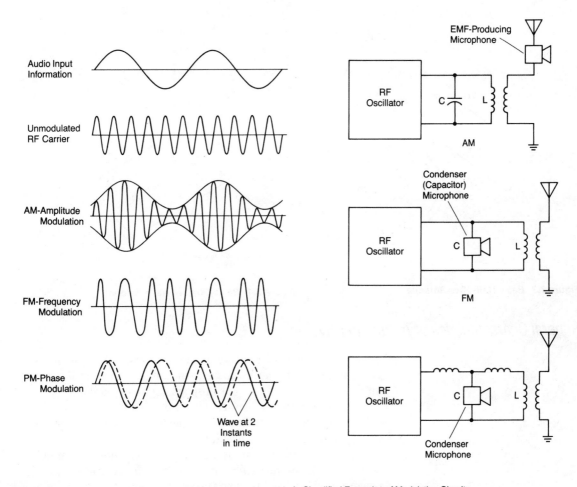

a. Waveforms

b. Simplified Examples of Modulation Circuits

Figure 3.2 Comparison of Various Methods of Modulation

Antennas are usually classified according to the frequency range in which they are used and their relative length. The length must be at least a quarter wavelength for efficient transfer of a signal's energy. Wavelength is the distance a signal of a given frequency travels in space in the time it takes the signal to complete one cycle. It takes much longer to complete, with respect to the wavelength, a cycle of a low frequency signal than it does a high frequency signal. As a result, low frequency antennas are large with long elements and high frequency antennas are small with short elements. Two very common antennas are the basic half-wavelength horizontal (Hertz) shown in *Figure 3.3* and the basic quarter-wavelength vertical (Marconi) antennas shown in *Figure 3.4*. Antennas are covered in greater depth near the end of this chapter.

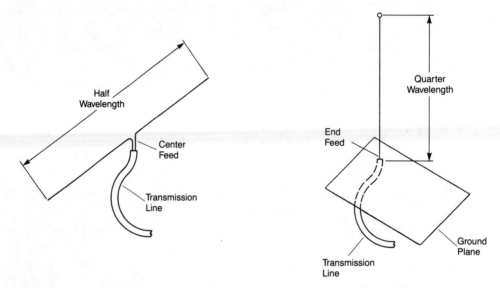

Figure 3.3 Basic Half-Wave Antenna   **Figure 3.4 Basic Quarter-Wave Antenna**

General Characteristics of Transmitter Systems

The simplest form of a radio transmitter consists of a means of generating the carrier radio frequency signal, modulating it with intelligence, and radiating or propagating the modulated RF wave from an antenna. An RF oscillator provides the desired signal which may be modulated by the intelligence through the appropriate modulation circuitry.

Large RF power amplifiers require a considerable input (excitation) from the oscillator stage. In order to prevent the power amplifier from loading the master oscillator driving it, buffer amplifiers are connected between the oscillator output and the input to the power amplifier stage. Their purpose is to isolate the oscillator from the following stages and minimize changes in the oscillator frequency that occur with changes in load.

Transmitters contain resonant or tank circuits which must be tuned to the correct frequency to ensure the transmission of the correct carrier frequency.

AM TRANSMITTER

The basic AM transmitter is shown in *Figure 3.5*. The oscillator, which generates a crystal-controlled frequency, drives the RF buffer amplifier. The buffer amplifier, which isolates the oscillator from the power amplifier, feeds the driver section. The driver section, which is a combination voltage and power amplifier, provides the necessary input to the final RF power amplifier stage.

These power stages are usually Class C, pulsing the tank circuits into oscillation. The modulation section consists of an intelligence source (in this case a microphone), several stages of linear audio amplification, and a modulator.

Oscillator

An oscillator capable of producing the desired radio frequency signal must be used in a transmitter. The degree of stability necessary, the single frequency or range of frequencies to be generated, and the signal drive required from the oscillator are important factors which govern the choice of an oscillator circuit. Crystal oscillators are usually employed in single frequency transmitters because of their extreme stability. If a range of frequencies are required, different crystals are selected or frequencies are divided down from a master crystal-controlled oscillator. Otherwise, traditional tuned circuits are used to set frequency.

Figure 3.6a shows an Armstrong transistor oscillator adapted for crystal control. Because many factors introduce slight variations in an oscillator's frequency, the ordinary LC oscillator is not suited for applications where a stable, constant frequency over long periods of operation is necessary. In *Figure 3.6a*, a quartz crystal is used in place of the LC tank circuit to provide the stability.

Most new transmitter designs requiring operation over a range of frequencies make use of frequency synthesizers to generate the highly accurate and stable frequencies used for the transmitter carrier. This method of digital synthesis of the frequencies desired, shown in *Figure 3.6b*, provides a better approach to critical tuning and maintains the rigid stability restrictions required for transmitting station frequencies. Frequency synthesis is achieved by employing digital IC logic circuits to obtain any exact frequency from one single fixed-frequency stable oscillator. Such synthesis is achieved by multiplying and dividing the fixed stable frequency by factors to obtain the desired output frequency. In *Figure 3.6b* the divided frequency signal is fed to a phase-locked loop (PLL) circuit. The PLL circuit synchronizes the transmitter oscillator with the crystal-controlled oscillator's signal in phase as well as frequency.

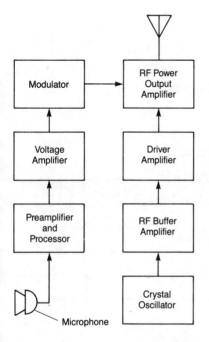

Figure 3.5   Block Diagram of a Basic AM Transmitter

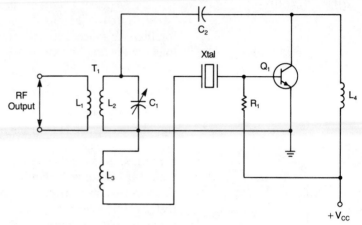

a. Crystal-Controlled Armstrong Oscillator

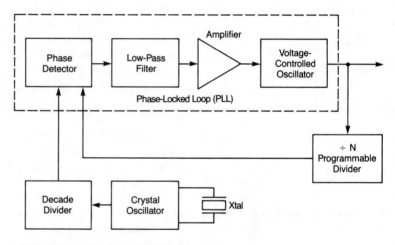

b. Digital Frequency Synthesizer with Phase-Locked Loop

Figure 3.6 Transmitter Oscillators

Frequency multipliers operate an oscillator at a lower frequency and feed its output to a frequency multiplier stage. Such a stage will produce an output of two, three, four, or five times the frequency fed to its input. It is usually a Class C RF amplifier with its output circuit tuned to resonate at a frequency some integer multiple of that fed to its input. Frequency doublers and triplers are quite common in high frequency transmitters, but quadruplers are somewhat less common. Frequency multipliers operating at more than a fifth harmonic are quite rare because the efficiency of the stage decreases greatly as the order of the harmonic is increased.

RF Buffer Amplifier

As mentioned previously, a buffer amplifier provides isolation between the oscillator and the power amplifier stages of a transmitter. If an oscillator drives a changing load impedance, the frequency of oscillation may be caused to fluctuate. As a result, a buffer amplifier is operated Class A to provide the minimum loading effect on the oscillator stage.

Driver

The buffer amplifier is sometimes all that is required to provide excitation for the final power amplifier stage on medium power transmitters. For transmitters with very large power outputs, one or more stages of amplification may be required to increase the drive power sufficiently to provide an adequate excitation signal for the final power amplifier. These stages are appropriately called driver stages. They are either "beefed up" buffer amplifiers or power amplifiers operating at lower current levels.

Power Amplifier

The radio frequency power amplifier is designed to deliver a large current to a load. Since Class C requires larger driving signals than Class A from a preceding stage, output current is produced during the peaked portion of each input cycle. These pulses of output current provide the required energy to replace that taken away from the parallel resonant circuit by the following stage. The flywheel action of the output resonant circuit permits the output signal to be sinusoidal even though the tube or transistor current is in the form of very non-sinusoidal pulsations.

Radio frequency amplifiers using transistors or triode vacuum tubes have undesirable interelectrode capacitances which produce circuit problems. Consequently, these devices tend to have sufficient feedback to cause them to self-oscillate, reducing efficiency. Oscillation can be prevented by use of a process called neutralization, in which a portion of output signal voltage is fed back to the input. The signal fed back by the neutralization network must be equal but opposite in phase when compared to the signal that is being fed back by the tube's or transistor's interelectrode elements. The regenerative signal which causes oscillation is then cancelled by the degenerative signal provided by the neutralization circuit, and the stage is said to be neutralized.

Figure 3.7 shows a neutralization circuit for a push-pull triode stage coupled to an antenna. The neutralization capacitors C_2 and C_8 are adjusted to minimize regenerative feedback.

Now that we've generated the carrier for transmission, let's look at how the information is modulated onto the carrier.

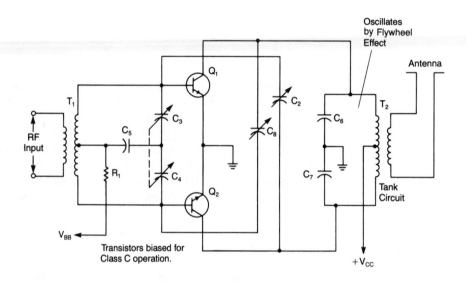

Figure 3.7   Neutralized Push-Pull RF Power Amplifier Stage

Audio Amplifier

Audio frequency voltages generated by a microphone, tape playback, or other audio signal source are common information inputs to a modulator. They are comparatively low level, usually less than 1 volt. It is necessary, therefore, that the audio signal be amplified to a level high enough to cause the proper amount of variation to modulate the RF carrier by changing its property per the chosen modulation technique. This required amplification is provided by the modulation preamplifiers.

Modulator

For audio input information, a modulator is essentially an audio output stage. The major difference is that the modulator output transformer has a different turns ratio than a conventional output transformer. The modulator is a linear audio power amplifier and may be operated Class A, Class AB, or Class B. If operated other than Class A, it must, of course, be a push-pull stage to provide linear amplification.

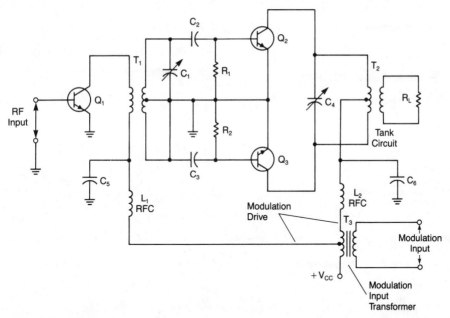

Figure 3.8   Collector Modulation Circuit

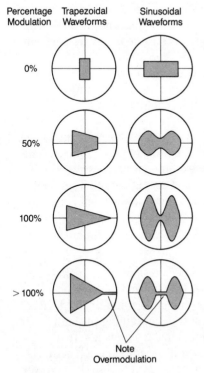

Figure 3.9   Modulation Waveform Patterns

A typical push-pull RF power output stage with collector modulation is shown in *Figure 3.8*. The modulation push-pull stage driving T_3 is very similar, therefore, only the modulation from output transformer T_3 is shown. Note that the RF driver stage as well as the RF output amplifier stage through T_2 must be modulated to achieve maximum modulation. This is necessary to avoid the swing into the saturation region typical of transistors.

Figure 3.9 shows the sinusoidal wave envelope and the trapezoidal waveforms associated with various percentages of modulation. The trapezoidal waveform is a means of indicating percent modulation on an oscilloscope screen, and is produced by using the audio signal to drive the horizontal deflection and the modulated RF signal to drive the vertical deflection. The sinusoidal audio waveform is used to internally trigger the horizontal sweep, while the modulated RF signal produces the vertical deflection.

The degree of modulation may be obtained from either the trapezoidal or the wave envelope oscilloscope presentation. Using measurements from the envelope pattern, *Figure 3.10* illustrates the calculation for percent of modulation.

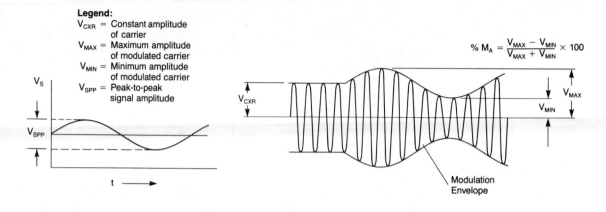

Legend:
V_{CXR} = Constant amplitude of carrier
V_{MAX} = Maximum amplitude of modulated carrier
V_{MIN} = Minimum amplitude of modulated carrier
V_{SPP} = Peak-to-peak signal amplitude

$$\% \ M_A = \frac{V_{MAX} - V_{MIN}}{V_{MAX} + V_{MIN}} \times 100$$

a. Audio Input to Modulator   b. Modulated Carrier

Figure 3.10   Percent of Amplitude Modulation

AM RECEIVER

A radio receiver accepts the transmitted RF signal which has been modulated and removes the information contained therein reproducing it into its original form. All radio receivers perform five basic functions:

1. Interception of the radio signal (antenna).
2. Selection of the desired signal from all others (tuning).
3. Demodulation of the modulated signal (detection).
4. Amplification (RF/IF/AF).
5. Reproduction of the information in a usable form (transducer).

Amplification is the only one that is not absolutely required for a functioning radio receiver. As an example, a simple crystal receiver performs all functions except amplification. This limits the crystal receiver's reproduction to headphones, but it can be, and is, a functioning receiver.

Superheterodyne System

The superheterodyne receiver has become standard in almost all radio communication applications. It employs the principle of heterodyning; i.e., two signals are mixed in a non-linear device, with the signal generated at the output containing the sum and the difference of the two input signal frequencies. In a superheterodyne receiver, the incoming modulated RF signal is mixed (heterodyned) with a signal generated within the receiver by the local oscillator, to produce a resultant output signal which is lower in frequency than the received modulated RF carrier. This lower frequency signal, known as the intermediate frequency (IF), contains the information that was modulated on the original carrier. It is then amplified and tuned in circuits called intermediate frequency amplifiers, demodulated, and applied to an audio amplifier and loudspeaker. *Figure 3.11* illustrates a basic amplitude modulated superheterodyne receiver in block diagram form.

Intercepting and Selecting the Signal

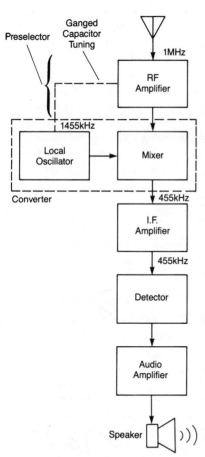

Figure 3.11 Block Diagram of a Superheterodyne Receiver

Signals radiated from transmitters are intercepted by the antenna and coupled into the receiver. The receiver must then select the desired signal from all the rest. We will call this circuitry the preselector. Many commonly call it a tuner or the tuning section. A preselector is all the circuitry before the converter. It consists mainly of the RF amplifier(s) and the tuned circuits. Selectivity and sensitivity, two very important parameters of any receiver, are largely determined by the preselector. Selectivity is the ability of the receiver to differentiate between the desired signal frequency and all unwanted frequencies and is determined largely by the number and quality of the tuned circuits. Sensitivity is a measure of weak signal detection. It is a function of the amount of amplification, or total number of stages used in the receiver. A large portion of this amplification is accomplished in the preselector circuitry and IF amplifier stages.

It might seem that a receiver could be designed for any degree of sensitivity merely by increasing the number of amplifier stages. Although the gain would increase, useable sensitivity would not. Stages of amplification not only amplify signals, they amplify noise present or add more of their own. Each additional stage increases the total noise level generated within the receiver and appearing at the output. Good sensitivity requires a high signal-to-noise (S/N) ratio at the output. Components and circuits must be selected for minimum noise generation.

The use of RF amplifiers in superheterodyne receivers ranges from none in the simplest, most economical receiver up to four stages in sophisticated communications receivers. A simple, inexpensive consumer-type receiver adequate for metropolitan reception of AM broadcast stations may contain no RF amplifier. It must, however, contain an RF section, which may only consist of the tuned circuits at the mixer input.

The major benefits of using RF amplification are: (1) better sensitivity; (2) improved signal-to-noise characteristics; and (3) improved image frequency rejection. For an explanation of image frequency, let's look at the converter section of the receiver.

Converter

Following the preselector in the receiver of *Figure 3.11* is the converter stage (shown within the broken line), consisting of a mixer and a local oscillator. Sometimes the mixer and local oscillator are contained in one device. The mixer stage performs the operation of frequency conversion (heterodyne action) to change a desired incoming signal to an intermediate frequency. To accomplish the heterodyning, it combines the frequency of the local oscillator, which is higher by a fixed amount, with the incoming signal frequency selected by the preselector. This enables the difference to always be the required IF frequency. In *Figure 3.11*, the incoming frequency is 1MHz, the local oscillator signal is 1.455MHz and the difference, or intermediate frequency, is 455kHz. The ability of the oscillator to maintain this difference for all received and tuned RF frequencies is called tracking.

An image frequency is defined as an interfering, transmitted signal whose frequency differs from the desired one by twice the IF frequency. The IF frequency of most broadcast receivers has been standardized to 455kHz.

Example 3-1: This example illustrates an image frequency problem. If the IF frequency is 455kHz, then a broadcast station separated from a desired station by twice 455kHz would be a possible image frequency problem.

For example,

$$455\text{kHz} \times 2 = 910\text{kHz}$$

If a station selected has a frequency of 570kHz, then a station with an assigned frequency of 1480 is a potential image frequency problem station.

$$910\text{kHz} + 570\text{kHz} = 1480\text{kHz}$$

This is possible because a station tuned to 570kHz has a local oscillator frequency of 1025kHz, to provide the 455kHz IF frequency.

If the unwanted station, 1480kHz, would appear at the input of the mixer, it also has a possible IF frequency of 455kHz because the difference between 1480kHz and the local oscillator frequency of 1025kHz is 455kHz. Thus, both stations, 570kH and 480kHz, would appear at the input of the IF amplifier, causing interference. The IF amplifier cannot distinquish the desired station from the image frequency station. To prevent the interference, image frequency must be rejected by the preselector stage of the superheterodyne radio receiver.

IF Amplifier

The IF amplifier is factory-tuned to a predetermined frequency. Thus, it can be expected to produce optimum gain (for high sensitivity) and sufficiently narrow bandwidth (for adequate selectivity). A narrow bandwidth improves sensitivity and selectivity at the expense of audio fidelity, since the higher sideband frequencies are squeezed out. The choice of the IF amplifier's frequency is a compromise of several factors. For example, the use of a low IF frequency results in slightly better gain and selectivity. However, these advantages may be offset by an increased susceptibility to image frequency interference.

Some receivers make use of components other than LC circuits for providing the IF selectivity. Crystal filters are becoming increasingly common. They have a quality factor (Q) of nearly 1000. Q is a circuit quality factor that is a measure of how well a circuit stores energy in its magnetic field. The higher the Q factor, the lower the R losses, and the sharper the selectivity. Mechanical filters are often used in communications receivers. The mechanical filter makes use of an input transducer, a mechanical resonant filter circuit similar to a tuning fork, and an output transducer. These mechanical filters may have an effective Q of several thousand.

Detector

The circuit used to demodulate or detect the impressed information from the carrier is the detector. There have been many types of electronic circuits used to perform this function. The simplest detector *(Figure 3.12)* is a diode "crystal detector," resistor and capacitor, where, by rectifying one half of the RF, the remaining amplitude variations become the representation of the impressed audio. The RF is filtered out by the resistor and capacitor to produce the original audio. In more complex circuits, the complete AM wave, containing the carrier with its upper and lower sideband frequencies (the sum and difference frequencies), is passed through a non-linear device, causing the heterodyning process to occur.

The output is fed to a low-pass filter, consisting of a capacitor and a resistor, which removes the RF carrier frequency and the sum frequencies generated in this mixing process. The difference frequencies which are the output of this low-pass filter, are the original information frequencies that were modulated onto the carrier at the transmitter.

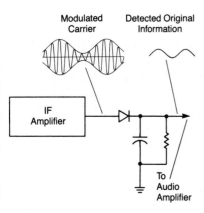

Figure 3.12 Simple Diode Detector

Automatic Volume/Gain Control

Any of the stages prior to the detector may be overloaded if very strong input signals are received. This can cause the output to be distorted. To overcome this distortion, a method of automatically controlling the gain of these stages prior to the detector has been developed.

Since the active devices depend upon the bias applied to them, these devices, used as amplifiers in the RF and IF stages, are supplied bias voltages that have been developed in the detector stage. This bias begins as an RF voltage, is rectified and filtered to remove the intelligence component from the signal. The result is a dc voltage whose level reflects the RF input signal. This dc voltage is used to control the gain of the RF and IF stages. A large dc voltage representing a strong signal increases the bias on the amplifiers and decreases the gain; weak signals decrease the bias and increase the gain.

Audio Amplifier

The purpose of the audio amplifier is to raise the power level of the information frequencies from the detector to a value sufficient to drive the loudspeaker of the receiver. It should have a frequency response to about 10kHz if reasonable fidelity is to be obtained. High fidelity receivers have audio frequency response to 20kHz. Communications receivers, however, may limit the audio response to no higher than about 3kHz, to decrease background noise output.

FM TRANSMITTER

The action of the modulating signal in an FM transmitter is to shift the frequency of the carrier about a center frequency. In an AM transmitter, modulation is usually performed at a relatively high signal level. However, in an FM transmitter, modulation is performed at low signal level only. Through the use of FM modulation, noise and interference from other stations are greatly reduced. *Figure 3.2* compared FM modulation to AM and PM.

Modulation

In the FM modulation circuit of *Figure 3.2b*, the resonant frequency of the oscillator is controlled by the inductance (L) and capacitance (C) of the tank (parallel resonant circuit) of the oscillator. The C value is determined by the capacitance microphone, which is in parallel with the inductor. With no sound, the oscillator produces its center or resting frequency. When the microphone is spoken into, the movable plate of the capacitor produces a changing capacitance which is proportional to the audio. This changing capacitance, therefore, causes the frequency of the signal produced by the oscillator to vary above and below its rest frequency. This is called carrier deviation.

There are several ways of viewing the signal produced by an FM wave. Two methods are shown in *Figure 3.13*. *Figure 3.13a* shows the FM wave in a time domain with the corresponding audio modulating signal that produces the complex wave. Notice that its frequency varies with the amplitude of the audio signal. The audio signal here is kept at a constant amplitude for simplicity. *Figure 3.13b* illustrates a combination of frequency domain for carrier versus time domain for the audio. The amplitude of the audio signal determines the amount of frequency deviation of the carrier signal from its rest or center frequency. The frequency of the audio signal, as shown in the time domain, determines the rate of the carrier frequency deviation. *Figure 3.13c* illustrates the side frequencies for an FM channel.

Modulation Index

Modulation index for FM is generally designated M_f and is equal to the maximum frequency deviation caused by the modulating signal deviation divided by the frequency of the modulating signal. Thus, the modulation index will be greater for a low frequency modulating signal than for a high frequency of the same amplitude.

$$M_f = \frac{f_d}{f_m} \tag{3-1}$$

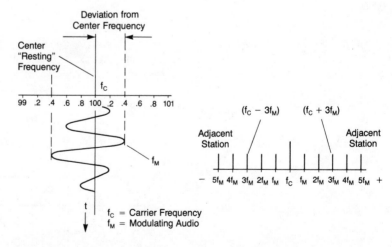

a. FM Wave in the Time Domain

b. FM Carrier Frequency Changed by Amplitude of Audio

c. Sidebands of FM Wave

Figure 3.13 FM Modulation Concept

FM Fidelity

Broadcast FM is noted for having higher fidelity than broadcast AM. This is not inherent with FM, but is the result of the standards of the Federal Communications Commissions for the FM and AM services. Because the AM band is crowded with stations and is low in frequency, being centered around 1MHz, the bandwidth allowed for each station is severely limited. The FM band is in the VHF range where there is more frequency spectrum available. Thus, each station is permitted much more bandwidth. Actually, FM requires more bandwidth for high efficiency (high modulation index) and high fidelity broadcasting than does AM. However, FM is less prone to noise and interference because amplitude variations are not detected as input information modulation.

Varactor Diode Modulator

FM modulation techniques usually involve some sort of variable capacitance component. All reverse bias diodes exhibit a junction capacitance that varies inversely with the amount of reverse bias. A diode that is physically constructed so as to enhance this characteristic is called a varactor diode. *Figure 3.14* shows a varactor diode FM modulator circuit. D_1, the varactor diode, has its reverse bias voltage varied with the modulating signal V_M. Bias changes vary the capacitance in parallel with the oscillator tank circuit, which produces a changing frequency output signal (FM) from the RF power amplifier to the antenna. Capacitor C_2 isolates the dc levels and the intelligence signal from the tank circuit while looking like a short to the high frequency carrier.

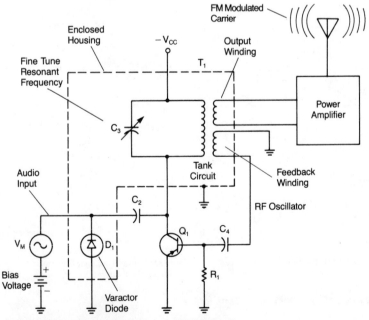

Figure 3.14 FM Modulator Using a Varactor Diode

Direct FM

Figure 3.15 shows a Crosby direct FM transmitter, which is an FM system utilizing direct generation of the FM wave. As shown, it contains an automatic frequency control (AFC) system. Since the modulated oscillator is LC controlled, its center frequency would tend to drift. Therefore, the output signal is sampled and compared with a crystal oscillator signal, the result of which is used to control the center frequency of the basic transmitter oscillator and hold it steady.

Commercial band FM transmitters in the broadcast band operate near 100MHz. It is difficult to produce maximum deviation at this high frequency and still maintain a high degree of linearity. Therefore, as shown in *Figure 3.15*, a low-frequency oscillator signal is modulated and then increased to the required transmission frequency by utilizing frequency multipliers.

Indirect FM

Indirect FM is produced by a phase modulation system using an Armstrong transmitter. The phase modulation stage is usually immediately after the oscillator and before the multipliers in an FM transmitter, thereby permitting the use of low power audio modulating signals. Proper linear frequency deviation over the maximum range can be maintained because of the small frequency change in the RF signal, and is maintained through the multiplier stages.

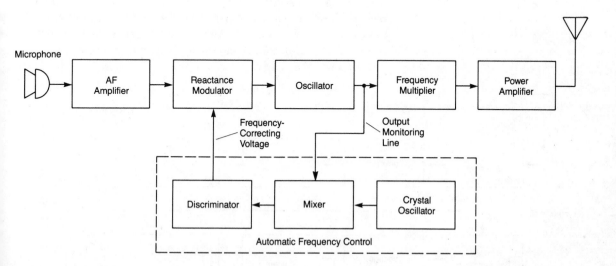

Figure 3.15   Block Diagram of a Crosby FM Transmitter

Emphasis and De-emphasis

Higher modulating frequencies tend to be of lower amplitude than lower frequencies. As a result, the high frequency signals tend to get lost in noise that might be present. To counteract this effect, pre-emphasis is commonly provided in FM signal transmissions. Pre-emphasis means that the relative strength of the high frequency components of the input information is increased before the signal is fed to the modulator. This, of course, upsets the normal mix of high and low frequency tones in the input information. To recover the signals properly, the process must be reversed at the receiver. This is called de-emphasis. If the noise signal remains constant through the system, the whole process — emphasis and de-emphasis — improves the signal-to-noise ratio. The pre-emphasis circuit is a high-pass filter while the de-emphasis is achieved with a low-pass filter.

FM RECEIVER

A block diagram of the FM receiver is shown in *Figure 3.16*. This may be compared with the block diagram of the AM receiver shown in *Figure 3.11*. If one were to examine an AM and an FM receiver, one would see significant physical differences in the way components are laid out. This is because frequencies used in FM receivers are so much higher. For example, the FM IF frequency is 10.7MHz as compared to the AM IF frequency of 455kHz. As a result, small lengths of wire have significant inductance, and stray capacitances become impedances that must be considered in the circuit performance. More IF amplifiers are used in *Figure 3.16* than the AM receiver because the higher frequencies in FM require more stages of gain to reach a desired level of sensitivity.

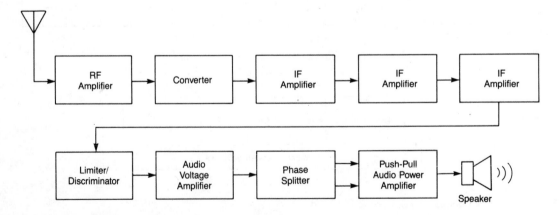

Figure 3.16   FM Receiver Block Diagram

Sometimes the IF amplifiers also function as limiter circuits in FM. The purpose of a limiter in an FM receiver is to remove unwanted amplitude modulation, which, if left in, can produce background noise if allowed to pass through the audio amplifier section to the speaker.

FM Discriminators

Another difference between the AM and FM signal is the replacement of a detector with a type of demodulator called a discriminator. The overall function of this circuit is the same as the detector in the AM receiver: that of removing intelligence from the carrier. However, the operation is much different, because the intelligence has been modulated on the carrier by way of frequency variations instead of amplitude variations.

Slope Detector
The easiest way to visualize an FM detector is by way of the slope detector as shown in *Figure 3.17*. *Figure 3.17a* shows the response curve of the tank circuit appearing in the collector of the limiter transistor shown in *Figure 3.17b*. As shown in *Figure 3.17a*, the resonant frequency of the tank circuit is designed so the IF center frequency is midway on the slope of the tank circuit response curve. When modulation occurs, the carrier frequency changes above and below the center frequency, producing a higher and lower proportional amplitude. This is rectified by the diode. The average value of the change appears across the RC circuit as an audio output. Because it can cause non-linearity and has a narrow bandwidth, the slope detector is not widely used in FM receivers, especially in equipment where high audio quality is important, but it is a circuit that demonstrates FM detection principles.

Phase Detector
Two popular circuits used for demodulation are shown in *Figure 3.18*. The operation of these two circuits is similar. The Foster-Seeley phase discriminator shown in *Figure 3.18a* produces an output amplitude that depends on the input frequency as well as the input amplitude. Thus, it must be preceded by a limiter stage to suppress amplitude variations. Its basic operation depends on the fact that frequency swings above and below resonance of a tuned resonant circuit. The swing causes the phase of the current and voltage of a secondary winding coupled to the tank circuit to change. Above resonance, the secondary circuit of the transformer becomes inductive. This shifts the phase of the applied voltage so that the current lags the voltage. As the frequency changes to below resonance, the phase of the applied

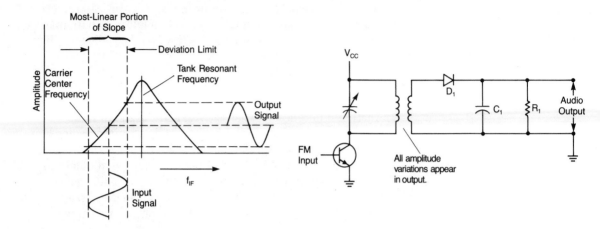

a. Slope Detector Response Curve   b. Slope Detector Circuit

Figure 3.17   Basics of Slope Detection Circuitry

voltage shifts so the current leads the voltage. This leading and lagging of the current with respect to the voltage causes the secondary voltages applied to the detector diodes and their load to vary, one increases while the other decreases. The sum of the two voltages is the input information output, and will be positive for above resonance, negative for below resonance, and zero at resonance.

Ratio Detector
The ratio detector shown in *Figure 3.18b* was developed to meet the need for an FM detector with amplitude rejection. The circuit needs no hard limiting before it is applied to the ratio detector, thus eliminating a function. The operation of the circuit is similar to that of the discriminator, with the exception that the voltages across the capacitors C_4 and C_5 are in the same direction. The output then is taken as a ratio of the voltage drops across these capacitors. The discriminator and ratio detector both have excellent bandwidths. Note that an AGC voltage is generated to adjust the IF amplifier gain just as for the AM receiver.

Phase-Locked Loop
The phase-locked loop *(Figure 3.6b)* is a means of demodulating FM using integrated circuits. The input frequency is fed to the phase comparator circuit with the voltage controlled oscillator signal. If the FM carrier frequency changes as a result of modulation, the output control signal will change as well. This changing control signal is then used as the intelligence.

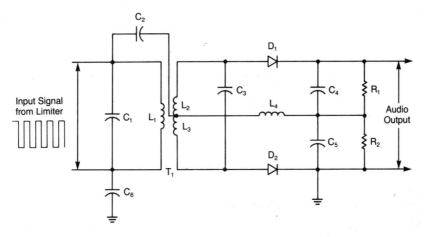

a. Foster-Seeley Phase Discriminator

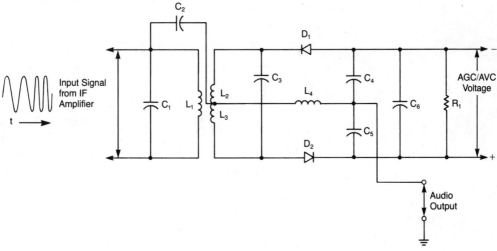

b. Ratio Detector

Figure 3.18   *Two Common FM Demodulator Circuits*

Quadrature Detector

The quadrature detector *(Figure 3.19a)* is a modern integrated circuit "reincarnation" of a simple, inexpensive demodulator used in vacuum tube circuits called a gated beam discriminator. The basic circuit is shown in *Figure 3.19a*. It has two signal paths for the signal received from the IF amplifier. The one path is marked V_1, the other path is marked V_2. In the V_2 path, the FM signal goes through a phase shifting network, which shifts V_2 90 degrees in relationship to V_1 if the FM signal is at its center frequency. This is the "no modulation" case shown in the waveform diagram of *Figure 3.19b*. V_2 shifts toward 0 degrees

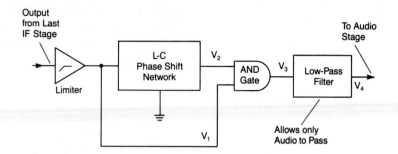

a. Block Diagram of Quadrature Detector

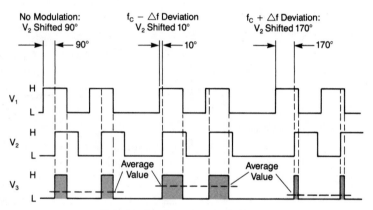

Note: Shading shows area of coincidence

b. Detector Operation Illustrated

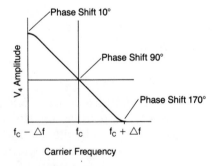

c. V_4 Output

Figure 3.19 Quadrature Detector Subsystem

phase shift with V_1 when the FM deviation is above center frequency, and shifts toward 180 degrees phase shift with V_1 when the FM deviation is below center frequency. The two modulation cases are plotted in *Figure 3.19b*, when the phase shifts are 10 degrees and 170 degrees respectively.

The voltages V_1 and V_2 are coupled to the inputs to an AND logic gate. They are essentially square waves formed by a limiter between the last IF stage and the input to the phase shifting network. The output of the AND gate V_3 is a high level voltage whenever V_1 and V_2 are at a high level. The output voltage V_3 is plotted on the waveform diagram of *Figure 3.19b*. The average voltage for each case is shown.

When V_3 is coupled to a low-pass filter, the resulting voltage V_4 is the original input information that modulated the FM carrier. *Figure 3.19c* shows the relative amplitude of V_4 with respect to the phase shift.

The 5 types of FM detectors are summarized as follows in *Table 3.1*.

Table 3.1 Types of FM Detectors

Type	Characteristics	Concept of Operation
Slope Detectors	No noise supression. Fair audio quality. Narrow bandwidth.	Operates on one slope of transformer. Diode detects induced amplitude variations.
Foster-Seeley Discriminator	No noise supression. Good audio quality. Wide bandwidth.	Detects phase shifts of voltage and current.
Ratio Detector	Suppresses noise. Good audio quality. Wide bandwidth.	Detects phase shifts of voltage and current.
Phase-Locked Loop	Suppresses noise. Good audio quality. Wide bandwidth.	Shifting FM carrier frequency causes a voltage-controlled oscillator signal to change control signal.
Quadrature Detector	Supresses noise. Good audio quality. Wide bandwidth.	The FM signal is split into 2 paths. One path shifts signal by 90 degrees. Two signals combined in AND gate, producing output at instants of coincidence.

Stereo Section/Audio Amplifier

The output of the FM detector may drive either the stereo demodulator and a matched pair of audio amplifiers, or for a monaural radio receiver, one audio amplifier. The quality and power output of the amplifier section used depends on the overall quality and expected use for the whole receiver. High fidelity performance requires amplifier circuitry capable of at least a few undistorted watts output over the entire audio frequency spectrum.

SPECIAL COMMUNICATIONS TECHNIQUES

In addition to basic AM and FM transmitter circuits, there are a variety of other specialized modulation techniques used to reduce bandwidth requirements, improve the signal-to-noise ratio, or otherwise improve the efficiency and quality of transmission.

Single-Sideband Communications

In the standard double sideband (DSB) amplitude modulation method of radio transmission, all information is contained in each sideband and none in the accompanying carrier. This is an inefficient method of modulation. Single sideband (SSB) principles have been used in telephone and some radio applications for a number of years. With the advent of improved solid state circuit techniques, the use of SSB is becoming more commonplace in radio transmissions.

In SSB, both carrier and one sideband are suppressed and only one of the intelligence-bearing sidebands is transmitted. Besides a reduction in bandwidth, SSB has definite advantages with respect to transmitter power, because all of the power is restricted to the intelligence-bearing part of the carrier. The net result at the receiver end is a tremendous system signal-to-noise ratio improvement.

The method of modulating the RF carrier in an SSB transmitter differs from DSB. The modulator for an SSB transmission is either a filter or a phase shift system. In the filter system shown in *Figure 3.20*, modulation occurs at low frequency and power levels, then the modulated signal is converted to a higher frequency and boosted in power for transmission. In the phase shift system, modulation occurs at a low power level at the frequency to be transmitted, then power amplifiers increase the modulated signal to the required power level for transmission. Of the two, the filter system is generally more expensive. The phase shift system requires fewer circuits, but adjustment of this system is quite critical, making it more difficult to maintain.

The reception of SSB signals requires some method of carrier insertion prior to detection, since the unmodulated carrier is not transmitted. Two methods have been developed: (1) an oscillator in the receiver that reinserts the carrier and (2) a pilot, or reduced power carrier, which is transmitted with the signal to reconstruct the composite signal at the receiver. Other than the carrier insert, a SSB receiver resembles a standard DSB AM receiver in most respects. It contains stable oscillators, a balanced detector and sharply tuned filters.

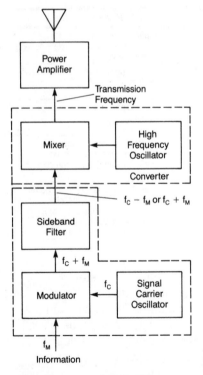

Figure 3.20   Filter System SSB Transmitter

FDM and TDM Multiplexing

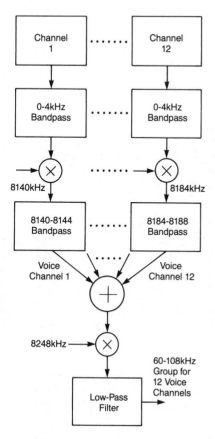

Figure 3.21 Frequency Division Multiplexing

Multiplexing is the process of combining two or more intelligence signals into a composite signal for transmission, and the separation of the received composite signal into individual intelligence signals. Through the use of the process, a number of communications channels may be combined into a composite signal which is then used to modulate a single RF transmitter. In simple terms, this means that many communications can be sent together over one transmission channel. The process has many applications, especially in digital communications. Multiplexing is accomplished by two distinctly different methods — FDM (frequency division multiplexing) and TDM (time division multiplexing). FDM generally uses SSB techniques.

Figure 3.21 is an example of FDM. Each channel, in this case a voice band, is kept separate from other channels by translating its reference frequency to a higher frequency band. The carrier frequency used for each channel is separated by the bandwidth of the voice band (4kHz). The only restriction on the number of channels is the carrier bandwidth capability. In *Figure 3.21*, it is 48kHz for 12 channels.

At the destination receiver, 4kHz bandwidth filtering networks tuned to the carrier frequency of each channel are used to separate the various channels. Detectors demodulate the carriers to recover the input information on each channel. FDM requires no synchronization since the input information to the system is transmitted continuously from source to destination.

Figure 3.22 details the principles of time division multiplexing. Under control of timing signals, each signal channel is placed in a given time slot. Digital data or sampled analog data can be placed in the time slot. At the receiving destination, the information is demultiplexed into the respective channels. TDM requires synchronization between the transmitter and receiver section, adding to the overall cost of the system.

Stereophonic Transmission and Reception

To transmit stereophonic sound over a broadcast station requires that both channels be transmitted independently without interfering with each other. This is accomplished with the modulation techniques of SSB and FDM. The two separate channels are appropriately combined to frequency modulate the carrier of the transmitter. In this way, an FM stereo-multiplexed system is compatible with a conventional monoaural receiver, so that a non-stereo receiver is able to deliver a combined single output. The bandwidth necessary to transmit the two stereophonic channels must be within the designated bandwidth of the commercial broadcast stations.

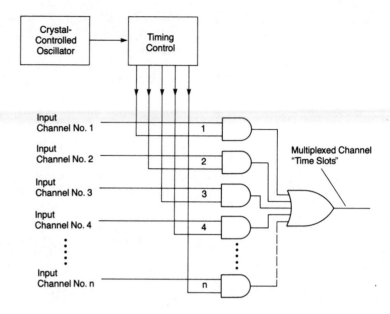

a. Circuit

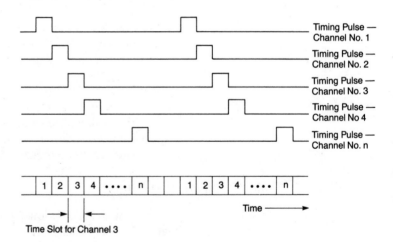

b. Timing Diagram

Figure 3.22   Time Division Multiplexing

Figure 3.23a is a block diagram of a stereo FM transmitter. The left and right channels are first fed through a high frequency pre-emphasis network, which increases the average level of the upper audio frequencies to improve the signal-to-noise ratio of the FM system. A matrix network combines the left and right channels in two ways. One produces (L + R) which is conventional monoaural audio. The other modifies the right channel through an inverter and adder circuit, thereby producing (L − R) audio.

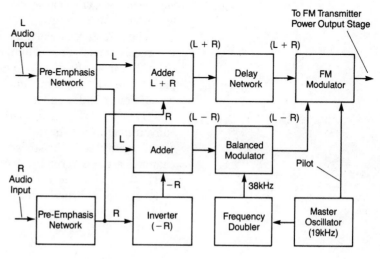

a. Encoder Section of a Stereo FM Transmitter

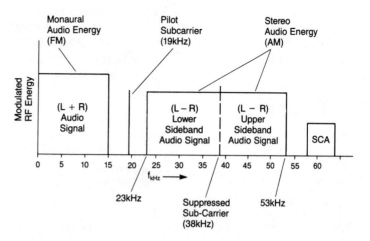

b. Composite Stereo Signal

Figure 3.23   *Stereo FM Signal Transmission*

The (L − R) signal is then amplitude modulated on a 38kHz carrier using DSB suppressed carrier techniques, which produces two sidebands, each containing the (L − R) information. Because of the time required for the (L − R) to go through the balanced modulator, a delay network is placed in the path of the (L + R) signal to maintain proper phase relationships between the left and right channel information. Because the receiver needs to reinsert the 38kHz carrier which was suppressed in the balance modulator, a frequency and phase reference for this carrier, called a pilot, is transmitted at 19kHz as well. *Figure 3.21b* shows a composite of the modulating signals fed to the FM transmitter.

The FM stereo receiver is identical to the standard monaural FM receiver up to and including the discriminator output. At this point, however, the discriminator output contains two circuit paths. The (L + R) signal goes through a low-pass filter which is cut off below 19kHz and fed to a matrix and de-emphasis network. The (L − R) DSB signal is fed through a band-pass filter to a conventional AM demodulator where it is mixed with a 38kHz signal generated in the stereo decoder. The left and right channels are recovered by electronically taking the algebraic sum and also the algebaic difference of the main monaural channel (L + R) and the subcarrier difference channel (L − R). Thus,

$$\begin{array}{cc} (L+R) & (L+R) \\ +\ \underline{(L-R)} & -\ \underline{(L-R)} \\ 2L & 2R \end{array}$$

As an additional source of revenue for FM stations, the FCC has authorized the broadcast of other services. These include subsidiary communications authorization (SCA) — commercial-free background music paid for by subscription by shopping malls, doctors' offices, etc. SCA is frequency multiplexed on the FM modulating signal with a carrier of usually 6-7kHz bandwidth. The SCA signal location is shown in *Figure 3.23b*.

Pulse Modulation

In normal AM and FM, some parameter of the carrier is varied continuously by the modulating signal. In pulse modulation, some pulse parameter such as pulse amplitude, width, or position is varied by the information signal.

The three basic forms of pulse-code modulation are shown in *Figure 3.24*. In the first, pulse amplitude modulation (PAM), the pulse amplitude is made to vary with the modulating signal amplitude. This is the simplest pulse modulation to create, in that the sampling of the modulating signal at a periodic rate is used to generate the pulses subsequently used to modulate the higher frequency carrier. It is the most susceptible to noise.

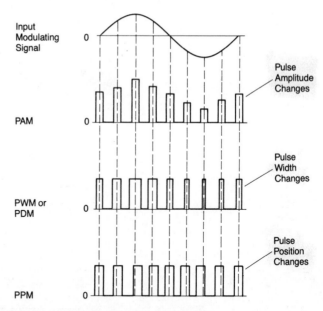

Figure 3.24   *Sampling Types of Pulse Modulation*

In pulse width modulation (PWM), also known as pulse duration modulation (PDM), the modulating signal varies the pulse width of the pulse. It provides superior noise performance to pulse amplitude modulation. It, along with the pulse position modulation (PPM) system, falls into a general category referred to as pulse time modulation (PTM) in that their timing, and not their amplitude, is the parameter varied by the intelligence.

In pulse position modulation (PPM), the position of the pulse relative to a reference pulse is made to vary with the intelligence. PPM has superior noise characteristics. At the receiver, the demodulated PPM pulse is typically converted to PWM first and then fed to a low-pass filter (integrator), the output of which is the original intelligence.

A fourth type of pulse modulation transmission is pulse-code modulation (PCM). PCM is a true digital process as compared to the other pulse modulating schemes, which are sampling processes. *Figure 3.25* shows PCM encoding. On the left side of the diagram are quantization levels. Along the bottom are time intervals. On the right side are the corresponding binary digital codes for the various quantization levels. At each sampling interval, the analog amplitude is determined and the closest quantization level is assigned. The analog-to-digital (A/D) converter puts out a series of pulses representing that level in the binary code. The code used in *Figure 3.25* is a 4-bit code which allows a maximum of 16 quantization levels since 2^4 equals 16. The use of a higher bit code would decrease the quantization error, but at the expense of transmission time and/or bandwidth.

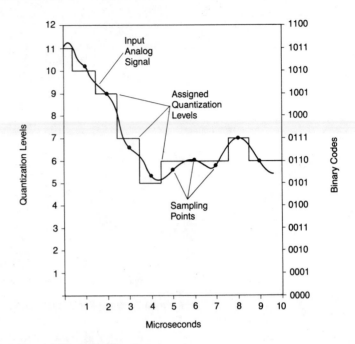

Figure 3.25 PCM Encoding

In any of the techniques requiring sampling for pulse modulation, the highest frequency component that can be reconstructed after sampling is a function of the sampling rate. Mathematically, it has been proven that the sampling rate needs to be at least twice the highest significant frequency component in the intelligence signal.

Modern digital communications requires the processing of binary (two level) intelligence by coding and decoding. The use of pulse modulation techniques is increasing rapidly in this application.

Digital Communications Techniques

Analog communications systems are prevalent, especially in telephone networks; however, digital communications systems are being developed to provide reliable communication for both analog signals which have been digitized, and for data which originates in digital form, such as from computers. Data transmission is probably the fastest-growing aspect of communications, chiefly because of the advent of the computer and microprocessor.

The basic elements of a digital communications system are illustrated in *Figure 3.26*. It consists of a piece of digital equipment as a source (a computer), a conversion unit (UART), a modem, a transmission link, and possibly equipment to interface to the transmission link. The rate at which digital data is transferred over the communications system in signalling events per second is termed baud. Common baud rates are 300, 1200, 2400 and 9600. It is commonly expressed, in some cases in error, as bits per second. As shown in *Figure 3.26*, the computer outputs are connected to the modem through a universal asynchronous receiver/transmitter (UART). The UART converts the parallel computer data into the serial data format required by the modem. The modem converts the digital codes into tones that can be sent over normal telephone lines. At the receive end, the process is reversed. Now, the modem is converting the tones to digital codes. If both synchronous and asynchronous capabilities are needed, USARTs are used.

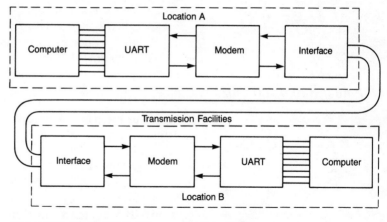

Figure 3.26   Typical Digital Communications System

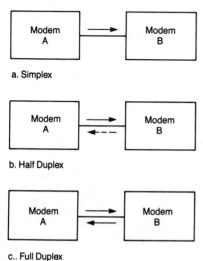

a. Simplex

b. Half Duplex

c.. Full Duplex

Figure 3.27   The Three Modes of Modem Operation

Transmission between two modems can be characterized in one of three ways: simplex, half-duplex, or full-duplex. This is illustrated in *Figure 3.27*. Simplex operation indicates transmission in one direction only. Half-duplex operation indicates operation in either direction, but in only one direction at a time. Full-duplex operation is transmission in both directions at all times.

TWO-WAY COMMUNICATIONS SYSTEMS

Commercial, Government, and Public Safety

Much two-way communication takes place by means of FM transmitters and receivers. These are usually combined in one system called a transceiver. One special feature of a transceiver may be the private line or channel guard function. Of the several techniques which can provide this feature, a common method is to use a control audio tone below 300Hz. This tone is below the low cutoff frequency for the audio section of the transceiver. Therefore, the control signal does not interfere with the message channel, but enables the receiver for the message. If it does not detect the tone, the received signal is inhibited by the audio circuit.

Another technique for achieving the private line feature is to send a digital code that the receiver recognizes, allowing the signal to pass through the receiver's audio section. If it does not receive this predetermined digital code, the receiver inhibits audio (called squelch). This feature greatly reduces unwanted reception and allows for a certain degree of privacy in the crowded channels of commercial bands.

Amateur Radio and Citizens Band

Amateur radio is undoubtedly one of the most popular and oldest hobbies in electronic communications. Much of the pioneering in communications has been done by these hobbyist.

Amateur radio and citizen's band (CB) radio service are often confused. The amateur radio services consist of twenty very wide frequency bands, with more scheduled to be allocated soon. CB communications equipment is limited to 40 operating low power channels in a single, very narrow band, in a part of the radio spectrum where satisfactory, reliable communications are possible for only a few miles. A block diagram of a CB transceiver is shown in *Figure 3.28*. We have discussed all the circuit functions contained in the block diagram. A mike switch usually controls transmit or receive.

CB operations must be by AM radiotelephone only, though single sideband has been authorized. The operating frequencies are from 26.965 to 27.405MHz. Amateurs (ham operators) can communicate by telegraphic code, teletype, television, home computers, and facsimile equipment, as well as by voice. Amateur operators may build or buy equipment and change it in any way desired, as long as it does not emit illegal signals. CB equipment must not be changed from the FCC-approved form in which it is sold.

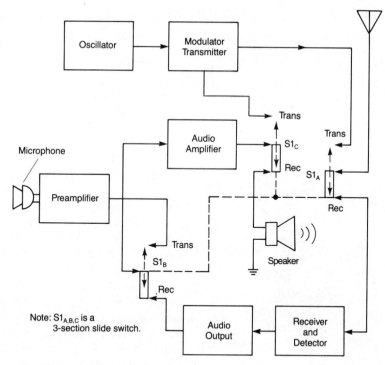

Figure 3.28 CB Transceiver

CB equipment is limited to 4 watts of power output to the transmitting antenna. Amateur stations may use as much as 1,000 watts of power, which is more than some commercial broadcast stations.

The term amateur means the on-the-air communications cannot be used for commercial gain in any way. Many of the foremost electronic engineers and technicians are avid ham operators. An operator's license and a station license (issued as one combined license) are necessary before any amateur equipment can be operated on the air, and are available only for citizens of the United States and nationals. With the recent changes in the FCC, the move is for the American Radio Relay League (ARRL) to take over the license examinations through the use of Volunteer Examination Coordinators (V.E.C.).

ANTENNAS AND TRANSMISSION LINES

Fundamental Concepts

In order for the radio frequency energy output from a radio transmitter to serve a useful pupose, it must reach a receiver. Usually, the RF energy (also referred to as radio waves) from a transmitter is applied to an antenna, from which it is radiated into free space, and then intercepted by the antenna of a receiver.

Radio waves propagated (transmitted) into free space are the same form of energy as light and heat. The speed at which the energy travels is the same as light, approximately 3×10^8 meters per second, or 1.86×10^5 miles per second. The basic principles of transmitting and receiving antennas are the same.

The propagation of a radio wave from an antenna may be explained in relatively simple terms by examining the dynamics of the electric and magnetic fields of force which exist about a conductor carrying a radio frequency alternating current. These changes in the field intensity about the conductor produce a moving field wave which travels away from the antenna.

Figure 3.29 shows the relationship between the electromagnetic and the electrostatic fields around a conductor that is carrying an RF signal. The greatest amount of charge accumulates at the ends of the antenna, and therefore produces the maximum electrostatic field between the ends, as shown by the solid lines. The resultant electrostatic field acts from the positive end of the antenna to the negative. The dashed lines show the apparent electromagnetic field concentration around the antenna. Since the ends of the antenna represent the highest impedance, the greatest current will occur at the center with the minimum current at the ends. Note the electromagnetic lines are around and perpendicular to the conductor while the electrostatic field is along the conductor.

The radio frequency energy is classified according to its frequency. The range of frequencies, called the spectrum, extends from below 1MHz to beyond several thousand megahertz. Also, radio waves are classified according to wavelength. As you recall, wavelength is defined as the distance the wave travels in space in the time required to complete one cycle. Since the speed of radio waves is three hundred million (300×10^6) meters per second, the wavelength in meters of any radio wave can be expressed as:

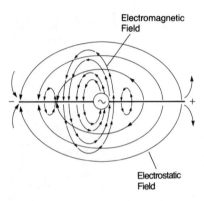

Electromagnetic Field

Electrostatic Field

Figure 3.29 Fields Around a Conductor Carrying RF Energy

$$\text{Wavelength} = \frac{\text{Velocity}}{\text{Frequency}} \qquad (3\text{-}1)$$

$$\lambda = \frac{3 \times 10^8}{f}$$

where f is the frequency of the signal of interest.

Antennas are generally designed to have a physical length equivalent to a fraction of (1/2, 1/4, . . .), or some multiple of, the wavelength of the radio frequency energy the antenna is supposed to handle. The amount of radiated energy from an antenna depends upon the amount of current in the antenna, and is greatest when the antenna reactance for the particular frequency is lowest. When this condition exists, the antenna is said to be resonant to the frequency of the applied signal.

Referring again to *Figure 3.29*, the travel of the charge in the antenna conductor causes points of voltage maximums to occur at the ends and a current maximum at the center. These distributions of current and voltage maximum and minimum points are referred to as standing waves.

Usually the polarization of an antenna (horizontal or vertical) is determined by the direction of the electric plane wave. Therefore, an antenna that has an electric field that is horizontal is said to be a horizontally-polarized antenna.

Common Types of Antennas

Many types of antennas are available for various applications. The characteristics of these antennas conform mainly to those of the half-wave horizontal or quarter-wave vertical antenna, of which most others are modifications. The half-wave antenna is called the Hertz and the quarter-wave the Marconi. *Figure 3.30* shows the voltage and current distribution and the corresponding impedance curves of half-wave and quarter-wave antennas.

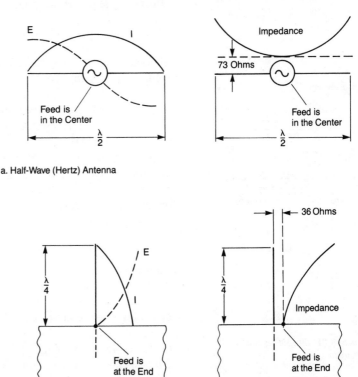

a. Half-Wave (Hertz) Antenna

b. Quarter-Wave (Marconi) Antenna

Figure 3.30 Two Basic Antenna Designs

The basic radiation pattern of an antenna depends primarily on the distribution of the current throughout its length, height and polarization. The height of the antenna above the earth determines, to a large extent, the amount of distortion of its free-space pattern by ground effects. A simple transmitting antenna radiates in all directions but with different intensities. The ability of an antenna to concentrate power in a given direction is called directivity. The antenna's length affects its directivity.

To produce optimum operation, an antenna should be tuned to resonate at the frequency on which it is to operate. The tuning may be accomplished by inserting either a capacitor or inductor in series with the antenna to electrically shorten or lengthen the antenna. If the antenna is shorter than required, a loading coil may be inserted in series with it, the wire of the coil acting as part of the required length of the antenna. An antenna that is physically shorter than necessary may be considered as having too little inductance. Thus, the loading coil increases the effective inductive reactance of the antenna. When an antenna is longer than required, a capacitor inserted in series with it has the effect of cancelling some of the excess inductive reactance, producing an effectively shorter antenna.

AM Broadcast Band, TV, and FM Antennas

Nearly all consumer-type AM receivers have a built-in ferrite rod (loopstick) antenna. This type of antenna is a highly efficient and compact interceptor of RF energy. The variable tuning capacitor is connected in parallel with it, establishing a resonant circuit that effectively responds to only one received station.

VHF and UHF antennas operate in the frequency range from 30 to 900MHz. The most common antennas in the frequency range for reception and transmission is the half-wave dipole antenna. The directive characteristics of the antenna and therefore the resultant concentration of radiated or received energy can be increased by adding driven or parasitic elements to form an antenna array, as is common in the TV antenna of *Figure 3.31.*

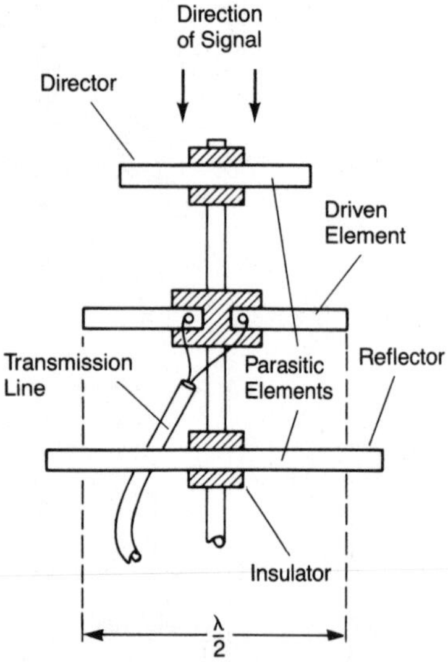

If a transmission line is connected to an element, it is referred to as a driven element, whether it is transmitting or receiving. An antenna element that is not connected to the transmission line will also develop a voltage by induction. This type element is called a parasitic element. There are two general types of parasitic elements — reflectors, which are behind the driven element and slightly longer, and directors, which are in front of the driven element and slightly shorter.

Figure 3.31 Simple Receiving TV Antenna

The re-radiated energy from the reflector tends to cancel the energy behind the antenna and add to the strength of the energy in front of the antenna. The re-radiated energy from the director has a phase relation to the field produced by the driven element such that its field will also aid in the forward direction and cancel in the reverse direction.

Sharper directivity can be obtained by increasing the number of parasitic elements. However, there is a practical limitation to the number of elements that can be used. Adding parasitic elements is similar to adding parallel loads, which reduces the radiation resistance of the antenna. Since the effect of parasitic elements on antenna directivity depends on element length and spacing, their use is restricted to a narrow band of frequencies for which they are designed.

Transmitting and receiving antennas for use in the microwave frequency spectrum are almost always highly directional. A microwave dish is a parabolic reflector that has a high directivity, because it collects radiation from a large area and concentrates it at the focal point where the antenna is located. Sometimes a small dipole or dipole array is used at the focus point of the dish to collect the focussed radiation. The array is pointed at the parabolic reflector.

Transmission Lines

A transmission line serves one basic purpose — to transfer electrical energy from a source to a load. When transferring low frequency energy a short distance, the transmission line presents no unusual problems. However, at radio frequencies even a short length of wire may take on characteristics like that of an LCR circuit. As in all electric circuits, in order to achieve maximum transfer of energy from a source to a load, impedances must be matched. A transmission line's parameters include impedance (ohms) and loss (dBs per foot).

A transmission line may take on one of many physical appearances. They are usually found as a pair of evenly-spaced conductors or a coaxial cable. The waveguide is a type of transmission line that is used at microwave frequencies.

At Radio Frequency
The electrical characteristics of common transmission lines are dependent primarily on their physical construction. The parallel wire type of transmission line looks very much like a capacitor with very long, thin plates. The longer the line, the more the capacitance. Also, since the conductors are long, when electrical energy is being passed through them, the magnetic field about them produces the property of inductance in series as well.

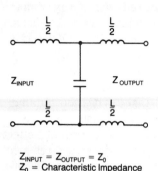

$Z_{INPUT} = Z_{OUTPUT} = Z_0$
Z_0 = Characteristic Impedance

Figure 3.32 Equivalent Circuit of a Transmission Line

The values of the capacitance and the inductance present in the transmission line depend primarily on the physical dimensions of the line. This capacitance, inductance, and the resistance of the wire produce a certain characteristic impedance, usually designated Z_O. The capacitive, inductive, and resistive qualities of the line are distributed evenly along the length of the line, though they are sometimes represented as lumped quantities when analyzing the line. The characteristic impedance of a transmission line is a constant value regardless of the length of the line. *Figure 3.32* is a schematic equivalent circuit of a transmission line.

Transmission lines are classified as tuned (resonant) or untuned (nonresonant) lines. A tuned line has standing waves due to a mismatched termination. An untuned line has no standing waves and is terminated in its own characteristic impedance. Since a tuned line does have standing waves, it is electrically equivalent to an antenna.

The degree of mismatch between the transmission line and the load determines the amplitude of the voltage and current reflected waves. The ratio of the maximum and the minimum of the wave is called the standing wave ratio (SWR). For maximum transfer of energy, a SWR as low as possible (near 1) is desirable. This is called a flat line.

An untuned transmission line is properly terminated at its load, allowing it to be extended to any reasonable length between the transmitter (or receiver) and the antenna. In many instances, the proper match is made by trial and error in connecting the line to the antenna for maximum transfer of power or minimum SWR.

The disadvantages of not having a perfectly matched (flat) line are:
1. The full generator power is not transferred to the load.
2. The transmission line insulation may break down as a result of high standing waves of voltage (when connected to a transmitter).
3. The existence of reflections increases the power loss up and down the line.
4. Noise problems are increased.
5. Reflected signals are created on video lines and appear as multiple images on a television receiver.

At Microwave Frequency
A phenomenon called skin effect occurs at high frequencies, and the higher the frequency, the more pronounced the phenomenon. This effect results in the electrons crowding to the outer surface of the conductor. Therefore, most of the copper loss in a coaxial line occurs in the thin, inner conductor where there is less surface. This is eliminated by the use of a waveguide. A

waveguide is a hollow pipe, usually rectangular, through which electromagnetic waves are conducted. The rectangular waveguide has a height about one-half its width for the usual voltage and current oscillation modes to occur. A common band of operation is the X band or the three-centimeter wavelength band, which has frequencies from 8.2 to 12.4GHz. This waveguide is about 3.0 centimeters wide and 1.5 centimeters high. They are constructed of brass, copper or aluminum. Sometimes the inner walls are silver plated to reduce the resistance loss.

The guide is capable of radiating energy into open space if it is excited at one end and open at the other. However, the open-ended type suffers from a mismatch in making the energy transfer into open space. This reflects most of the energy back down the waveguide, only a small part of it being radiated. If the mouth of the waveguide is flared out to form a cone or horn however, then this discontinuity to the open space may be overcome. If the flare angle of the horn is of proper value, the impedance will be matched. Thus, all the energy traveling forward in the waveguide will be radiated and we have made a transition from a transmission line to a radiating antenna.

Optical Fibers

An increasingly popular and revolutionary transmission line in communications systems is the optical fiber. Fiber optic systems are rapidly becoming competitive with other types of transmission lines. Some of the reasons for their increasing popularity are:
1. A fraction of the weight and size
2. No electromagnetic interference (EMI)
3. No crosstalk between adjacent transmission lines
4. Less attenuation than coaxial cable and waveguides
5. Extremely wide bandwidth
6. Rapidly decreasing cost
7. Conservation (they are made from sand, the most abundant material on earth)
8. Not electrically conductive which gives electrical isolation and safety from short circuits
9. Very rugged, almost inert to corrosive atmospheres
   Fiber optics communications systems are, however, still somewhat more expensive than equivalent electrical systems.

SUMMARY

In this chapter we have learned that all methods of radio transmission and reception have certain elements in common. They all must have modulators which superimpose the information to be transmitted onto a carrier. Thus, a particular modulation format is required. At the receiving end, there must be a circuit to demodulate the carrier, thereby recovering the original information. The three basic types of analog modulation are amplitude, frequency, and phase, all other types being special applications of these three.

Both AM and FM transmitters generate their carriers in similar ways, but the methods of modulation are completely different. In AM, the carrier is modulated by a signal applied to the RF output and/or driver stages. With FM, however, the carrier must be modulated well before the final output stage, since it is the frequency of the carrier that is being affected.

Both AM and FM receivers utilize the superheterodyne system, where a preselector tunes and amplifies the incoming signal, a converter changes the selected frequency to the required IF, and one or more tuned IF stages amplifies it. The difference is in the detection. In the demodulation of AM, the audio portion of the carrier is recovered by passing the signal through a non-linear device, which may be a solid state diode and appropriate filtering. In FM demodulation, a tuned circuit detects frequency shifts of the carrier and converts them into an equivalent audio. Carrier amplitude variations are supressed either by the detector itself or in amplitude clipping limiter stages that feed the detector.

Special modulating techniques have been developed, which include SSB, FDM, TDM, stereo multiplexing, and PCM. Each one has unique characteristics that make it most suitable for situations where the system achieves the maximum information throughput with the narrowest bandwidth, and highest S/N ratio.

Two-way radio communications are a specialized application of basic transmission and reception principles. Often both the transmitter and receiver are combined into one unit called a transceiver. Both AM and FM techniques are used. Amateur radio and CB use AM, because of the reduced cost, and commercial and professional is FM, because of its high fidelity and/or superior S/N characteristics. AM range is greatly improved by SSB, which concentrates the transmission power in the intelligence-bearing sideband.

Antennas and transmission lines are the transmitter's and receiver's link with each other via the electromagnetic wave medium. Although there are a wide variety of antenna designs, all of them are supposed to deliver the maximum possible signal with the least interference or inhibiting factors. The specifications describe this ability in terms of gain, polarity, impedance, etc. The higher the frequency of the RF, the more the signal appears to behave like light, hence the significant differences between commercial broadcast and microwave antenna systems. Coaxial cable transmission lines are used for commercial broadcast, waveguides for microwave systems. And light itself is being used as the carrier in fiber optic transmission lines. Such lines are free from electromagnetic interference, have wide bandwidths, reduced physical size, and excellent durability. Their use will increase significantly as the material cost is decreased.

CHAPTER 3 QUIZ

Handwritten notes:
AM Amplitude modulation
Fm Frequency modulation
Pm Phase modulation
IF Amp is FActory tuned to A predetermined frequency
IF intermediate Frequency
RF - RAdio Frequency

1. Most of the selectivity of a superheterodyne receiver is produced in the:
   a. RF amplifier.
   b. detector.
   c. IF amplifier.
   d. converter.

2. Oscillators used to generate the carrier frequencies for broadcast stations are:
   a. LC controlled.
   b. multivibrator controlled.
   c. RC controlled.
   d. crystal controlled.

3. Neutralization is used in RF amplifiers:
   a. to prevent oscillation.
   b. to keep them oscillating steadily.
   c. to help start them oscillating when power is applied.
   d. never - it is used in oscillators.

4. In an AM transmitter the modulator:
   a. generates the carrier frequency.
   b. adds intelligence to the carrier signal.
   c. amplifies the carrier signal.
   d. rectifies the carrier signal.

5. Where is demodulation accomplished in a superheterodyne receiver?
   a. In the local oscillator
   b. In the detector
   c. In the IF amplifier
   d. In the RF amplifier

6. In an AM superheterodyne receiver, the automatic gain control (AGC) voltage is produced in the:
   a. discriminator.
   b. mixer.
   c. IF amplifier.
   d. detector.

7. A characteristic of an AM wave is:
   a. constant amplitude.
   b. constant frequency.
   c. continuously varying amplitude.
   d. constant phase.

8. The ratio detector is superior to the phase discriminator because it:
   a. is more linear.
   b. is more sensitive.
   c. responds to amplitude variations.
   d. requires less limiting before it.

9. The reception of an SSB signal requires some method of carrier reinsertion for:
   a. demodulation.
   b. stability.
   c. sensitivity.
   d. high fidelity.

10. Time division multiplexing (TDM) uses:
    a. SSB.
    b. number of channels in time slots.
    c. amplitude modulation.
    d. CB channels.

AUDIO AND VIDEO CIRCUITS AND SYSTEMS

INTRODUCTION

Audio and video technologies are very similar. Not only do the design practices and types of components used have much in common, but television is a system that combines both media. Because of this overlap, audio and video concepts have been combined in this chapter.

This chapter begins with an audio section. It covers the fundamentals of audio systems — microphones, speakers, and tape and disc recording and reproduction. Special attention is given to that traditional enemy of audio — background noise, and how the latest technology has virtually eliminated it.

A major portion of the rest of the chapter covers television. TV is introduced with an overview of basic concepts, followed by a step-by-step description of the functional subsystems within an operating monochrome (black-and-white) receiver.

Color television is introduced with a synopsis of the principles of color, and how they have been applied to a practical television system that is compatible with existing monochrome broadcast standards. Then the operation of color television systems and circuits are covered.

Next the theory of operation of most of the common television options and accessories are covered. This includes fine tuning, automatic color control, remote control, and projection techniques.

The material on color television is presented in terms of traditional methods so that the reader can better understand the principles of operation. Current "state-of-the-art" practices may be different, but they are merely functional improvements resulting in better performance, often at a lower cost.

Multiple television distribution systems are discussed next. Cable television, master TV systems, and satellite concepts are included.

Finally, the operating principles of home video cassette recorders (VCRs) are described. This includes an explanation of the difference between the VHS and Beta formats.

AUDIO RECORDING/REPRODUCTION

Audio components and systems have been changing tremendously as a result of high technology innovations in the electronics industry at large. The result has been a steady, upward climb in the quality of sound offered to the consumer, while cost has been declining.

Microphones

A microphone is a transducer which changes sound waves into an electrical ac voltage of equivalent frequency and relative amplitude. When sound waves act against the diaphragm of a microphone, the compressions push it inward, while rarefactions allow it to return to its idle position. Thus, the sound wave causes the microphone to produce voltages equivalent in amplitude and frequency to the air pressure variations.

Microphones fall into the following categories depending on how they produce an electrical signal:
1. Variable resistance (carbon)
2. Magnetic induction (dynamic or variable reluctance)
3. Piezoelectric effect (crystal and ceramic)
4. Capacitor (condenser)

Each one has its special performance, durability, and cost considerations. The magnetic induction type is by far the most commonly used for professional applications, such as recording studios and broadcast, because of its wide, flat frequency response, excellent sensitivity, and "natural sound" characteristics. The piezoelectric variety has been generally used for consumer applications for years because of its low cost, high voltage output, and ruggedness. In recent years, it has been replaced by the condenser microphone, which has superior fidelity and sensitivity.

Speakers and Speaker Systems

Most speakers (loudspeakers) are one of two types; dynamic or electrostatic. Dynamic speakers depend upon the interaction of two magnetic fields, one produced by a permanent magnet and the other produced by the audio signal current passing through a voice coil. The electrostatic speaker operates by the repelling and attraction of capacitor-like plates being used as diaphrams. The audio signal controls the electric field which causes these plates to vibrate. This method is generally used for high frequency speakers, called tweeters.

The ability of the speaker cone to move the surrounding air mass for a given amount of electrical power applied to the speaker's voice coil determines the efficiency of the speaker. The design of the cone and of its suspension is important for proper frequency response and low distortion.

A loudspeaker may have excellent low frequency response, but if the reproduced sound contains too much bass compared to the high frequency response, a booming sound results. A speaker with excellent high frequency response can, because of the absence of low frequency response, sound thin or tinny.

Combination Speaker Response

Balance can be reached between low and high frequency responses. The best solution is to use a combination of low frequency response speakers (woofers) and high frequency response speakers (tweeters). This is called a 2-way speaker system. In addition, a third speaker may be used that has a response between these extremes, called a mid-range speaker. Special filters, called crossover networks, route those frequencies that each speaker can faithfully reproduce to the proper speaker. For the low and mid-frequencies, the speaker enclosure is about as important as the speaker itself in determining the overall sound quality. The matching of the speaker to the enclosure for specific overall response is a science in itself.

Tape Recording and Reproduction

A popular means of recording and playing back information is by means of the magnetic tape cassette or open reel-to-reel format. For any format, the magnetic tape is moved across the tape head, an electromagnetic induction coil. The tape is made of a very thin layer of finely-powdered magnetic material, usually iron oxide or chromium dioxide particles, which have been deposited on a suitable backing material. During recording the audio signal is fed through an amplifier to the tape recorder recording head along with a high frequency (60kHz) bias signal. The purpose of the ac bias voltage is to place the audio signal into the liner portion of the hysteresis magnetic curve of the oxide coating on the tape. (The concept is analagous to the dc biasing of the transistor for Class A operation.) As the tape is moved past a micro-gap on the recording head, the changing magnetic field caused by the changing audio, causes a magnetized pattern to be set up on the tape. During playback, when the tape is moved past a head again (it may be the same one used for recording), the magnetic pattern induces a corresponding voltage in the head, which is now connected to the input of the amplifier, making it a playback head. The more expensive recorders use separate heads for recording and playback.

Before recording new information, the tape is passed by an erase head, which when excited by a bias-erase oscillator signal, rearranges the magnetic pattern on the tape representing the sound (intelligence) and thus erases the recorded information.

Disc Recording and Reproduction

The grooves of a phonographic record vary from side to side, corresponding to the audio signal recorded on them. The phonograph pickup (cartridge) converts the grooved modulations into mechanical vibrations, which it then converts into electrical energy. The transducer portion of the phonograph pickup converts the mechanical movement of the needle (stylus) to an electrical signal of the same frequency. The transducer works on one of two principles. It is either velocity-responding, such as the variable reluctance or dynamic pickup (the familiar magnetic cartridge), or it is amplitude-responding, such as the crystal or ceramic capacitance pickup.

The differences between the different types of pick-ups are their electro-accoustical parameters, durability, and cost. The dynamic pickup is preferred for the better quality audio systems because of its superior compliance (ability to accurately track a phonograph groove with minimal force), wide frequency response and low distortion. Its negatives are its fragility, lower output voltage and higher cost.

Most pickups are stereophonic. They respond independently to the two sides of the stereo groove. When these pickups play monophonic records, the two channels respond equally, producing a monophonic sound.

Noise-Reduction Techniques

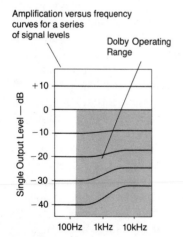

Amplification versus frequency curves for a series of signal levels

Dolby Operating Range

As the level of sound decreases, the amount of boost given to the signal for the higher frequencies is increased.

Figure 4.1 Dolby Dynamic Pre-Emphasis

Dolby System

In the past, the reduction of noise has primarily been achieved by passive filter networks in the high frequency range (scratch filters). Low frequency passive filter networks (rumble filters) are then used to reduce noise, like hum and rumble originating from phonograph turntables. A more modern system makes use of dynamic signal compression and expansion during recording and playback processes, to reduce the inherent noise levels in these media.

The Dolby [1] system is an outstanding noise reduction system. In addition to fixed pre-emphasis and de-emphasis techniques, the Dolby system uses a 25 microsecond time constant. However, instead of it being fixed in attenuation, it varies with the amplitude of the signal in the higher frequency range. Since noise interference is predominant in the high frequency range, the Dolby solution to this problem provides varying degrees of high frequency boost. Changes in frequency response as a function of signal level are shown in *Figure 4.1*. The weaker high frequency signals are given significantly greater

[1] Dolby is a trademark of the Dolby Corporation.

amplification than the stronger signals, the amount of pre-emphasis and subsequent de-emphasis in the receiver varies, depending on the loudness of the signal at any instant. Thus at the higher volume levels, where background noise is drowned out by the music, less high frequency pre- and de-emphasis is required. At lower volumes, however, the background noise can become more obvious, requiring the level of the upper frequencies to be increased at the recorded end and decreased at the playback end. With these techniques, the Dolby system is highly effective in minimizing high frequency tape noise (hiss) and results in better quality tape recordings.

Digital Techniques

Another noise-reduction technique, which also all but eliminates circuit-caused distortion, is digital sound. Basically, the digital system involves converting the complex analog audio wave from the microphone to a digital code. This coded format, if maintained throughout the mastering process and the reproduction process up to the input of the high fidelity amplifier, results in an audio signal that is a flawless replica of what originated at the studio microphone output. Because a digital code cannot be unintentionally altered by the processing electronics or the recording medium, there is no circuit-generated background noise nor distortion added anywhere between the original recording session and the final conversion back to analog.

For the consumer playback market, the digital signals have always been reconverted to analog for traditional record pressings and the copying. This has been the weakest link in the chain ending at the consumer's stereo.

What has been widely-promoted as "digital sound," still has used the traditional analog disc or tape format for the consumer's playback medium. The recently-introduced Compact Disc[2] (CD) format bridges the analog playback gap by providing a digitally-encoded disc medium to the public. The intelligence is encoded in the form of microscopic (0.16 × 0.6 micrometers) bumps and plateaus, representing 1s and 0s on the surface of a plastic disc with a shiny aluminized coating. The disc is read by a laser pickup mechanism, which focuses a less than hair-thin light beam on the disc's surface. A "1", which is a tiny bump, scatters the reflected laser light, whereas a "0", which is a tiny plateau, reflects the light back into the optics, where a light sensitive pickup device detects it. The processing electronics appropriately interprets the reflected image, outputting a continuous stream of digital data, which is decoded by the D/A (digital-to-analog) converter to produce the high fidelity, stereophonic analog signal required by the input of home audio amplifiers.

[2] Compact Disc is a trademark of the Sony Corporation.

The medium solves not only the background noise level problem, but increases the dynamic range (the difference between the largest and smallest possible amplitude) to that of the limitations of the human ear.

The disc is only 120 millimeters across, but can store the digital data for 74 minutes of program material. It is recorded only on one side.

BASIC TELEVISION SYSTEM

The television system involves much of the electronic technology included in AM and FM radio transmission and reception. In the television system, the visual information in the scene is converted by the television camera tube to an electrical signal, which is processed in a manner similar to that of sending audio signals to the radio receiver. These electrical variations, which correspond to the televised scene, are used to reassemble the image on the screen of a cathode-ray tube (CRT).

The television transmitter is shown in a functional block diagram in *Figure 4.2*. The television transmitter has two functions — visual and sound transmission. Both the picture signal, which is transmitted AM, and the sound signal, which is transmitted FM, are radiated from a common antenna. Separate transmitters having different power outputs are used, however.

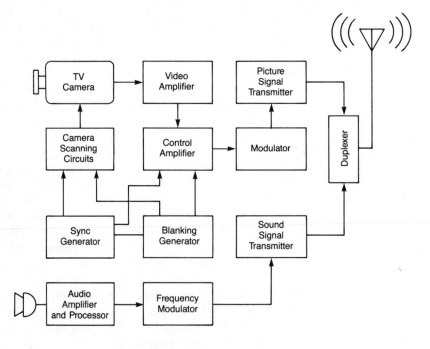

Figure 4.2 Block Diagram of a Basic Television Transmitter

Scanning and Picture Information Transfer

The breaking down of the picture into a mosaic suitable for transmitting and reassembling these received elements to produce the televised picture is done by a linear scanning process. Television, like motion picture photography, creates the illusion of motion by a rapid presentation of slightly different successive scenes. This phenomenon is possible because of the persistence of human vision and the persistence of the fluorescent screen of the CRT.

The United States NTSC (National Television System Committee) television picture is scanned in a sequential series of horizontal lines, one after the other as shown in *Figure 4.3*. A rectangular pattern with a 4:3 width-to-height aspect ratio is formed by 525 evenly spaced, nearly horizontal parallel lines that are traced 30 frames per second. As shown in *Figure 4.3*, each frame is made up of two 262.5 line fields interlaced together.

The horizontal scanning signal steadily moves the electron beams in the camera and in the picture tube from left to right, making the trip across in approximately 53 microseconds. It then abruptly flies back (called the retrace time), returning the beam to the left side in less than 10 microseconds. This sweeping motion is repeated at a frequency of approximately 15,750Hz, or scans per second.

Simultaneously, a 60Hz linear sawtooth signal deflects the horizontal sweeping beam uniformly downward in 1/60 second. Thus, only 262.5 (1/60 × 15,750) horizontal lines, or one field, are traced per vertical sweep. The vertical sweep causes a downward slant of the horizontal scanning lines, seen in *Figure 4.3*, but not easily discernible on the picture tube screen because of the horizontal sweep's much faster frequency. This vertical sweep is just enough to leave space between lines for the next vertical sawtooth to interlace. The second 262.5 line field is also traced in 1/60 second. The two fields (525 line frame) thus take twice as long (1/30 second), making a total of 60 single fields or 30 interlaced fields (frames) per second. Thus, each frame is divided into two parts so that 60 views of the scene are presented to the eye each second. The division of a frame into two parts (fields) cannot be accomplished simply by a shutter as in the motion picture projector, because the picture in television is reproduced one element at a time. Instead, the same effect is obtained by interlacing horizontal scan lines in groups, one with the odd-numbered lines and the other with the even-numbered. Each group with odd or even lines is called a field. Thus, two fields then make the total frame. Interlaced scanning allows for 60 fields per second instead of 30, virtually eliminating image flicker.

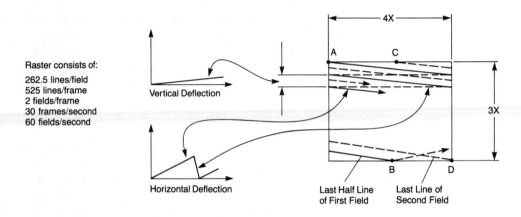

Raster consists of:

262.5 lines/field
525 lines/frame
2 fields/frame
30 frames/second
60 fields/second

Figure 4.3   Interlaced Scan Pattern for Television Pictures

Transmitter/Receiver Synchronization

When the video signal arrives at the receiver and is processed, it must have a means of synchronizing with the televised scene exactly as scanned at the transmitter camera tube, i.e., when the TV camera begins scanning line one at the upper left of the televised scene, the receiver must also begin scanning line one on the CRT. The speed of the receiver scanning line must duplicate that of the transmitter scanning line so that the top of the scene would appear where it should, and not in the middle of the screen or elsewhere. When the horizontal beam reaches the end of the bottom line of the televised scene, it must retrace back to the beginning of the top line (vertical flyback or retrace) without being seen. This must occur simultaneously at both transmitter and receiver. Therefore, besides developing video and audio signals, the system must generate synchronizing and blanking signals to be used by the receiver, so that it stays in step with the transmitter. When the vertical oscillator is out of synchronization, the reproduced picture image will crawl up the screen or jump downward. The horizontal oscillator running out of synchronization will cause the image to tear diagonally.

There are two sets of synchronization signals in a black-and-white picture — the horizontal and the vertical. The electron beam at the receiver must be blanked out (turned off) during vertical and horizontal retrace. This blanking is accomplished by a signal strong enough so that the electron beam is turned off, while the scanning (sweep) circuits retrace the beam. During each blanking interval, a sync pulse is transmitted, so that it is not seen on the screen. The vertical retrace occurs when about 500 lines have been displayed on the screen. The horizontal scanning continues during vertical retrace, so several lines occur as the beam is pulled from the lower right to the upper left corner of the screen. About 20 lines (lines 505 to 525) are not part of the lighted screen (raster).

The sync generator at the television station serves as the system's basic timing unit — generating, shaping and arranging in proper sequence all the pulses necessary to control the interlaced scanning process. The basic timer is a crystal-controlled oscillator. Since the interlaced fields that make up one frame occur 60 times per second, the vertical retrace in the receiver must be synchronized with the vertical retrace at the transmitter by means of the vertical sync pulses, which occur each 1/60 of a second. The vertical blanking interval is a relatively long time — about 1000 microseconds, compared to the 3 microseconds required for each horizontal line. Therefore, horizontal sync pulses are transmitted during the vertical blanking time to keep the receiver's horizontal oscillator in synchronization.

A keying circuit, which arranges the sync pulses in proper sequence to form a composite sync signal, is generated to ensure a tightly synchronized television system. The composite television signal containing the synchronization signals is shown in *Figure 4.4*. The synchronizing waveform consists of three distinct functional type pulses — the horizontal sync pulses, the equalizing pulses, and the vertical sync pulses. The equalizing pulses occur in two groups of six each before and after each vertical sync pulse block. They serve the threefold function of ensuring equidistant interlacing, of enabling production of identical vertical intervals between fields and between frames (alternate fields), and of maintaining horizontal synchronization during vertical retrace intervals.

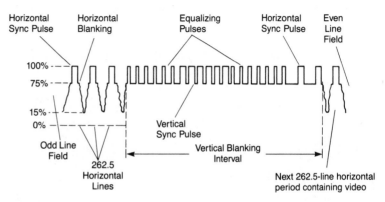

Figure 4.4 Composite Television Picture Signal — Vertical Blanking Interval

The Composite Video Signal

The three components of the composite video signal are:
1. Camera signal variations representing the image
2. Blanking pulses
3. Sync pulses.

The only parts of the transmission that remain constant are the peaks of the sync pulses and the blanking levels. The top of any sync pulse is the maximum value of the emitted carrier (100% modulation). The blanking level (pedestal level) is 75 percent of the peak value. The reference black level, which will produce the darkest black in the transmitted picture, is approximately 70 percent of the peak level. The reference white level, which produces the whitest white, is 12.5 percent of the peak value. This is illustrated in _Figure 4.5_. Notice that the picture signal can be any level from the reference black to the reference white level which is it's most negative level. The transmitted image is a negative image. This was done so that noise spikes would be less-noticeable on the received picture by driving into the "blacker-than-black" region of the waveform.

A television camera generates voltages whose amplitudes vary in accordance with brightness levels of the picture elements being scanned. This is video information. Along with the sync and blanking pulses, this information makes up the composite video signal that is transmitted as sidebands of a station carrier. The lines of video information that are generated by the camera are broken up by the insertion of the relatively short duration blanking and sync pulses. However, the small amounts of the picture that are lost during the brief vertical and horizontal retrace periods are not noticeable to a viewer at the receiving end.

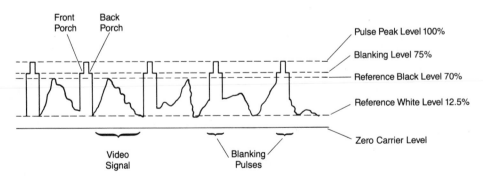

Figure 4.5 _Relative Levels of Composite Video Signal_

Camera and Picture Tube Operation

Camera Vidicon

There are several types of television camera tubes. A widely-used type is the vidicon. The vidicon is relatively inexpensive, simple and compact in size. *Figure 4.6* shows the construction of a vidicon camera tube. The light sensitive area at the front of the tube consists of three very thin layers which are light active. The first is a transparent conductive film. Next is a semiconductor, photoresistive layer deposited on the conductive film. Finally, a photoconductive mosaic layer is developed on the semiconductor layer.

The middle semiconductor layer has the property of extremely high resistance when the dark portion of the scene exists on the film, but its resistance reduces drastically when light strikes it. The area between the photoconductive mosaic islands and the conductive film act as tiny capacitors whose dielectric leakage is directly dependent on the light intensity of these areas. There are over a million individual separate areas which act as tiny capacitors, with the photoresistive layer acting as the dielectric and the photofilm as the other common capacitor plate. Therefore, the dielectric leakage is variable and dependent on the amount of light striking each tiny area. An electron beam scans across the mosaic areas so as to charge up each of the tiny capacitors. Light on the mosaic area discharges the mosaic capacitors through the load resistor (R_L in the figure). The scanning electron beam recharges the capacitors, producing a video signal voltage drop across the resistor R_L that is proportional to the light intensity at the individual areas being scanned.

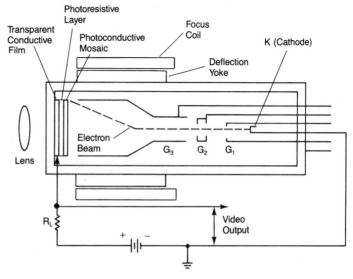

Figure 4.6   Vidicon Camera Tube

The electron beam that does the scanning starts at the cathode of the electron gun at the rear section of the vidicon. Electrons are "boiled" off the cathode by heating it to a high temperature with a filament heater. Its intensity is set by the bias voltage between the cathode and the first grid. Grid 2 is positively charged and accelerates the beam of electrons that emerge through the aperture of the first grid. Focusing is provided by the magnetic field action of the focus coil and also by the electrostatic lens effect set up between the second and third grid. Scanning is produced electromagnetically with horizontal and vertical coils in the deflection yoke located around the midsection of the vidicon.

Camera Plumbicon

The Plumbicon[3] is similar to the vidicon except that it has a lead oxide target plate on which the image is focused. Its advantage is that it has less residual image on the photosensitive area when the scene changes, than the vidicon type.

Black and White Picture Tube

The black-and-white (monochrome) picture tube, shown in *Figure 4.7*, that is used in a television receiver is a cathode-ray tube (CRT). It makes use of electromagnetic deflection (as compared to electrostatic deflection used in oscilloscopes). The much greater deflection angle of the CRT used in television receivers makes electromagnetic deflection the practical choice for this application. The television picture tube CRT consists of: an electron gun, a fluorescent screen, and an Aquadag[4] coating on the inside of the glass envelope. The electron gun consists of: a combined heater cathode, a small metal cylinder with a hole in one end, which serves as a grid, and then two more metal cylinders used for focusing, and accelerating the electron beam toward the screen. The aquadag coating on the inside of the screen is the gray metallic substance that acts as an accelerating anode. It has a high positive potential of about six to twenty thousand volts (depending on tube size), which accelerates the electrons to a high enough velocity so that when they strike the fluorescent screen on the face of the CRT, they produce a spot of light.

The intensity of the spot produced on the screen is controlled by the bias voltage between the cathode and the first grid — the more negative the grid with respect to the cathode, the fewer electrons that can pass through its hole and the less intense is the spot produced on the screen. Intensity can be manually controlled by changing the grid voltage bias with a brightness control.

---

[3] Plumbicon is a trademark of N.V. Philips of Holland.
[4] Aquadag is a trademark of Acheson Industries, Inc.

As the electron beam accelerates to the screen, it is deflected across the face of the picture tube screen by means of horizontal deflection coils and up and down by vertical deflection coils. These coils are placed around the neck of the CRT on the outside as shown in *Figure 4.7*. This set of deflection coils is called the deflection yoke assembly.

The electron beam is made up of electrons, but it also contains heavy negative ions. These ions serve no useful purpose and, if allowed to strike the screen, burn it. Early model TV sets used an ion trap, a small magnet positioned on the neck of the CRT to permanently deflect the heavy ions beyond the edge of the screen. In CRTs today, ion burn is prevented by an aluminized screen which is a thin film of aluminum deposited on the back of the phosphor on the inside of the CRT. The film is porous to the small electrons, but blocks the passage of the larger ions. An additional feature of the aluminized film is that it acts like a mirror reflector, which produces about twice the light output as CRTs without this film. The type of picture tube is referred to as an aluminized-screen picture tube.

The video signal creates variation in beam current during the scanning process by varying the voltage between the first grid and the cathode. The varying electron beam produces a spot on the screen which varies in intensity. As a result, a picture is produced on the screen. This is termed intensity modulation of

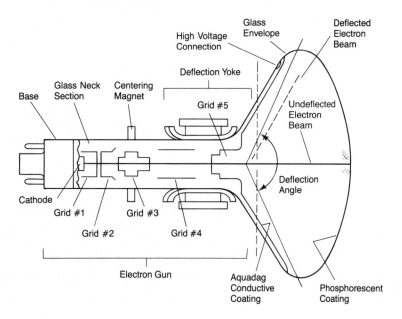

Figure 4.7 Black-and-White Television Picture Tube

the CRT beam. Either the grid or the cathode can have the signal voltage applied. The vertical and horizontal blanking pulses drive the grid negative (or the cathode positive) during its duration which darkens the screen during retrace. Since the sync pulses occur during this blanking interval, they are not seen on the screen.

Sound System

The sound transmitter is essentially the same as an FM broadcast station. However, it has a narrower deviation (25kHz). As with FM radio broadcast, TV sound transmission uses pre-emphasis and de-emphasis to improve the signal-to-noise ratio. *Figure 4.2* shows the sound signal path from the microphone through the sound signal transmitter. The audio signal is frequency modulated on an audio carrier that is 4.5MHz above the picture carrier.

BLACK-AND-WHITE TELEVISION RECEIVERS

The functional analysis of the television receiver circuit reveals that it is basically a superheterodyne receiver. *Figure 4.8* shows a typical block diagram of a monochrome receiver. The tuner, which is sometimes called the front end, contains the RF amplifier, the mixer and the local oscillator. The output of this stage is the intermediate frequency (IF). The sound and video signals are amplified together through the IF stages, but are separated at the video detector. The 4.5MHz sound carrier and its sidebands are fed through a sound IF amplifier, an FM detector, an audio amplifier stage, and on to a speaker. The sync pulses are separated from the composite video signal after the video detector and fed to their respective deflection circuits to control the vertical and horizontal scanning of the picture tube in synchronization with the scanning of the camera at the transmitter. The video signal containing the picture information is amplified to control the beam intensity of the CRT.

Tuner

A television receiver must be capable of tuning over a very wide frequency range and it must have a linear response over the 6MHz bandwidth of each channel. The VHF tuner has three sections: an RF amplifier, a mixer, and an oscillator. The oscillator frequency is always higher than the RF picture carrier by an amount equal to the IF frequency.

During conversion, the signal oscillator signal beats, (hetrodynes) with the picture carrier, producing the IF signal, which is the numerical difference between the oscillator frequency and the picture and sound RF carriers. The oscillator frequency is 45.75MHz above the received station's picture carrier and 41.25 MHz above the station's sound carrier. For a high quality picture and sound, the IF frequency produced by the tuner must be exactly coincident with the tuning of the IF amplifier section.

Because of the high frequencies and low-level signals, component positioning, lead routing, and shielding are critical. Older TV tuners used a rotating mechanical channel switch mechanism. Many modern tuners use electronic voltage-controlled capacitors and phase locked loops to control the tuning. All of these requirements call for the tuner to be a self-contained assembly.

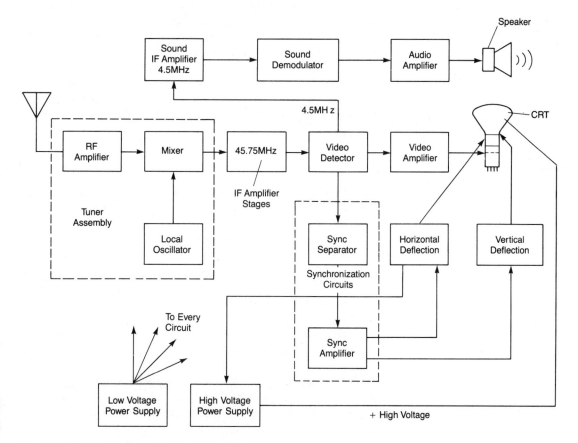

Figure 4.8   Block Diagram of a Monochrome TV Receiver

Video IF Amplifiers and Detector

The IF amplifier in the TV set performs the same function as in the radio receiver, that of amplifying frequencies within a certain bandwidth. The picture and sound signals travel together through the IF amplifier — the sound IF carrier at 41.25MHz and the picture at 45.75MHz. They travel on through the tuned amplifiers to the point where they are separated after the video detector. The video detector is often a low-level solid state diode. The detector's function is to demodulate the composite (video) signal (much as happens in a simple AM radio receiver), send the synchronizing signals to the sync separator, send the sound FM sidebands to the sound IF, and couple the video signal to the video amplifiers and on to the picture tube. The output from the detector to the video amplifier is the composite video signal.

Fine detail in the picture of the televised scene produces high sideband frequencies. This results in wide bandpass requirements of the IF amplifier. Screen size of the CRT also affects bandpass requirements. A large screen requires a wide bandpass to obtain maximum resolution of the fine picture detail. With a small screen, such detail is unnecessary. Overall, the bandwidth requirement is somewhere between 3MHz to 4MHz, depending on the screen size. High Q resonant circuits, called wave traps, are used in the IF section to shape the response curve and to reject certain frequencies that may interfere with the picture and sound. There are usually at least three IF amplifier stages.

Video Amplifier

The purpose of the video amplifier is to boost the weak signal that exists at the detector output to the level required for good picture contrast. The number of stages of video amplification is usually two or three in a black-and-white receiver.

The video information produced by the television camera is referenced to a dc voltage that corresponds to the average level of background illumination of the scene being televised. This same dc level must be maintained in the receiver, or the overall brightness will fluctuate — dark scenes will appear brighter than normal and light scenes will be too dark. Therefore, direct coupling between the detector and the CRT or some means of dc restoration is necessary.

In order to have good picture quality, the video amplifier must have a reasonably flat frequency response from 30Hz to 3-4MHz again depending upon the size of the picture tube. Loss of low video frequencies reduce the contrast for large picture objects and cause smearing of edges. Loss of high frequencies results in poor resolution, and a soft-to-blurred picture.

There are two controls that are found in the video amplifier circuitry: brightness and contrast. The brightness control sets the intensity of the CRT beam current by setting a bias level and therefore the average raster brightness is controlled directly. The contrast control is a gain control in a video amplifier stage. It usually adjusts the amount of degeneration used in the video amplifier. Maximum degeneration produces low stage gain and minimum picture contrast. The contrast control for the picture is analagous to the volume control for the sound. The picture contrast is determined by the peak-to-peak amplitude of the composite video signal that reaches the picture tube control element. Excessive contrast is often caused by too much signal in the video amplifier.

Horizontal and Vertical Deflection

As previously shown in *Figure 4.3*, the screen raster is produced by simultaneously deflecting the CRT beam, horizontally and vertically. The function of the vertical sweep section is to deflect the beam up and down at a constant rate. The horizontal sweep section sweeps the beam sideways over 15,000 times per second. As shown in *Figure 4.3*, the waveforms deflect the beam at a uniform rate on the screen. The horizontal deflection circuit sweeps the beam from left to right, while the vertical deflection circuit sweeps the beam down from top to bottom at a much slower rate. Besides beam deflection, the horizontal sweep circuit performs a number of secondary functions, such as developing the high voltage for the CRT and producing keying signals for various circuits in the receiver, such as the automatic gain control.

The horizontal and vertical sections each contain an oscillator and an amplifier, and sometimes a driver. The oscillators are free running, non-sinusoidal types. The frequency of each oscillator is controlled by its respective hold control. The hold controls set the free running frequency within the control range of the sync pulses, thus enabling the sync pulses to keep each oscillator locked in to match the sweep frequencies of the transmitted image.

The deflection waveform used in the electromagnetic deflection system is a trapezoidal wave. That is, it consists of a step voltage combined with a slightly non-linear sawtooth voltage. This signal input produces an electromagnetic field at the deflection coils that increases and sweeps the beam linearly either across or up and down the screen. The output from the vertical and horizontal deflection amplifiers is fed to the deflection yoke (electromagnetic coils) around the neck of the picture tube. The varying field produced penetrates the glass tube and deflects the beam as described as illustrated in *Figure 4.3*.

Horizontal Output/High Voltage Section

The horizontal section requires a more powerful output signal than the vertical section because it must sweep the beam a greater distance, and because its output has several functions:

1. Horizontal beam deflection by providing yoke drive
2. Pulse source for the high voltage transformer
3. Keying pulses for other circuits
4. Boost voltage for other circuits

As the sawtooth level builds up in the horizontal output amplifier, it reaches its maximum level and then suddenly drops to zero, supplying the retrace drive. The waveform is similar to the waveform shown in *Figure 4.3*. The magnetic field around the horizontal yoke collapses rapidly, inducing a high amplitude flyback EMF across the transformer secondary which is connected to the yoke. The secondary winding is a step-up coil consisting of many turns of wire to produce high voltage from the sharp drop in current during retrace. A damper diode, which is present in every television high voltage section, suppresses the "flywheel effect" oscillations that would otherwise follow each high voltage pulse. This high voltage is rectified to produce the 15,000 to 25,000 volts dc anode accelerating voltage for the picture tube.

The high voltage (flyback) transformer not only provides the high voltage pulse just described, but it also serves as an impedance-matching device between the output of the horizontal output amplifier and the yoke's horizontal deflection coils. In addition, it has separate windings or taps to supply triggering (keying) voltages to several other circuits to keep them synchronized, and is a source of high voltage (boost voltage) to other circuits.

Vertical Output

The vertical output deflection circuits are amplifiers similar to the horizontal output circuits, and provide the current needed to drive the vertical windings of the deflection yoke during the scanning process. These circuits amplify the output of the vertical oscillator to a level necessary to drive the coils in the deflection yoke with sufficient power to produce a changing magnetic field strong enough to deflect the electron beam from the top of the screen to the bottom. This circuit is also used to shape the waveform so that the current that drives the yoke produces a linear vertical sweep. The circuit sometimes makes use of output signal feedback to the driver stage to improve circuit linearity.

In addition to driving the yoke, the vertical output deflection circuit also provides blanking pulses to the cathode-ray tube to blank out the picture during vertical retrace from the bottom of the screen to the top after each scanned field.

The amplifier stages that make up the vertical output section may also contain linearity adjustments. These are basically biasing networks that control the operating point of the transistors. To produce a linear vertical sweep so the image is not stretched nor squeezed, the current through the yoke must change at a uniform rate. This is accomplished by operating the output stage as a Class A linear amplifier.

Synchronization Circuits

Referring again to *Figure 4.8*, the synchronization (sync) section controls the timed operation of the vertical and horizontal sweep oscillators. The sync section is driven by the composite video signal, and the sync signals contained therein are riding on top of the blanking pulses (see *Figure 4.4*). This sync separator has a clipper circuit which clips off the sync pulses and passes them to the sync amplifier. The sync amplifier has integrator and differentiator circuits. Because the horizontal sync pulses are much more narrow than the vertical sync pulses and have a faster repetition rate, simple RC filter circuits can be used to separate the horizontal from the vertical pulses.

Figure 4.9 shows signal waveforms when the incoming sync pulses are passed through an integrator circuit to separate the vertical sync and a differentiator circuit to separate out the horizontal sync. The differentiator circuit acts as a high pass filter, passing the horizontal sync pulses on to the horizontal oscillator. The integrator circuit acts as a low-pass filter, taking the vertical sync pulse and building up a charge on the integrating capacitor, thereby producing an output pulse waveform.

The vertical sync pulse is very wide as compared to the horizontal pulse, but it has serrations at half-line intervals so that complete rejection of horizontal sync pulses during this time does not take place in the differentiating circuit. Although the wide portions of the pulses are rejected, each serration produces a differentiated output pulse which keeps the horizontal oscillator synchronized during the time that the vertical sync pulses occur. Because these serrations in the vertical sync pulse tend to produce irregularities in the output waveform, two or more sections of integrators are generally utilized.

Audio Circuits

The TV sound carrier is frequency modulated. As previously discussed for *Figure 4.8*, after the video IF stages and video detector, the audio and the video are separated, and the audio is detected, amplified and fed to the speaker.

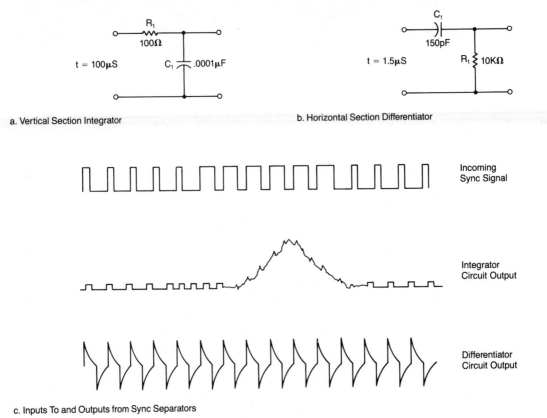

a. Vertical Section Integrator

b. Horizontal Section Differentiator

Incoming
Sync Signal

Integrator
Circuit Output

Differentiator
Circuit Output

c. Inputs To and Outputs from Sync Separators

Figure 4.9 Separation of Vertical and Horizontal Synchronization Pulses

The sound takeoff circuit is composed of one or more tuned circuits (traps) resonant at 4.5MHz. The tuned circuits accept the 4.5MHz sound signal while rejecting the video of the composite signal. Thus, video is not coupled to the sound section, and sound is not coupled to the video section. The sound section is very similar to an FM receiver. It has a sound IF tuned to 4.5MHz and a sound IF limiter to eliminate any amplitude variations of the signal before being applied to the FM detector. Recall that because the sound is FM, clipping of the amplitude variation does not distort the sound. Amplitude modulated signals, generated by the video blanking and sync pulses, could produce a strong, objectionable buzz in the sound if overall video gain is too high.

The limiter couples the signal to a FM detector circuit, such as a ratio detector, or a quadrature detector to demodulate the sound from the FM signal. A volume control varies the amount of signal voltage coupled from the detector to the audio amplifier stages.

There may be two audio amplifiers: a voltage amplifier to increase the signal level, and a power output amplifier to develop the necessary power to drive the speaker. The better console sets use a high fidelity audio section, and some television receivers are capable of stereo reproduction. Other TV stations simultaneously broadcast their sound on a FM radio broadcast frequency, so that stereo sound can be received and reproduced through a standard FM stereo receiver. (This is called a "stereo simulcast".)

COLOR TELEVISION SYSTEM

The color television system as defined by NTSC is an extension of the standard monochrome arrangement with the additional circuits included to insert, extract and synchronize color information. Color transmissions using this system are compatible with the black-and-white television system.

Color Fundamentals

Color is the characteristic of light energy that produces the sensations of brightness, hue and saturation. Brightness is the amount of luminance or the intensity of a color. Hue is the wavelength or frequency of the color (i.e., its position in the electromagnetic spectrum), and saturation is the property that denotes the absence of white light. Thus, a color that contains no white light is a saturated or pure color. When white light is mixed with a color, it becomes desaturated as in the case of the pastel colors. The color television system uses these principles to reproduce the color scenes on the screen.

The FCC has specified a color system for transmission based on the three primary colors, Any hue, brightness, or saturation can be reproduced with acceptable accuracy using the three primary colors. For example, when colors of the same saturation are mixed additively in proportions of 30 percent red, 59 percent green and 11 percent blue, white light is produced.

Basic Color Television System

A color television camera separates the primary hues from the televised scene. It has three basic camera tubes arranged as shown in *Figure 4.10*. Each tube in the camera receives its light input through an optical filter that passes a single color — one red, one green and one blue. The image of the object after passing through the lens assembly, is optically split in three directions and presented to each of the filters of the respective camera tube.

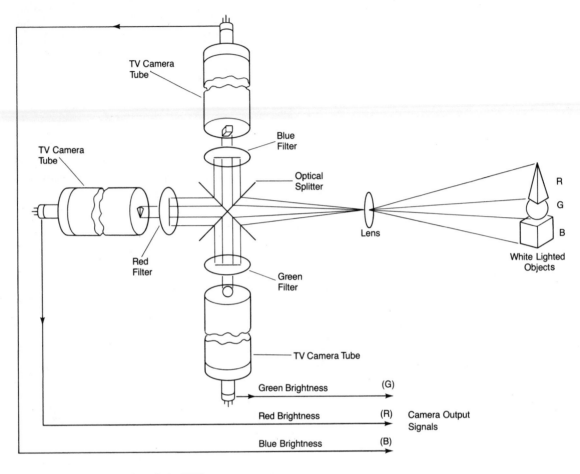

Figure 4.10 Basic Three-Tube Color TV Camera

Since each filter permits only its own color to reach the camera tube, a substantially independent brightness voltage is obtained from each of the camera tubes. The amplitude of each signal is proportional to the mount of reflected light of each primary color that strikes the mosaic surface of its respective camera tube.

If only one camera tube were available to receive the object's image, without a light filter, the signal output from the tube would be representative of all three primary colors mixed together in the right proportions. This is called the Y or luminance signal. The luminance signal is the video signal to produce the picture in a standard black-and-white television receiver.

Color Signals

The method of development of the color signal is illustrated in *Figure 4.11*. The output of each color tube is combined in a matrix circuit to produce the luminance signal Y. Luminance signal $+Y$ is fed directly to the mixer, but also is fed through a phase inverter to produce a $-Y$ signal. This is because the FCC standard requires a negative image. The blue signal is added to the $-Y$ signal producing a $(B-Y)$ out of the matrix. Similarly, a $(R-Y)$ signal is developed. Since G is present in the Y signal, the $(G-Y)$ signal is not transmitted because it is derived at the receiver from the $(R-Y)$ and $(B-Y)$ signals. The $(B-Y)$ and $(R-Y)$ signals are further processed in the IQ matrix where a phase adjustment is made. The output with in-phase components added is I, and with 90 degrees out of phase components added is Q. Q is called the quadrature signal.

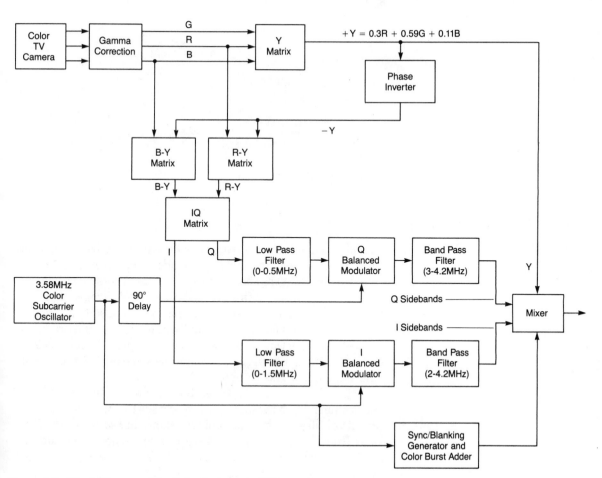

Figure 4.11   Block Diagram of the Color System of a TV Transmitter

The amplitude of the I and Q signals determines the saturation (absence of white) of the colors. The phase vector developed between the two determines the hue (actual color) produced on the receiver CRT screen. The I and Q signals make up the color information, and together are called the chrominance (C) signal. The I signal modulates a 3.58MHz subcarrier directly in a balanced modulator, while the Q signal modulates the same 3.58MHz subcarrier delayed by 90 degrees.

The output of the balanced modulators are sidebands which represent the color information. When they are produced in balanced modulators, the carrier is suppressed and therefore must be regenerated at the receiver. In order to maintain the proper overall phase relationship, a sample of the color subcarrier is transmitted during the horizontal blanking interval after the horizontal sync pulse as shown in *Figure 4.12*. These eight cycles of the 3.58MHz reference subcarrier are called the color burst signal.

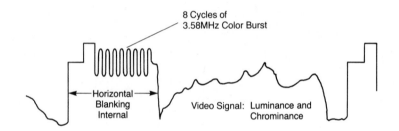

Figure 4.12   Color Burst Signal

Color Picture Tubes

The most popular color picture tube design, which has been in use since 1953, has been the three-gun shadow-mask picture tube (patented by RCA) as shown in *Figure 4.13a*. The three basic internal components of this type tube are the electron gun assembly, the shadow mask and the phosphor dot screen. Each gun is the same as for the black-and-white TV tube and produces an electron beam that is focused to the same point on the shadow mask so that the beams pass through the same perforation but at different angles. This is shown in *Figure 4.13*.

The shadow mask contains about one-half million tiny perforations. Each beam, therefore, strikes the phosphor dot screen at a slightly different point as shown in *Figure 4-13b*. The beam from the red electron gun strikes the red dot, the beam from the green gun strikes the green dot and the beam from the blue gun strikes the blue dot.

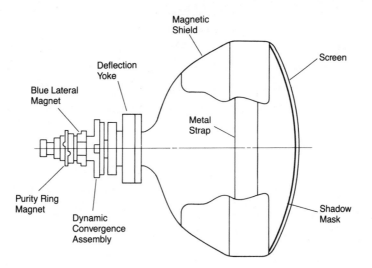

a. External Appearance

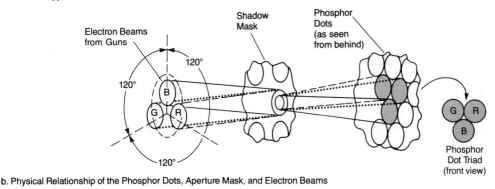

b. Physical Relationship of the Phosphor Dots, Aperture Mask, and Electron Beams

Figure 4.13 Shadow Mask, Three-Gun Color Picture Tube

This action is the same at any point on the screen so that if the red and blue guns were turned off and the green gun was operating, then a green field would be displayed over the field of the color picture tube.

The CRT has a deflection yoke mounted on the tube neck just as in a black-and-white picture tube. In addition, a dynamic convergence assembly and a permanent magnet assembly is mounted behind the yoke. The purpose of the magnet assembly is to cause static convergence of the three electron beams at the shadow mask so they pass cleanly through the same hole in the center area of the shadow mask. The dynamic convergence assembly consists of electromagnetic coils. Specially shaped current waveforms in these coils change the beam deflection so that convergence of the three beams can be obtained over the whole screen. Misadjustment of this convergence magnet assembly will produce color fringing at the edges of objects and shapes displayed on the CRT.

A second type of color picture tube, the Trinitron[5], is shown in *Figure 4.14*. Here the red, green and blue phosphors are utilized, but instead of being dots, are in vertical stripes on the picture tube screen. Instead of a shadow mask, an aperture grill is formed with slots instead of holes. Each slot has the same width as the color phosphor stripe. Therefore, the beam from the red gun strikes the red phosphor stripe, the green strikes the green, and the blue strikes the blue. The aperture grill picture tube operates from the same electrical signal waveform as the shadow mask picture tube. However, because of its comparative simplicity, only six picture tube adjustment controls are required, compared to two or three dozen controls utilized by the typical shadow mask tube convergence circuitry.

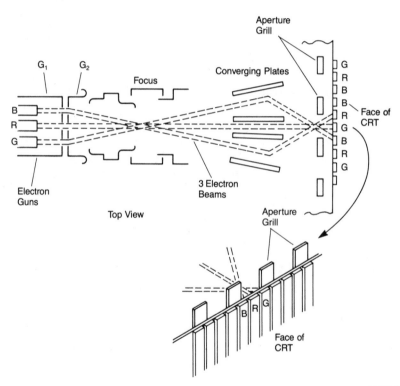

Figure 4.14   Trinitron Color Picture Tube

COLOR TELEVISION RECEIVER

Figure 4.15 shows the color television receiver in block diagram form. The shaded blocks indicate stages used only in the color receiver. The unshaded blocks are sections that appear in both the black-and-white and the color television receivers.

[5] Trinitron is a trademark of the Sony Corporation

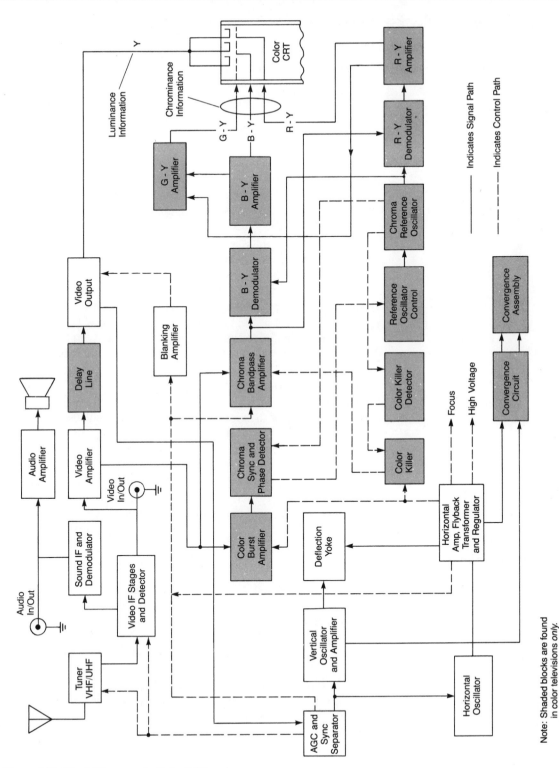

Figure 4.15   Block Diagram of a Color TV Receiver

Sections Common to Black-and-White and Color Receivers

The tuner unit and IF stage are nearly identical in both types of receivers. The selected picture and sound signals are amplified in the RF amplifier and then coupled to the mixer. The picture signal includes video, sync, equalizing, and blanking pulses, as well as the chrominance and the color burst signals.

The operation of the stages from the tuner to the video detector are the same as for the black and white circuits, except the IF bandwidth is wider — 6MHz, instead of 3-4MHz.

The detected signals are amplified in the first video amplifier. A 3.58MHz trap in this circuit prevents the chrominance signals from entering the video amplifier. From the video amplifier, the sync, blanking and luminance signals are applied to the one microsecond delay line. The delay line, which is a six-inch long air-core coil, is designed to delay the blanking and luminance signals by the same amount of time that the chrominance signals are delayed in the chroma section. In this manner, all the signals that are coincident at the transmitter also appear coincident at the picture tube. The output of the delay line is amplified, applied to the video output stage and applied, in a positive-going polarity, to the cathode of the picture tube.

Portions of the signal from the video output are also applied to the sync separator and the AGC amplifier. The sync separator extracts the positive-going horizontal and vertical sync pulses from the output of the video output. These sync pulses are then applied to the vertical and horizontal oscillators, respectively. The AGC circuit automatically adjusts the gain of the RF and IF sections to compensate for differences in signal strength at the receiver. The amplitude of the sync pulses from any particular television transmitter is normally constant. Their amplitude is therefore proportional to signal strength and they may be used as the basis for determining the necessary receiver gain (AGC).

Bandpass Amplifier and Color Killer

The chroma bandpass amplifier, in association with the color killer circuit, is either on or off. If a color signal is being received, the color killer circuit turns it on, otherwise, with a black and white signal, it is off. On black and white signals, the chroma amplifier is off to reject possible interference that could produce color streaks during black-and-white program reception.

In addition, the color killer circuit operates as an automatic gain control for the chrominance signal during color reception. That is, the output chroma signal is held at about the same level whether the input signal is strong or weak.

The output from the video amplifier is fed to the burst amplifier and also the chroma bandpass amplifier. The bandpass amplifier has a rising frequency response that peaks at 4.2MHz. The amplified output of the bandpass amplifier is fed in parallel to each demodulator where the I and Q sidebands are sampled for the chrominance information they contain.

Burst Amplifier, Subcarrier Oscillator and Color Synchronization

The burst amplifier supplies a strong color burst signal, which originated from the station transmitter. It serves two purposes: color sync and chroma switching. The signal at the burst gate input consists of chrominance IF sidebands and the color burst. The output of the burst amplifier contains only the burst of 3.58MHz signal. The chroma is eliminated by limiting the bandpass of this amplifier to about 0.5MHz and by gating (keying) the stage to conduct for the duration of the burst signal only. Gating is accomplished during horizontal retrace by a high amplitude horizontal sweep pulse that is obtained from the horizontal output stage.

A 3.58MHz color subcarrier is required to demodulate the chrominance sidebands. Because the station subcarrier is not transmitted, an equivalent subcarrier must be generated at the receiver. The signal developed by the chroma reference crystal oscillator is an unmodulated voltage of constant amplitude. Its frequency and phase must be precisely controlled for proper color. Normally a varactor diode is used to provide precise control of the oscillator. A feedback loop, where a sampling of the oscillator is applied to a phase detector for comparison with the color burst, provides proper phase locking of the signal to provide a normal synchronized color condition; i.e., the correct hue of the picture is present on the screen.

Loss of color sync shows up in various ways. If the oscillator frequency is off by a small amount, the result is a rainbow pattern of horizontal bars called "barber pole effect." The greater the frequency error, the greater the number of bars. If the oscillator frequency is correct but the wrong phase, colors may all be present but of the wrong hue. If the oscillator is far off frequency or is not working at all, a black-and-white image results.

Color Demodulation and Matrixing

All colors are derived from just the chrominance signals developed at the station. These are the I and Q sideband signals produced by modulating the 3.58MHz subcarrier with the camera outputs as explained for the transmitter. Each sideband represents certain colors. Colors associated with the I sideband are red and all of its secondary colors, that is, yellow, magenta and variations of these. Colors associated with the Q sideband are blue and the secondary color cyan and its variations. Each color corresponds to a specific phase angle of the signal with respect to the reference 3.58MHz subcarrier. As just discussed for the color burst and subcarrier oscillator, the receiver oscillator is synchronized to the transmitter oscillator by the color burst signal.

The phase angle of the chrominance signal is constantly changing based upon the color of the scene detected by the camera. The vector addition of the phased signals produces the hue, and the instantaneous vector amplitude is the saturation level of the color.

Matrixing

The chrominance signal and the synchronized 3.58MHz oscillator signal are applied to each demodulator. Note that there are only two demodulators; a $(R - Y)$ and $(B - Y)$ demodulator. There is no $(G - Y)$ demodulator. Recall from the discussion of the transmitter, green was not transmitted as such. It is reproduced at the receiver by a mixture of the $(R - Y)$ and $(B - Y)$ signals. The output of $(B - Y)$ and $(R - Y)$ demodulators are fed to the $(B - Y)$ and the $(R - Y)$ amplifiers, respectively. Particular proportions $(-0.51(R - Y)$ and $-0.19(B - Y)$ of the $(R - Y)$ and $(B - Y)$ signals are fed to the input of the $(G - Y)$ amplifier. The outputs of these amplifiers, $(R - Y)$, $(B - Y)$, $(G - Y)$, are fed to the grids of the color picture tube where control of the electron beams occurs. In *Figure 4.15*, the net bias between grid and cathode with $- Y$ applied to the cathode and $(G - Y)$ applied to the grid is $(G - Y) - (- Y)$, or G. In like manner, R and B signals are the resultant bias on the other grids that intensity modulate the electron beams of the three separately controlled electron guns.

The color produced on a CRT screen at any given instant is determined by the relative bias voltage between grid and cathode, produced by the chrominance signal to each of the three guns. Primary colors are produced when there is output from only one amplifier that drives the grid; the other two beams would be cut off ("in the black"). For example, the $(B - Y)$ amplifier output only would produce a blue screen. In *Figure 4.15*, the complete video signal is recombined by applying it to the cathode. In some TV sets this combination process takes place in the demodulators or output amplifiers. Sometimes the output amplifiers are called matrix amplifiers because the mixing process is called matrixing.

Static and Dynamic Convergence

As mentioned previously, the holes in the shadow mask are positioned very accurately directly behind the center of each triangle of red, blue and green dots. A normal picture is obtained only when the beam of each gun strikes its corresponding color dots on the screen. This occurs only when all three beams converge in each and every hole in the shadow mask. This represents the ideal condition of color purity. Improper adjustment of purity and/or convergence results in a noticeable and distracting color fringing on a black-and-white picture and a bleeding around the images of a color picture. When the color purity adjustments are correct, activating the red, green and blue guns in sequence will produce pure red, green and blue rasters on the screen. With all three guns on and the beam currents balanced correctly, the raster is uniform, neutral white.

As the electron beams are deflected toward the outer edges of the screen, the distance from the electron guns to the screen becomes greater than it is while the central region is being scanned. This varying distance must be progressively compensated for as an electron beam moves away from the center screen. Center-area screen convergence is determined largely by the adjustment of permanent magnets mounted over the electron guns around the outside of the CRT neck. These magnets are called static convergence controls. Screen convergence toward the edge is controlled by horizontal and vertical electromagnets mounted over the electron guns also around the outside of the CRT neck. These are called dynamic convergence coils.

Convergence Adjustments

A complete and accurate convergence set-up requires the injection of a test pattern as shown in *Figure 4.16*, usually from a dot and crosshatch generator. The misconverged test pattern is shown in *Figure 4.16*. Note the separation of colors along the edges. The procedure itself is usually divided into two sections, static adjustments and dynamic adjustments.

The static adjustments (see *Figure 4.17a*), which are performed first, involve the alignment of the centermost area of the test pattern for minimum color separation by moving the purity rings and permanent magnets in their supports. These adjustments are located in an assembly mounted just behind the deflection yoke.

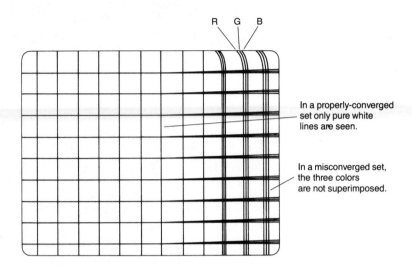

R G B

In a properly-converged
set only pure white
lines are seen.

In a misconverged set,
the three colors
are not superimposed.

Figure 4.16   *Crosshatch Test Pattern Showing Misconvergence*

The dynamic adjustments (see *Figure 4.17b*) involve the alignment of the remainder of the test pattern by using potentiometers and slug-tuned coils mounted on the small control board called the convergence board. These controls vary the amplitudes and waveforms of ac drive signals input to the convergence coils mounted on the static magnets around the picture tube neck. These convergence coils produce a magnetic field, which in combination with the permanent magnetic fields, interract with the three electron beams to deflect them into proper convergence. These ac drive signals are obtained from the horizontal and vertical output circuits (see *Figure 4.15*).

There is a lot of interaction between static and dynamic adjustment. For example, static adjustments, while adjusted for convergence at the center of the screen, affect every square inch of CRT surface; therefore, multiple adjustments of each are necessary. When both adjustments are properly made, the screen picture should look as uniformly defined as the left two-thirds of the test pattern of *Figure 4.16*

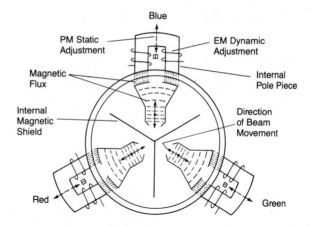

a. Convergence Assembly Mounted on the Neck of Picture Tube

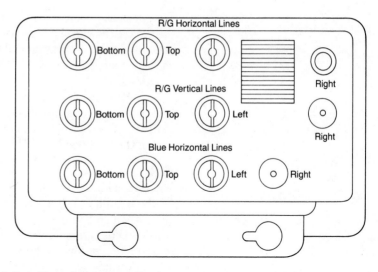

b. Typical Dynamic Convergence Board

Figure 4.17   Convergence Assemblies

TELEVISION RECEIVER OPTIONS AND ACCESSORIES

Complex functions involving numerous components and circuits have been added to the basic television receiver. These functions make the television more reliable or easier to operate, or add features for the enjoyment of the user.

Automatic Fine Tuning

In the past few years, there have been many improvements and innovations in tuner design. The biggest improvement is the all-electronic varactor tuner that eliminates troublesome mechanical contacts. Automatic fine tuning (AFT) was an optional feature for years, but with the advent of the varactor, AFT has become a standard feature. AFT maintains a stable local oscillator frequency with no need for periodic manual adjustment of the fine tuning control. Drift in the local oscillator frequency results in a deterioration of reception of picture, color and sound quality. Some sets equipped with AFT have an off/on (disabling) switch on the front panel. When off, the oscillator is controlled by the manual fine tuning in the normal manner.

Automatic Color Control and VIR

ACC

The automatic color control (ACC) circuit automatically controls the gain of the chroma bandpass amplifier, and therefore, the amount of color saturation and intensity of the reproduced color on the screen in accordance with the strength of the received signal.

Setting the adjustment is usually made by judging how well skin tones are being reproduced on the screen. This circuit can be compared to an automatic gain control (AGC) which controls the gain of the tuner and the IF strip.

VIR

The vertical interval reference (VIR) is a circuit that provides for the automatic adjustment of color signal amplitude and tint (saturation and hue) based on a transmitted reference signal. This development furnishes the most consistently accurate color reproduction on the CRT.

A completely integrated circuit color TV makes use of a VIR IC. The VIR IC requires no adjustment and is fabricated on a single 24-pin dual in-line package. Additional information, which is required to provide the VIR adjustment, is contained in line 19 which occurs during the vertical blanking interval. It contains reference signals for the chroma bandpass and color burst amplifiers and the IQ phase relationship. In addition, there is luminance and black level data, which when combined with the color correction, produces a perfectly balanced image.

Remote Control

A remote control unit allows the user to control the receiver from a remote, handheld transmitter. A basic remote control system is limited to essential functions only, such as channel selection, on/off and volume. These are enough when the other receiver circuits are automatically controlled. However, for sets not automatically controlled, the more elaborate remote control systems control other functions such as brightness, contrast, and color intensity and tint.

Of the transmission mediums used — acoustical, a visable light beam, infrared light beam, and RF — acoustical and infrared are most common.

Either an electronic oscillator that drives an ultrasonic transducer (30-50kHz) or spring-loaded hammers that strike tuned metal rods are used by the remote control unit for the acoustical system. The infrared system has two or more infrared light-emitting diodes in the remote unit that emit coded light pulses that represent the various functions. To minimize errors, the coded light pulses are sent twice for each transmission. The radiated light pulses bounce off the surrounding walls and fixtures in the room to arrive at the receiver.

Audio/Video Tape Recorder Output

With the interest in home video recording has come an interest in video accessories to enhance the picture quality and provide for special video effects. Early vintage TV receivers had no outputs for video or audio; therefore, even though the accessories needed only audio and video, there was no way to use these accessories except by RF connections to the antenna terminals. TV receivers are now available with video and audio input/output jacks. The video input/output jack essentially breaks into the receiver after the demodulator and before the output signal to the video output amplifier (see *Figure 4.15*). In fact, some sets have an additional video output power amplifier.

Digital Display Systems

A modern solid-state color television receiver may make use of many digital techniques. The channel number in use, the correct time, or both may be displayed in a separate, constant display, or may be displayed briefly on the screen superimposed on the picture. Character-generating IC ROMs are used in the latter case.

Projection Screen Techniques

The first CRTs used in television receivers used electrostatic deflection. The deflection angle limited the size of the screen because of the length of the tube required. Electromagnetic deflection removed a large part of this limitation. With CRTs using electromagnet deflection, a 110-degree angle of deflection permits a large screen in a relatively short envelope. Even so, a limitation still exists and the 25-inch screen has become somewhat of a de facto maximum.

Projection television allows the image to be optically projected so that it appears greatly enlarged on a special screen. It was first used for theater programs and industrial and educational purposes. However, it is now becoming more popular in home video systems.

In a typical educational system, a separate front projection picture tube is used for each of the three primary colors — red, blue and green — and the images combined on a special high-efficiency screen. The screen diagonal measurements are from five to seven feet. Such systems are difficult to set up and align and have restricted viewing angles of between 30 and 60 degrees for maximum brightness.

Home projection systems are virtually all rear projection types. An optical system within the cabinet focuses the image from a single special color picture tube on the rear of a special flat screen. Such screens usually are less than four feet, thus viewing distances are limited, but adequate for home use.

MULTIPLE TELEVISION INSTALLATION SYSTEMS

Transmission by broadcast stations with elecromagnetic links between antennas to individual receivers is not the only way that television is distributed to consumers. Cable TV provides a distribution system with coaxial cable. Master antenna television systems are used for distributing a signal from a single receiving antenna to large numbers of television receivers, such as in hospitals, hotels or educational facilities.

Television broadcast used to be limited to line-of-sight transmission – to about 100 to 150 miles. But now, communications satellites serve as relay stations that allow worldwide television transmission.

CATV and MATV

The community antenna television services (CATV) system requires the construction of entirely new transmission facilities by way of coaxial cables throughout a service area. Existing installed power line and telephone line facilities are used in many cases to physically mount the cable. Formerly, CATV systems were utilized only in fringe and far fringe areas, where reception was made difficult or impossible because of low signal levels. However, CATV systems are now being used in high signal level areas where multipath propagation is a problem (RF signals bounce off large objects such as buildings, causing multiple TV images). A single antenna site, which may be on top of a hill, mountain or skyscraper, is employed. Separate high gain and properly oriented antennas are used for each active channel. Compromises are thereby avoided and reception is optimized across the entire TV spectrum. The signals from the antenna site are conducted to the TV receiver locations by way of coaxial cable.

A master antenna television system (MATV) is essentially a CATV system on a smaller scale. MATV systems are usually an integral part of apartment, hotel or condominium complexes. TV signals are taken off the air, processed and distributed over coaxial cable just as in larger CATV installations. Some MATV systems even include satellite receiving capabilities and offer one or more premium-pay TV services.

Cable Television

Cable TV began as CATV. A community antenna was used at a remote location to feed TV signals to receivers in that area. Today, cable TV has developed far beyond such isolated systems into huge systems that tie together whole metropolitan areas. Cable TV does not have the channel restrictions of broadcast TV where channels must be allocated to prevent signal interference.

A cable system requires a converter box for the selection of the desired channels. Each channel is converted to an open channel on the TV receiver. Many late model TV receivers offer a tuner that can select the cable channels directly without the need of a converter. The problem that is encountered, however, is that the premium-pay services offered by cable TV, such as the movie channels, usually have a signal that is electronically scrambled. The circuits for descrambling are built into the converter from the cable company. As a result, the consumer must use the cable company converter at a monthly fee, or not receive the channel.

The starting point for a cable signal is called the head-in. Here the broadcast signals picked up by the antennas are amplified, adjusted for level and fed into the trunk line for distribution to consumers. In addition to downstream signals from the head-in to the subscriber, many cable systems are designed for upstream service from subscriber to the head-in. The same cable is used for both directions, but separate amplifiers are needed. Downstream communications is in the frequency band from 50 to 300MHz; upstream communication is in the band of frequencies between 5 and 30MHz.

Figure 4.18 shows a two-way cable amplifier system. This two-way communication system provides subscribers with services such as shop at home, voting, surveys, and an opportunity to "pay as you view" for special programs. For the latter, the system becomes an electronic box office collecting from subscribers as they view movies or specially produced programs.

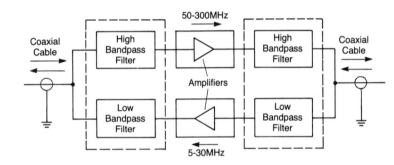

Figure 4.18   Two-Way Cable TV Amplifier System

Satellite Antenna Systems

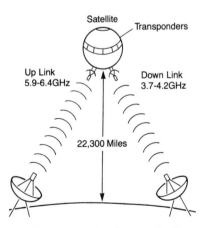

Figure 4.19   Satellite Communication System

The best way to overcome line-of-sight limitations is put the transmitting antenna very high. The ultimate in height for a transmitting antenna is a satellite. The satellite serves as a relay station between earth stations at different locations. In this way, satellite communication is achieved easily over thousands of miles.

Figure 4.19 shows the elements of a satellite communications system. The satellite height of 22,300 miles is used because this height provides a geostationary orbit. That is, the time for one orbit matches the 24 hours for one rotation of the earth on its axis. As a result, the satellite appears to be still with respect to the earth.

The frequencies used for satellite communication are microwaves in the gigahertz (GHz) range. Uplink frequencies are 5.9 to 6.4GHz; downlink frequences are from 3.7 to 4.2GHz. The transponders in the satellite are essentially wide-band amplifier repeaters, accepting signals on the uplink frequencies and retransmitting on the downlink frequencies. One transponder with a 40MHz bandwidth can send one TV channel, 1200 voice channels, or a 24 megabit data channel. The television pictures from a satellite can have excellent quality. Since FM is used for the satellite transmission, the picture has virtually no noise. Also, with a 40MHz channel bandwidth, high frequency definition can be much better than that of the standard 6MHz channel. Satellites can have many transponders. Early models had two, but future satellites will have 50 or more.

VIDEO CASSETTE RECORDERS

A video cassette recorder (VCR) is a type of video tape recorder (VTR). Video tape recorders have been used in the broadcast television industry for about 30 years. They are based on the same electromagnetic principles that are used in audio tape recording. A video tape recorder has the ability to record on magnetic tape and play back electronic video signals coming from a video camera or other video source. When recording audio signals, the typical range of frequencies is from 50Hz to 15kHz. Typical video signals, however, go from dc (0Hz) up to about 4.2MHz.

Principles of Video Recordings

In order to improve the increased frequency response required for video signals, three techniques are used:.
1. Frequency modulation of the video signals.
2. Using record/playback heads that have very narrow (micro) gaps.
3. Increasing the relative velocity between magnetic tape and heads by using high speed rotating heads.

All of these methods are used simultaneously. First, the video signal is converted to an FM signal by an FM modulator before recording on tape. Upon playback, the FM signal from the video heads is amplified and limited to remove amplitude variations. After limiting, the constant amplitude playback signal is demodulated to convert the FM signal back into the original video signal. Because most tape noise is related to amplitude variations, FM overcomes the problem of tape noise.

Second, the narrower the record/playback head gap, the shorter the wavelength of the signal that can be handled, and hence, the higher the frequency of the signal that can be recorded and played back. Also, the smaller and more densely-packed the magnetic particles on the tape, the wider the frequency range.

Present day video head gaps are microinches in width, but there is a physical limit on how small a head gap can be economically manufactured. Because of this limitation, it is necessary to increase the relative speed between head and tape to accommodate the required video frequency range. One way is to increase the linear tape speed to increase the writing speed, but unfortunately, this requires an unreasonable length of tape, so practical recording times are not possible. Instead of using linear tape at a high speed, the video heads are also moved in a circle, the rotation producing a relatively high speed between the head and the tape. While the video heads rotate in a horizontal plane, the tape passes the head producing a recorded track diagonally across the tape called a helical scan. This helical scan is shown in *Figure 4.20*. There are at least two rotating heads placed 180 degrees apart on the drum that make successive tracks on the tape as shown.

The video signal is coupled to the video heads by use of rotary transformers. The two video heads are connected to rotary coils which correspond to the stationary coils that are mounted on the lower stationary drum. The two sets of coil windings (rotary and stationary) form the rotary transformer, to couple the video heads to the remaining circuits.

The rotating mechanism containing the video heads is called the head drum. Two magnets mounted on the head drum are used to generate a pulse signal, which is used to control drum braking. By accurately controlling the drum braking, the speed of rotation is controlled.

The VCRs that are popular for consumer use are units that provide long playing time. These are so called "high-density recording" units because the linear speed of the tape has been slowed so the recording tracks of *Figure 4.20* are packed as closely together as possible. The guard band shown is eliminated and the tracks butt up against each other. Guard bands were necessary in studio tape recorders to eliminate crosstalk between the tracks. Crosstalk is eliminated in consumer VCRs by techniques known as azimuth recording and phase inversion. Azimuth recording varies the head gap orientation to tape for adjacent tracks and phase inversions add noise signals together at different phase angles.

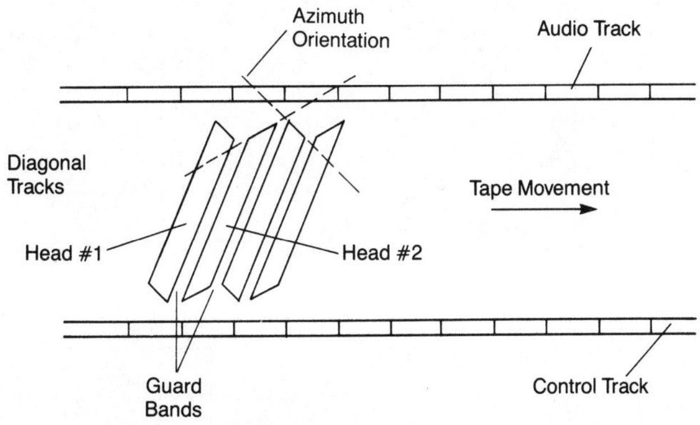

Figure 4.20   Helican Scan Recording

At the same time the video is being recorded by the rotating heads, a track of control pulses and the audio signals are recorded linearly by stationary heads along the edge of the tape (see *Figure 4.20*). The control track is used to control the speed of the tape, for timing marks, and to locate position on the tape. An erase head is mounted separately on the opposite side of the video heads from the audio and control head stack. It erases the tape ahead of any new recording that is made.

VHS and Beta Formats

There are two types of home entertainment VCRs in common use — Beta and VHS. The Beta system was developed and manufactured by Sony Corporation under the trade name Betamax[5]. The VHS (Video Home System) system is used by a majority of the other major manufacturers.

The two systems, although similar in operation and identical in overall purpose, are not at all compatible. The video cassettes of the two systems are different sizes and thus, are not physically interchangable. Even if the VHS recorded tape could physically be moved across the Beta cassette playback heads, there would be no playback, because different frequencies and recording techniques are used for the two systems.

The Beta system has the video heads mounted in a drum that rotates, whereas the VHS system uses a cylinder. The drum or the cylinder, which is referred to as the scanner, rotates at a speed of 1800 rpm for both Beta and VHS to match the field frequency of the TV scan. *Figure 4.21a* shows a functional diagram of a Betamax system in the record mode. The playback mode is shown in *Figure 4.21b*. Beta systems have a 688kHz carrier for the chrominance signals; VHS has a 629kHz chrominance carrier.

---

[5] Betamax is a trademark of the Sony Corporation

BASIC ELECTRONICS TECHNOLOGY

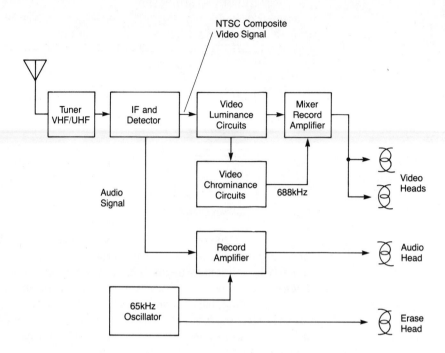

a. Record Mode Subsystems

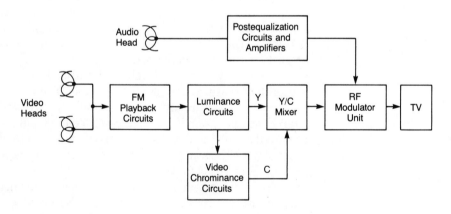

b. Playback Mode Subsystems

Figure 4.21   Block Diagram of Betamax VCR System

The azimuth recording angle (*Figure 4.20*) for Beta is plus or minus 7 degrees, which results in a 14 degree difference between head 1 and head 2. VHS uses a plus or minus 6 degree azimuth difference (12 degree difference between head 1 and head 2).

The phase inversion system for VHS is also entirely different from that used in Beta. The phase of the 629kHz color signal being recorded on head A is advanced in phase in increments of 90 degrees at each successive horizontal line. At the end of four lines, therefore, the 629kHz signal is back to the original phase. In the Beta system, the chrominance signal is 180 degrees out of phase from the in-phase signal on track B. Because the phase inversion signals add vectorially from track to track, the phase inversion techniques are used to reduce significantly or eliminate crosstalk of the chrominance signal. This is especially important on the long playing cassette where the guard bands between tracks are eliminated.

Special Features of VCRs

The distinction between special and standard features is not a clear line. Most VCRs have built-in VHF and UHF tuners that work in conjunction with electronic timers which permit the user to view one program on the TV receiver while recording another program on the VCR from a different channel. The automatic timer provides for unattended recording. In order to scan through the tape for particular scenes, many machines are capable of presenting a picture while the tape is moving at fast forward or rewind speed.

SUMMARY

In this chapter we have learned microphones and speakers are really electromechanical transducers, converting sound to electrical energy and vice versa. The ideal transducer will make this conversion without adding its own coloration, referred to as distortion. Records and tape systems are electromechanical formats that allow electrical variations representing sound to be stored for future use.

Two electronic techniques have been developed to practically eliminate background noise; Dolby noise reduction and digital sound. Dolby uses dynamic pre-emphasis and de-emphasis, whereas digital techniques exclude noise as a potential component of the signal.

Television works on the principle of the high speed, continuous division of an image into individual picture elements as lines of a screen raster, like a mosaic, are scanned. The amplitude of the electrical signal corresponds to the intensity of light picked up by each element. Repeated 30 frames a second, the scan gives the illusion of a continuous image in motion. When combined with synchronization and sound information, a very complex signal results. This signal is transmitted over a single 6MHz wide channel, and intercepted by the receiving antenna, where it is applied to the television set's input.

The typical monochromatic receiver consists of a tuner, a video IF strip, a detector, video amplifier, a sweep section, synchronization circuits, and an audio section. The tuner selects the one RF carrier that is to be processed, amplifies it and converts it to an intermediate frequency for further amplificaton and unwanted carrier rejection. The detector outputs the composite video signal, feeding it to the video amplifiers. Also, the detector circuitry allows the FM sound carrier to be detected and sent to the audio section for further amplification, demodulation, and audio amplification. The composite video signal also contains the horizontal and vertical synchronization pulses. These are extracted, amplified and supplied to the appropriate sweep oscillators, allowing them to lock-up the picture on the TV screen with the originating camera timing. The horizontal sweep section also generates the high acceleration voltage required by the CRT.

The color television is based on a system that is compatible with the pre-existing black-and-white system. At the camera, the color image is broken into three image signals, each one representing a selected part of the light spectrum. This color video is transmitted in two parts — as luminance information and chrominance information. The luminance carries the brightness and picture detail, and the chrominance the hue information.

The color receiver processes this composite signal just like a monochrome receiver, until the detector output. Then the color circuits reconstruct the hue information, while the video circuits amplify the luminance. Both are fed to the picture tube simultaneously to provide a complete image.

Because the color picture tube is a three element system, special convergence circuitry and yoke assemblies are required to direct the individual electron beams to the right dot with the correct phosphor color.

The technology of distribution of television RF signals includes the various hard-wired cable systems and the newer satellite methods.

Current video-audio recording techniques are concerned with the efficient transfer of information to magnetic tape. By using compacted information on narrow tape tracks; high-speed, rotating heads scanning the tape diagonally; high recording density, low noise tape; precision mechanics; and sophisticated electronics, a high-quality continuous-color video image is transferred to, stored on, and played back from the magnetic tape medium.

CHAPTER 4 QUIZ

1. The width-to-height aspect ration for a TV picture is:
   a. 5:4.
   b. 4:5.
   c. 4:3.
   d. 3:4.

2. To reduce the flicker of a TV picture, _____ is used.
   a. a raster
   b. a single field
   c. high speed scanning
   d. interlaced scanning

3. The background light pattern on a TV screen without signal is called a:
   a. flood.
   b. pilot.
   c. raster.
   d. ion.

4. The blanking level of a composite video signal is ___75___ percent of the maximum value of the emitted carrier.
   a. 100
   b. 75
   c. 50
   d. 25

5. The most widely used TV camera tube is the:
   a. vidicon.
   b. Plumbicon.
   c. iconoscope.
   d. Trinitron.

6. The intensity of the spot on a CRT is controlled by the relative voltage between the cathode and the:
   a. anode.
   b. aquadag.
   c. grid.
   d. heater.

7. TV sound is transmitted by:
   a. DSB.
   b. FM.
   c. AM.
   d. SSB.

8. The sound intermediate frequency (IF) is:
   a. 455kHz.
   b. 1.5MHz.
   c. 3.58MHz.
   d. 4.5MHz.

9. Fine detail in the picture of a televised scene produces:
   a. noise.
   b. high sideband frequencies.
   c. interference to CB channels.
   d. low frequency video.

10. The two controls found in the video amplifier of a TV receiver are:
    a. brightness and contrast.
    b. fine tuning and channel selection.
    c. volume and tone.
    d. intensity and tint.

11. The amount of intensity of a color is its:
    a. luminance.
    b. hue.
    c. chrominance.
    d. saturation.

12. A color that contains no white light is a/an _____ color.
    a. pastel
    b. subdued
    c. impure
    d. saturated

13. The color subcarrier reference is transmitted:
    a. during the vertical blanking pulse.
    b. at the same time as the video.
    c. at the same time as the horizontal sync.
    d. during horizontal blanking after the horizontal sync.

14. The most popular color picture tube has been the _____ type.
    a. one gun
    b. three gun
    c. Trinitron
    d. chromatron

15. To maintain proper phase relationship between the video luminance and blanking signals and the chrominance signals, the TV receiver makes use of a:
    a. phase corrector.
    b. delay line.
    c. phase splitter.
    d. sync separator.

16. The amplitude of the _____ from any particular television transmitter is normally a constant.
    a. sync pulses
    b. video level
    c. audio level
    d. video power

17. The signals developed at the station from which all colors are derived are the _____ signals.
    a. R and G
    b. Y and Q
    c. I and Q
    d. hue and luminance

18. A moving rainbow pattern of color bars on a receiver screen would mean:
    a. picture tube needs convergence.
    b. chroma oscillator failed.
    c. loss of chroma signal.
    d. loss of color sync.

19. A color receiver has no:
    a. G - Y demodulation circuit.
    b. R - Y demodulation circuit.
    c. mixer oscillator.
    d. black-and-white video circuitry.

20. Static convergence adjustments are made:
    a. for a white dot at the center of the screen.
    b. for color crosshatch lines around the edge.
    c. on a black-and-white TV receiver.
    d. for a pure red screen.

POWER SUPPLIES

INTRODUCTION

All electronic circuits require some source of power from which to operate. A power supply, which is an essential component of every electronic system, may be as simple as a single chemical dry cell to as complex as an uninterruptible power supply for a large computer system.

In this chapter, only power supplies which convert alternating line current to direct current will be discussed. Devices like chemical dry cells or solar cells, which convert chemical or solar energy directly into electricity, will not be considered. However, included in the discussion will be the basic electronic components of power supplies (transformers, diodes, etc.) the principles of operation, and the advantages and disadvantages of the various types of circuit designs.

GENERAL POWER SUPPLY

The purpose of a power supply in a system is to provide the electrical energy that a system's circuits require for normal functioning. For most electronic systems, the source of energy required is a constant voltage that can supply a varying amount of current, or a constant current at some set voltage level. The power supply must be able to maintain this constant voltage or current level even if its own ac input varies, or if the demand for energy by a circuit or the system should change. This is commonly referred to as power supply load changes. A general block diagram for power supplies with these capabilities is shown in *Figure 5.1*. The diagram shows the four main power supply sections, along with the typical waveforms at the input through the output of each section. This is the type of power supply covered in this chapter. Its input signal is the ac line voltage (typically 110-117 volts) and its output is a constant dc voltage. Let's begin with the transformer.

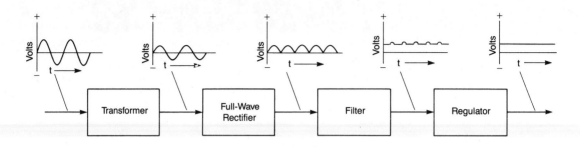

Figure 5.1   Block Diagram of a Basic Electronic Power Supply

TRANSFORMER PRINCIPLES

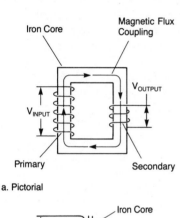

a. Pictorial

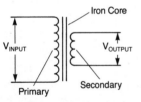

b. Schematic

Figure 5.2   Iron Core Transformer

The transformer has two major purposes in the power supply. It provides circuit isolation from the line input and it supplies the required voltage levels using various turns ratios to the secondary. It consists of two or more coils of wire (inductors) wound together so that energy from one of the coils (called the primary) can be efficiently magnetically coupled to the other(s) (called secondaries). When an alternating current is made to flow in the primary winding, energy is electromagnetically coupled to the secondary winding(s) with the aid of an iron core. The iron core serves to concentrate the magnetic field generated by the primary winding thereby providing good coupling to the secondary windings. *Figure 5.2* shows a transformer with one primary and one secondary winding wound on an iron core. *Figure 5.2a* is a pictorial drawing, and *Figure 5.2b* shows the corresponding schematic symbol.

If 100 percent of the power applied to the transformer's primary is coupled to the secondary, the transformer has no losses and is considered to be perfectly efficient. As a result, it can generally be assumed that primary winding power equals secondary winding power. Typically, efficiency is in the 80 to 90 percent range, but the best transformers may be in the upper 90 percent range. Transformer losses generate heat.

Turns Ratios

The magnetic flux produced by the current flowing in the primary winding as a result of the voltage applied induces a voltage in the secondary winding. If the number of turns in the secondary winding N_S equals the number of turns in the primary winding N_P, the primary voltage V_P equals the secondary voltage, V_S. However, if the number of turns is not the same in the two windings, the voltages will not be the same.

If the primary voltage is known, the secondary voltage can be determined by using the transformer's turns ratio. The turns ratio is the ratio of the number of secondary turns to the number of primary turns, $N_S:N_P$. For example, if the primary winding has 250 turns and the secondary has 50 turns, the turns ratio is 50/250, or 1:5. This means that there is one secondary turn for every five primary turns. Since induced voltage is directly proportional to the number of turns, the ratio of secondary voltage V_S to primary voltage V_P equals the turns ratio. In mathematical terms,

$$\frac{V_S}{V_P} = \frac{N_S}{N_P} \qquad (5\text{-}1)$$

Thus, if the turns ratio and the primary (input) voltage is known, the secondary voltage can be calculated using equation *5-1*.

Example 5-1: A transformer has a turns ratio of 2:5. If the input voltage, V_P, is 400 volts, what is the secondary voltage?

By rearranging equation *5-1*, the secondary voltage can be determined as

$$V_S = \left(\frac{N_S}{N_P}\right) V_P \qquad (5\text{-}2)$$

Substituting into equation *5-2* gives

$$V_S = \left(\frac{2}{5}\right) 400V$$

or

$$V_S = 160V$$

Conservation of Energy

As previously mentioned, power supply transformers can be used to increase or decrease the input voltage to a level required by the system. To increase the voltage, the secondary must have more turns than the primary, and the transformer is called a step-up transformer. To decrease the voltage, the secondary must have fewer turns than the primary, and the transformer is called a step-down transformer.

The law of conservation of energy states that energy can be neither created nor destroyed. Transformers step up or step down input voltage, but do not create nor destroy energy. This is the basis for saying that the primary power in a transformer equals the secondary power. Power is the rate at which energy is used. The power consumed by the load connected to the secondary windings(s) comes from the primary winding via the electromagnetic coupling of the two windings.

By definition power in watts is current multiplied by voltage.

$$P = IV \qquad (5\text{-}3)$$

Therefore, primary power is

$$V_P = I_P V_P \qquad (5\text{-}4)$$

and secondary power is

$$V_S = I_S V_S \qquad (5\text{-}5)$$

Equating the two terms and rearranging gives

$$\frac{I_P}{I_S} = \frac{V_S}{V_P} \qquad (5\text{-}6)$$

Substituting the turns ratio from equation *5-1* for V_S/V_P and rearranging gives

$$I_S = \left(\frac{N_P}{N_S}\right) I_P \qquad (5\text{-}7)$$

Equation *5-2* stated that the secondary voltage was directly proportional to the turns ratio N_S/N_P. Equation *5-7* states that the secondary current is inversely proportional to the turns ratio N_S/N_P. In other words, if the transformer is a step-up transformer, the secondary voltage will be increased over the primary voltage, but the secondary current will be decreased from the primary current by the same proportion to keep the primary and secondary power equal.

Example 5-2: A transformer with a turns ratio of 3:1 has a primary voltage of 24 volts and a primary current of 1.5 amperes. What is the secondary power, voltage and current?
Secondary power equals the primary power; therefore (equation *5-3*)

$$P_P = P_S = 1.5A \times 24V$$

therefore

$$P_S = 36 \text{ watts}$$

Secondary voltage is found by using equation *5-2*.

$$V_S = \left(\frac{3}{1}\right) 24V$$

$$V_S = 72V$$

Similarly, using equation *5-7*, secondary current can be found as follows:

$$I_S = \left(\frac{1}{3}\right) 1.5$$

$$I_S = 0.5A$$

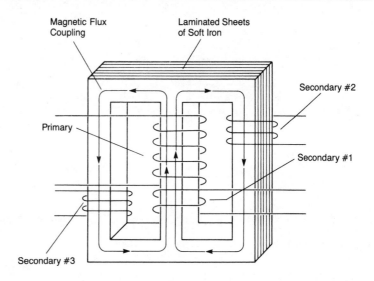

Figure 5.3 Shell-Type Core Design

Transformer Construction

Most power supply transformers are wound on a laminated soft iron shell core illustrated in *Figure 5.3*. The soft iron provides an easy path for the magnetic flux and the laminations help to minimize losses in the core caused when magnetic flux induces small electrical currents in the core, (called eddy currents). These currents heat up the core.

Some power supplies use transformers having more than one secondary winding in order to provide multiple output voltages. These are indicated in *Figure 5.3* and *Figures 5.4a* and *5.4b*. *Figures 5.4a* and *5.4b* are schematic drawings of two types of transformers. *Figure 5.4a* is a multiple secondary winding transformer and *Figure 5.4b* is a single secondary, but it is tapped in the center, providing two outputs if needed. One output can be obtained across each half of the secondary, or a single output is available across the full secondary. The transformer with separate secondaries is used where the circuits supplied must be electrically isolated, or have very different voltage and current requirements.

RECTIFIER CIRCUITS

The function of the rectifier section of the power supply is to convert the transformer's alternating current output to direct current. The active elements are the semiconductor diodes, which conduct current in only one direction.

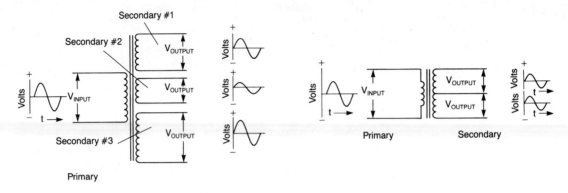

a. Multiple Secondary Windings

b. Center-Tapped Winding

Figure 5.4   *Transformer Secondary Winding Designs*

Half-Wave Rectifier

Figure 5.5a shows the simplest type of rectification, the half-wave rectifier circuit. A single diode is connected in series with one of the transformer leads. When a load, R_L is attached at the output, current flows only when the transformer voltage forward biases the diode. During alternate half-cycles, the diode is reverse biased. The voltage developed at the output *(Figure 5.5b)* is a series of half cycle pulses, each with the same polarity. The average value is shown as a dotted line on the plot of the output waveform. Between the pulses are intervals when the output is zero volts, because the recitifier circuit delivers current to the load only during the positive alternation of the secondary voltage.

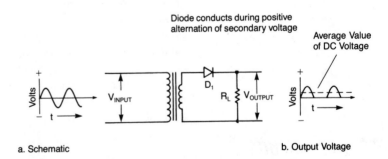

a. Schematic

b. Output Voltage

Figure 5.5   *Half-Wave Rectifier Circuit*

Full-Wave Rectifier

A circuit which converts both halves of the ac input to a dc output is called a full-wave rectifier. The circuit illustrated in *Figure 5.6* uses a center-tapped transformer and two diodes, D_1 and D_2, to provide full-wave rectification. The center tap is common ground and is a common return for the two half-wave rectifiers which alternately conduct. Each diode delivers current to the load in the same direction when its secondary terminal, the one to which the diode is connected, is positive with respect to the common (ground) point.

The full-wave rectifier eliminates the gaps between the pulses of dc that were characteristic of the half-wave output. This circuit, since it uses only half of the secondary winding at any instant, requires a transformer with an ac rms full secondary output voltage approximately twice the dc level at the output. The full-wave rectifier output is more efficient source of power and is easier to filter than a half-wave rectifier output. Also, its average value of dc voltage is much higher than for the half-wave rectifier.

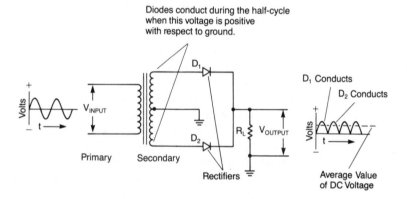

Figure 5.6 Full-Wave Rectifier Circuit (Center-Tapped Secondary)

Bridge Rectifier

The full-wave bridge rectifier, as shown in *Figure 5.7a*, does not need a center-tapped transformer to function, but it requires four diodes. When the top secondary lead is positive and the bottom lead negative, as shown in *Figure 5.7b*, diodes D_2 and D_4 are forward biased and electron flow is as indicated. The secondary delivers power to a load through a circuit completed through diode D_4 to ground, through ground to the load R_L connected at the output, and through diode D_2.

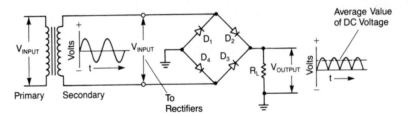

a. Bridge Configuration

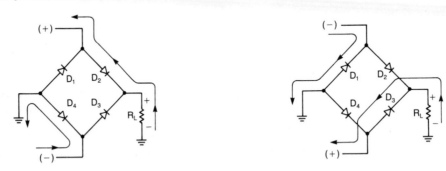

b. Current Flow for First Half of Alternation

c. Current Flow for Second Half of Alternation

Figure 5.7 *Full-Wave Bridge Rectifier Circuit*

During the next alternation of the ac input, the top secondary lead is negative and the bottom lead positive. Diodes D_1 and D_3 and the load device complete the circuit, as shown in *Figure 5.7c*. Each alternation delivers power to the load just as for the full-wave rectifier. Observe that current flow through the load is always in the same direction. The average value of the dc voltage is approximately the same as for the two diode full-wave rectifier, being different only by the additional diode voltage drops. Note that the common negative reference point for the output voltage is the common point between diodes D_1 and D_4.

Three-Phase Half-Wave Rectifier

The circuit diagrammed in *Figure 5.8* is a half-wave rectifier circuit for a three-phase input. Each phase is producing an output load voltage similar to the output voltage of *Figure 5.5*, but displaced from each other in time by 120 degrees as shown. The circuit consists of three rectifiers, one for each phase winding. The input and output waveforms are shown in the figure.

Notice that the output voltage never drops to zero because at least one of the phases is always conducting. This output is said to exhibit less ripple than the single phase circuits, because the change in output voltage is much less, and the average dc value is much greater than for the single phase half-wave rectifier of *Figure 5.5*. The ripple is the small variation in voltage riding on the top of the output waveform.

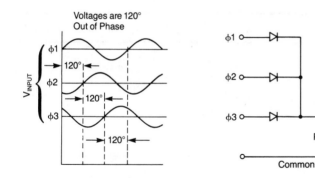

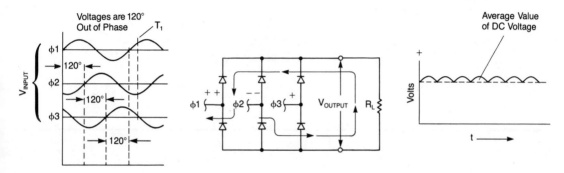

Figure 5.8   *Half-Wave Three-Phase Rectifier*

Three-Phase Full-Wave Rectifier

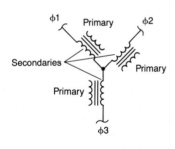

a. Three-Phase, Y-Transformer Secondaries
Supply Rectifier Circuit Below

Even less ripple is output by the three-phase full-wave rectifier, shown in *Figure 5.9b*, supplied by the three-phase source in *Figure 5.9a*. The circuit is called a three-phase bridge, and it uses six diodes driven by secondary voltages from a three-phase Y-connected transformer. Full-wave rectification results in a reduced ripple level because each alternation is supplying current to the load, which means a cleaner, higher average value dc voltage. Electron flow through the load is indicated in *Figure 5.9b* when phase 1 is more positive than phase 3, and phase 2 is negative, as at time T_1.

Table 5.1 summarizes the characteristics of the rectifier circuits previously described. Resistors are used to represent the loads in the circuit diagrams, and the output waveforms are drawn on the same time scale as the input signal. The average dc value is given in the table as a fraction of the peak value of the secondary voltage. Ripple frequency is specified as a multiple of the input frequency.

b. Rectification Circuitry

Figure 5.9   *Full-Wave Three-Phase Rectifier*

Table 5.1. Rectifier Circuit Summary

Name	Schematic	Output Waveform	Average Output	Ripple Frequency
Half-Wave			$0.318V_P$	f_{INPUT}
Full-Wave Center Tap			$0.636V_P$	$2f_{INPUT}$
Full-Wave Bridge			$0.636V_P$	$2f_{INPUT}$
Half-Wave Three-Phase			$0.826V_P$	$3f_{INPUT}$
Full-Wave Three-Phase Bridge			$0.955V_P$	$6f_{INPUT}$

Diode Specifications

In all of these rectifier circuits, the important diode specifications are: 1. forward dc current, 2. reverse breakdown voltage, 3. peak surge current. While forward biased, a diode must be able to conduct enough current to satisfy all other sections of the power supply in addition to the load. If the rectifier drives a capacitive-input filter, the diode conduction time is greatly reduced. During this short time the diode must be able to replace the charge on the filter by conducting high-current pulses. The maximum amplitude (current) of these pulses is directly proportional to the capacitance of the filter. Any replacement diode should have at least the same maximum forward current specification as the original diode. During the reverse bias period, the diode must not break down from the inverse voltage, which may equal twice the peak secondary voltage.

The surge current parameter specification is very important because most rectifiers are connected directly to a filter circuit that looks like a capacitive load. When the power supply is first energized, the capacitive load charges rapidly through the diodes, causing high surge currents. Many power supplies have filter capacitances of several thousand microfarads. In these, a resistor called a surge resistor is connected in series with the capacitor charge circuit to protect the diodes. For filter capacitors under about 1000 microfarads, surges occur too quickly and are sufficiently limited in amplitude to damage most rectifier diodes.

FILTER CIRCUITS

None of the rectifier circuits examined previously produce a steady clean dc voltage, but only a pulsating dc called ripple. Most electronic systems require a highly stable dc power supply voltage with minimal ripple. The function of the filter section is to minimize the ripple in the dc signal output from the rectifier. All power supply filters are essentially low-pass filters; ideally they pass the dc (0Hz) to the output, while attenuating fundamental and harmonic frequencies greater than 0Hz, including those produced by signal processing.

Ripple and Ripple Factor

Figure 5.10 is a convenient model for analyzing the ripple content of a dc signal. As the figure indicates, ripple is the variation in the dc level of the power supply's output. It is approximated as a dc voltage that has an average value V_{DC} and a sinusoidal voltage superimposed on it with a peak amplitude of v.

No filter can totally eliminate the variations, but they are designed to minimize v while maximizing V_{DC}. The ratio of the rms value of v to the output dc voltage, V_{DC}, is an indicator of the relative amount of variation in the dc output. The ratio expressed in equation *5-8* is called the ripple factor.

$$\text{Ripple Factor} = \frac{V_{RMS}}{V_{DC}} \qquad (5\text{-}8)$$

Example 5-3: The average dc output of a power supply is 5 volts, and the ripple measures 0.57 volts peak. What is the ripple factor?

The rms value of the ripple when the peak value is given is 0.707 of the peak value. Therefore,

$$V_{RMS} = 0.707 \, (0.57V)$$
$$V_{RMS} = 0.4V$$

Therefore, using equation *5-8*, the ripple factor is

$$RF = \frac{0.4V}{5V}$$

or

$$RF = 0.08$$

Sometimes ripple factor is converted to a percent by multiplying by 100.

$$RF = 0.08 \times 100\%$$

or

$$RF = 8\%$$

In this example, the effective ripple is eight percent of the total dc output.

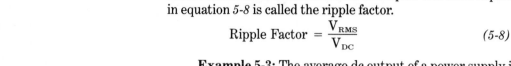

Figure 5.10   Ripple Content of a DC Voltage

Simple Capacitor Filter

A simple, commonly used filter is a single capacitor connected across the output of the rectifier circuit as shown in *Figure 5.11*. The input is a full-wave rectified voltage. Some ripple is still present at the output, but it is much less severe. The capacitor charges to the peak value of the rectified voltage, and it discharges through the load during the gaps between rectified pulses. However, if it is properly designed, it discharges only a small amount, the output remaining relatively constant. The rms value of the ripple can be estimated by equation *5-9*,

$$V_{RMS} = 2.4 \, \frac{I_L}{C} \qquad (5\text{-}9)$$

where I_L is the current drawn by the load (in milliamperes) and C is the filter capacitor value (in microfarads).

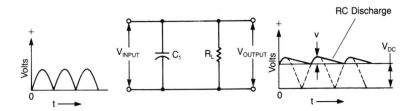

Figure 5.11 Simple Capacitor Filter

The same formula can be rearranged to solve for the capacitor value as shown in equation *5-10*. This is the value of C in microfarads required in order to keep the ripple voltage at a particular amount at a given milliamperes of load current.

$$C = 2.4 \frac{I_L}{V_{RMS}} \qquad (5\text{-}10)$$

Example 5-4: What value filter capacitor is required to keep the ripple below 0.5 volts rms for a 5 volt power supply and a load resistance of 2 kilohms?

The 5 volts is derived from a 60Hz full-wave rectified source. Load current, I_L, is found by using Ohm's law

$$I_L = \frac{V_{DC}}{R_L} \qquad (5\text{-}11)$$

Substituting values gives

$$I_L = \frac{5V}{2 \times 10^3 \Omega}$$

or

$$I_L = 2.5mA$$

The capacitor value in microfarads, therefore, from equation *5-10* is

$$C = \frac{(2.4)\,(2.5)}{0.5V}$$

or approximately

$$C = 12\mu F$$

Although equation *5-9* is only an approximation, it does provide results which agree well with actual circuit measurements. This equation assumes that the ac input to the rectifier section has a frequency of 60Hz, and that it is full-wave rectified. For other frequencies, use equation *5-12*:

$$V_{RMS} = \frac{144I_L}{fC} \qquad (5\text{-}12)$$

Where I_L is again in milliamperes, C is in microfarads, and f is frequency in hertz.

RC Filter

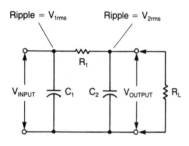

Figure 5.12   RC Filter

Figure 5.12 shows a simple capacitor filter followed by a resistor and a second capacitor. This network reduces ripple even further beyond the simple capacitor filter on a full-wave rectified source, but it also reduces the dc output voltage because of the drop across the resistor. The greater the current drawn by the load, the lower the available dc output voltage. To arrive at a required output dc voltage at a certain load current would require that the input voltage level be increased over that used for a simple capacitor filter.

To calculate the approximate value of ripple from this filter, first calculate the ripple for the input capacitor as though it were a simple capacitor filter, using either equation *5-9* or equation *5-12*. Let's assign the notation V_{1RMS} to it. An approximation for output ripple, V_{2RMS} then is given by equation *5-13*.

$$V_{2RMS} = V_{1RMS}\left(\frac{X_{C2}}{R_1}\right) \qquad (5\text{-}13)$$

This approximation assumes that X_{C2} is smaller than R_1 by a factor of 5 or more. X_C must be estimated using 0.159/fC, where f is 60Hz for a half-wave rectified input, or 120Hz for a full-wave input, and C is in farads.

Pi-Type Filter

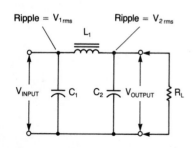

Figure 5.13   Pi Filter

The RC filter discussed in the previous section required a compromise to minimize ripple while maintaining the correct dc output voltage. Increasing the series resistor value decreases the ripple, but it also decreases the output voltage.

The filter in *Figure 5.13* uses an inductor, (L_1) called a filter choke, instead of a resistor, to provide a high ac impedance with little dc resistance. This minimizes the reduction of the output voltage while contributing to the minimization of ripple.

To calculate the ripple level at the filter output, first find V_{1rms}, the ripple across the input capacitor C_1, using the equation for the simple capacitor filter (either equation *5-9* or *5-12*).

Then, if the filter is connected to a full-wave rectifier, use equation *5-14*

$$V_{2RMS} = V_{1RMS} \frac{1.77}{L_1 C_2} \text{ (For Full-Wave Rectifiers)} \qquad (5\text{-}14)$$

to estimate the output ripple, $V_{2(RMS)}$. If the filter is connected to a half-wave rectifier, the 1.77 constant in equation *5-14* is changed to 7.09 and becomes

$$V_{2RMS} = V_{1RMS} \frac{7.09}{L_1 C_2} \text{ (For Half-Wave Rectifiers)} \qquad (5\text{-}15)$$

In both equations *5-14* and *5-15*, L_1 is in henries and C_2 is in microfarads.

L-Type Filter

All the filters covered so far use a capacitor across the output of the rectifier section. This capacitor charges for only a portion of the input cycle, so very high current surges are used for charging during these short periods. The rectifier diodes must be able to withstand these current surges.

The L-Type filter circuit shown in *Figure 5.14*, holds the peak diode current to a level about the same as the average load current. It has an inductor of L henries at the input instead of a capacitor.

For a full-wave rectified 60Hz input, the output ripple voltage from this L-Type filter is approximated by

$$V_{RMS} = 0.53 \frac{V_P}{L_1 C_1} \text{ (For Full-Wave Rectifiers)} \qquad (5\text{-}16)$$

where V_P is the peak value of the rectified input voltage and C is in microfarads. If the input is half-wave rectified, the constant 0.53 is replaced by 2.5, and the ripple is

$$V_{RMS} = 2.5 \frac{V_P}{L_1 C_1} \text{ (For Half-Wave Rectifiers)} \qquad (5\text{-}17)$$

This filter's disadvantage, like the one preceding it, is the increased size, weight, and cost of the inductor device.

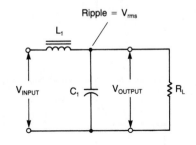

Ripple = V_{rms}

L_1

V_{INPUT} C_1 V_{OUTPUT} R_L

Figure 5.14 L-Type Filter

Voltage Multiplier Circuits

In capacitive input filters the capacitor charges to approximately the peak voltage of the rectified input. By modifying the filter design, it is possible to obtain output voltages that are two or more times greater than this peak voltage. Such circuits are called voltage multipliers. They are used where voltages up to several times the line input and only moderate currents are required.

Figure 5.15a shows a half-wave doubler. It combines a rectifier with a filter to produce an output dc voltage which is approximately twice the peak voltage of the ac input. To analyze its operation, refer to *Figure 5.15b*. The transformer secondary winding has an output of V_P peak volts, is positive at the top, negative at bottom. Diode D_1 is forward biased and conducts, causing C_1 to charge through the current path shown to V_P with the polarity shown. Diode D_2 is reverse biased and does not conduct.

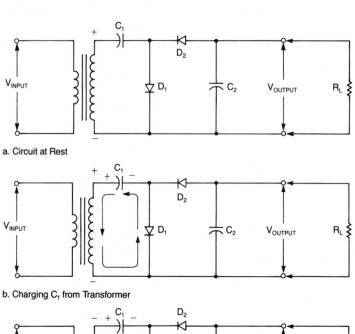

a. Circuit at Rest

b. Charging C_1 from Transformer

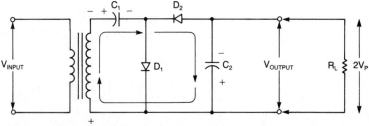

c. Charged C_1 + Transformer EMF Combine Across C_2

Figure 5.15   *Half-Wave Voltage Doubler Action*

When the transformer polarity reverses, as in *Figure 5.15c*, D_2 is forward biased and D_1 is cut off. D_2 conducts, which charges C_2 through the path shown to the polarity shown. However, the voltage across C_2 is the combination of the transformer peak voltage plus the charge across C_1. Since these two are series aiding, the total voltage across C_2 is twice the peak value. Thus, the output voltage is $2V_P$, twice the peak value of the input. As long as the load current through R_L does not discharge C_2 faster than the filter circuit can keep it charged, the output voltage will be maintained.

Figure 5.16 shows a voltage doubler with an additional diode-capacitor section, which results in a voltage tripler. Additional diode-capacitor sections can be added to produce quadruplers, and so on. Full-wave versions of these voltage multipliers are also used in some systems. *Figure 5.17* shows a full-wave voltage doubler.

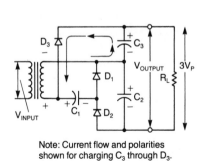

Note: Current flow and polarities shown for charging C_3 through D_3.

Figure 5.16 Half-Wave Voltage Tripler Circuit

REGULATOR CIRCUITS

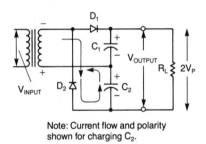

Note: Current flow and polarity shown for charging C_2.

Figure 5.17 Full-Wave Voltage Doubler Circuit

The function of a regulator circuit is to reduce variation in the output voltage level, by compensating for changes in load or in input line voltage. All but the simplest power supplies have some type of regulator circuit. Because there is some dc resistance in the components of the power supply, load current will cause some voltage to be dropped inside the supply across these internal components. If the load should be changed, the internal drop will also change. As a result, the output voltage (the load voltage) depends on the characteristics of the load.

Also, often the peak value of the ac line voltage will vary. Since a power supply's output depends on the peak level of the input, line variations will result in output variations.

Concept of Voltage Regulation

The example in *Figure 5.18* will aid in explaining voltage regulation. A power supply is connected to a variable resistance load. In *Figure 5.18a*, the load is disconnected through the open switch, and the power supply voltage is at its maximum value or the no-load voltage, V_{NL}. In *Figure 5.18b*, the load is connected and load current flows, dropping some voltage internally to the supply. The resulting output voltage is called the full-load voltage, V_{FL}. In an ideal supply, the no-load and full-load voltages would be equal. In practical systems, the difference in the two values is an indicator of the power supply's ability to regulate the output voltage to the desired value.

Output Voltage vs Load Current

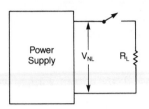

a. Power Supply Unloaded — Maximum Output Volts

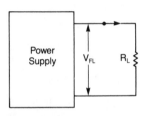

b. Power Supply Fully Loaded — Reduced Output Volts

Figure 5.18   Effect of the Load on Output Voltage

Figure 5.19 is a graph of the output voltage as a function of the load current. The resistance of the load and hence the current is varied from no load to full load. Ideally, this graph would be a perfectly horizontal line, but the output voltage drops slightly in any practical system as the load current increases. To compare the regulation properties of power supplies, the difference in the no-load and full-load voltages is divided by the full-load voltage. The result is multiplied by 100 to express the answer as a percent. In mathematical terms,

$$VR\% = 100\% \frac{(V_{NL} - V_{FL})}{V_{FL}} \qquad (5\text{-}18)$$

For an ideal supply, VR = 0 percent because the no-load voltage V_{NL} and the full-load voltage V_{FL} would be equal. Therefore, low percentages of voltage regulation are desirable, and the smaller the percent regulation the better the power supply.

Example 5-5: What is the voltage regulation of a power supply whose no-load voltage is 25.5 volts and whose full-load voltage is 25 volts?

Substituting directly into the equation *5-18* gives

$$VR\% = 100\% \frac{(25.5 - 25)}{25}$$

or the percent voltage regulation is

$$VR\% = 2\%$$

Well-designed power supplies may have regulations of less than 0.01 percent.

Current Regulation

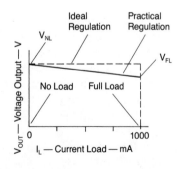

Figure 5.19   Output Voltage Versus Load Current

In some applications, power supplies are required which provide constant currents rather than constant voltages. A current regulator circuit should provide the same current for all values of loads, but the output voltage is allowed to vary with load impedance. *Figure 5.20* shows the extreme situations under which a current regulator must perform. In *Figure 5.20a* the load resistance is zero (because of the shorting switch) so that a constant current is flowing into a short circuit. This is the maximum load current that would flow. It is considered as I_{SC} for this case. In *Figure 5.20b* there is a normal load present. Typically, full-load constant current I_{FL} is somewhat less than short-circuit constant current I_{SC}, as shown in *Figure 5.20c*. The difference is used to calculate the percent current regulation.

Note:

SC = Short Circuit
FL = Full Load
NL = No Load

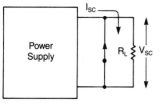

a. Shorted Output

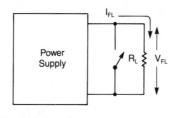

b. Full (Normal) Load

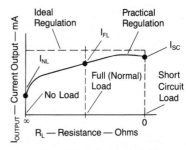

c. Output Current Versus Increasing Load

Figure 5.20   Effect of the Load on the Output Current

Equation *5-19* for constant current regulation is exactly analogous to equation *5-18* for voltage regulation. It is

$$\text{IR\%} = 100\% \frac{(\text{I}_{\text{SC}} - \text{I}_{\text{FL}})}{\text{I}_{\text{FL}}} \qquad (5\text{-}19)$$

In the following paragraphs most of the regulators discussed are voltage regulators, because these are much more commonly used. The last section will cover the fundamentals of current regulators.

Zener Diode Regulator

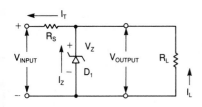

Figure 5.21   Zener Diode Regulation

A simple but effective voltage regulator is the zener diode circuit diagrammed in *Figure 5.21*. The zener diode is reverse biased in the breakdown region by the input voltage from the filter section. When a zener diode operates in this designed breakdown condition, its voltage remains almost constant over a wide range of currents flowing through it.

In this circuit, the diode is chosen to have a breakdown equal to the desired output voltage of the power supply. The series resistor is chosen to limit the zener current to a maximum safe level when no load is connected. When a load is connected, zener current drops, but its voltage remains constant as long as the current load does not exceed a maximum value.

The load is connected in parallel with the zener diode. The current in the series resistor I_{T} is the sum of load current I_{L} and zener current I_{Z}. I_{T} through the series resistor remains constant because the voltage across it, $\text{V}_{\text{IN}} - \text{V}_{\text{Z}}$, is constant. At the zener and load, I_{T} divides, some passing through the zener and the remainder flowing in the load. If the load draws too much of the current, the zener current will not be sufficient to sustain breakdown, and the regulation will not be maintained.

Example 5-6: A zener diode regulator circuit, like the one in *Figure 5.21*, uses a 150 ohm series resistor and a diode whose breakdown voltage is 6.2 volts. The input voltage to the regulator is 13.9 volts, and the zener diode requires at least 1 milliampere reverse current to keep it in the regulation state. What is the smallest load resistance for which the regulator will continue to function?

The current through the series resistor is

$$I_T = \frac{V_{INPUT} - V_Z}{R_S} \qquad (5\text{-}20)$$

substituting in the values gives

$$I = \frac{(13.9V - 6.2V)}{150\Omega}$$

or

$$I = 51mA$$

If at least one milliampere must flow through the diode, a maximum of 50 milliamperes may flow in the load. The resistance of this load is

$$R_L = \frac{V_Z}{I} \qquad (5\text{-}21)$$

Substituting values gives

$$R_L = \frac{6.2V}{50mA}$$

or

$$R_L = 124\Omega$$

In the example just given, the diode must be capable of dissipating 6.2 volts times 51 milliamperes (equation *5-3*), or 316 milliwatts of power. This would be the requirement when no load is connected.

The series resistor must be able to dissipate

$$P = (V_{INPUT} - V_Z)(I_T)$$
$$P = (13.9V - 6.2V)(51 \times 10^{-3})$$

or

$$P = 393mW$$

Shunt Regulator

The zener diode regulator circuit of *Figure 5.21* is called a shunt regulator because the regulating device is in parallel with the load. The circuit regulates voltage by shunting more current away from the load in order to reduce output voltage, or by shunting less current from the load, thereby increasing output voltage. The resulting voltage drop across R_S determines the output voltage.

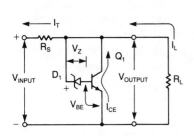

Figure 5.22   Transistor Shunt Regulator Circuit

Figure 5.22 illustrates a shunt regulator using an NPN transistor (Q_1) along with a zener diode (D_1). In this circuit, the zener voltage plus the base-to-emitter voltage of the transistor equals the load voltage. If load voltage should attempt to increase or decrease, V_{BE} changes in the same direction.

If R_L increases, I_L decreases, which increases the load voltage and V_{BE}. Increasing V_{BE} causes the transistor to draw more current, I_{CE}. Increasing I_{CE}, increases I_T and drops more voltage across R_S, the series resistor, thereby decreasing the load voltage to compensate for the original increase in load voltage caused by the increase of R_L. If V_{BE} should decrease due to load changes that cause the load voltage to decrease, the transistor draws less current I_{CE}, which results in a compensating increase in the load voltage.

Series Regulator

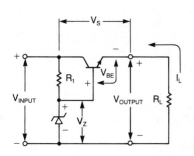

Figure 5.23   Transistor Series Regulator Circuit

Series regulators are designed by employing a control device in series with the load. *Figure 5.23* shows a series regulator using a zener diode to fix the voltage at the base of an NPN transistor. This time, the zener voltage minus the transistor's V_{BE} equals the output (load) voltage. Let's see how it works. Suppose the load voltage increases. Since the zener voltage is fixed, an increase in load voltage results in a decrease in V_{BE}. A decrease in V_{BE} causes the transistor to conduct less current, which increases its resistance, which causes a larger series voltage drop across the transistor, which decreases the load voltage to the proper level and compensates for the load current change.

In all of these regulator circuits, the regulating device operates as an "automatic variable resistor." Its resistance changes so as to provide more or less current to the load, thereby keeping the voltage constant.

Feedback Regulator

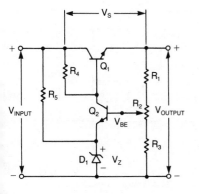

Figure 5.24   Feedback Regulator Circuit

Figure 5.24 shows a regulator whose output voltage can be easily changed. The range of output voltages can be regulated from almost as low as the zener breakdown voltage (a transistor V_{BE} away from V_Z) to almost as high as the unregulated input voltage (the V_{CE} voltage of Q_1 must not go lower than about 1 to 2 volts to keep Q_1 in the linear operating range). Potentiometer R_2 is used to set the desired output level.

Resistors R_1, R_2, and R_3 form a sensing network to detect changes in the output voltage. Output voltage changes cause V_{BE} input changes to transistor Q_2 which amplifies the variation and controls the conduction of the series pass transistor, Q_1, to compensate for the original output voltage change. R_4 is a load resistor for amplifier Q_2 and R_5 sets the idling current through the zener diode.

Integrated Circuit Regulator

In recent years many general purpose power supplies have been designed using integrated circuit voltage regulators. Inexpensive, compact IC regulators like the one shown in *Figure 5.25a* are available for a wide range of output voltages and currents. The device is about the same size as a conventional plastic case power transistor. The unregulated input voltage must be a few volts higher than the desired output for proper operation of the regulator. *Figure 5.25b* gives an operational block diagram of the IC three-terminal regulator. An error sensing amplifier compares the output voltage against a reference, represented by the zener diode. The error amplifier controls the conduction of a series pass transistor. The integrated circuit protects itself against excessive power dissipation by limiting the transistor current to a safe level and by shutting itself down if the internal temperature exceeds a safe level. *Figure 5.25c* shows how a three-terminal regulator can be used for an adjustable voltage regulator.

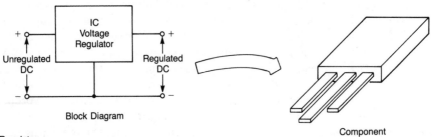

a. IC Voltage Regulator

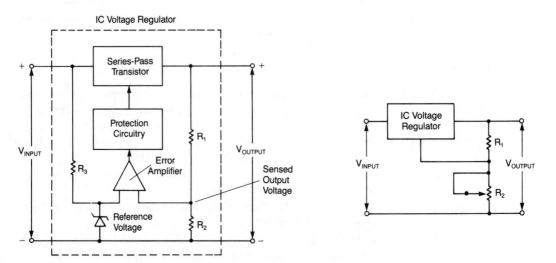

b. Block Diagram of IC Regulator

c. IC Variable-Voltage Regulator Circuit

Figure 5.25 Monolithic IC Regulation

Variable Voltage IC Regulators

For more precise power generation and control, IC voltage regulators are available with more package pins to provide adjustable output voltage, multiple outputs, and overload protection. Voltages may be variable over a wide range of output levels at some maximum current. *Figure 5.25c* shows how external components are added to such a regulator to provide a variable output voltage regulator.

Point of Use Regulation

Integrated circuit regulators have created a trend in system design toward point-of-use regulation. That is, individual subsystems have their own regulators on the printed circuit board instead of having a single regulator in the power supply. Thus, unregulated dc voltages are distributed around the system as source for the IC regulators. These tiny regulators help to isolate individual subsystems from any detrimental effects of other subsystems. Switching transients, circuit malfunctions, and other events which might affect the power supply output are, in most cases, confined to the printed circuit board on which they occur.

Switching Regulator

All the regulator circuits described so far suffer from a common malady. They are all relatively inefficient, because they regulate for load or line variations by dissipating power internally in the form of heat. This inefficiency exists because the internally-dissipated power is lost and not delivered to a load. As load power requirements increase, internal dissipation increases and so does inefficiency. Large series and shunt regulators must be cooled with heat sinks, fans and special heat transfer assemblies. To prevent the power supply from dominating the size and weight of many products, power supply designers have developed alternate approaches to regulator design. The switching regulator is one such alternative.

As the waveforms in *Figure 5.26* indicate, the series pass transistor in a switching regulator does not conduct continuously. Instead, it is either saturated or cut off by a control oscillator, outputting a series of pulses. These pulses are filtered to produce the output voltage. Regulation may be accomplished by varying either the pulse repetition rate or the duty cycle. Energy is stored in the electromagnetic field of L_1 between pulses. The filter is designed so as to output the average dc voltage of the pulse train.

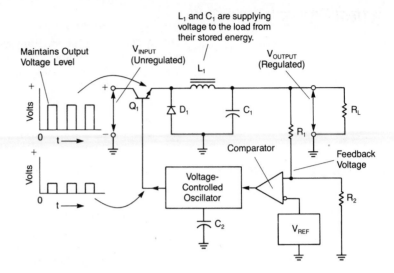

Figure 5.26　Switching Regulator Circuit

As *Figure 5.26* illustrates, the output voltage level is fed back to a VCO (voltage controlled oscillator). When the output voltage decreases so the feedback voltage is below a reference, the oscillator is triggered to charge C_2 for a given time. The oscillator is controlled by a comparator, which senses the output voltage through a resistor divider network (R_1, R_2). These resistor values program the regulator for the desired output voltage. During the time the oscillator is on, an output pulse turns on the series pass transistor Q_1. The current through Q_1 raises the output voltage level required to turn off the oscillator. The number of pulses produced by Q_1 in a given time is determined by how fast the load reduces the output voltage. Because of the LC filter design, output voltage is directly proportional to the transistor's on time. The diode D_1 protects the transistor from the inductive kick of the filter, L_1, that occurs when the transistor switches from saturation to cutoff. Thus, the oscillator outputs a non-sinusoidal pulse whenever the output voltage drops below a threshold level to restore the dc voltage level, the frequency of recurrence depending upon the load requirements.

Typical operating frequency ranges for various types of switching regulators are from 10kHz to 500kHz allowing the filter components to be quite small. The transistor dissipates relatively little power during saturation and cutoff (the only mode of operation), as compared to a linear series regulator. As a result, switching regulated power supplies may be as small as one-third to one-half the volume and weight of a typical series regulator supply.

Current Regulator

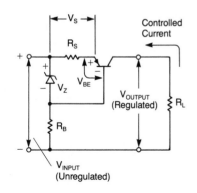

Figure 5.27 Current Regulator Circuit

The fundamentals of constant current regulator operation are illustrated in the circuit of *Figure 5.27*. Note that a PNP transistor is used. The transistor bias V_{BE} equals the difference between the zener diode voltage, and the voltage drop V_S across the emitter resistor, R_S. If the load current increases, the voltage V_S increases. Because V_Z is constant, V_{BE} decreases. When V_{BE} decreases, collector current decreases to compensate for the original increase in load current. Corresponding changes cause the transistor current to increase if there is an original decrease in load current due to the load changing. If the input voltage increases, it would tend to increase the load current, which would set up the compensating changes, just discussed, to keep the current constant.

Constant current supplies are most often used in instrumentation settings. Current-sensitive devices like magnetic cores, meters, relays, fuses, transistors, and diodes are among the many devices commonly operated with constant current power supply sources.

POWER SUPPLY TESTING

Defective power supplies usually affect the performance of the entire system because of the common power supplied to the total system. Sometimes these defects are caused by failures within the power supply, but some apparent power supply problems are caused by failures in the other parts of the system. The system's subsystems are the load on the supply. If a system problem occurs that indicates a power supply problem, it must be established that the subsystem loads have not changed before assuming that any fault lies with the power supply.

In the discussion that follows, it is assumed that the load meets the system specifications, and that the fault definitely lies with the power supply. One way to determine this is to substitute a second power supply and observe system operation. If the system operates properly, the power supply is at fault.

Regulated power supply problems are usually limited to one of two categories. Most component failures cause either loss of regulation or excessive ripple. Loss of regulation causes improper (or zero) output voltage; excessive ripple results in a large ac signal component on the output voltage.

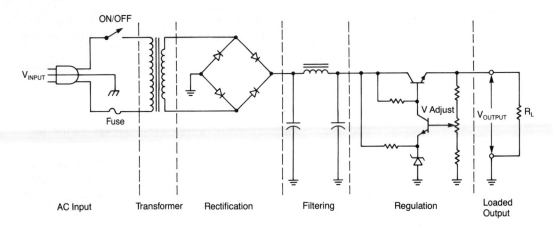

ON/OFF

V_{INPUT}

Fuse

V Adjust

V_{OUTPUT}

R_L

AC Input   Transformer   Rectification   Filtering   Regulation   Loaded
                                                                                                       Output

Figure 5.28   Complete Power Supply

Isolating Power Supply Problems

Figure 5.28 is a complete series regulated power supply schematic. The four sections — transformer, rectifier, filter, and regulator — have been identified by the broken-line partitions. Testing this power supply usually requires that a load be simulated and that a digital voltmeter and an oscilloscope be available. Waveform observations and voltage measurements must be made as the load is varied from a high resistance (light) load to a low resistance (heavy) load. An output voltage that is too high or too low usually indicates a filter or regulator problem, while no output is usually indicative of a rectifier or transformer problem. Excessive ripple is most often associated with filter failure, but it may be caused by regulator malfunction in some cases.

Transformer Testing

In a power supply like the one diagrammed in *Figure 5.28*, a faulty transformer will usually result in a blown fuse. Typical transformer problems include shorts between turns in either the secondary or primary windings, or windings shorted to the core or shield material. If such shorts do not cause fuses to blow, they may cause the transformer to overheat, or they may cause the output voltage to drop significantly.

Power transformer windings may open, instead of shorting. In this case, fuses will not blow, but output voltage will be zero. Open or shorted windings in transformers can be verified by resistance checks. If fuses are not blown, voltage measurements may be used to verify transformer operation. If there is primary voltage but no secondary voltage, either the primary or secondary winding could be open.

Rectifier Circuit Testing

When rectifier diodes fail, they are either open or shorted. If the fuse is not blown, an observation of the waveform at the rectifier output can provide much information about the state of the rectifier. For example, a full-wave rectifier with an open diode operates as a half-wave rectifier. An improper waveform (which can be viewed on an oscilloscope) will detect the problem. An open diode will also cause the output voltage to be lower than normal.

A shorted rectifier diode should cause a fuse to open. It also may cause a second diode to go bad, either shorting or opening. On alternate half cycles the secondary winding is short circuited, causing excessive transformer current. Locating the shorted diode requires resistance checks. It may be necessary to measure both the forward and reverse resistances of the diodes to establish the location of the fault. The forward resistance should be only a few ohms, whereas the reverse resistance should read thousands of ohms, the exact value depends upon the electrical characteristics of the diode under test.

Filter Testing

Low-pass filters like those used in dc power supplies use capacitive shunt elements and resistive or inductive series elements. An open shunt element causes the output voltage to drop and to exhibit excessive ripple. A filter capacitor usually develops current leakage before it shorts, causing it to get warm. Should the shunt element short, it may blow the fuse. If not, the unregulated dc voltage will be much lower than normal, and the transformer will be operating at a higher temperature than normal.

An open resistor or inductor in the series arm of the filter will cause output voltage to be zero. Simple voltage checks can isolate an open series element. A shorted resistor or inductor may cause a fuse to open, but it is more likely to produce excessive ripple at the output of the supply. The input to the regulator may also be slightly higher than normal. Again, resistance checks are used to verify that a series element is shorted.

Regulator Testing

The regulator is the most electronically complicated section of a power supply. Its overall operation is best tested by varying the load resistance while observing the output voltage. Significant variation in the output voltage indicates a regulator malfunction.

Under normal operating conditions, regulator problems are indicated by too high or too low load voltages, or by zero voltage. The most common cause of zero output is an open series-pass transistor. This fault also causes the unregulated input to rise slightly because no current is being drawn by the regulator circuitry.

Most of the regulator circuits discussed use a zener diode to establish the reference voltage for the control transistor. If this diode shorts, it would cause the output voltage to be very low. It may also cause the series-pass transistor to overheat. Higher than normal output voltage indicates that the regulator is not responding to changing load requirements. The sensing elements are usually resistors, which are quite reliable, so the prime suspect is the error amplifier circuit. It may be a transistor in a linear regulator, or it may be the voltage controlled oscillator in a switching regulator. These problems are most easily isolated by using dc voltage measurements and oscilloscope waveforms.

SUMMARY

In this chapter, we have learned that transformers are used to step up or step down the ac line voltage into the required operating voltage. Rectifiers, which convert the transformer's ac output into dc, may be configured in several different ways, but generally those arrangements providing full-wave rectification are preferred.

Filtering, which is accomplished primarily by capacitors, is required to smooth out the pulsating dc supplied by the rectifiers. Capacitors in combination with inductors or resistors provide superior filtering, as compared to a single capacitor

Regulation is a means of insuring proper power supply voltage or current stability under conditions of varying load or ac line voltages. Circuits, each with one or more semiconductor devices (usually a zener diode) at their functional heart, provide the required circuit control. With the advent of all the regulator circuitry in integrated circuit form, it has become common practice to distribute unregulated dc through a system and provide regulated supply voltages at each subsystem with IC regulators.

CHAPTER 5 QUIZ

1. Converting ac to dc is a function of which power supply section?
   a. Transformer
   b. Rectifier
   c. Filter
   d. Regulator

2. If 110VAC is applied to the primary of a transformer with a 1:10 turns ratio, what is the secondary voltage?
   a. 1.0 volt
   b. 11.0 volts
   c. 110 volts
   d. 1100 volts

3. Neglecting losses, how much power is dissipated in the secondary of the transformer of the previous question if the primary current is 0.1 ampere?
   a. 11 watts
   b. 9 watts
   c. 1.1 watts
   d. 0.1 watts

4. A short circuit between turns in a power transformer secondary is likely to produce what effect?
   a. Open filter choke
   b. Excessive ripple
   c. Shorted series-pass transistor
   d. Reduced output voltage

5. Power supply filters are what basic type?
   a. Bandpass
   b. Band reject
   c. Low pass
   d. High pass

6. For 60Hz ac input, a full-wave rectifier produces what frequency output?
   a. 120Hz
   b. 60Hz
   c. 30Hz
   d. 20Hz

7. A transformer with a 1:20 turns ratio requires how much primary current to produce 5 amperes secondary current?
   a. 25 amperes
   b. 4.0 amperes
   c. 0.25 amperes
   d. 0.04 amperes

8. What is the ripple factor if a power supply has 240 millivolts rms ripple on an average dc output of 12 volts?
   a. 0.24
   b. 0.02
   c. 0.5
   d. 2.0

9. What is the percent regulation if output voltage is 23.8 volts under full load, but 24.2 volts with no load?
   a. 40.0 percent
   b. 2.4 percent
   c. 2.0 percent
   d. 1.7 percent

10. A full-wave rectifier using two diodes requires a:
    a. simple capacitor filter.
    b. series-pass transistor.
    c. center-tapped transformer.
    d. zener diode reference.

11. A filter capacitor affects the power supply output by:
    a. reducing the ripple level.
    b. reducing the dc level to the average.
    c. increasing the dc level to the peak values.
    d. increasing the no-load output.

12. A shorted series-pass regulator transistor results in:
    a. excessive ripple level.
    b. always too high dc volts out.
    c. too low dc volts out.
    d. zero output voltage.

13. In a voltage regulator, if the load resistance decreases, the effective resistance of the series-pass transistor:
    a. increases.
    b. decreases.
    c. stays the same.
    d. may increase or decrease.

14. In a current regulator, if load resistance decreases, the effective resistance of the series-pass transistor:
    a. increases.
    b. decreases.
    c. stays the same.
    d. may increase or decrease.

15. If a full-wave rectifier circuit operates as a half-wave circuit, what is the most likely problem?
    a. Shorted filter
    b. Open transformer
    c. Shorted diode
    d. Open diode

16. A power supply whose output is 51 volts with no load outputs only 40 volts when fully loaded. This is a result of:
    a. poor regulation.
    b. poor filtering.
    c. normal operation.
    d. shorted transformer secondary.

17. Switching regulators typically operate at what frequency?
    a. 25kHz or higher
    b. 1kHz
    c. 120Hz
    d. 60Hz

18. The output voltage level in a zener regulated voltage supply is determined by the:
    a. transformer turns ratio.
    b. series resistance.
    c. zener breakdown voltage.
    d. filter capacitance.

19. What is the biggest advantage of switching regulators over linear regulators?
    a. Lower ripple
    b. Better regulation
    c. Greater efficiency
    d. Simpler filtering

20. Shorted power transformer windings are not likely to cause which of the following symptoms?
    a. Blown power supply fuse
    b. A distorted sine wave
    c. Transformer overheating
    d. Reduced output voltage

TEST EQUIPMENT

INTRODUCTION

Test equipment allows technicians and engineeers to monitor, and sometimes to intervene in the operation of electrical devices. The test equipment becomes an extension of their eyes, ears, and hands to help them determine how well the devices being tested are performing.

In this chapter, we will cover the common test equipment used for measuring and displaying voltages, currents, and frequencies. The heart of many measuring devices, the common electromechanical meter movement, is covered, as well as how the circuitry connected to it determines its units of measure. This is followed by basic bridge circuits, which are used in many precision measurement applications.

The oscilloscope, perhaps the most versatile type of test instrument, is given the greatest amount of attention. It can perform the functions of most other instruments, such as voltage measurement and frequency measurement (indirectly), but it's invaluable for direct viewing of waveforms. In addition, much of its technology appears in other instrumentation.

Also discussed are the basic signal generators which are used to provide an input test signal with known characteristics. By connecting measurement test equipment to the output of the circuit under test, the condition of the circuit can be determined.

In addition to test equipment designed for testing circuits, some test equipment is designed for testing components. In this category is the common semiconductor testing apparatus, which is also briefly described.

Special attention is given to test probes, which are common to almost all test equipment. It will be pointed out why they are much more than simply a conductor used to transfer a voltage sample from the circuit under test into the testing device.

Finally, the technology of data communications circuitry testing is addressed.

The equipment covered in this chapter represents most of the types available. Those devices not specifically covered are largely variations of the basic units that are included.

BASIC METER CIRCUITS

For more than fifty years, the most widely used of all test equipment has been the volt-ohm-milliammeter — or VOM as it has been popularly called. The instrument is relatively inexpensive, yet can accurately make the most often-needed measurements: ac and dc volts, ohms, and dc milliamperes.

Meter Movements

The heart of the VOM is the moving coil meter movement. A coil of wire, which is mounted so that it can rotate, is suspended between the poles of a permanent magnet. When current flows through the wire, an electromagnetic field forms around the coil which interacts with the permanent magnet field surrounding it. This electromagnetic field attracts or opposes the field of the permanent magnet, depending upon the direction of current flow, so that the coil is made to rotate about its axis. This basic principle, which is involved in every moving coil meter movement, is shown in *Figure 6.1*.

A similar coil with many turns of wire and with a pointer needle attached to it is shown in *Figure 6.2*. The coil is supported by jeweled pivot bearings and is suspended within the field of a permanent magnet. The needle moves along a calibrated scale as the coil rotates. The distance moved is proportional to the amount of current in the coil. A balance is obtained between the force of rotation of the coil produced by the current flowing through it, and the mechanical force of the springs connected to oppose the rotation. These springs are wound in a spiral at the top and bottom of the coil as shown in *Figure 6.2*. The amount of current required for full-scale deflection is the sensitivity of the meter. Most meter movements require one milliampere or less for full-scale deflection. To read a meter with the greatest accuracy, view it from a point directly in front of the meter scale to minimize parallax error.

This type of moving coil meter, known as a permanent magnet moving coil instrument, is very similar to the original meter developed almost 100 years ago by the French physicist Jacques Arsene D'Arsonval. The D'Arsonval meter movement has been improved until it is more sensitive, comparatively rugged, and easily transported. With special circuits, it readily adapts to indicate current and voltage values higher than its basic range, as you will soon learn.

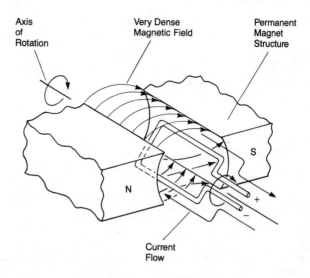

Figure 6.1 Basic Principles of Electromagnetic Torque

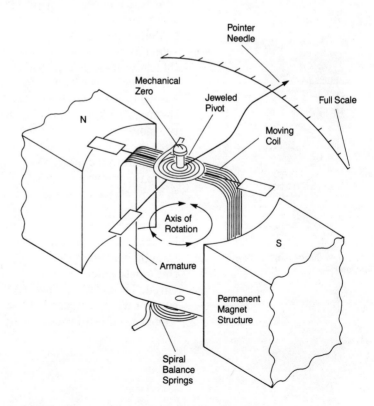

Figure 6.2 Detail of a Common Moving Coil Assembly

Current and Voltage Meters

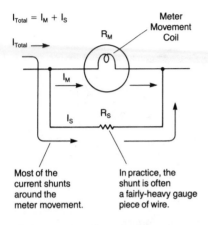

$I_{Total} = I_M + I_S$

$I_{Total} \rightarrow$

R_M

I_M

R_S

I_S

Meter Movement Coil

Most of the current shunts around the meter movement.

In practice, the shunt is often a fairly-heavy gauge piece of wire.

Figure 6.3 The Shunt Bypass

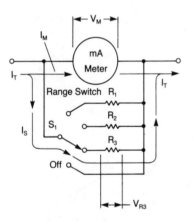

$\leftarrow V_M \rightarrow$

I_M

mA Meter

I_T

Range Switch R_1

R_2

S_1

R_3

Off

I_S

I_T

$\leftarrow V_{R3} \rightarrow$

Figure 6.4 Simple Switch Multi-Range Ammeter

DC Current Measurements Using a D'Arsonval-Type Meter Movement

Meter movements are utilized extensively to measure the direct current in a circuit. To obtain this measurement, the meter is connected in series with the load so that all, or a sample of, the current through the circuit also flows through the meter.

The meter movement coil has a small amount of resistance; hence, maximum pointer deflection, called full-scale deflection, is produced by a very small current. Therefore, if large currents are to be measured, a very low resistance conductor, called a shunt, must be connected in parallel with the meter movement to carry most of the current around the meter coil. As expected from Kirchoff's current law, the current is divided in inverse proportion to the resistance of the meter coil, as compared to the resistance of the shunt. Therefore, a small fixed percentage or sampling of the total current will always flow through the meter coil. *Figure 6.3* illustrates how the shunt is arranged with the meter movement and how the current flow is divided.

A simple way to make a multi-range ammeter is shown in *Figure 6.4*. A rotary switch connects different values of shunts across the meter. This circuit, however, presents a problem when switched from range to range. During the intervals when the switch is between contacts, all of the current will flow through the meter movement alone and probably will seriously damage the meter by overloading it. A circuit of this kind must have a special type of switch with make-before-break contacts. When the movable contact is being moved from one terminal to another, the movable contact touches the next terminal before it breaks with the previous terminal. Notice that the Off position places a short across the meter movement. This short causes CEMF to damp the meter movement. This protects it during physical movement, as when it is carried from place to place.

A more practical method of switching between shunts is shown in *Figure 6.5*. This is called a universal shunt or Ayrton shunt. This circuit makes use of a simpler, less expensive switch than the make-before-break type. At no time can full current pass through the meter movement, since the shunt portion is hard-wired. The position of switch S_1 determines how the circuit current will be divided between the meter and the shunts. Most VOMs use this universal shunt circuit.

Example 6-1: The circuit shown in *Figure 6.3* is to be used as a 50 milliampere ammeter. The meter movement has a sensitivity of 1.0 milliampere and an internal resistance of 90 ohms. What value shunt resistor, R_S, should be used?

The total current flowing is the sum of the current through the meter, plus the current through the shunt:

$$I_T = I_M + I_S \qquad (6\text{-}1)$$

Since the meter and shunt are in parallel, the voltage across the meter and shunt are equal:

$$E_S = E_M \qquad (6\text{-}2)$$

Since

$$E = IR \qquad (6\text{-}3)$$

Therefore,

$$I_S R_S = I_M R_M \qquad (6\text{-}4)$$

Transposing terms

$$R_S = \frac{I_M R_M}{I_S} \qquad (6\text{-}5)$$

and since the shunt current is the difference between the total current and the meter current:

$$R_S = \frac{I_M R_M}{I_T - I_M} \qquad (6\text{-}6)$$

Substituting values gives

$$R_S = \frac{(1\text{mA})(90\Omega)}{(50\text{mA} - 1.0\text{mA})}$$

or

$$R_S = 1.84\Omega$$

Therefore, the shunt must have a resistance of 1.84 ohms.

Precautions for Ammeter Use

There are four precautions which should be remembered when using an ammeter:

1. The meter should always be connected in series with the circuit in which the current is being measured. Never connect an ammeter directly across a battery or other voltage source.
2. Polarity must be observed when connecting the meter. Reversed polarity causes the meter pointer to deflect backwards against the mechanical stop, possibly bending the pointer.

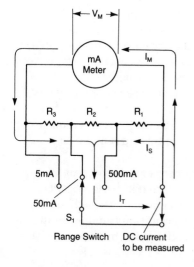

Figure 6.5   Ayrton or Universal Shunt Ammeter

3. When using an ammeter with several ranges, always start with the highest range. Decrease the current range until deflection giving as near to full scale as possible is obtained. This will give the most accurate reading of the current being measured.
4. Whenever transporting an ammeter, the range switch should be in the Off position or the highest current range position.

Voltage Measurements Using a DC Current Meter

Voltage can be measured using a dc milliampere meter movement if a resistor is connected in series with the meter movement, as shown in *Figure 6.6*. Of course, the meter face must have appropriate scales to indicate the measured voltage. The addition of this series resistor, referred to as a multiplier resistor, converts a basic milliammeter movement into dc voltmeter. The value of the multiplier resistor required to extend the voltage range is calculated from Ohm's law and Kirchoff's laws governing series circuits for voltage drops. Voltage measuring circuits require only a small current. It is the magnitude of this current which determines the meter deflection.

Example 6-2: The 1.0 milliampere meter movement described in example *6-1* is to be converted into a 0-100 volt voltmeter. What value multiplier resistor is to be used?

By Ohm's law, the full-scale current that can flow is equal to the voltage applied to the total circuit divided by the sum of the two series resistances:

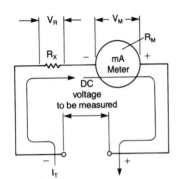

Figure 6.6 Converting a Basic Milliammeter to Measure Voltage

$$I_{FS} = \frac{V_{FS}}{R_M + R_X} \qquad (6\text{-}7)$$

and

$$I_{FS} = \frac{V_{FS}}{R_T} \qquad (6\text{-}8)$$

Rearranging equation *6-8* gives

$$R_T = \frac{V_{FS}}{I_T}$$

Substituting into the equation

$$R_T = \frac{100V}{1mA}$$

$$R_T = 100k\Omega$$

The unknown resistor must be the difference between the total resistance and meter resistance:

$$R_X = R_T - R_M \qquad (6\text{-}9)$$

Substituting values into equation *6-9*

$$R_X = 100k\Omega - 90\Omega$$

or

$$R_X = 99,910\Omega$$

Therefore, the series multiplier resistor must have a value of 99,910 ohms.

A multi-range voltmeter may be obtained by the addition of a number of multiplier resistors together with a range switch. *Figure 6.7a* shows a multi-range voltmeter which has a four-position switch and four multiplier resistors. The higher the resistor value switched into the circuit, the greater the voltage value which can be measured.

A significant cost factor in meter circuit manufacture is the custom resistance values needed to complement the fixed meter resistance. A variation of the multiplier resistor circuit shown in *Figure 6.7a* is shown in *Figure 6.7b*. The advantage of this circuit is that all the multiplier resistors, except R_1, have standard resistance values. The only custom value resistor required is R_1.

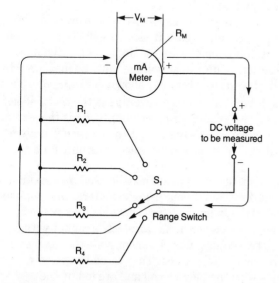

a. Circuit Requiring Custom Resistor Values

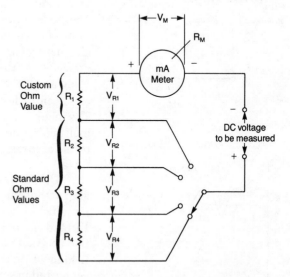

b. Circuit Requiring Mostly Standard Resistor Values

Figure 6.7 *Two Multi-Range Voltmeter Circuits*

Sensitivity of a Voltmeter

The ohms per volt (ohms/V) is called the sensitivity of the voltmeter. The sensitivity of the voltmeter is specified by the manufacturer and is frequently found printed on the scale of the instrument.

If the sensitivity is known, then the resistance that the voltmeter will have for any particular voltage range can be determined. The sensitivity is the reciprocal of the full scale deflection current of the basic movement.

A voltmeter should have very high resistance, to minimize the current drawn from the circuit under test. This means that the meter movement itself should be as sensitive as possible.

Precautions for Voltmeter Use

The precautions to be observed when using a voltmeter are:
1. The correct polarity must be observed.
2. The voltmeter is always connected across the component whose voltage drop is to be measured. Although harmless to the instrument, the series connection would give a meaningless reading.
3. When using a multi-range voltmeter, always start on the highest voltage range and then decrease the voltage range until a reading as nearly full scale as possible is obtained.
4. Whenever transporting a voltmeter, it should be in the off position or the highest voltage range position.

Measuring AC Voltage

The basic D'Arsonval movement responds to the average or dc value of the current through its coil. It usually will not respond to alternating current; if it does, the voltage indication will not be even close to the actual value. An ac voltage must be measured by using a rectifier bridge in the circuit, as shown in *Figure 6.8*. This circuit provides a dc current that is an average of the rectified ac. The meter scales must be calibrated accordingly. R_X is the series multiplier resistor which allows the circuit to measure voltage in terms of current flow. This type circuit is accurate only for a sine wave.

Other types of meter movements may be used to measure an alternating current directly without using rectifiers. One popular movement is an electrodynamometer as shown in *Figure 6.9a*. Instead of a permanent magnet, it has an electromagnet with a fixed coil split into two equal parts. These provide the magnetic field in which the moving coil rotates. The two coil halves are connected in series with the moving coil and are fed by the current under measurement.

This type of meter will respond to the rms value of the current regardless of the wave shape. The rms value is slightly greater than the average value of the current as shown in *Figure 6.9b*.

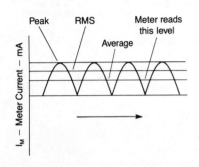

a. Circuit

b. Waveform to Meter

Figure 6.8 Using the DC Milliammeter to Measure AC Voltage

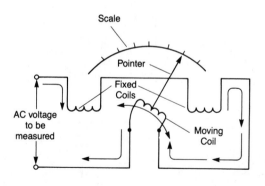

a. Circuit

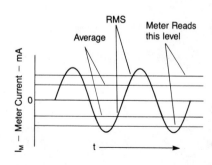

b. Waveform to Meter

Figure 6.9   Electrical Circuit for an Electrodynamometer

Resistance Measuring Meters

Because of the relationship between resistance, voltage, and current as expressed by Ohm's law, resistance also may be measured using a basic dc meter movement and a source of voltage. The ohmmeter measures resistance in terms of the magnitude of current allowed to flow by the unknown resistance. Obviously, the lower its resistance, the greater the current flow; hence, the more the milliammeter needle will deflect. The meter scale is appropriately calibrated so that zero ohms is at full scale (maximum current flow) and infinity ohms is at zero current flow.

A circuit illustrating a series-type ohmmeter is shown in *Figure 6.10*. The series ohmmeter is the most popular type circuit. The available current from the internal battery, which is used to power the ohmmeter circuit, gradually decreases with use and age so that it can't supply enough current to drive the meter to full scale. Therefore, the meter will not read zero ohms when terminals A and B are shorted together, which represents zero ohms for R_x. Therefore, R_4, called an Ohms Zero control, is made variable so it can be adjusted to compensate for the battery aging.

A shunt type ohmmeter may also be constructed using a basic meter movement and a battery, as shown in *Figure 6.11*. The shunt type ohmmeter is particularly suited to the measurement of very low values of resistances.

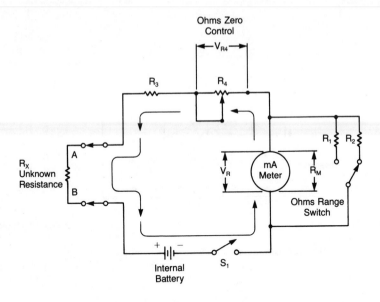

Figure 6.10   Circuit for a Simple Series Ohmmeter

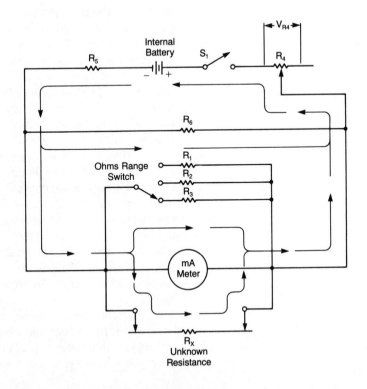

Figure 6.11   Circuit for a Simple Shunt Ohmmeter

Multimeters

The milliammeter, ac and dc voltmeters, and ohmmeter all have been combined into a single instrument. This instrument is referred to as a multimeter, or more commonly, a volt-ohm-milliammeter (VOM). A function switch connects the appropriate circuits to the meter movement. Additional functions are available on some VOMs with the use of adapters, probes, and additional jacks for the probe leads on the front of the instrument.

Most VOMs have ac voltage ranges. To measure ac voltage, follow the procedure exactly the same as for dc voltage, except that the terminal polarity need not be observed for ac, and of course, the function switch must be set to ac.

For making ac voltage measurements, a VOM uses rectifiers in its circuit as shown in *Figure 6.8*. In the ac function, the meter responds to both ac and dc voltages which may be present. Voltage readings are accurate for purely sinusoidal ac quantities. To measure ac voltages only, a capacitor of the correct capacitance must be placed in series with one of the meter leads to block the dc. Of course, you can insert this capacitor externally, but for convenience, most VOMs have a jack on the front, or a position on the function switch, labeled Output. This jack, or function position, inserts a capacitor inside the meter in series with the test lead. The Output label is used because, when used in this manner, the VOM may be referred to as an output meter, and may be used for signal tracing in audio amplifiers.

A dB scale also is included on many VOMs for audio measurements. To measure dB, set the function switch to the ac voltage position and use the output function. The dB scale usually is calibrated for a value of 600 ohms for the circuit impedance. Where the circuit load impedance is other than 600 ohms, the dB scale is not correct.

The reference level of power generally used in communication work is one milliwatt of power is dissipated when 0.775 volt rms is across a 600 ohm load. This is designated as 0 dBm. The dB scale is accurate only for sinusoidal signals and for resistive loads of 600 ohms. One of the ac voltage scales is used to measure dBm directly. For other values of dBm, the range switch is changed and the appropriate number of dBm are added to or subtracted from the actual reading. The dBm adjustment values are usually printed on the meter scale or given in the user's manual.

Safety Precautions for VOMs

Meter movements may be damaged by electrical overloads or mechanical shock. Sometimes the overload will drive the pointer against the mechanical stop (called "pegging the meter") so hard as to cause mechanical damage even if the coil is not damaged.

In VOM-type instruments, always start with the range switch higher than is likely to give a mid-scale reading to protect the meter from unexpected overloads. Then, if necessary, switch to a more sensitive setting. Some instruments are overload-protected but this precaution still should be observed.

When not actually making resistance or current readings, the function switch should not be left in the Ohms, Milliampere or Microampere positions. This reduces the possibility of damaging the meter if it is mistakenly connected to a voltage source. If a VOM doesn't have an Off position, leave it set for dc volts on the highest voltage range when it's not in use.

When transporting a VOM, if there is an Off position on the unit, make sure it is in that position to provide maximum damping to inhibit meter movement.

Meter Loading

The loading effect of a voltmeter depends on its ohms/volt characteristics, the voltage range to which the meter is set, and the total impedance of the circuit under test. The resistance measured across the terminals of a voltmeter is the load resistance that the meter presents to the circuit under test. This resistance will draw current from the circuit and affect the measured value. Since the voltmeter is connected in parallel with the circuit under test, the loading effect decreases the voltage drop across the circuit or component under test as shown in *Figure 6.12a*.

Since a dc current meter is placed in series with the circuit under test, it causes an additional voltage drop in the series circuit path. Thus, the sum of the resistances of the meter and the circuit is larger than the circuit's resistance before the ammeter is inserted. Therefore, the current measured will be less than was actually flowing in the circuit before the ammeter was inserted. This is illustrated in *Figure 6.12b*.

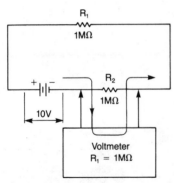

Meter reads 3.33V instead of the 5V
expected if it were not loading the circuit.

Meter reads 9mA instead of the 10mA
expected if it had no internal resistance.

a. Effect of a Voltmeter on Circuit Measurement

b. Effect of an Ammeter on Circuit Measurement

Figure 6.12   Effect of Meter Loading on Circuit Conditions

ELECTRONIC METERS

The main disadvantages of a VOM are its low sensitivity and changing input impedance. An electronic voltmeter overcomes these problems.

Electronic voltmeters, ammeters, and ohmmeters make use of active devices such as field-effect transistors and operational amplifiers to generate an output current which is used to supply the indicating device proportional to the parameter that is being measured. A typical electronic voltmeter has an input impedance of more than 10 megohms, and some have as much as 100 megohms. Also, the input impedance is the same for all ranges, making true circuit voltages easier to determine.

Solid-State Multimeters

One of the most useful and versatile electronic instruments capable of measuring dc and ac voltages, as well as dc current and resistance, is a solid-state multimeter. The solid-state multimeter is a descendant of the popular vacuum-tube voltmeter (VTVM). Though probably no longer in production, many VTVM's are still in service. The VTVM usually obtains its power from a 117 volt ac supply, wereas the solid-state multimeter is generally battery operated.

The solid-state multimeter basic operations are similar to the conventional VOM, but the electronic circuitry makes it more sensitive, thus, it has less loading effect, especially on low voltage ranges. A simplified version of a solid state multimeter is shown in *Figure 6.13*.

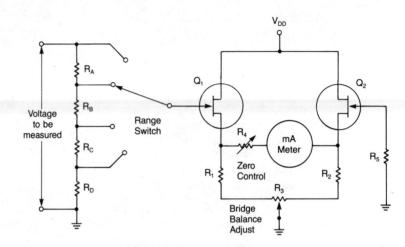

Figure 6.13   Solid-State (FET) Balanced Bridge Electronic Multimeter

To measure ac voltages with a solid-state multimeter, some form of rectification must be used. A full-wave rectifier is the simplest way to accomplish this, but the same problem exists here as with the VOM; that is, the waveshape must be sinusoidal for accurate measurements.

The solid-state multimeter also makes resistance measurements somewhat differently than a conventional VOM. A constant value of current from a constant current source is caused to flow through the unknown resistance. The voltage drop is then measured across the unknown resistance and the value of the resistance is read from the scale calibrated according to Ohm's law. A simplified diagram of this type of circuit is shown in *Figure 6.14*.

Differential Voltmeters

When an extremely accurate measurement of an unknown voltage is required, a differential voltmeter or potentiometer provides the best results. The principle of operation is illustrated in *Figure 6.15*. To make the measurement, a precision divider, which is calibrated in volts is adjusted so that the meter movement reads zero. In this null condition, neither the source nor the reference supplies current to the meter. The differential voltmeter presents a theoretically infinite impedance to the source under test; therefore, it has virtually no loading effect. Of course, this is the optimum way to measure voltage.

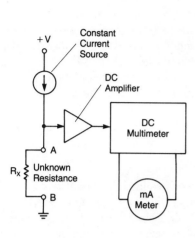

Figure 6.14 Solid-State Ohmmeter Circuit

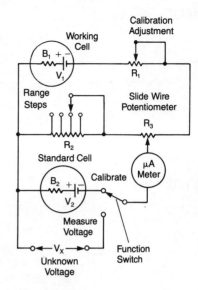

Figure 6.15 Basic Potentiometer Circuit

Vector Voltmeter

If the phase difference and the amplitude between two voltage waveforms at two points are to be measured simultaneously, a vector voltmeter is used. This instrument is very useful in making amplifier gain and phase shift measurements, as well as filter transfer function measurements. A vector voltmeter is generally used in the radio frequency range and covers a band from 1MHz to approximately 1GHz. It has output jacks to drive a plotter, and is available with digital readout.

Impedance Meter

A vector impedance meter (VIM) is similar to the vector voltmeter, except the VIM has an internal ac voltage source, usually a Wien bridge oscillator. Impedance measurements are concerned with both magnitude and phase angle of a component and a VIM will make these measurements over a frequency range from about 5kHz to 500kHz. The component with unknown impedance is connected across the terminals of the instrument and the desired frequency is selected by turning the front panel frequency adjustment control. The two front panel meters indicate the magnitude of the impedance and the phase angle directly. The VIM also has output jacks to drive a plotter, and is available with digital readout.

Audio Meter

If all audio signals were sine waves, a voltmeter with a dBm scale could be used, and an accurate reading relating both the electrical and acoustical variations could be obtained. Unfortunately, audio signals are complex waves and their rms amplitude is not 0.707 times the peak. The dBm meter is for sinusoidal measurements, whereas the VU (volume unit) meter may be used for any audio frequency waveform to indicate the average energy level of speech or music program material.

Digital Multimeters

Digital voltmeters have been available for many years, but for some time were quite expensive. They were found only in military, scientific, and commercial laboratories, and were built by only a few sophisticated instrument manufacturers. Today, however, microelectronics and integrated circuit technologies have allowed the production of digital voltmeters and digital multimeters at greatly reduced cost. The digital multimeter generally has the same functions as the conventional VOM.

The digital readout of a digital multimeter eliminates the parallax error common in an analog instrument when the pointer is viewed from an angle other than 90 degrees. By eliminating this error, as well as errors caused by the mechanics of the moving coil meter, the digital multimeter is usually more accurate.

Special purpose probes are also available to extend the function and range of digital multimeters. Even the lower priced digital multimeters have features such as automatic zeroing and overload protection, making them a useful addition to any workbench.

BRIDGE CIRCUITS

Bridge or null circuits have been used extensively for many years to measure electronic component values of resistance, inductance, and/or capacitance. With the rapid growth of digital measuring instruments, it might seem the bridge circuit should have outlived its usefulness. However, many applications in instrumentation and control still employ the bridge circuit for detecting and measuring parameters directly, making an understanding of this circuit valuable now and for years to come. The bridge circuit principle of operation is that it compares the value of an unknown component to the accurately known value of another component, which is referred to as a standard.

The Wheatstone Resistance Bridge

The most fundamental bridge circuit is the Wheatstone type. All the others are variations of this basic circuit. The bridge consists of three parts: (1) the voltage source, (2) the four resistive arms, and (3) the null detector. The resistive Wheatstone functions with either ac or dc voltage to power it. For dc, the null detector is usually a galvanometer-type microammeter or other sensitive current meter with zero at center scale. When an ac source is used, the null detector must detect the presence of ac current or voltage.

Figure 6.16 shows a dc Wheatstone resistance bridge. The current through the null detector is dependent on the voltage between points C and D. If this voltage is zero, the currents through the four arms are equal, and the bridge is said to be balanced. The sensitivity of the null detector determines the amount of unbalance that may be detected.

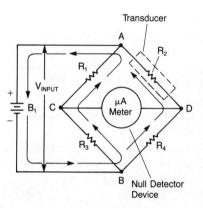

Figure 6.16 DC Wheatstone Bridge Circuit

The Wheatstone bridge circuitry used in instrumentation and control begins in a balanced state. One of the bridge arms may be a transducer sensitive to a stimulus parameter, such as force (as in a strain gauge), temperature (as in a thermistor), or light (as in a photoresistive cell). Under a condition of zero stimulus, the output voltage is zero. When a change in the stimulus occurs, the output voltage is directly proportional to the value of the change in stimulus, which unbalances the bridge. The detector can be directly calibrated in the units of stimulus, or the change in current can be amplified and used to control something.

AC Impedance Bridge

Figure 6.17 shows a simplified ac impedance bridge circuit. Both the amplitude and the phase of the voltages at A and B must be equal for balance.

Capacitance Bridge

For many years, a popular application of the ac version of a Wheatstone bridge has been included in a service-type capacitance bridge. These bridges can measure the resistance of resistors as well as the capacitance, insulator-caused leakage current, and the dielectric resistance of capacitors. The circuit for a simple capacitance bridge for small capacitors is shown in *Figure 6.18a*. It is common practice to replace the values of Z_3 and Z_4 with precision potentiometers calibrated in capacitance values (microfarads, picofarads, etc.).

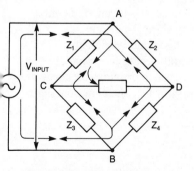

Figure 6.17 An AC Impedance Bridge

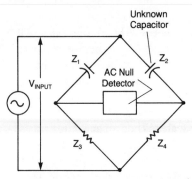

a. Simple Capacitance Bridge for Small Low-Loss Capacitors

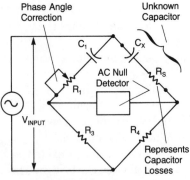

b. Capacitance Comparison Bridge for Large High-Loss Capacitors

Figure 6.18 Two Capacitance Measurement Bridges

OSCILLOSCOPES

Figure 6.18b shows a capacitance bridge for measuring large value, electrolytic capacitors. Precision potentiometer R_1, in series with C_1, provides the means to balance out the phase angle (power factor), resulting from the series resistive losses represented by R_S, in the unknown capacitor. The power factor of a capacitor is the cosine of the angle between its impedance Z, and series resistance R_S, and indicates the amount of power losses to be expected.

Consideration of Resistive Losses

In ac circuit analysis, capacitors and inductors are considered to be perfect reactances. In reality, however, capacitors and inductors have resistive losses. A real component is represented by its equivalent circuit; for example, components C_X and R_S in *Figure 6.18b* represent a real capacitor.

Series and parallel RC and RL equivalent circuits are used in place of the Z_S (series impedance) in the ac bridge circuit. Instead of measuring the R of a component with a bridge, the quality factor, Q, is measured. The Q of an inductor defines the quality of the component as a ratio of the component's series reactance-to-series resistance.

The accuracy of bridge measurements is reduced by high loss components, high frequency signal inputs, and either very large or very small unknown impedances. High frequencies decrease bridge accuracy because of stray capacitance and inductance in the bridge's variable resistors. When the unknown impedance is very small or very large, the residual capacitance of the bridge and the capacitance of the leads must be taken into account.

The meter is an extremely useful device, but it responds only to a dc signal or averages a changing signal to provide a measurement of one parameter — the signal level. The oscilloscope displays a real-time graphic representation of electronic circuit activity. The oscilloscope provides an accurate display of voltage change no matter how fast the changes occur (within the oscilloscope's capabilities).

Basic Oscilloscopes and Their Circuits

The two-dimensional graph drawn by an oscilloscope allows the user to measure almost anything that can be converted into a voltage. In most applications, the oscilloscope shows a graph of voltage on the vertical axis and time on the horizontal axis. This display presents far more information than is available from any other single piece of test equipment, such as frequency counters or multimeters.

The basic oscilloscope consists of four sections, as shown in *Figure 6.19*. The vertical circuitry deflects the trace in a vertical plane, the horizontal section deflects (sweeps) the trace in a horizontal plane, and the trigger section controls the starting time of each horizontal deflection. The display section is the cathode-ray tube (CRT) and its support electronics.

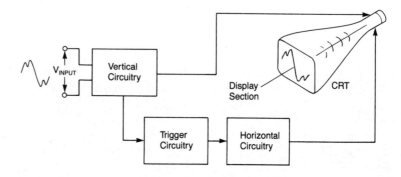

Figure 6.19 *Simplified Block Diagram of the Oscilloscope*

Display

The heart of an oscilloscope is the cathode-ray tube (CRT), illustrated in *Figure 6.20*. It is a special display vacuum tube that performs the same function as the picture tube in a television receiver. It has three main sections besides the glass envelope — the electron gun assembly, the deflection section, and the phosphor screen. The electron gun produces a sharply-focused beam of electrons which is accelerated toward the screen by a high positive voltage. When this beam hits the screen, it activates the phosphor so that a spot of light is produced on the face of the screen. This spot must be focused into a fine dot to obtain a sharply-defined waveform on the screen. The Intensity control on the front panel controls the voltage between the cathode and the first grid or control electrode, adjusting the brightness of the trace.

The focusing of the oscilloscope's electron beam on the CRT screen is accomplished by a combination of three electron lenses. The focus control is the primary focus adjustment to cause a very small dot to appear on the screen. The astigmatism control is the secondary focus control and it mainly adjusts the roundness of the spot.

After the electron beam leaves the electron gun, it passes between the vertical deflection plates and then the horizontal deflection plates. If the voltage between both pairs of the deflection plates is zero, then the electron beam would pass straight through and strike the center of the oscilloscope screen.

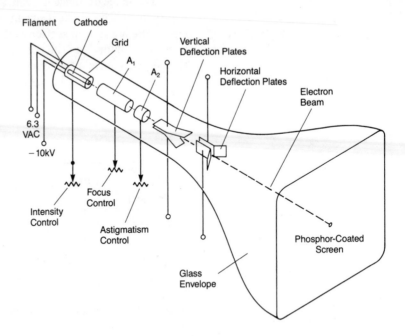

Figure 6.20 Internal Construction of a Cathode-Ray Tube

However, when one plate of a pair has a positive potential with respect to the other, the electrons in the beam are attracted towards the positive plate. This causes the beam to bend toward the positive plate and the spot appears on the screen away from center.

Most oscilloscopes have a grid pattern called the graticule, that is etched into the outside face of the CRT, or is a separate plastic overlay that fastens over the face of the CRT. The graticule is used to make amplitude and time measurements on a displayed waveform.

Vertical

The vertical drive for the graph on the CRT is supplied by the vertical deflection amplifiers. The vertical system takes the input from a jack on the front of the oscilloscope and develops differential outputs. The input coupling switch for the vertical channels allows selection of either ac or dc coupling.

The vertical deflection system must meet strict specification requirements. It must faithfully reproduce the signal that is applied to the input on the screen, maintaining frequency bandwidth, rise time, amplitude, and harmonic content. A block diagram of the vertical deflection system is shown in *Figure 6.21* (light blocks).

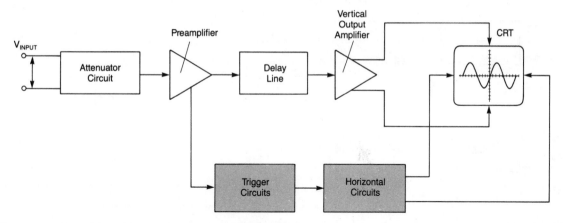

Figure 6.21   Block Diagram of a Vertical Deflection System

The vertical attenuator consists of a number of resistance and capacitance voltage dividers that are controlled by the Volts/Div switch. These voltage dividers usually allow for selection of vertical deflection factors in the 1-2-5 sequence. For example, the voltage ranges might be 0.1, 0.2, 0.5, 1, 2, 5, 10, etc., volts per division. A multi-purpose oscilloscope, or laboratory oscilloscope, is capable of accurately displaying signal levels from millivolts to many volts.

To make voltage measurements, the vertical deflection must be calibrated. Calibration is accomplished by applying to the vertical input an internally generated sine or square wave of a known voltage. A calibration control, often a screwdriver adjustment accessible at the front panel, is adjusted until the known voltage is accurately indicated on the CRT. The appropriate control located in the center of the Volts/Div switch must be set to calibrate when the calibration is performed and when accurate amplitude measurements are to be made. At other times, the variable control provides continuously variable change in the scale factor between each range of the Volts/Div settings. The variable Volts/Div and the vertical step attenuator (Volts/Div rotary switch) may be considered as fine and coarse attenuators, respectively.

Oscilloscopes are much more useful if they have two separate vertical channels. Dual beam and dual trace are two techniques employed to obtain multi-trace images on the screen. Dual beam CRTs have two separate electron guns, thus, they are more expensive to manufacture. In the dual trace oscilloscope, a CRT with a single electron gun is used, with the two or more channels being alternately connected at a rapid rate to the final vertical amplifier by an electronic switch. *Figure 6.22* shows a technique for obtaining dual trace.

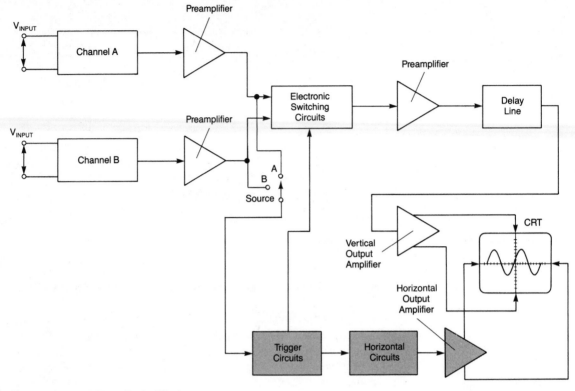

Figure 6.22 Dual Trace Vertical System

The oscilloscope may operate either in Alternate mode or in Chopped mode for dual trace display. In the Alternate mode, the electronic switch alternately connects its inputs from the output of the Channel A preamplifier and the Channel B preamplifier to the main vertical amplifier. The switching takes place between each sweep of the horizontal circuit, thus, the switching rate of the electronic switch is synchronized to the horizontal sweep rate. The CRT spot traces Channel A on one sweep, Channel B signal on the next sweep, Channel A on the next sweep, etc.

In the Chopped mode of operation, the electronic switch switches at a rate of several hundred kHz and is independent of the horizontal sweep rate. In this mode, the switch successively connects Channel A and Channel B waveforms to the main vertical amplifier, chopping very rapidly many times during each sweep. This allows small segments of each channel signal to be fed to the main vertical amplifier, so that both signals are displayed during the same sweep. An advantage of the chopped mode over the alternate mode is the elimination of display delay between the two vertical signals. This is important when measuring time delays. A disadvantage is that the chopped method limits the upper frequency of the signal displayed to a fraction of the switching frequency.

Other modes of operation are available, too. Many oscilloscopes are provided with an Add mode of operation in the vertical section. In this mode, the Channel A and Channel B signals are algebraically combined and their sum displayed as a single waveform on the screen of the oscilloscope. Some oscilloscopes also have a polarity inversion switch on one or both of the vertical channels.

Many times the leading or falling edge of a waveform is used to activate the trigger circuit and start the trace sweep. A delay line is inserted into the vertical deflection channel to delay the signal that is applied to the vertical input so it reaches the vertical deflection plates at a slightly later time than it would otherwise. The time that the vertical signal is delayed is sufficient to allow the trigger and horizontal circuits to begin operation. In this way, the leading edge of the waveform can be seen even though it was used to trigger the horizontal sweep. If the delay line were not used, only the portion of the waveform following the trigger point could be seen.

Horizontal

To draw a time graph, the oscilloscope must have a horizontal deflection voltage which sweeps the dot across the screen from left to right with a constant and known velocity. When it reaches the right-hand side, the deflection voltage must return the beam rapidly to the starting position on the left-hand side of the screen, ready for the next sweep. This is accomplished by the horizontal deflection section (light blocks) as shown in *Figure 6.23*. The long, upward-sloping portion of the ramp waveform (ramp) sweeps the beam from left to right, and the short, downward sloping portion (retrace) returns the beam to the left.

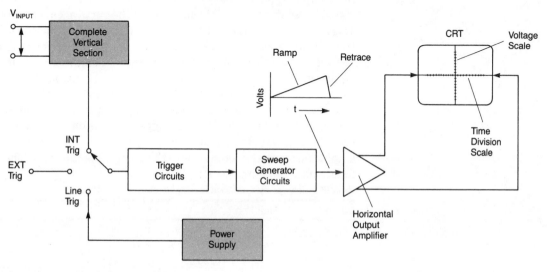

Figure 6.23   Horizontal Deflection System

The ramp voltage waveform produced by the sweep generator is initiated by the trigger circuit. If the ramp is linear, as it is in good quality oscilloscopes, the horizontal beam movement can be calibrated directly in units of time, making it possible to measure time between events. Because it is calibrated in time, the sweep generator is often called a time base generator. The sweep speed is determined by the Time/Div selector switch and a variable sweep speed control. The variable control must be in the Cal position for accurate time measurements. The ramp voltage is fed to the horizontal deflection amplifier, which drives the horizontal deflection plates to sweep the electron beam across the CRT screen.

Trigger System

The trigger circuits interface with the vertical section and the horizontal section as shown in *Figure 6.23*. The display section draws the waveform on the screen under control of the vertical section which supplies the signal that moves the trace up and down, and the horizontal section which provides the left-to-right sweep in the form of a time axis. The trigger circuit, which is usually controlled by the input signal to the vertical axis, determines when the left-to-right movement of the electron beam begins. If each sweep of the time base did not begin at the same relative point on the signal being displayed, the display on the screen would jitter and jump, or would be meaningless, cluttered lines. The trigger controls allow adjustment of the trigger point to achieve a stable display of the desired portion of the waveform.

The controls located in the trigger section include the Trigger Source switch, the Coupling control, the Trigger Slope control and the Level control. The Trigger Source switch selects the particular signal that determines the triggering point. This signal is usually obtained from either of the vertical channel (Int Trig), an external signal connected to a trigger input jack on the front of the oscilloscope (Ext Trig), or a sample of the power line voltage (Line Trig). The precise trigger point on the waveform is determined by the Slope control and the Level control. The Coupling control determines if an external triggering source is to be directly coupled or with dc blocked by a capacitor. The Slope control determines whether the trigger point is on the rising or the falling edge of the signal. The Level control determines the amplitude along that edge where the trigger point occurs. These functions are summarized in *Table 6.1*.

Table 6.1   Trigger Functions in Normal or Automatic Mode

Control	Function
Trigger Source	Selects signal to be used as trigger point.
Coupling	Direct or capacitor coupling of external trigger source.
Trigger Slope	Trigger point used from rising or falling edge.
Level	At what point on the edge of the signal will be the triggering threshold.

With all the combinations possible by setting the trigger switches, the trigger circuit can operate in two modes. The Normal mode is the most useful because it handles a wider range of trigger signals than the other triggering mode. A disadvantage of the Normal mode is that it does not permit a trace to be drawn on the screen if there is no trigger; for example, when no vertical input is applied or when the vertical input is only dc. The Automatic mode overcomes this disadvantage. After each sweep, a trigger is automatically generated again and the time base is automatically retriggered. In this mode, there will always be a trace on the screen. The position of the trace can be adjusted with the vertical and horizontal position controls.

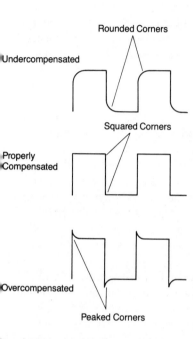

Figure 6.24 Oscilloscope Test Probe Compensation

Probes

The vertical input terminals of the oscilloscope are connected to the circuit under test via a probe. The multitude of probes available can generally be divided into two classes — current probes and voltage probes. For most applications, the probes which come with the oscilloscope are voltage probes and are usually the passive-attenuator type. These probes attenuate the signal applied to the vertical input from the circuit under test by 10 times. For example, if the circuit voltage is 10 volts, the input to the vertical amplifier is one volt. In voltmeter measurement applications, connecting a probe to a circuit can produce loading. The use of an attenuator probe greatly reduces this loading.

The standard way of adjusting or compensating a probe is to connect a square wave to the oscilloscope and adjust the probe's compensation adjustment so that the square wave's leading edge corner is square — not rounded-off or peaked. Improperly and properly-compensated probes will produce the results shown in *Figure 6.24.*

Triggered Oscilloscope Operation

The two basic measurements made with an oscilloscope are voltage amplitude and time between events. Almost every other measurement is based on these fundamental ones.

Measurements of amplitude and time are more accurate when the signal covers a large area of the screen because the resolution is improved. To make an amplitude measurement, connect the probe to the input of one of the vertical channels. Set all the variable controls to their calibrated position, which is usually a detent in the rotation of the knob. Connect the probe to the oscilloscope's test signal output, and, if necessary, adjust the probe compensation and the vertical amplifier calibration.

Connect the probe to the circuit under test. Set the Trigger Source switch to Internal for the particular vertical channel where the signal to be displayed is connected. Adjust the Trigger Level control to obtain a stable trace of the waveform, and adjust the Volts/Div switch and the Time/Div switch until the waveform, or the portion of the waveform of interest, covers as large an area of the screen as possible. Use the vertical and horizontal position controls to position the waveform as necessary. For amplitude measurement, count major and minor divisions on the center verticle graticule line, and multiply the number of divisions by the Volts/Div setting for time measurement, count major and minor divisions across the center horizontal graticule line between the points of interest, and multiply the number of divisions by the Time/Div setting.

Pulse measurements are very important in work done with digital and data communications equipment. Some of the important points of pulse measurement are shown in *Figure 6.25*. Three fundamental measurements of the pulse are rise time, pulse width, and pulse repetition time. These parameters are shown in the figure, as well as the other parameters of overshoot, ringing, and tilt.

The phase relationship between two or more waveforms having the same frequency may be measured on the oscilloscope. There are two common methods to measure phase shift. One way is to put one waveform on each channel of a dual channel oscilloscope. Set the mode switch to chopped, and set the sweep trigger for the channel that is displaying the waveform that is to be the reference. Increase the sweep speed until the maximum horizontal distance that can be viewed occurs between corresponding points on the two waveforms.

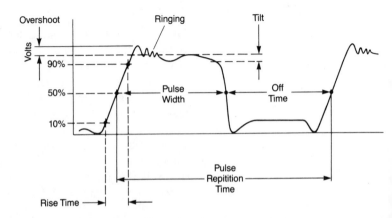

Figure 6.25 *Measurement of Typical Pulse Waveform Parameters*

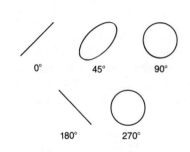

a. Typical Phase Shift Patterns for Various Angular Differences

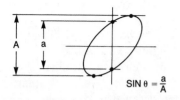

$$SIN\ \theta = \frac{a}{A}$$

b. Mathematical Relationship Between Pattern and Phase Angle

Figure 6.26 Phase Measurements with Lissajous Patterns

The phase shift is the difference in time between the two corresponding points, divided by the period of the waveform displayed, and multiplied by 360 to give degrees. Any dual trace oscilloscope permits this method of measuring phase. Some oscilloscopes have special circuits (discussed later) that allow the delay to be measured much more accurately and the delay is read directly frtely and the delay is read directly from calibrated controls.

The other way to measure phase shift (of sinusoidal signals only) involves using a Lissajous pattern. This is a very common application of the X-Y mode of operation. To make any phase measurement between sinusoidal signals, the signals must be of the same frequency or of perfect multiples. *Figure 6.26* shows a display of phase shift patterns and the X-Y technique for phase measurements.

The X-Y function of the oscilloscope may be used to advantage any time there are two physical quantities that are interdependent and not time dependent. Examples include motor speed versus torque, and plotting the current-to-voltage relationships between electronic devices. To make X-Y measurements, the oscilloscope's horizontal amplifier must be connected to an external input so that the time base generator and trigger circuits are bypassed. Some oscilloscopes have a separate jack on the front for external horizontal deflection. Some use the external trigger jack.

Specifications

Probably the most popular specification in advertisements of oscilloscopes is bandwidth. Bandwidth is the range of frequencies between the lowest and highest frequency at which an oscilloscope can display a sine wave with a 30 percent (maximum) reduction in signal amplitude. Since most oscilloscopes have a response to dc, bandwidth usually refers to the highest frequency that can be displayed with a 3dB maximum error. Most oscilloscopes have a gradual rolloff in response at the high-frequency end. This means that an oscilloscope may be useful far beyond its stated bandwidth, but for monitoring only, not for accurate measuring.

Another important specification is the rise time of the vertical amplifier. This specification gives an indication of how well the oscilloscope will reproduce pulse waveforms and the fastest rise time it can measure. The rise time of the oscilloscope must be faster than that of the pulse to be measured. Rise time and frequency response are closely related specifications. In the horizontal section, sweep frequency range will determine how much waveform detail can be displayed for high-frequency signals.

Special Features

Dual Time Base Measurements

Delayed sweep measurements are based on the use of two linearly-calibrated time bases, the delaying time base and delayed sweep. The delaying time base allows the operator to select a specific delay time. When this time has lapsed, the delayed sweep starts. The delayed sweep is typically a decade or two faster than the delaying time base and offers additional horizontal expansion or resolution. The combination of these two sweeps offers additional flexibility and increased accuracy of time interval measurements of complex waveforms. Small time intervals within a larger waveform are expanded. The principle of operation is shown in *Figure 6.27*.

Storage

Two major types of storage methods are available — CRT and digital. CRT storage is made possible by special cathode-ray tubes that have the ability to retain and display a waveform on their tube face long after the waveform ceases to exist. Popular types of CRT storage are variable persistance and bistable.

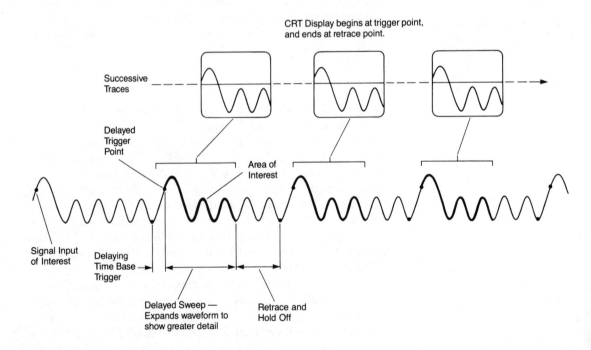

Figure 6.27   Dual Time Base Display

In a digital storage oscilloscope, input signals are sampled and the samples are stored in a digital memory. The stored samples are recalled from memory to reconstruct the original waveform for display. A digital-to-analog converter takes the signal from the memory and converts it to analog voltages capable of driving the CRT vertical deflection system. The memory is scanned several times per second. Thus, before the display on the screen fades out, it is constantly being renewed (refreshed) by the data stored in memory. The trigger point is only a reference, and it is possible to view the signal before the trigger. This allows for both post-triggered and pre-triggered viewing.

FREQUENCY GENERATORS

Signal generators have been designed for every frequency requirement of electronic equipment. Included in this broad spectrum are signal sources from the subsonic through the microwave frequencies, and now even laser signal sources. This section is limited to the more common devices, however.

Audio Generator

The audio generator usually produces sine waves and square and sometimes triangular waves. A typical audio generator has a calibrated output attenuator to control output signal level. A variable control in conjunction with a step control varies the output frequency over the range of frequencies from below 20Hz to about 20kHz, although some may range as high as 100kHz. Audio signal generators generally have an output impedance of 600 ohms. In addition, special features include a dc offset adjustment, and voltage-controlled frequency and voltage-controlled amplitude inputs.

A pulse, as measured on a cathode-ray oscilloscope, is shown in *Figure 6.25*. Fundamentally, the difference between a pulse generator and a square wave generator is that the pulse generator has a variable duty cycle. (Duty cycle is the ratio of on time to on + off time.)

RF Generator

As a group, RF signal generators produce output frequencies from just above the audio range through the top of the UHF band (3000MHz). However, any specific generator covers only a portion of this spectrum. The output may be a sine wave, or a complex wave rich in harmonics. Most RF generators have a provision for modulating the output with an audio signal, originating internally or from an external source. Output impedance is usually 50 ohms.

Frequency Synthesizers

A new type of signal generator that has become very popular in the last few years is shown in *Figure 6.28*. This highly versatile, programmable signal generator has applications in a very wide variety of automated systems. Frequency synthesizers permit fast, accurate frequency switching from either local or remote programmable control.

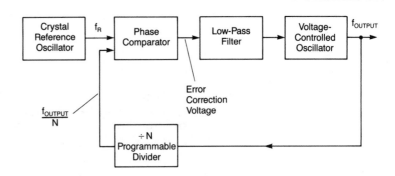

Figure 6.28 Basic Frequency Synthesizer

Sweep Generators

A sweep generator is used with an oscilloscope to give a visual representation of the frequency response of a tuned circuit. For years, it has been the standard instrument employed in aligning tuned circuits in wideband applications, such as the intermediate frequency amplifiers of television receivers. The sweep frequency generator supplies an FM signal, with a center frequency and deviation that may be adjusted by controls on the front panel. The center frequency is usually frequency modulated by 60Hz from the power line or from a low frequency audio oscillator inside the sweep generator. The amplitude of this sweep voltage determines the amount of deviation from the center frequency, known as sweep width. An accurately calibrated RF marker generator is used in conjunction with the sweep generator to identify frequency points on the response curve. (See *Figure 6.29*.)

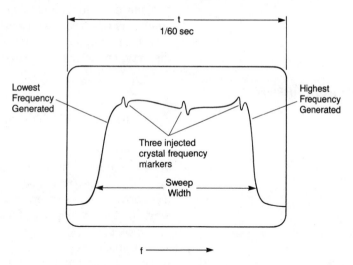

CRT display curve also is used to show the response of a
circuit under test for a band of frequencies.

Figure 6.29   *Oscilloscope Display from a Sweep Generator*

INSTRUMENTS FOR ANALYZING ELECTRONIC SIGNALS

Analyzing electronic signals, primarily in the frequency domain,
is an important measurement concept. A complex wave, or
distorted waveform, consists of multiple sinusoidal frequencies,
each harmonically related. A wave analyzer performs the function
of a frequency-selective voltmeter, which may be tuned to each
frequency independently, thereby measuring the amplitude of
one signal component while all other frequencies are rejected.
The frequency-selective bandwidth of a wave analyzer is very
narrow, usually somewhere in the range of one percent of the
frequency selected.

Harmonic Distortion Analyzer

Harmonic distortion is one of the five types of distortion created
in communications equipment, including audio and ultrasonic
sound systems. Non-linear transfer functions in amplifiers
generate harmonically-related frequencies from a pure,
fundamental tone stimulus. The ratio of these harmonic
frequency components to the amplitude of the fundamental is
called total harmonic distortion (THD). It's generally given in
percent.

A harmonic distortion analyzer consists of a narrow-band
rejection filter and a broad-band detector. Measurement consists
of two steps: First, the meter is set to 100 percent with the total
signal input. Then the rejection filter is switched into the circuit

to remove the fundamental so only the harmonic and noise content of the signal is measured. The ratio of the two measurements is a close approximation of the total harmonic distortion which can be read directly from the meter in percent.

Spectrum Analyzers

Spectrum analysis is the study of energy distribution across the frequency spectrum of a given electrical wave. The spectrum analyzer is an instrument that graphically plots amplitude versus frequency from a selected portion of a frequency band. A heterodyne spectrum analyzer consists of two instruments — a superheterodyne receiver and a CRT oscilloscope. A simplified block diagram of a basic spectrum analyzer is shown in *Figure 6.30*.

A modern spectrum analyzer is an extremely sophisticated instrument, and may include such operator-convenience features as digital display, store and recall of control settings, automatic zoom-in, and track functions. All of these may be controlled by a microprocessor system, which is programmable via the IEEE-488 BUS from a remotely-located computer. The 488 BUS is an interconnection bus standardized by the Institute of Electrical and Electronics Engineers for interfacing various test instruments or test equipment. Conforming to the 488 BUS standard makes it easy to connect equipment together.

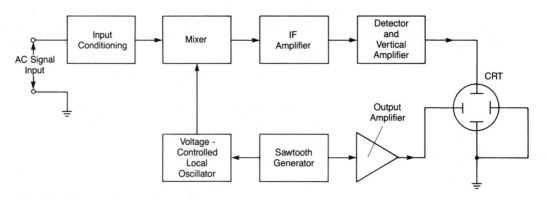

Figure 6.30   Block Diagram of a Basic Spectrum Analyzer

Frequency Counter

A frequency counter is an instrument designed to measure the number of events per unit of time, such as sinusoidal frequency or pulse period. It makes its measurement by comparing the unknown frequency or time interval to a known frequency or time interval which is generated by the instrument's circuitry.

With faster and faster digital circuits appearing throughout the electronics industry, time interval measurement techniques with a high degree of resolution become increasingly useful. When applications require a large number of frequency or time measurements involving many changes of the front panel settings, a universal frequency counter with IEEE-488 capability is desirable.

SEMICONDUCTOR COMPONENT TESTING

The category of instruments included in this section may be divided into the quick-check, service-type tester and the laboratory-quality semiconductor tester. Most of the fast go/no-go in-circuit semiconductor testers are designed to detect only major defects rather than make quantitative measurements. Instead of actually measuring the value of resistance, the scale is usually marked off in red, yellow, and green which indicate bad, questionable, and good.

Dynamic Transistor Tester

Transistor testers have evolved from a simple conduction tester, which was little more than an ohmmeter with a socket to plug in the transistor, to very sophisticated laboratory-quality transistor testers which perform many tests on many different kinds of devices under dynamic operating conditions. These make it possible to collect a full range of accurate test data on the semiconductor device parameters.

Curve Tracers and Plotters

A curve tracer draws a graph of one parameter of a device and how it varies when another parameter changes. For example, the input voltage (or current) and output voltage (or current) may be easily plotted on the screen of the CRT. This instrument has been used for many years in the research laboratory, but current technology has made possible the reasonably-priced service bench version.

Curve tracers come in two basic forms: as complete units or as adapters. *Figure 6.31* shows a functional block diagram of a complete curve tracer. The portion of the figure to the right of the dashed line may be replaced by a simple oscilloscope. If so, the portion on the left would be replaced by a curve tracer adapter, greatly reducing the cost of the instrument. For the small shop, experimenter, or infrequent user, this often represents the most economical way to own a curve tracer.

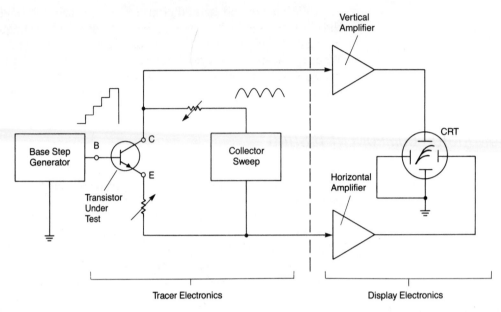

Figure 6.31 **Block Diagram of a Transistor Curve Tracer**

IC Testers

Measurement problems in digital circuits are quite different from those in analog circuits. One of the most popular devices used for troubleshooting digital integrated circuits is the logic probe. The simplest has a single lamp that indicates the logic states by being either full on, full off, or dimly lit. Another type has two or three different colored indicator lamps to indicate the logic states. Either type quickly indicates the logic state of a particular pin on an integrated circuit.

Another very useful digital test probe is the logic pulser. It injects a single pulse of proper amplitude and polarity into a circuit at a particular point. Its purpose is to drive a low-to-a-high or a high-to-a-low state. This is useful for forcing the inputs of integrated circuits to change states, so that the outputs may be observed with a logic probe. Some pulsers can also inject pulse trains.

The family of probes may be completed by the addition of a current tracer probe. Its purpose is to locate very low-impedance faults to check current sources and current sinks on a printed circuit board. It functions by sensing the magnetic fields produced by fast-rise-time pulses produced by the logic pulser.

Another useful tester for digital integrated circuits, the logic clip, is easy to use and very handy. It clips on a TTL or CMOS IC and lets the user observe the logic state of up to 16 pins of an integrated circuit at once.

Logic probes have memory functions that allow them to capture noise spikes (glitches). The most commonly provided features are: (1) high/low pulse identification; (2) pulse train identification; and (3) stretching capability for short pulses.

Logic Analyzers

For digital circuit testing, the logic analyzer has assumed a role similar to that of the oscilloscope for analog circuit testing. Like the oscilloscope, it is a highly flexible instrument that can be connected to many circuit points relatively easily, and provides a clear visual display for the operator. Modern logic analyzers put modular data acquisition and pattern generation into a single mainframe, with flexibility and analytic power not possible earlier.

TEST PROBES

Test probes and test leads are much more than the point of interface between the circuit under test and the test equipment. When a circuit is probed to take measurements, the test probe and leads become a part of both circuits simultaneously. Probes and leads are the external part of the test equipment's internal circuitry. Therefore, they must be matched to the test apparatus input network for such parameters as impedance and frequency response. Any probe/lead set should accurately transfer a sample of the signal or voltage, with a minimum of interference to the circuit under test. The sample should be applied to the input network of the test apparatus in a form that can be accurately measured.

Each piece of test equipment has its own set of probes designed for specific applications. Give careful consideration to using the proper probes and leads to ensure accuracy and to avoid damaging equipment. Never indiscriminantly interchange test lead/probe sets between different models of test equipment. Some of the common types of probes are discussed in the following paragraphs.

General Purpose

The general purpose probe allows the test equipment to perform within its rated frequency and voltage range. It often contains a passive attenuator circuit which decreases circuit loading, while reducing the signal reaching the test instrument's input.

High Voltage

The high voltage probe has a very high resistance internal series resistor and extra-high voltage molded insulator body to permit the voltage measuring device to safely and accurately read voltages up to 50kV.

Demodulator

The demodulator probe has an internal diode and frequency compensation network to allow the modulation component of an RF signal to be viewed on an oscilloscope. The RF signal frequency may even be well above the frequency limit of the oscilloscope. Similar probes are also used for voltmeters.

Since tuned circuits are easily detuned by any probe connection, special precautions must be taken to ensure the least loading effect, such as using a low capacitance capacitor in series with the probe. This so-called loose coupling method serves to isolate the probe from the circuit under test.

Low Capacitance

The low capacitance probe is used to measure ac in circuits where a general purpose probe would load the circuit too much. This type of probe has a low-value internal capacitor in series with the probe tip, along with a small network of frequency-compensation components. The connecting test lead is a low capacitance shielded-type cable.

Cables

The test probe cabling must meet the appropriate requirements for breakdown voltage, distributed capacitance, and shielding. For high voltage measurements, most of the voltage is dropped across the high voltage probe's internal resistor, leaving only voltages in the hundreds range to be applied to the cable conductor. Thus, voltages are quite reasonable between the inner conductor and the shield. Of course, high frequency attenuation is most pronounced with high values of cable capacitance. This affects both RF and pulse measurements.

Grounding

Whenever circuit measurements are made, the test equipment common lead must be connected to the correct point in the circuit under test to provide a return. If the common lead is connected to the test equipment chassis ground, which in turn, is connected to the power line ground, the operation of the circuit under test may be altered, or worse, the circuit may be damaged. Each case must be considered before connecting the common lead.

Caution: Before connecting the ground lead to the circuit under test, make sure the circuit is not operated directly from the ac power line, but is powered through a transformer!

Wherever high frequencies or low signal levels are involved, and shielded cable is used, the ground lead pigtail should be kept very short.

DATA COMMUNICATIONS TESTS AND MEASUREMENTS

Troubleshooting a data communications network used to be an awesome task. The situation usually included several technicians working with room-sized test sets, trying to make sense out of many knobs, switches, flashing neon lights, and a maze of connecting cables tapping the data communications network. Today, most tests can be made with a small portable unit.

Breakout Box

Probably the most fundamental tool available to isolate problems in a data communications system is the breakout box. It is a hand-held device inserted in a data communications link between two devices. It is low-priced and highly portable. The unit allows the user to determine the status of all data, control, and clock signals on the data communications link, at the interface or port.

Bit Error Rate Tester

The bit error rate test (BERT) involves generating a known data sequence into the transmitting modem, observing the received sequence at the distant modem and evaluating that sequence for errors. The bit error rate is expressed as a ratio of bits received in error, to the overall bits sent. This is an indication of the overall link performance.

Data Transmission Test Sets

A data transmission test set is a high-performance service instrument that provides the service technician with the means to locate problems in a data communications network that elude even the BERT. Although it usually contains a BERT, it also contains built-in diagnostic routines with a keypad entry on the front panel, and a programmable mode that allows for automatic transmission, reception, and examination of data. Provision for storing the data is also included in these test sets. It may be used to monitor, analyze, test, and troubleshoot data communications interfaces, as well as operate as a serial data transmission monitor. It can also function as a modem simulator for off-line testing of the data terminal equipment (DTE).

In this chapter, we have learned that most analog meters use the D'Arsonval-type, moving coil milliammeter or microammeter movement as the indicating device, whether the input signal is dc, ac, or RF. Series and/or parallel resistor circuits are used directly with the meter movement so that only a fixed percentage (sampling) of the true current or voltage in the circuit under test is presented to the meter movement itself. Other circuit configurations are used ahead of the resistor circuitry to allow the dc meter to measure ac, audio, and RF, and to decrease circuit loading. These configurations include the use of rectifiers, op amps, and compensation networks. The accuracy of any reading is greatly reduced if the measuring device loads the circuit under test.

Bridge circuits are widely used for measurement because of their great accuracy. They have virtually no loading effect on the circuit under test, and make a measurement by comparing the unknown quantity to a precision standard.

The oscilloscope, which is the most versatile single piece of test equipment for analog circuits, displays fixed or changing voltages on a CRT in real time. By plotting the input voltage against a predetermined time base, accurate measurements of voltage (amplitude) and time are possible, as well as overall waveform interpretations.

A wide variety of frequency generators are available for injecting the appropriate ac signal into circuits and electronic devices. The outputs of these circuits are fed into electronic analysis equipment, which presents information as to how the injected signals have been changed.

Semiconductor components are tested by connecting them to test equipment that approximately simulates operating conditions. The performance parameters of the component are presented via a meter reading or oscilloscope-type display.

Nearly all test equipment uses test probes to sample the signal or voltage. Probes are a very critical part of the test instrument, since they simultaneously interface with the circuit under test and with the test device input. There are a wide variety of probe types. Some are limited to very specialized purposes, making possible types of measurements not otherwise within the design of the test instrument.

The field of data communications, which has been undergoing an explosive technological growth, had outgrown the test equipment available to service it. That has now changed, and some compact and sophisticated test equipment can be purchased. Microelectronics test equipment is available to accurately and efficiently troubleshoot almost any equipment or software failure in the digital and computer fields.

CHAPTER 6 QUIZ

1. The meter movement most commonly used in measurements is the:
   a. dynamometer.
   b. D'Arsonval.
   c. electrostatic.
   d. iron vane.

2. To increase the current measurement of a basic meter, use a:
   a. divider.
   b. adder.
   c. multiplier.
   d. shunt.

3. When a meter movement is used as a voltmeter, a resistor is connected:
   a. in series.
   b. in parallel.
   c. across it.
   d. as a shunt.

4. The ohms-per-volt rating refers to a _____ test instrument specification.
   a. voltmeter
   b. wattmeter
   c. ammeter
   d. ohmmeter

5. An Ayrton shunt has the advantage of:
   a. less resistance.
   b. a lower cost switch.
   c. faster operation.
   d. cooler operation.

6. Before resistance is measured with a VOM:
   a. send it in for calibration.
   b. adjust voltage Cal.
   c. adjust zero ohms.
   d. adjust line voltage.

7. The loading effect of a voltmeter results from:
   a. drawing current from the circuit.
   b. adding a series resistance.
   c. too high a range.
   d. none of these.

8. To measure the ac component only of a voltage with a VOM, use the:
   a. Output function. +
   b. Ohms function.
   c. Input function. —TO GRd
   d. DC Volts.

9. The 0dBm reference on a VOM is:
   a. 1 milliwatt and 600 ohms.
   b. 0 milliwatts and 500 ohms.
   c. 0 volts and 600 ohms.
   d. 1 volt and 500 ohms.

10. The input resistance of an electronic voltmeter:
    a. is low.
    b. is constant.
    c. changes with the range.
    d. is 600 ohms.

11. When the Wheatstone bridge is balanced, there is no current through the:
    a. multiplier.
    b. ratio arm.
    c. battery.
    d. galvanometer.

12. The purpose of the sweep generator in an oscilloscope is to:
    a. vary the gain.
    b. move the beam vertically.
    c. sync the vertical.
    d. move the beam horizontally.

13. The horizontal axis of an oscilloscope represents:
    a. voltage.
    b. time.
    c. current.
    d. power.

14. To measure phase with an oscilloscope, the X-Y method makes use of a:
    a. linear sweep.
    b. time base.
    c. cross-hatch pattern.
    d. Lissajous pattern.

15. Triggering of the sweep generator when in the X-Y mode is:
a. not used.
b. external.
c. internal.
d. line.

16. The variable resistance component that varies the voltage between the cathode and the grid of a CRT is:
a. vertical position.
b. focus.
c. intensity.
d. trigger level.

17. When an oscilloscope has a dual trace feature, it is alternate or:
a. chopped.
b. split.
c. delayed.
d. added.

18. The curve tracer is an application of the oscilloscope to display:
a. transistor characteristics.
b. modulation patterns.
c. time waveforms.
d. reflection waveforms.

19. When an oscilloscope displays individual frequency components, is it called a:
a. laboratory scope.
b. spectrum analyzer.
c. vector scope.
d. radar scope.

20. A programmable signal generator available today is a:
a. frequency counter.
b. function generator.
c. sweep generator.
d. frequency synthesizer.

AUDIO, RADIO AND TELEVISION TROUBLESHOOTING

INTRODUCTION

An electronic system is an arrangement of circuits made up of components connected together to perform a particular function. Each component in the circuit has a part to play in the operation of the system. Since they are interdependent, the failure of any component can drastically change the overall operation. To understand the impact of a component failure, one must have a comprehensive understanding of the operational characteristics of the equipment.

In this chapter, we will provide an overview of servicing through examples. Nearly all of the circuit concepts have been covered in other chapters and the reader should already have some familiarity with them; therefore, the emphasis here will be on cause-and-effect analysis. However, this chapter is not intended to be a reference on servicing however, which would require at least a volume in itself.

Initially, a logical way to analyze complete systems is introduced. Then some transistor circuits are analyzed in detail, to show how defective components may be located by the effect they have on the voltage levels. Then servicing techniques for audio, radio receivers, transceivers, commercial two-way radio, and television receivers are covered. This is followed by an analysis of the procedures involved in actually making the repair. Finally, the supplies needed to perform repairs are addressed, and the chapter ends with some safety precautions.

ELECTRONIC SYSTEM TROUBLESHOOTING

A Logical Procedure

Skillful troubleshooting requires knowledge of circuit theory and circuit operation. Of course, practical experience helps too. A systematic and logical approach must be followed to effectively troubleshoot any electronic system. To do otherwise will most assuredly result in much wasted time, as well as the possibility of doing further damage to the device.

Seasoned troubleshooters make use of "seven" senses (the basic five, plus intuition and common sense) to locate and correct the problem. Observation and correct interpretation of the symptoms provide the first clues to possible trouble areas, because it is futile to try to locate a fault that is vaguely defined. Accurately defining the fault usually means that a functional test of the equipment must be made. Knowledge of what is normal and acceptable performance, taking into account the device's age, is also important. A brief history of the problem often indicates whether the problem is a gradual deterioration or an instantaneous failure. This may be important to taking corrective action towards heading off another, similar failure.

The troubleshooting procedure should begin with visual inspection; that is, a careful examination of the equipment for clues. Burned or discolored components, loose wires or components, blown fuses, etc. are all clues, and may be shortcuts to finding the trouble before anything more sophisticated is attempted. In some cases, this may be all that's required to isolate the problem; however, most troubles will require moving on to the next procedure.

The following steps form a simple procedure to isolate the defect in the equipment:

1. Accurately identify the symptoms. This often takes only a few moments, but usually saves time and labor. Recognition of abnormal operation is important. Study of technical manuals, data sheets, and troubleshooting charts is necessary to properly understand the symptoms before attempting any trouble analysis.
2. Localize the trouble to a major function or module where possible. This is sometimes difficult because functioning units are often interrelated.
3. Isolate the trouble within the major module to the component or circuit level. Signal tracing with an oscilloscope is often the most efficient procedure to pinpoint trouble in a signal path.
4. Locate the specific fault within the unit. At this point, in addition to using an oscilloscope to check the waveforms against those in the instruction manual or schematic diagram, voltage and resistance measurements must be made to isolate the defective components. Compare these readings with the normal readings or the component values and recall the principle of operation of the circuit. Then analyze the results to determine which component is probably defective. Once it's found, do the actual repair. Usually, more effort and time is expended to find the trouble than to make the actual repair or correction.

Types of Signal Paths

The paths of signals through a piece of equipment can be categorized into one or more of six basic types which are illustrated in *Figure 7.1*. These are useful concepts to understand when performing signal tracing.

The most common is a linear path *(Figure 7.1a)*, which is analogous to a series circuit arranged so that the output of one circuit feeds the input of the following. A variation of the linear path is the meeting path *(Figure 7.1b)* where one or more signal paths come together, or a separating path *(Figure 7.1c)* where one or more signal paths branch away. A combination of separating and meeting *(Figure 7.1d)* is a path in which the stage has multi-inputs and multi-outputs. A feedback path *(Figure 7.1e)* is where the signal from one point in the circuit is returned back to a preceding point in the same circuit. A switching path *(Figure 7.1f)* contains some means of changing the path from one route to another so that it provides a different signal path for each switch position. Although *Figure 7.1f* shows switching added to the meeting path, switching may be added to any of the other path types. Throughout the rest of this chapter, wherever we discuss signal flow, refer back to these six types of signal paths, and identify the one which applies.

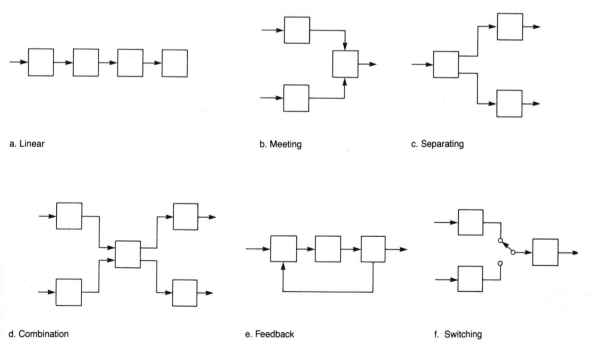

a. Linear

b. Meeting

c. Separating

d. Combination

e. Feedback

f. Switching

Figure 7.1 Six Basic Types of Signal Paths

Variations in Troubleshooting Procedures

Signal tracing of actual real-time signals is not the only technique used to isolate troubles. Signal injection (substitution) of known test signals is accomplished by injecting an appropriate signal from an external source, such as a signal generator, into the circuit or system. The injected signal is then moved from point-to-point while the system's operation is observed or certain parameters are monitored with test equipment. An inoperative stage or one with inadequate performance will be apparent.

Usually a troubleshooter relies exclusively on signal tracing or signal injection. However, a combination of the two techniques is probably the most effective where a signal is injected and an oscilloscope is used to follow its progression from stage to stage.

Sometimes voltage measurements are required, especially when a power supply distribution problem or incorrect bias voltages are suspected. Even in-circuit resistance measurements are sometimes useful.

CAUTION: Resistance measurements must be performed with all power to the device under test Off, and all power supply capacitors discharged.

BASIC SOLID-STATE TROUBLESHOOTING

Vacuum-tube equipment is becoming increasingly scarce, as almost all new electronic equipment is solid-state. Though the same basic test and trouble-locating principles apply to solid state as to other types of equipment, there are methods which are better for solid-state circuitry.

Analysis of Voltage Measurements in a Typical Transistor Circuit

Two techniques for making voltage measurements on a transistor are:
1. Directly from element-to-element of the transistor.
2. From a common reference point to each of the three elements of the transistor.

Measuring the voltages between common ground and each element is usually the most practical method. *Figures 7.2a* and *7.2b* show typical transistor stages using PNP and NPN transistors, respectively. The voltage values are measured between ground and the indicated element. Notice that the corresponding elements of *Figure 7.2a* and *7.2b* have the same voltage, but the polarities are opposite.

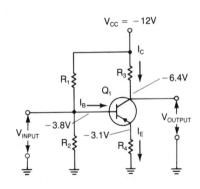

a. PNP Transistor

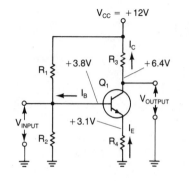

b. NPN Transistor

Figure 7.2   Class A Transistor Amplifier Operating Voltages with Ground Reference

Before considering any fault conditions, the normal operation of the circuit should be understood. Recall that in a transistor, the emitter current is equal to the collector current plus the base current.

$$I_E = I_C + I_B \qquad\qquad (7\text{-}1)$$

For transistors with high current gain, the base current is very small in comparison with the collector current, so that the collector and emitter current are almost identical. The normal condition of bias for a Class A stage is for the base-emitter junction of the transistor to be forward-biased to the Q-point and base-collector junction to be reversed-biased. The forward-biased base-emitter junction means that very small changes in the input voltage, either positive or negative, result in large changes in the emitter-collector current which is proportional to the base current. That is, if the base current is doubled (by doubling the base voltage), the much larger collector and emitter currents will also double. Thus, the output is an amplified reproduction of the input.

A linear-operating transistor amplifier is shown in *Figure 7.3*. The changing output current flowing through R_3 produces large changing voltage drops across it proportional to the changes in the input signal. The voltage drop across R_3 with no input signal should be such that it allows equal swing in voltage in a positive and negative direction. To accomplish this, the collector voltage V_C should be about half the supply voltage with no input signals.

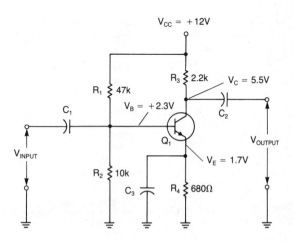

Figure 7.3   Class A Silicon Transistor Amplifier Showing Typical Voltages with Ground Reference

The values of the bias components, R_1, R_2, R_4, must be chosen so the transistor operates in its linear portion. Usually, the current through R_1 and R_2 is sufficiently larger than base current so that, with no input signal, the voltage V_B is practically constant regardless of changes in base current caused by temperature changes. V_B is the forward bias voltage between base and emitter. It is typically about 0.7 volt for a silicon transistor and about 0.2 volt for a germanium transistor.

Transistor voltages as specified in service literature are generally given from the element of the transistor to a common or ground point. As we said earlier, this is the most common method of measuring transistor voltages, although some technicians prefer to measure the transistor voltages from element-to-element to directly measure the bias at the transistor junctions. However, this latter method may load the circuit and upset the biasing voltages so that true readings are not possible. The ohms-per-volt rating of the measuring instrument used for the values given on the schematic is usually given in the service literature. The measuring instrument used should be at least as sensitive as the one listed.

The voltage across the transistor from V_C to V_E gives an indication of the current flow through the transistor. If V_C almost equals V_E, then the transistor is in saturation (hard conduction) because V_B is too high, or there is a short between the collector and emitter terminals. On the other hand, if there is a large voltage drop (approximately equal to V_{CC}), then the transistor is not conducting. This indicates either that the transistor is not forward-biased ($V_{BE} = 0$) or that the transistor is defective.

Table 7.1 shows how voltages at the elements of the transistor in the circuit shown in *Figure 7.3*, measured with respect to ground, can be used to analyze a failure in this single-stage transistor amplifier.

Table 7.1 Defective Component's Effect on Voltage Readings

Component Defect	V_B	V_E	V_C
Normal Voltages	2.3	1.7	5.5
Open R_1	0.0	0.0	12.0
Open R_2	3.3	2.6	2.7
Open R_3	0.74	0.1	0.1
Open R_4	2.4	2.0	12.0
Open C_1, C_2, C_3	2.3	1.7	5.5
Shorted C_3	0.7	0.0	0.1

Transistor Defects	V_B	V_E	V_C
Open CB Junction	0.75	0.1	12.0
Shorted CB Junction	3.0	3.0	2.3
Open EB Junction	2.3	0.0	12.0
Shorted EB Junction	0.1	0.1	12.0
Shorted CE Junction	2.3	2.5	2.5

Think of the overall circuit as a complicated series-parallel configuration, with the transistor being a tapped resistor, whose resistance can change. When R_1 is open, the current in R_2 and the base is zero. Therefore, since the transistor is cut off, both the emitter and base voltages are zero. With the transistor cut off, there is no collector current and the voltage drop across the collector load R_3 is zero, and the collector voltage itself is the same as the supply voltage, V_{CC}, or 12 volts.

If R_2 should open, the base voltage would tend to rise. The current that was flowing through R_2 now tries to flow into the base of the transistor. The base current increases to a value that saturates the transistor. The collector voltage is then almost the same as the emitter voltage (V_{CE} saturation) since the transistor conducts heavily.

If R_3 opens, the collector current is zero and any emitter current must be the same as the base current. With the small current flowing in the base emitter circuit, the small R_4 resistance value causes a small voltage drop. Thus, V_E is a small voltage with the E_B junction acting like a forward-biased diode and dropping about 0.7 volts across the junction.

The remaining circuit conditions are to be analyzed in a similar way. Open capacitors in linear circuits generally cause no change in dc voltages and can most easily be found by signal tracing with an oscilloscope. Leaky or shorted capacitors do affect dc voltage readings, however.

Testing Solid-State Devices

Transistors are very long-life, reliable components, usually lasting for the life of the system. Occasionally transistors become leaky, but for the most part, when they fail, they fail catastrophically; that is, they become open or shorted. Unlike vacuum tubes, which are subjected to heat-related factors, transistors rarely deteriorate so that their parameters change. Often transistor failure is caused by other component failures; therefore, when a defective transistor is found, it is wise to check other components in the circuit, if possible, before replacing the transistor.

In-Circuit Testing
A transistor must be forward-biased to turn it on. If forward bias is normal (greater than 0.6 to 0.7 volts dc for silicon transistors) and removing this forward bias produces no change in conduction, the transistor is probably defective. If the forward bias is removed, the transistor should turn off. One way to remove the forward bias is to connect the base to the emitter, as shown in *Figure 7.4*. This places both elements at the same potential,

removing the forward bias. A good transistor will not conduct under this condition, therefore, no voltage drop should appear across the collector load or the emitter resistor. A voltage drop across either of these components indicates current flow.

> *CAUTION: Be very careful not to short the base to the collector, which could forward bias the transistor into maximum conduction, thereby destroying it.*

The base of a transistor operated as a Class A amplifier must be capable of causing collector current to increase as well as decrease. Removing the bias (as was done above) is a way to determine if the transistor can decrease collector current, but to increase the collector current, forward bias must be increased. One way to do this is to reduce the effective value of R_1 by paralleling it with a resistor of comparable value as shown in *Figure 7.5*. If the voltage drop across the emitter or collector resistor increases, the current has increased.

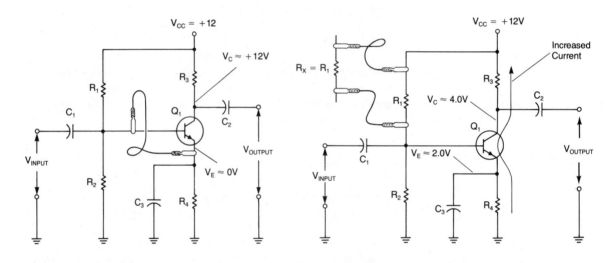

Figure 7.4 Shorting the E-B Junction Will Turn a Good Transistor Off

Figure 7.5 Increasing Forward Bias Voltage Increases Current Through E-C Circuit

Out-of-Circuit Testing

When the dc voltage measurements and the in-circuit checks indicate a possibly defective junction transistor, the suspicion can be confirmed by removing the transistor from the circuit and measuring its resistance with an ohmmeter. Consider the transistor to be electrically equivalent to two diodes with the base as a common element and measure the forward and reverse resistance of each diode with an ohmmeter. A substantial difference in resistance should be noted (at least a 50:1 ratio) when the ohmmeter leads are reversed in polarity when connected across any one diode. Although this test can be made in-circuit, the dc paths in parallel with the transistor junction when it is in the circuit affect the readings. In-circuit ohmmeter tests are valid only if all dc paths are taken into account when interpreting the readings. This is difficult to do; therefore, out-of-circuit tests are more conclusive.

The ohmmeter connections with the expected readings are shown in *Figure 7.6a* for an NPN and *Figure 7.6b* for a PNP transistor. (Note: The polarity of the ohmmeter voltage may not correspond to the marked polarity on the input of the meter. Consult the User's Manual to determine the true polarity.) The Rx1 range of the ohmmeter should not be used, because it may allow excessive current to flow through the transistor and damage it. Also, very high resistance ranges should be avoided, because they sometimes use a higher voltage internal battery, which could damage some voltage-sensitive transistors. Whatever range is chosen, it should be used for both forward and reverse measurements.

If both forward and reverse readings are very low, the transistor is shorted. If both readings are high, the transistor is open. If the readings are nearly the same value, the transistor is incapable of amplifying. Actual resistances will depend on the ohmmeter range, the ohmmeter's battery voltage, and the characteristics of the particular transistor being checked.

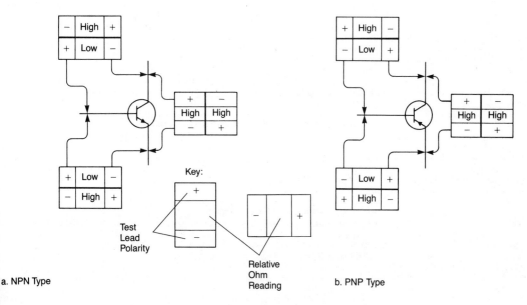

a. NPN Type

b. PNP Type

Figure 7.6 *Comparative Ohmmeter Readings When Checking Junction Transistors*

The junction field-effect transistor may be tested using an ohmmeter, as shown in *Figure 7.7.* The high resistance path of the operator's body provides the required bias, and by changing the fingertip pressure on the leads, the ohmmeter reading should change.

CAUTION: Do not use this method for testing MOSFET transistors.

Of course, transistor testers are more reliable than the ohmmeter method. A basic transistor tester tests only the dc gain and leakage parameters. Laboratory-type testers test ac gain, frequency response, and noise. Substituting a known good semiconductor into the circuit is best, since no cost-effective test method can completely duplicate operating conditions.

Silicon control rectifiers (SCRs) also may be tested with an ohmmeter also, as shown in *Figure 7.8.* They are either on or off — a very high or very low resistance. When turned on by the application of a forward bias to the gate, the resistance drops to a low value, and stays low until current from cathode to anode is stopped. The SCR then turns off and becomes a high resistance again.

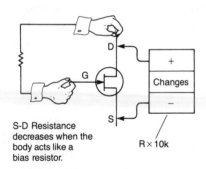

S-D Resistance decreases when the body acts like a bias resistor.

$R \times 10k$

Figure 7.7   Checking an FET with an Ohmmeter

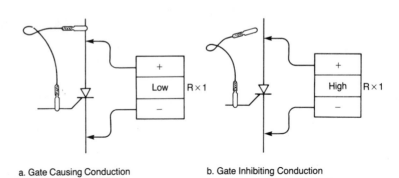

a. Gate Causing Conduction   b. Gate Inhibiting Conduction

Figure 7.8   Checking an SCR with an Ohmmeter

AUDIO EQUIPMENT TROUBLESHOOTING

Troubleshooting audio equipment involves the same approaches and procedures discussed earlier in this chapter on the transistor amplifier; that is, signal tracing, signal injecting, and voltage measurements.

Common Problems

Although many types of malfunctions occur in audio equipment, they can all be classified into one of three categories:

1. Output signal weak or nonexistent.
2. Output signal distorted.
3. Output signal contains noise.

The audio system consists of three subsystems: the intelligence or signal source, the amplifier system, and the output transducer (speaker system). The subsystems are connected together by cables and connectors, which can also be a source of trouble. In the case of a weak or non-existent output signal, if a click is heard from the speaker when the power switch is turned on and off, and/or fairly loud noise is heard with the volume turned up, the output section of the amplifier, the speakers, and the power supply can usually be ruled out as a source of trouble, at least for the moment. If a click cannot be heard, then these sections are suspect. After this preliminary test is made, either signal injection or signal tracing may be employed.

If the symptom is a weak output, then the output of each subsection should be checked with an oscilloscope while it is being injected with the proper level input signal.

CAUTION: Always make sure the amplifier output is under load — either with a speaker or a carbon resistor of a wattage rating appropriate for the amplifier output.

Distortion Measurements: Parameters and Techniques

We have already learned that there are five types of audio signal distortion: frequency, phase, harmonic, intermodulation, and transient intermodulation. A preliminary check may be made of an audio system with an audio generator and an oscilloscope, as shown in *Figure 7.9*. First, set the bass and treble controls to center position or "flat". The basic test may be made at a frequency of 1kHz with the amplifier output driven to its maximum rated value. The rms power output is determined by the following equation:

$$P_{RMS} = \frac{E_{OUTPUT}^2}{R_L} \qquad (7\text{-}1)$$

After it is determined whether or not the amplifier can produce its rated output power, the frequency distortion, better known as frequency response, may be obtained by reducing the signal until the output is at 1/10 of maximum power. Maintain the input level constant while varying the frequency of the input signal above and below 1kHz and observe (or plot) the output signal level.

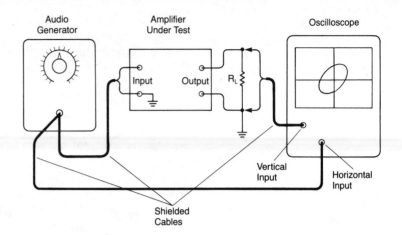

Figure 7.9 Sine Wave Test of an Audio Amplifier

To check for phase distortion, connect the oscilloscope as shown in *Figure 7.9* to produce a Lissajous pattern. Connect the vertical input terminals across the output load resistor. Connect the horizontal input terminals across the amplifier input terminals. Vary the frequency of the input signal again and note whether oscilloscope waveform pattern gives an indication of phase shift changing with respect to frequency.

Harmonic distortion may be measured with an oscilloscope, but the calculations are complex. It's much easier to measure percentage of distortion directly with a harmonic distortion meter as shown in *Figure 7.10*.

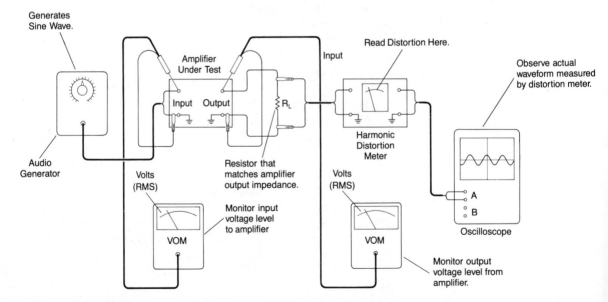

Figure 7.10 Total Harmonic Distortion Test of an Amplifier

Intermodulation distortion is related to harmonic distortion because both are caused by nonlinearities in the amplifier. An intermodulation distortion test involves a two-tone test that is most easily performed with an intermodulation distortion meter as shown in *Figure 7.11*. In this set-up, 6kHz and 60Hz signals are combined and fed into the amplifier under test. In the IM distortion meter, the presence of beat frequencies (intermodulation distortion) is detected and measured.

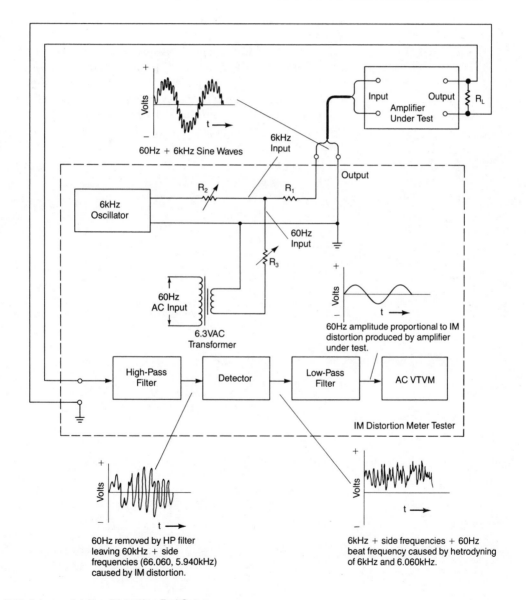

Figure 7.11   Intermodulation Distortion Test Setup

Distortion Measurements Using Square Waves

An audio system may be tested with a square wave signal to illustrate such parameters as phase response and frequency response. The square-wave method offers a simple, inexpensive, and credible technique of observing how linearly an amplifier is operating. *Figure 7.12* shows typical output waveform patterns caused by amplifier distortion with a perfect square wave applied to the input. Adjusting the bass and treble controls will greatly change the shape of the waves, because they affect amplifier response.

An interesting demonstration of the interreaction of amplifier output distortion and speaker (load) response characteristics is to monitor with an oscilloscope the square wave output of an audio amplifier driving a speaker. Carefully pressing on the speaker diaphram changes its frequency response characteristics, causing the square wave driving the speaker to also change.

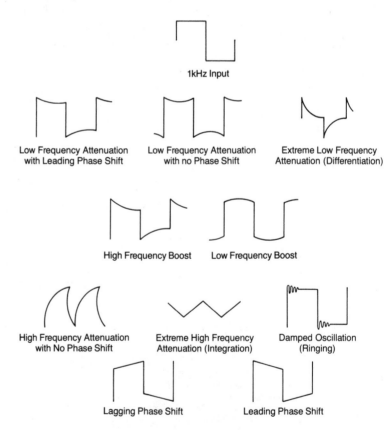

1kHz Input

Low Frequency Attenuation with Leading Phase Shift

Low Frequency Attenuation with no Phase Shift

Extreme Low Frequency Attenuation (Differentiation)

High Frequency Boost

Low Frequency Boost

High Frequency Attenuation with No Phase Shift

Extreme High Frequency Attenuation (Integration)

Damped Oscillation (Ringing)

Lagging Phase Shift

Leading Phase Shift

Figure 7.12   Square Wave Distortion Interpretation

Noise Source Tracing

Noise is any unwanted signal that appears mixed into the desired signal in an operating system. Noise is usually caused by the thermal agitation of electrons in semiconductors and resistors. Since the preamplifier sections of the amplifier systems are most-susceptible to noise-generating components, these sections are usually built with so-called low-noise components. Hum in sound equipment is usually caused by poor ground connections, faulty contacts (usually on plugs not fully seated into the jacks), or by defective filter capacitors in the power supply.

The noise quality of an audio amplifier is usually expressed as signal-to-noise ratio. This is the ratio, expressed in decibels, of the rated output power of the amplifier to the noise component of the output power. In a properly operating amplifier, the signal-to-noise ratio should be from $-50dB$ to $-80dB$, depending upon the quality of the amplifier. To accurately make this measurement, follow the test set-up and procedure recommended in the equipment's service literature.

The source of the noise may not be in the signal path at all, but in a component in the power supply. The supply could be injecting the noise throughout the system, but the earliest stages are the most susceptible, making it appear that they are the source.

To isolate the source of the noise using the oscilloscope, find the point of greatest amplitude and trace it back to its source. A complete and accurate schematic diagram of the circuit may be required.

BROADCAST RADIO RECEIVERS

The basic troubleshooting techniques are the same for all designs of radio receivers. The first step, analyzing the symptoms, is very important. Most symptoms can be classified in one of the following categories:
1. Inoperative receiver (dead or weak output)
2. Distorted output
3. Noisy output
4. Intermittent operation
5. A tuning problem, (drifting from the received station or an uncalibrated tuning dial)

AM Radio

The most common type of radio receiver design is the superheterodyne system. This receiver can be further classified into single conversion, double conversion, communications receiver, single sideband, double sideband, radio telegraphy, broadcast, citizens band, and special purpose.

The majority of AM receivers employ single conversion. *Figure 7.13* shows a single conversion AM superheterodyne of the broadcast type. If this AM receiver seems inoperative, first determine if there is any sound at all coming from the speaker. A no-output trouble symptom may or may not be accompanied by white noise (hissing noise) from the speaker when the volume control is turned to maximum. White noise is a circuit-generated noise, primarily generated in the RF sections. If noise is present, the audio sections are operating at normal gain. The RF sections are also probably operating at normal gain. The problem most likely lies in the oscillator section. This can be determined by testing it for a sine wave output with an oscilloscope or voltmeter. If the oscillator is operating properly, the next most likely cause is the RF input circuit. The closely-meshed plates of the antenna tuning capacitor could be slightly bent and shorted, or the RF antenna coil could be open.

If the receiver is completely dead (no noise coming from the speaker), first check any fuse or circuit breaker on the receiver. Then check the power supply output voltage. If it is OK, a signal injection test can be made to localize the defective stage. The "half-split" technique is usually the fastest way of locating the trouble. Be sure the volume control is turned up. The first logical point at which to inject a signal would be at the input of the audio amplifier at the volume control, and it should be an audio signal. If a tone is heard in the speaker, then the trouble lies toward the antenna. Inject an RF signal modulated with an audio tone from the signal generator at the proper frequency at the antenna.

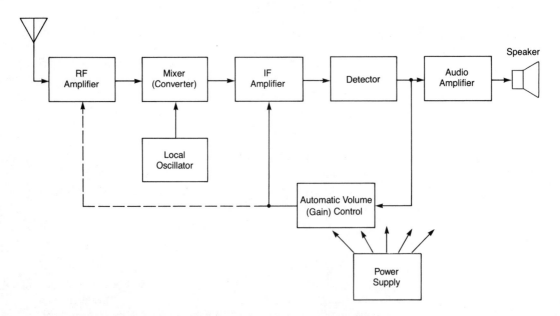

Figure 7.13   Single Conversion AM Broadcast Band Superheterodyne Radio Receiver

If there is no tone in the speaker, move the point of injection, changing the frequency as required, toward the speaker until the tone is heard in the speaker. When the defective stage has been localized, apply the techniques of troubleshooting solid state stages to isolate the trouble to one or more components.

Distortion in the output of an AM receiver can be isolated by inserting a good quality audio tone at the volume control at the proper level, and noting the output of the speaker. The output waveform can be analyzed for distortion using an oscilloscope. Clipping of the test signal is a common form of distortion and indicates an overloaded stage. Clipping before the detector section is likely to be the result of a defect in the automatic gain (volume) control (AGC/AVC). The usual cause of distortion in audio stage is improper bias levels, often caused by leaky or shorted coupling capacitors.

FM Radio

Most troubleshooting procedures applicable to AM receivers also apply to broadcast FM receivers. However, there are a few differences.

No AGC action is utilized in the IF stages of an FM receiver. Also, the last IF stage is sometimes overdriven to form a limiter stage. AGC action is usually employed only in the RF stage of the receiver.

FM radios, as well as AM/FM radios, usually make use of integrated circuits for the IF stages, the detectors and the audio. The techniques used to troubleshoot an IC unit are basically the same as those used for the transistor type. Both types of components have an input, an output, and bias voltage requirements. For example, an oscilloscope can be used to check the gain of a stage. If the oscilloscope test indicates a problem, dc voltage measurements at the IC terminal can be analyzed for deviations from normal to determine if the IC is defective or if an associated circuit component which supplies the voltage is defective.

A major difference between AM and FM receivers is the FM receiver's susceptibility to drift. This is because the local oscillator in the FM receiver operates at a much higher frequency than the AM oscillator (oscillator is at 99MHz and above), and is therefore much more unstable. AFC (automatic frequency control) circuitry produces an error voltage in proportion to the amount by which the oscillator drifts away from its correct frequency. The error voltage controls the oscillator frequency. The failure of the receiver to stay locked on the tuned station indicates a likely AFC problem.

Stereo Decoders

If the FM receiver functions properly except for no stereo separation between the left and right channel, then the trouble is probably in the stereo multiplex decoder circuit. A block diagram of an FM receiver employing a matrix stereo decoder is shown in *Figure 7.14*. Normal separation between the left and right channel may be anywhere from 20dB to 50dB, but separation less than 20dB is an indication of a trouble in the decoder. Inadequate separation is often caused by an open or shorted capacitor in the decoder circuit. A total loss of stereo effect probably indicates that the 38kHz oscillator is not functioning. If the two channels are drifting back and forth, the oscillator is not locking up with the 19kHz transmitted subcarrier.

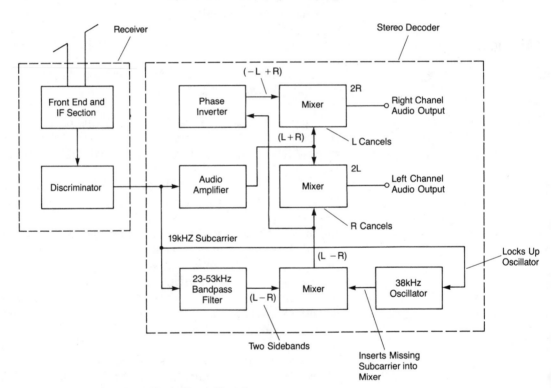

Figure 7.14   FM Receiver Employing a Matrix Stereo Decoder

CITIZENS BAND TRANSCEIVERS

Citizens band (CB) transceivers operate in the 27MHz band, are limited to a 4 watt antenna input, and are usually double sideband, although single sideband is becoming more common. The following discussions are applicable to both CB and amateur radio.

Servicing Techniques

Operating a transmitter without a load connected to it will damage the output stage. Normally the antenna is the load, but servicing requires the use of a dummy load to minimize RF radiation.

Since most CB sets operate with a 50 ohm antenna and transmission line, they require a 50 ohm dummy load. The resistor should be non-inductive (wirewound resistors have too much inherent inductance),that is, carbon or carbon composition. Lamps are often used for dummy loads for communications service work because they are inexpensive, readily available, and glow when the transmitter is on. The very popular #47 lamp, which is commonly used as a pilot lamp in many electronic instruments, provides approximately a 50 ohm impedance and the power dissipation required of a CB dummy load.

For accuracy, it is important that the RF power of the CB be measured with an RF-type wattmeter. A wattmeter should have a capability of 5 watts for a standard CB and be capable of handling up to 15 watts peak envelope power (PEP) for SSB.

A number of inexpensive test sets are available specifically for testing the performance of a CB transceiver. Most combine functions such as power output, standing wave ratio (SWR), field strength, and percent modulation. Some fairly sophisticated CB transceiver testers have many special functions incorporated which allow them to be easily connected to oscilloscopes, frequency counters, and signal generators for rapid, convenient and complete testing of the CB.

Transmitter Section Maintenance

The transmitter can be divided into three basic sections:
1. The low level frequency generation, which is generally a frequency synthesizer.
2. The driver section, which is an intermediate power amplifier.
3. The power amplifier stage, which feeds the RF signal to the antenna.

The RF signal is amplitude modulated by feeding the audio from the push-pull output transformer secondary to the collectors of the final RF power amplifier. The signal is fed from the RF power amplifier to the antenna through a low-pass pi-filter which removes harmonics that may have been generated in the driver or final amplifier stage.

Except for the higher power encountered in the driver and the final stage, the RF amplifier stages and the frequency generating circuits (frequency synthesizer) are serviced the same as in radio receivers. The manufacturer's service notes and FCC regulations should be carefully adhered to when making any tuning adjustments in the transmitter section.

Basically, the transmitter section should be checked for:
1. correct frequency.
2. power output.
3. percentage of modulation.

The percentage of modulation can be checked with a modulation meter or an oscilloscope. The modulation must not exceed 100 percent. The two popular methods for using the oscilloscope to check for percentage of modulation are the direct and the trapezoidal methods.

Receiver Section Maintenance

The receiver section of the CB transceiver is similar to an AM broadcast receiver. The major difference, other than the frequency of operation, is that dual conversion circuitry may be used.

Antenna-Related Noise Problems

Transceiver noise problems are often caused by the antenna and lead-in, or outside electrical noise sources. The CB antenna may not be performing properly because of shorts or opens in the coaxial cable lead-in or the antenna loading coil. Open or corroded connections, or broken shielding where the lead-in connects to the antenna is also a common cause of noise or poor performance.

The SWR (standing wave ratio) meter is the most useful test instrument for checking antennas. It can be used to tune the antenna for an optimum impedance match. If there is a mismatch or improper adjustment, the CB will not perform properly. The ideal SWR is 1:1 but this is rarely, if ever, achieved. If the antenna has a good SWR reading at the lower channels, but gets progressively worse at the higher channels, then the antenna is probably too long.

An ohmmeter with long test leads may be used to check antenna continuity from the plug on the transmitter and of the coaxial cable to the antenna. Shorts in the antenna or coaxial cable often can be found by setting the ohmmeter to its highest resistance range, and measuring between the shield ground and the center connector of the plug on the transmitter end of the cable, while the cable and the antenna are being shaken. Any indication of an intermittent short should be checked out and repaired.

Even a properly-installed mobile CB transceiver can have a noise problem. Its origin is usually traced to the spark plugs, the alternator, or the voltage regulator of the vehicle. The most common source of interference is ignition noise, which occurs as a popping sound synchronized with the speed of the engine. This noise is either conducted through the automobile's electrical distribution wiring harness or radiated to the antenna. Most automobiles have noise suppressor ignition wire and noise suppressor spark plugs to control it. Noise elimination kits are available that include several bypass capacitors and/or choke coils to be connected at various points in the vehicle's electrical system.

COMMERCIAL FM TWO-WAY RADIO TROUBLESHOOTING

Most FM radio transceivers come with 1, 2, or 3 specific frequencies of operation in the range of 150-174MHz or 450-470MHz. Transceivers which operate in the 800-900MHz range are becoming increasingly popular.

Typical Two-Way Radios

A modern two-way radio uses narrow-band FM, which gives it an advantage in signal-to-noise ratio. Narrow-band FM occupies the same spectrum space as a comparable AM transmitter signal. FM channels are spaced 20kHz apart in the 150MHz and 450MHz bands, with a deviation of about 5kHz.

The two basic ways that modulation is achieved in commerical two-way radio transmitters are direct (Crosby) and indirect (Armstrong). Both make use of reactance modulators with a varactor connected across a tank circuit. A change in the varactor capacitance causes the oscillator frequency to change in the direct method; or, in the case of the indirect method, the output to change phase.

The RF amplifiers in the FM transmitter are often utilized as frequency doublers or triplers; that is, the output of the amplifier is tuned to two or three times the input frequency. Both the carrier frequency and the deviation are doubled or tripled in a frequency multiplier.

Figure 7.15 shows the block diagram of the typical FM radio telephone transmitter section. Note that a total multiplication factor of 24 is obtained through the chain of multipliers (Both the carrier frequency and the deviation are multiplied by the same factor.). Therefore, to obtain a carrier frequency deviation of 4.8kHz, the modulator must produce a deviation of 200Hz. An accurate frequency counter is needed to trace this type of system.

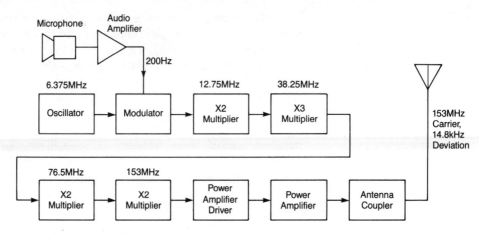

Figure 7.15   FM Radio-Telephone Transmitter

A typical two-way radio receiver section is shown in *Figure 7.16*. When troubleshooting the transmitter or the receiver sections of the transceiver, it is logical to further divide the system into subsections. If the receiver is dead, inject a 455kHz modulated FM test signal at the input of the third IF amplifier. With the volume and squelch control adjusted as required to permit audio output, determine if the signal gets through to the speaker. If it does, the trouble is toward the input of the receiver. If it does not, it is either in the third IF amplifier, the detector, the audio stages, or the squelch system. Assuming it does not get through the speaker, subdivide again with an audio tone at the volume control. Disable the squelch so that it is not gating the audio amplifier off. If the audio amplifier works, check the squelch circuits to see if they can disable and enable the audio amplifier. From the results of this test, determine if the trouble is in the squelch circuit or in the third IF or detector. In this way, the trouble can be pinpointed to one or two stages.

Most transceivers used in two-way radio have a troubleshooting checklist in the service manual. After the trouble has been localized to one or two stages, take pin voltage measurements to isolate the trouble down to a few components.

Special Circuits

Many transceivers include a feature that minimizes unwanted reception and allows for a certain degree of privacy on the extremely busy communications channels. Known as channel guard or private line, the system allows the selective unsquelching of receivers by the transmission of a special tone or binary codes. This coded information modulates the RF carrier below 300Hz, when voice communications are not carried, but is responded to by the receivers' squelch circuitry whenever the appropriate tone or code is received.

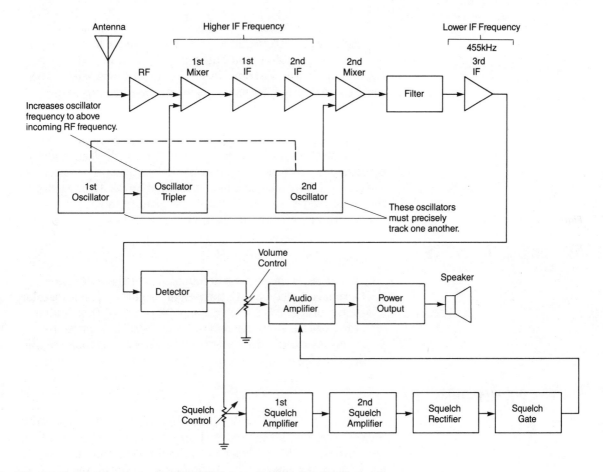

Figure 7.16 Dual Conversion Two-Way FM Transceiver (Receiver Section)

Another feature found on some two-way radios is a noise reduction system. One method samples the RF energy reaching the antenna at a frequency near the channel that is being received. It then applies cutoff bias pluses to the RF amplifier stage of the receiver to silence it for the very short duration of the impulse noise bursts. Silencing the receiver for this short period of time does not perceptably remove desired information from the received signal. This method of suppression by blocking the undesired noise and passing only the desired information to the speaker is far superior to the alternative methods of bypassing or shielding for noise picked up by the receiver.

An oscilloscope and signal generator are the test instruments used to check these subsystems. The manufacturer's service data are essential for servicing these circuits, for they provide the theory of operation, schematic diagram, important voltages and waveforms, and troubleshooting guidelines.

Protection Circuits

Several types of protection circuits are found in commercial two-way radio transmitters that are not often found in low-power CB transmitters. Protection circuits generally shut down the final power amplifier of the transmitter when conditions exist that could cause damage; for example, an increase in temperature caused by an overloaded output. Temperature sensors on the power amplifier transistor circuit board sense this increase and activate the protection circuit to remove power from the circuit.

Some transmitters have a time-out relay which shuts down continuous transmission after a certain length of time to prevent the transmitter from being held in a keyed-on position. Again, the proper way to test these circuits is given in the manufacturer's service information.

TELEVISION RECEIVERS

Any television receiver must accomplish three basic things:
1. Reproduce a picture with the proper brightness, and in a color set, the proper color.
2. Reproduce the proper sound to accompany the picture.
3. Synchronize the picture, so that what is received is an accurate reproduction of what is sent by the TV transmitter.

Analysis of Symptoms

Before beginning any service procedure, be sure all user controls are set correctly. If they are, and service controls adjustment will not solve the problem, then troubleshooting methods must be used. To troubleshoot a malfunctioning TV receiver, the technician must mentally divide the receiver into functional sections and have a clear idea of their operation. With the functional block diagram of the TV receiver in mind, assessment of the symptoms of the malfunctioning television will help to isolate the section in which the problem exists. For example, if there is no sound, but the picture is normal, the trouble must be in the path of the sound signal through the receiver that is not common to the picture. If the picture is also faulty, those sections of the receiver which are common to both sound and picture paths should be suspected of being defective.

Table 7.2 shows some common symptoms of monochrome receivers with a logical analysis of the sections suspected to be in trouble. Always consult the television service data because sometimes subsystems that are functionally unrelated may actually have some common circuitry. (Such circuitry usually was designed to reduce manufacturing cost). For example, the audio output may receive its power source from a voltage divider in the vertical circuit.

Table 7.2 Cause-and-Effect Analysis of a Typical Monochrome TV Receiver

Symptom	Probable Causes
1. No picture, no sound, no raster	A problem in the power supply since none of the subsystems are operational
2. Normal sound, no raster	A problem in the horizontal and/or vertical oscillator stages or high voltage power supply; defective CRT or incorrect CRT bias
3. Normal sound and raster, but defective or no picture	A problem in the video amplifiers after the sound take-off point; defective CRT
4. Normal raster, but defective or no sound and picture	A problem in the RF amplifier, antenna system, IF amplifier, AGC, or video amplifiers prior to the sound take-off
5. Picture shrunk at top and bottom, but good quality picture otherwise; sound normal	A problem in the vertical sweep sections, or in the section of the power supply that supplies the vertical sweep

Sweep Failures

The sweep (deflection) circuits in the receiver generate the vertical and horizontal sweep signals, amplify them and drive the deflection yoke on the CRT. The horizontal sweep section also drives the high voltage power supply. Vertical deflection circuit failure results in failure of vertical sweep action, therefore, only a bright horizontal line appears across the center of the screen. Loss of horizontal sweep is rarely seen as a bright vertical line because horizontal sweep circuit failure also results in loss of high voltage to the CRT anode. *Figure 7.17* shows some effects that various sections have on the picture.

Other defects that may occur in both vertical and horizontal deflection circuits, including the deflection yoke, may affect the linearity of the picture. It may be squeezed together or pulled apart on one side, both sides, or top or bottom.

RF, IF, Video and Sync

The antenna and transmission line supplies all area TV signals to the tuner section. The tuner circuitry selects a particular channel signal, amplifies that signal and converts it to an IF signal. The IF amplifiers further amplify and filter the signal before passing it to the sound and video stages. Since both the video and sound signals come through the RF and IF sections, failure or inadequate performance in either section will usually affect both the picture and sound.

If the signal is interrupted in the tuner, but the IF amplifiers are operating, there is usually dense snow on the screen and loud hissing in the sound. Snow is caused by noise generated and amplified in the IF amplifier stages. These stages are operating at maximum gain, because the AGC section is trying to get these stages to amplify a non-existent signal.

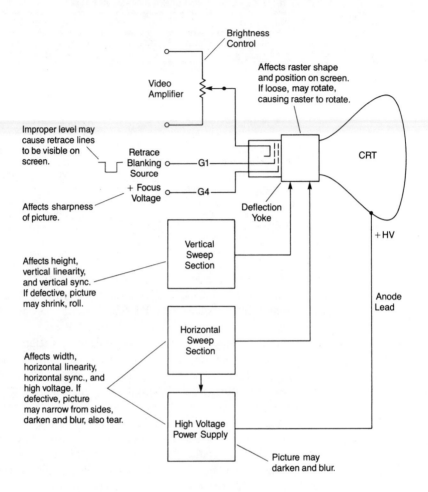

Figure 7.17   Block Diagram Showing Possible Sweep Section Trouble Sources

Intermittent tuner contacts in mechanical tuners are also a common problem, but a good tuner spray will usually clean them. If there is no snow and no picture, the problem could be either just before or after the video detector.

The take-off point for the 4.5MHz sound signal varies with receiver designs. If the sound take-off point is before the video amplifier, then trouble in the video amplifier affects only the picture. Between the video section, which provides the video signal to the CRT, and the sweep circuits, which provide the raster, are the synchronization circuits. Sync section trouble is indicated when the raster is normal, but the picture rolls and/or tears and adjustment of user controls (Vertical and Horizontal Hold) will not lock-in the picture, but will bring it very close to synchronization.

Color Symptom Analysis

Difficulties in obtaining proper color display on the screen can be caused by improper adjustment of the receiver controls. For example, a misadjusted fine tuning control can result in complete loss of color signal information. Misadjustment of the color amplitude control can result in no color or oversaturated color. The hue (or tint) control varies the phase of the color signal, thus, it determines the correct coloring of the picture. All the user controls and service controls should be checked for proper adjustment before more extensive troubleshooting is attempted.

A color television receiver includes all of the circuitry found in a standard black-and-white receiver, plus a chrominance section, convergence electronics, and a color CRT. Thus, if a picture is displayed on the CRT, but has little or no color, or if the color synchronization is unstable, then the color signal processing sections are the most likely cause of the trouble. Sometimes the RF/IF circuitry may attenuate or alter the color information part of the signal while affecting the monochromatic part of the image very little.

The color TV receiver should be observed in operation to determine what trouble symptoms exist. Some common color trouble symptoms along with their probable causes are listed in *Table 7.3*.

Table 7.3 Cause-and-Effect Analysis of a Typical Color TV Receiver

Symptom	Probable Causes
1. Color tinted areas on a black and white picture, or color blotches	Purity rings out of adjustment; CRT needs degaussing
2. Some colors more vivid than others	Misadjusted drive or screen controls; defective color demodulator stage
3. Entire screen predominantly one color	Defective demodulator; Misadjusted drive or screen controls; defective CRT
4. Loss of color	Defective demodulator stage; color killer control improperly set; bandpass amplifier or color oscillator defective
5. Loss of color sync	Defective oscillator crystal or weak or defective color oscillator; defective reactance control circuit; defective burst amplifier
6. Color fringing at edges of objects and/or 2 or 3 color lines where there should be 1 line	Misconverged
7. Faded colors	Defective CRT; improperly adjusted bias on CRT; improperly adjusted screen and drive controls; weak demodulator amplifiers
8. Color smears, loss of detail	Loss of Y signal
9. Moving color bars	Loss of color sync
10. Poor flesh tone colors	Incorrect setting or defective tint control; defective color demodulator(s)

Set-Up Procedure

In color television, the term set-up refers to the process of making three types of adjustments.
1. Purity
2. Gray-scale
3. Convergence

Purity refers to the relative non-contamination of each of the primary colors (red, green and blue) by the other two colors. Purity problems are a CRT-caused defect and are not related to the color demodulator. Gray scale refers to the accuracy with which the relative intensity of the three CRT electron beams is maintained to reproduce gray tonal values from black to white. Inaccurate gray scale tracking causes the overall raster to have a color tint to it. Convergence refers to the accuracy with which the three electon beams in the CRT strike only their appropriate phosphor dot on the inner face of the screen.

The following adjustments should be made before starting convergence procedures:
1. High Voltage
2. Focus
3. Height
4. Vertical Linearity
5. Width
6. Horizontal and Vertical Centering
7. AGC

A general set-up procedure consists of the following five steps which are usually performed in the order listed. To speed up the operation, start by correcting the most obvious and serious problems before going through the entire procedure.

1. Degaussing — Demagnetize the shadow mask with a degaussing coil.
2. Purity — Adjust purity rings for pure red center screen area; adjust yoke position for pure red at outer area of the screen.
3. Static Convergence — Connect a dot/crosshatch generator to the RF terminals of the receiver and use the permanent magnets in the convergence assembly on the CRT neck to converge all three colors in the center area of the screen.
4. Dynamic Convergence — The dynamic convergence controls are located on a separate printed circuit board. Normally all vertical controls for the red and green beams are adjusted first, then the horizontal controls for the red and green beams are adjusted. Then the blue beam vertical and horizontal controls are adjusted in the same order. Due to the interaction of the dynamic convergence controls, most adjustments may have to be repeated several times.

5. Color Temperature (Gray-scale) — With the CRT service switch set to the Service position, adjust individual color screen and/or drive controls following the manufacturer's recommended method. This establishes correct bias levels so the three color levels are always in the right relative proportions to each other.

These procedures may vary slightly for different set designs depending on the year of manufacture and hence the state-of-the-art at the time. Generally, the newer the set, the easier it is to converge. Old or defective color CRT's may not converge well; therefore, some sets may fail to provide a satisfactory picture no matter how much adjusting is done. In this case, troubleshooting is the next step.

CRT Testing

A CRT tester checks for cathode emission level, shorts between elements in the gun(s), and gas (deterioration of the vacuum). For three-gun color tubes, each gun is checked separately.

Defective CRTs may sometimes be successfully restored to acceptable operation. Shorts between electron-gun elements may be burned off by placing the two short-circuited gun elements across a high voltage developed by the CRT tester. Cathode emission may be increased by rejuvenation using the CRT tester to burn off the cathode contamination, or by installing a filament voltage booster.

Standard Test Patterns

Standard test patterns are used to determine the performance level of a televison receiver and to provide an objective standard for adjustments.

The monochromatic test pattern shown in *Figure 7.18* permits a technician to make an objective evaluation of video quality of either monochrome or color receivers.

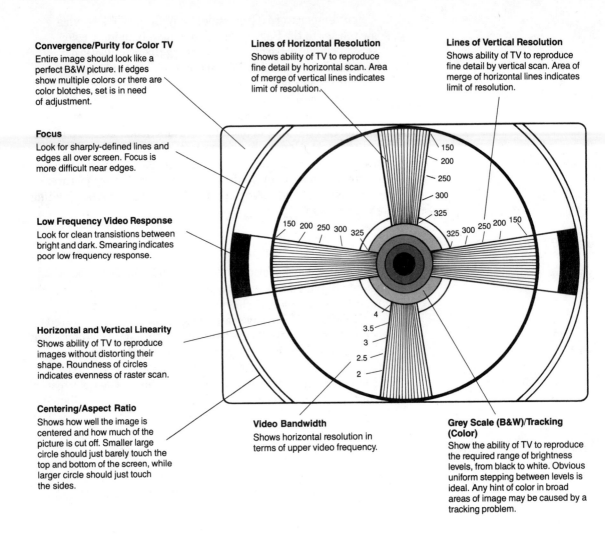

Convergence/Purity for Color TV
Entire image should look like a perfect B&W picture. If edges show multiple colors or there are color blotches, set is in need of adjustment.

Focus
Look for sharply-defined lines and edges all over screen. Focus is more difficult near edges.

Low Frequency Video Response
Look for clean transistions between bright and dark. Smearing indicates poor low frequency response.

Horizontal and Vertical Linearity
Shows ability of TV to reproduce images without distorting their shape. Roundness of circles indicates evenness of raster scan.

Centering/Aspect Ratio
Shows how well the image is centered and how much of the picture is cut off. Smaller large circle should just barely touch the top and bottom of the screen, while larger circle should just touch the sides.

Lines of Horizontal Resolution
Shows ability of TV to reproduce fine detail by horizontal scan. Area of merge of vertical lines indicates limit of resolution.

Video Bandwidth
Shows horizontal resolution in terms of upper video frequency.

Lines of Vertical Resolution
Shows ability of TV to reproduce fine detail by vertical scan. Area of merge of horizontal lines indicates limit of resolution.

Grey Scale (B&W)/Tracking (Color)
Show the ability of TV to reproduce the required range of brightness levels, from black to white. Obvious uniform stepping between levels is ideal. Any hint of color in broad areas of image may be caused by a tracking problem.

Figure 7.18 Standard Monochromatic Television Test Pattern

Table 7.4 indicates what kinds of electronic parameters and circuits are involved.

The color bar test pattern shown in *Figure 7.19* indicates how accurately the hues are being demodulated and reproduced. (Without this test pattern, the most accurate way of making this assessment is to tune in a program and observe flesh tones.)

The positions and colors of the bars represents the relationship between the hues and the I-Q rector phase angles. Adjusting the television receiver's tint (hue) control changes the phase angle of the I-Q vector with reference to the burst signal.

Table 7.4 Using Standard Monochrome Test Pattern for Troubleshooting

Image Parameter	Electronic Parameters and Controls/Circuits/Sections Involved
Lines of horizontal resolution	Overall video bandwidth; picture tube quality; focus
Lines of vertical resolution	Accuracy of vertical interlaced scanning; focus
Horizontal and vertical linearity	Horizontal and vertical sweep and drive circuits; yoke; linearity and size controls settings
Centering/aspect ratio	Horizontal and vertical sweep and drive circuits; linearity and size controls settings; centering rings (B&W only) or purity rings around CRT neck
Focus	Quality of CRT and correct voltages on electron guns; setting of focus control
Gray scale/tracking	Video detector; video amplifiers; quality of CRT; setting of brightness and contrast controls; setting of CRT screen and drive controls
Low frequency video response	Video detector; video amplifiers
Convergence/purity (for color TV only)	Convergence circuitry; convergence coils; static convergence magnets around CRT neck; purity rings; external magnetic field

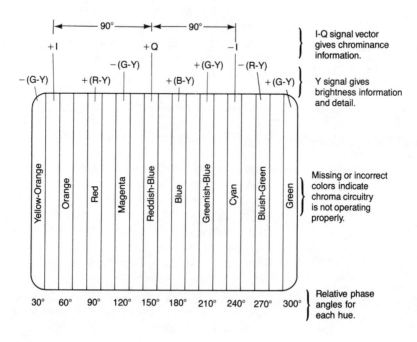

Figure 7.19 Standard Color Bar Pattern

By examining the raster pattern, and the phase angle waveforms produced on a special color television oscilloscope, called a vectorscope, the chrominance circuitry may be accurately analyzed.

These two common test patterns are available from certain test instruments, and also, are usually transmitted by most television stations before normal programming each day.

COMPONENT-LEVEL CONSIDERATIONS

Connectors, Sockets, Terminals, and Circuit Boards

Many electronic equipment failures are caused by mechanical problems — usually a connection or contact failure — rather than an electronic component failure. One must keep in mind that each connector, socket, and terminal represents a potential problem area, and that for most equipment, they far outnumber the discrete components.

Connections are either of two types: soldered or friction (pressure). Improperly soldered connections can become intermittent or totally open from mechanical and thermal shocks. Friction-type connections can become oxidized. Screws on terminal board connections can become loosened. Circuits boards may develop hairline breaks in the lands. Sometimes components may break loose from their circuit board contact points.

Applying moderate mechanical shock and stress, such as tapping or flexing, to all suspect connections while the device's operation is being monitored should be tried before any large-scale testing or disassembly effort is begun. Resoldering suspect connections or cleaning connector contacts sometimes is all that is needed to restore acceptable operation.

Determining if Components are Good or Bad

Once a certain component is suspected of being defective, how does one determine if it really is? If a known good part is available, the substitution method is preferred. If the new one solves the problem, the old one must be defective. If, however, the replacement does not cure the problem, either the new part is also bad, or the defect lies elsewhere. Another possiblity is that other circuit problems are damaging this component.

Components may often be tested out-of-the circuit using an ohmmeter as discussed in previous chapters, or by using the appropriate tester. The tester will more closely subject the component to normal operating conditions, but these results still do not always indicate how well it will perform in a circuit. This is especially true of high frequency (RF) circuits.

Sometimes components have intermittent problems which show up only when the circuit has been operating for a while. This is generally a heat-related problem, which sometimes can be found by subjecting the suspect component to thermal shock. A hot soldering tool or hair dryer brought near (but not touching) can be used to heat a component, and a shot of pressurized refrigerant can be used to cool it. Alternately heating and cooling it may cause the failure to occur. Often it's the component's connection that's bad, rather than the component itself.

Choosing the Right Replacement

The criteria for choosing the best replacement part depends on the type of part involved, and the apparatus being repaired. Sometimes only the manufacturer's exact recommended part will work, other times a generic substitute will do just fine. The following guidelines will provide some guidance.

For semiconductors, using the exact same type is the safest method. Cross-reference guides will often point to a good substitute, or if the operating parameters are known, the technician may choose a good replacement. Before choosing an alternate type, make sure that its voltage and current ratings are adequate, so at least it will not short out nor overheat.

For resistors, replacement with the same resistance value and tolerance is important. The wattage rating should be the same rating or higher. Some circuits require special resistors, such as low-noise types or precision values, to maintain circuit S/N specifications.

For capacitors, the capacitance and tolerance of the replacement should be the same, and the voltage rating should be the same or higher. Also, the dielectric material and construction are important in some applications. When replacing electrolytic capacitors, voltage ratings that are a lot higher than the original value often will not work properly.

Power, driver, and flyback transformers almost always must be replaced with the identical or a nearly-identical type, because of mounting requirements, winding specifications, and voltage ratings. Replacement components for the high voltage section must be chosen carefully with regard to insulation and voltage ratings.

Component Removal and Replacement

When the source of the problem has been narrowed to the defective component(s), a certain amount of common sense and precautions should be used while doing the repair. The following guidelines should be kept in mind.

1. For socket-mounted parts, do not bend the leads of the new part more than necessary for a fit. Trim off excess lengths as required.
2. For soldered-in parts, heat-sink the leads to prevent heat damage to the components. Use careful soldering practices, and be cautious of nearby components.
3. Position the replacement exactly as the original. Route the leads the same way, and if they are bare, insulate them with spaghetti tubing if necessary.
4. An insulated gate field-effect transistor, such as a MOSFET, must be treated with extreme care to prevent destroying it from static discharge. In-circuit, the MOSFET is just as rugged as a bipolar junction-type transistor. Out of the circuit, however, it is subject to damage from static charge when handled or moved in any way. The leads are generally shorted together to prevent damage before it is inserted in the circuit. Usually the short is removed only after it is soldered into the circuit. The person should touch a grounded point with both hands before handling the FET and, preferably, wear a wrist ground strap while handling it. To ensure proper grounding of the soldering iron, connect a clip lead from the barrel of the solder tool to the chassis in which the FET is mounted. A soldering gun should never be used when working with IGFETs. The soldering tool tip must be at ground potential.

To make certain that the replacement component is installed correctly, pay close attention to lead identification. Some devices are polarized, so note which lead goes where. Socket-mounted components are usually keyed in some way, although it may be possible to physically insert them incorrectly. Some component leads are identified by the shape of the package, a tab, notch, or an imprinted dot.

Many transformers have the leads identified by the color of the insulation on the leads, but the replacement may not use the same color code. Flyback transformers usually have numbered terminals, but again, the replacement may not use the same numbers.

Mount all power-type devices on their heat sinks exactly as the manufacturer did, using heat-conducting silicon grease, and insulators as required. Always check the component manufacturer's technical literature to make certain that the lead arrangement of the new part is physically identical to the defective part.

BASIC SUPPLIES

To perform maintenance and repair of electronic equipment, three kinds of supplies are needed in addition to some hand tools:
1. Test equipment
2. Consumables
3. Service information

Test Equipment

The amplifiers, radio receivers, CB units, and television receivers as previously discussed all require much of the same test equipment. *Table 7.5* lists the basic equipment for most types of electronic service needs, and *Table 7.6* lists some of the more specialized equipment.

Table 7.5   Widely-Used Test Equipment

Test Device	Comments
VOM or Multimeter	Use for all electronic circuits. Voltage section should be at least 20,000 per/V sensitivity, but higher is preferred. Should be able to read in millivolt range and as low as 0.25 ohms. Electronic type is best, since it doesn't load the circuit under test.
Oscilloscope	Use for signal tracing, waveform analysis, modulation check, hum and noise tracing, voltage measurement. Triggered type is best. Dual trace type is not necessary for analog circuitry.
AF/RF Generators	Use for signal injection for signal tracing, approximate gain measurement. AF generator must also have square wave output for checking amplifier distortion.
Signal Injector Probe	Use for quick location of a dead amplification stage. Should have an audio tone rich in harmonics for RF use.
R-C Substitution Box	Use for trying new capacitors and resistors. Commercially available, but you may want to build your own, using most-often needed component values.
Sweep/Marker Generator	Use for aligning radio and TV RF and IF sections, and for a quick test of overall bandpass. Use with oscilloscope.
Auxiliary Power Supply	Use when a system's own power supply is suspect.
AC Isolation Transformer	Use whenever the equipment under test is not operated through an internal power transformer. (A safety must.)
Variable Power Transformer	Use when low or high line voltage is causing component failures. Useful for testing power supply regulators.

Consumable Supplies

Expendable materials and chemicals are an essential part of all servicing. *Table 7.7* lists the most commonly used supplies.

Table 7.6   Specialized Test Equipment

CB/AMATEUR RADIO

Test Device	Comments
Electronic Frequency Counter	Accurately measures the frequency for each channel.
SWR/RF Power Meter (Combined Test Set)	Checks impedance match between RF transmitter output and antenna. Measures the power input to the antenna.

AM/FM STEREO RECEIVER

Test Device	Comments
Sweep/Marker Stereo Generator	Provides needed signals to allow complete alignment of receiver.

COLOR TELEVISION

Test Device	Comments
High Voltage DC Voltmeter Probe	Use to measure CRT high voltage. Necessary to set high voltage before performing convergence.
Color Generator: DOT/ Crosshatch/Color Bar	Use to generate test pattern for convergence and setup of color TV. Also for color and convergence circuit troubleshooting.
Degaussing Coil	Use to demagnetize CRT and nearby metal. Use prior to any convergence adjustments.
Vectorscope	Use to test and align the color circuits.
CRT Tester/Rejuvenator	Use to determine if a CRT has low emission, internal shorts, or is gassy. Can use it to repair a defective CRT.
TV Analyzer	Multiple-use test instrument. Provides many types of signals and voltages needed to check TVs. Also provides standard test patterns.

Table 7.7   Consumable Supplies

Material	Application/Comments
RTV	Use it as a general bonding material. Especially useful because it dries pliable, making it useful as a sealer. It is impervious to water and most chemicals. It has good high voltage insulation properties.
Silicon Grease	Use it for mounting power components on heat sinks. It helps to conduct heat from the device to the sink.
Solder/Rosin Flux	Use it for general-purpose soldering. The higher the tin content, the better the solder (60% tin/40% lead is considered a high-quality grade). Don't use acid core solder, because it will corrode the connection.
Control Cleaner/Lubricant	Use it for deoxidizing potentiometers and contacts. It should leave little or no residue.
Can of Pressurized Refrigerant	Use it for finding intermittent components and connections.
Insulating Tape	Good quality plastic tape. Avoid using friction tape, because it doesn't adhere very well.
High Voltage Dope — Putty and Spray	Use it when repairing or replacing components in the high voltage section. Suppresses corona and arcing problems.

Service Information

Often equipment must be serviced with only a schematic diagram, and most schematic diagrams will show the important voltages and waveforms. However, it is much easier and better if the manufacturer's complete service information is available. Typical service information includes schematic diagrams, instructions for adjustments and alignment, lists of components, and their part numbers, voltage and resistance charts, and sometimes, part number cross-reference lists, troubleshooting charts and flow diagrams. Manufacturers may also supply service bulletin updates and engineering changes which should be kept with the service manuals.

Some independent technical publishers supply servicing data, too. These packages of diagrams are sold through electronics parts distributors. In addition, service manuals may be obtained upon request from the manufacturer of the equipment for a small fee.

To find substitute components, parts manufacturers supply cross-reference guides which indicate which of their own parts may be substituted for other manufacturer's equipment parts. Most electronics parts suppliers carry these cross-reference guides. A good rule to follow, however, is to compare the specifications of the original to those of the substitute before installing it, because occasionally a mistake is made in the cross-reference literature.

SAFETY PRECAUTIONS

Proper safety awareness can minimize the likelihood of injury to people and/or damage to the equipment. Although every situation is a little bit different, certain precautions and common sense are always applicable.

Never automatically assume that power is off. Take the extra moment to check, and the safest way is to unplug the unit. Sometimes the larger filter capacitors can store a charge long after the system is turned off. Discharge them to the appropriate ground point.

All ac power line-operated equipment that is not powered through its own internal transformer must be plugged into an isolation transformer. Since the chassis or circuitry may be connected to the hot side of the line without the isolation transformer, the technician's body could become a path to ground for the power line. It only takes a current of 10 milliamperes through the heart to interfere with its normal rhythm; if the B+ supply output voltage is above 50 volts, it too becomes a potential source for a lethal shock.

The high voltage section of any television receiver is a dangerous area. The CRT anode voltage varies from about 7kV for a small black-and-white receiver, to upwards of 26kV for a 25-inch color receiver. The high voltage systems for the larger receivers can supply a much larger current, too. The flyback transformer and other high voltage components are often enclosed in a cage for your protection. Exercise extreme caution when working in this area. These voltages are extremely dangerous.

The CRT is electrically a large capacitor, and it may hold a charge long after the power is shut off. The anode terminal should be discharged to chassis ground before working on it.

Whenever working near an operating high voltage section, keep as much distance as possible. Even though everything is insulated, these high voltages and frequencies have a way of ionizing the insulation and the air, and discharging to anything in the vicinity.

SUMMARY

In this chapter, we have learned that to successfully troubleshoot and repair electronic equipment, one must analyze it in terms of functional blocks, with each one processing a signal and passing it to the next block. Once the defective block has been located, the defective component can generally be identified by analyzing waveforms, and by measuring voltage, current, and/or resistance.

The same principles of troubleshooting are applicable to audio, radio, and television. A complete understanding of how the subsystem and circuits work and relate to each other, and what is normal operation, is necessary to find the cause of the defect. Anything less is haphazard.

When a defective component is suspected, a methodical procedure must be followed to repair the equipment and restore operation. This procedure includes looking for bad connections, testing the component, getting the proper replacement, and installing it.

Successful servicing requires that the proper test equipment and other supplies be available, and that conservative safety practices be followed.

As one gains experience, one develops his (her) own technique and shortcuts. Until that point is reached, follow the traditional methods and the recommendations of the electronic manufacturers.

CHAPTER 7 QUIZ

1. The first step in a logical troubleshooting procedure is to:
   a. locate the specific fault.
   b. isolate to a specific circuit.
   c. analyze symptoms.
   d. localize to a major module.

2. A signal path where the output of one circuit feeds the input of the next is:
   a. linear.
   b. meeting.
   c. separating.
   d. switching.

3. Bias for a typical transistor amplifier stage is:
   a. EB junction reverse, CB junction forward.
   b. EB junction forward, CB junction reverse.
   c. EB junction forward, CB junction forward.
   d. EB junction reverse, CB junction reverse.

4. In linear circuits (Class A), _____ usually cause no change in dc voltage
   a. open resistors
   b. shorted resistors
   c. open capacitors
   d. shorted capacitors

5. If forward bias is removed from a transistor:
   a. the transistor will be turned off.
   b. the transistor will overheat.
   c. base current will go high, collector will stop.
   d. base current will stop, collector current will go high.

6. If collector voltage V_C equals V_{CC}, then:
   a. I_C is zero.
   b. this is normal.
   c. the transistor is good.
   d. the transistor is shorted.

7. If the EB voltage of a silicon transistor measures 0.7 volts:
   a. look for a shorted EB junction.
   b. the transistor is open.
   c. base current will be zero.
   d. this is normal.

8. On a good transistor, if an ohmmeter is connected to the EB junction, it reads high resistance; then the leads are reversed and when connected:
   a. it should read zero.
   b. it should read a low resistance.
   c. the ohmmeter should read a high resistance again.
   d. the transistor will be destroyed.

9. A fast and inexpensive method to determine an amplifier's frequency response is to use a:
   a. square wave test.
   b. harmonic distortion analyzer.
   c. spectrum analyzer.
   d. transient intermoduation test.

10. In a transmitter output stage feeding an antenna, if SWR indicates an impedance mismatch, the problem will cause:
    a. driver oscillator clipping.
    b. output stage overheating.
    c. transmitted background noise.
    d. distorted modulation of the carrier.

11. Clipping of the audio signal in a radio receiver may be caused by:
    a. ac power supply filter.
    b. an open transistor in the mixer.
    c. a shorted speaker.
    d. an overloaded stage.

12. A loss of stereo separation in an FM receiver would probably indicate:
    a. a defective converter.
    b. a shorted power amplifier transistor.
    c. loss of the 38kHz oscillator.
    d. loss of the local oscillator.

13. When transistors fail, they usually:
    a. short or open.
    b. become weak.
    c. become leaky.
    d. become noisy.

14. If the base of a transistor is shorted to its collector:
    a. it will cut off I_C.
    b. it will saturate.
    c. it will be reverse-biased.
    d. its base lead will be opened.

15. If the horizontal section of a TV receiver fails:
    a. a bright horizontal line results.
    b. a bright vertical line results.
    c. no raster results.
    d. the picture rolls from top to bottom.

16. On a color receiver, color fringing on a black-and-white picture is usually caused by:
    a. color sync loss.
    b. misconvergence.
    c. color demodulator failure.
    d. low high voltage on the CRT.

17. Which TV picture defect would not show up on a standard black-and-white test pattern when viewed on a color television?
    a. Deterioration of video bandwidth
    b. Sweep non-linearity
    c. Non-convergence
    d. Chroma demodulator inaccuracy

18. In a typical color receiver, if there is an acceptable black-and-white picture, and good sound, but no color, which is not a possible cause?
    a. Color convergence isn't working.
    b. Tuner isn't fine-tuned properly.
    c. Color demodulator circuits aren't working.
    d. IF strip is having a bandpass problem.

19. When choosing a substitute capacitor for a power supply filter, ignoring which parameter can do the most harm to the system?
    a. Capacitance
    b. Type (electrolytic, paper, mylar, etc.)
    c. Voltage
    d. Physical size

20. In a color television receiver, plugged-in but power switch set to the Off position, which area is probably "safe" from being a source of electric shock?
    a. The high voltage anode lead
    b. Power supply electrolytic capacitors
    c. The power transformer secondaries
    d. The ac input wiring

DIGITAL CIRCUITS

INTRODUCTION

Digital electronics technology has become a part of every aspect of what used to be analog-based technology only. Digitizing has made possible a much greater degree of accuracy, control, miniaturization, and cost-effectiveness, not previously possible. Yet whether we are dealing with a pocket four-function calculator or a sophisticated mainframe computer, a child's remote control toy or a communications satellite, the technologies are all based upon certain fundamental concepts.

The backbone of all digital techniques is comprised of the numbering systems, the basic logic devices, and the logic rules. To successfully apply these three items to achieve functioning systems, a whole technology has been developed consisting of digital components, circuits, and design practices to perform the required electronic manipulations.

In this chapter, we will cover the concepts which will provide some insight as to how those manipulations occur. We'll start with the basic digital concepts. This section includes a comparison between analog and digital circuits, followed by a synopsis of the commonly used numbering systems, and concluding with information about encoding.

The next sections explains the basic logic gates and combinational logic circuits. Nearly all other digital circuits use these basic gates and circuits as building blocks.

With this foundation established, the remainder of this chapter is more technology- and component-oriented. We'll begin this part with an introduction to the discrete devices and circuit techniques which make up a functioning system. The various families of logic components are identified and discussed, then component-level functional circuits are explained. Next these functional circuits are combined into digital arithmetic circuit configurations that actually perform a useful function — taking an input, manipulating it, and providing a result.

Finally, in discussing data handling and display methods, we explain some of the finer points of circuit design. These include bus structure, three-state bus interfacing devices, analog to digital conversion, display devices, and interfacing techniques.

BASIC DIGITAL CONCEPTS

Review of Analog and Digital

Signal-processing electronic circuits may be classified into one of two types: analog or digital. In analog circuitry, there is a continuous and direct relationship between a physical quantity described, measured, or controlled, and the electrical energy present. By comparison, in digital circuitry, this relationship exists when the electrical energy is present and absent (on and off) in a predictable and controlled way. The relationship is abrupt (on/off) and may be indirect (coded).

A comparison between analog and digital concepts is shown in *Figure 8.1*. In the analog circuit of *Figure 8.1a*, as the control R_1 is turned through its range, the output voltage will vary continuously from 0 to +5 volts. In the digital circuit of *Figure 8.1b*, the voltage at the output terminal will be +5 volts when the switch S_1 is open (off), or it will be 0 volts when the switch is closed (on).

Number Systems Used in Digital Circuits

Counting in any system should begin with 0. Each digit in a number contributes to the magnitude of the number by multiplying the number of the digit by the weighting factor of that digit position. The basic distinction between numbering systems is this weighting factor. Various digital numbering systems have four common elements:

1. In a number system, the number of values that a digit can assume is equal to the base in that number system.
2. The largest value in the number system is always one less than the base.
3. Each digit position multiplies the digit's value by a weighting factor for that digit position, to determine the digit's contribution to the magnitude of the number.
4. A carry from one position to the next higher position increases the digit's value equal to the base times its previous value.

The most common numbering systems, decimal, octal, binary, and hexadecimal, are explained in the following examples.

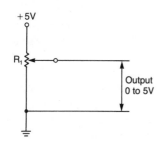

a. Analog

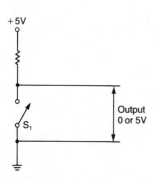

b. Digital

Figure 8.1 Comparison Between Analog and Digital Electrical Circuits

Decimal

Example 8-1: Decimal is the base 10 number system, the system we use in our everyday life. The largest number of digits per position is 10, (0-9) and the largest digit is 9. Consider the decimal number 657. Each digit position represents the following weighted values:

Digit Positions	MSD		LSD
	10^2	10^1	10^0
Positional Weighting Factors	Hundreds	Tens	Units
Magnitudes	6	5	7

Therefore,

$$(6 \times 10^2) + (5 \times 10^1) + (7 \times 10^0) =$$
$$600 \quad + \quad 50 \quad + \quad 7 \quad = 657_{10}$$

Octal

Example 8-2: Octal is one of the number systems commonly used in work with computers. Octal is the base 8 number system. The largest number of digits is 8 (0-7), and the largest digit is 7. Consider the octal number 432. Each digit position represents the following weighted values:

Digit Positions	MSD		LSD
	8^2	8^1	8^0
Positional Weighting Factors	Sixty-Fours	Eights	Units
Magnitudes	4	3	2

Therefore,

$$(4 \times 8^2) + (3 \times 8^1) + (2 \times 8^0) =$$
$$256 \quad + \quad 24 \quad + \quad 2 \quad = 282_{10}$$

Example 8-3. To convert from base 10 to base 8, divide the decimal number by 8 successively. The remainders that occur form the octal digits. The last remainder is the MSD (most significant digit) of the octal number, and the first remainder is the LSD (least significant digit):

$$\frac{282}{8} = 35 \quad \text{with remainder of 2}$$

$$\frac{35}{8} = 4 \quad \text{with remainder of 3}$$

$$\frac{4}{8} = 0 \quad \text{with remainder of 4}$$

Therefore,

$$282_{10} = 432_8$$

Binary

The binary number system is used in the digital computer, because it uses only two digits, 1 and 0, which can represent the on and off states of digital circuits. The base in the binary system is 2, thus, the largest number that can be expressed by a single digit is one less than 2, or 1. The method of converting binary numbers to decimal numbers is similar to that used in the octal system, except each positional place has an increasing power of 2. Since digits can have only a value of 0 or 1, a number greater than 1 causes a carry to the next position.

Converting from base 2 to base 10 is quite simple. If there is a 1 in a given position, the weight of that digit position is added. If a 0 is in a digit position, the weight of that digit position is not added.

Example 8-4: Consider the binary number 11010. Each digit position represents the following weighted values:

Digit Positions	MSD				LSD
	2^4	2^3	2^2	2^1	2^0
Positional Weighting Factors	Sixteens	Eights	Fours	Two	Units
Magnitudes	1	1	0	1	0

Therefore,

$$(1\times2^4) + (1\times2^3) + (0\times2^2) + (1\times2^1) + (0x2^0) =$$
$$16 + 8 + 0 + 2 + 0 = 26_{10}$$

To convert decimal to binary, divide successively by 2, keeping the remainder. The remainder from the first division gives the LSD of the binary number, and the final remainder is the MSD.

Hexadecimal

An important number system used in computer work, is the hexadecimal (Hex) system. It is base 16, thus, the largest digit is 15. However, since 15 requires two digit positions, more symbols must be used than in the decimal system. 0 through 9 are used for the first ten numbers and A through F are used for the remaining six. This relationship is summarized in *Table 8.1*.

The conversion of hexadecimal to decimal is identical to conversions in other bases except the digit positions are weighted by powers of 16. The primary purpose for using hexadecimal numbers in computer work is to represent binary numbers which tend to be very long. The conversion back and forth between binary and hexadecimal is fast and easy as shown in examples *8-5* and *8-6*.

Decimal	Hexadecimal
0	0
:	
:	
9	9
10	A
11	B
12	C
13	D
14	E
15	F
16	10
17	11
18	12
19	13
20	14
etc.	

Table 8.1 Hex Notation

Example 8-5: Convert 1101100110110011 from binary to hexadecimal.

The number is first separated into groups of four bits, and a hexadecimal digit is substituted for the decimal value of each group of four binary bits:

Magnitude in Binary	1101	1001	1011	0011
Magnitude in Decimal	13	9	11	3
Magnitude in Hex Notation	D	9	B	3

To convert hexadecimal to binary, the reverse procedure is used.

Example 8-6: Convert the hexadecimal number BEAF to its binary equivalent:

Magnitude in Hex Notation	B	E	A	F
Magnitude in Decimal	11	14	10	15
Magnitude in Binary	1011	1110	1010	1111

Electrical Levels and Digital Quantities

In a digital system, information is represented by pulses. These pulses may represent binary numbers, letters, or punctuation. *Figure 8.2* shows signals that might be encountered in a digital system, as viewed on a multiple-trace oscilloscope or a logic analyzer. A digital clock is a pulse generator that generates pulses with a precisely controlled period. These pulses control the timing of the entire digital system.

Binary Codes

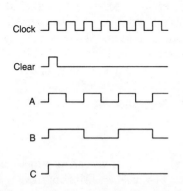

Figure 8.2 Clock Pulses Synchronize All Other Digital Activities

Signals that represent binary numbers, which in turn represent letters or characters in various codes, may occur in either parallel or serial form. In serial numbers, the binary places, or powers of 2, are represented by a group of pulses that occur in sequence during a specified time interval as shown in *Figure 8.3*. This figure shows a binary number (25) in serial pulse train form and also in the serial level pulse train form. The advantage of using serial form is that only one wire (plus the common) is needed to move the pulses from place to place. The disadvantage is that it takes more time to transmit a number than using the parallel form.

A binary number represented in parallel form requires a separate line (wire) for each binary place. However, this disadvantage is offset by the advantage of speed, because a complete number can be transmitted in a single time interval. *Figure 8.4* shows the waveforms on five parallel lines representing five numbers in five time intervals.

Digital electronic equipment uses two voltage levels to represent the 1s and 0s of binary numbers. These 1s and 0s are grouped together using various coding schemes to represent information, such as numbers, letters, punctuation marks, and control characters.

The human operator of a piece of equipment works best with decimal numbers rather than any of the other number systems. However, the digital equipment must work with binary numbers. One solution to this problem is to use binary-coded decimal (BCD) numbers. Binary-coded decimal is a way of representing decimal numbers using the binary symbols of 0 and 1.

To express a decimal number in BCD, the binary equivalent of *each* decimal digit is inserted into the corresponding position in the BCD number. This is done by representing each of the digits of the decimal number by four binary digits (bits). Four bits are required to represent a decimal digit, because the decimal numbers 8 and 9 require four binary digit positions. The binary, octal, hexadecimal and BCD, configurations used to represent decimal digits are shown in *Table 8.2*.

To convert binary-coded decimal to decimal form, arrange the digits in groups of four, starting from the far-right side. If the last grouping on the left has fewer than four digits, insert 0s to the left to fill the group. The decimal equivalent of the number can then be found by writing the decimal equivalent of each group of four digits. This process is simply reversed to convert a decimal number to BCD as shown in example *8-7*.

Example 8-7: Find the BCD equivalent of 764_{10}.

Decimal	7	6	4
BCD	0111	0110	0100

To convert BCD to binary form, it is necessary to first find the decimal equivalent and then to find the binary equivalent of the decimal number. There is no convenient method of converting directly from BCD to binary. Likewise, to convert binary form to BCD, it is necessary to first find the decimal equivalent of the binary number, then to find the BCD equivalent of the decimal numbers using four bits to express a decimal digit.

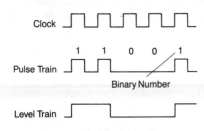

Clock, Pulse Train, Binary Number, Level Train

Figure 8.3 Comparison Between Serial, Pulse and Level Train Waveforms of the Binary Number 11001 (25 Decimal)

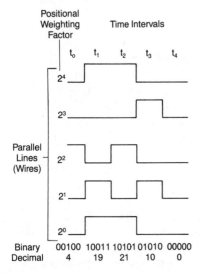

Figure 8.4 Five Numbers in Parallel Form

FUNDAMENTAL LOGIC GATES

The circuits that perform digital switching functions may include simple switches, relays, diodes, and transistors. Most of the digital circuits used in actual practice consist of combinations of individual parts to perform a specific function. Most modern equipment uses integrated circuits that contain one or more functions within a package that are ready to use.

Decimal	Binary	Octal	Hexadecimal	Binary Coded Decimal	
0	0000	0	0		0000
1	0001	1	1		0001
2	0010	2	2		0010
3	0011	3	3		0011
4	0100	4	4		0100
5	0101	5	5		0101
6	0110	6	6		0110
7	0111	7	7		0111
8	1000	10	8		1000
9	1001	11	9		1001
10	1010	12	A	0001	0000
11	1011	13	B	0001	0001
12	1100	14	C	0001	0010
13	1101	15	D	0001	0011
14	1110	16	E	0001	0100
15	1111	17	F	0001	0101

Table 8.2   Number Systems Compared

Basic Boolean Operations and Truth Tables

Combinational logic circuits make decisions based on the input. These logic operations follow the rules of a mathematical system known as Boolean algebra. In Boolean algebra, only two constants exist: 0 and 1. Although any number of variables may be used, each of these must assume the values of these constants only. Expressions that may be rather complex are expressed in the much simpler form of a truth table, a systematic listing of all the possible combinations of the states of the input (variables) and corresponding outputs assigned to each combination.

OR, AND, NOT Functions

There are only three basic logic functions in digital circuits and Boolean algebra: AND, OR, and NOT. These are summarized in the truth tables in *Figure 8.5*. Variables in Boolean algebra correspond to the input conditions on a logic circuit called a gate. *Figure 8.5* also shows an electrical equivalent and the standard logic symbol of each logic gate.

Boolean expressions of logic functions are normally written as equations, which are variables joined by operators. The raised dot ($\cdot$), which is normally used for a product symbol, is read as "AND" in Boolean, and the plus sign ($+$) is read as "OR." The equal sign ($=$) separates the variables from the output function, F. As in ordinary algebra, many times the dot is omitted and the variables are written together with no space; for example, AB is the same as A·B.

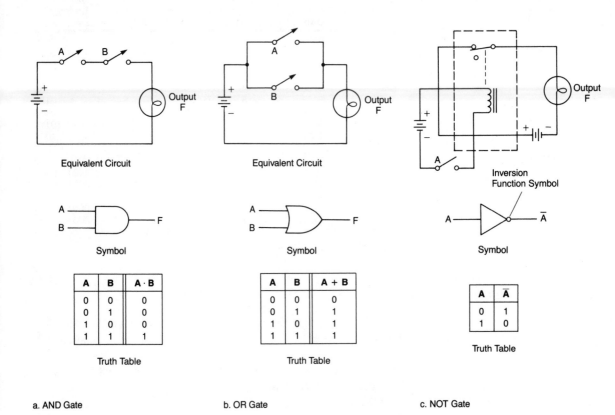

Equivalent Circuit

Equivalent Circuit

Inversion
Function Symbol

Symbol

Symbol

Symbol

A	B	A · B
0	0	0
0	1	0
1	0	0
1	1	1

Truth Table

A	B	A + B
0	0	0
0	1	1
1	0	1
1	1	1

Truth Table

A	Ā
0	1
1	0

Truth Table

a. AND Gate

b. OR Gate

c. NOT Gate

Figure 8.5 Basic Logic Functions

Example 8-8. The Boolean equation, $F = (AB) + (AC)$ is read as:

Function equals (A AND B) OR (A AND C).

The complement, or NOT function, is represented by a bar over a variable or constant. If the bar is over variables connected by an operator, the operation is performed before the inversion; otherwise the operation is performed after the inversion. The NOT function symbolizes an inverter electronic circuit and simply reverses or inverts the logic state of the input variable. For example, if a logic 1 is applied to the input of an inverter, a logic 0 results at the output.

Combinational Circuit Analysis

A combinational logic circuit is a network of logic gates which are interconnected to perform a desired function. The logic operators OR, AND and NOT can be connected so that all other possible switching functions can be realized. An analysis of a combination of these logic gates results in an equation describing the function performed by the group of gates. *Figure 8.6* shows an example combinational logic circuit, in equivalent switch form and in logic symbol form, and the Boolean equation representing the function performed. Notice that the AND gate in *Figure 8.6b* has three inputs. Multiple input logic gates are commonly available with as many as ten inputs.

Two of the more important laws of Boolean algebra are DeMorgan's laws. His first law says that the complement of an OR function is equal to the AND function of the complements. This law gives the circuit equivalency and Boolean expression identity shown in *Figure 8.7*.

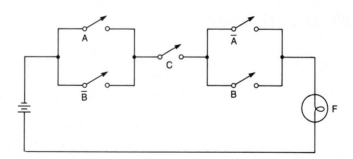

a. Switching Circuit Equivalent

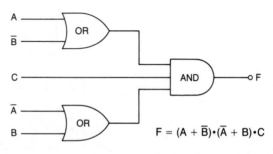

b. Logic Circuit

c. Boolean Expression

$$F = (A + \overline{B}) \cdot (\overline{A} + B) \cdot C$$

Figure 8.6 Combinational Logic

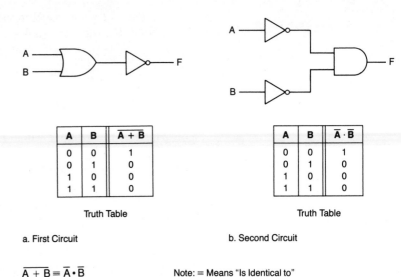

A	B	$\overline{A + B}$
0	0	1
0	1	0
1	0	0
1	1	0

Truth Table

a. First Circuit

A	B	$\overline{A} \cdot \overline{B}$
0	0	1
0	1	0
1	0	0
1	1	0

Truth Table

b. Second Circuit

$$\overline{A + B} \equiv \overline{A} \cdot \overline{B}$$

Note: ≡ Means "Is Identical to"

c. Boolean Expression

Figure 8.7   Equivalent Forms of DeMorgan's First Law

NAND and NOR Functions

It is very common for inverters to be combined with the circuitry of AND and OR gates. Connecting an inverter to the output of an AND gate produces a modification called a NAND (short for NOT-AND) gate. When the inverter is connected to the output of an OR gate, the result is a NOR gate. The NAND and NOR gates with their truth tables are shown in *Figure 8.8*. Note that the little circle on the output lead at the symbol represents an inversion of the gate.

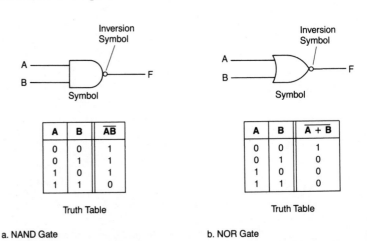

A	B	$\overline{AB}$
0	0	1
0	1	1
1	0	1
1	1	0

Truth Table

a. NAND Gate

A	B	$\overline{A + B}$
0	0	1
0	1	0
1	0	0
1	1	0

Truth Table

b. NOR Gate

Figure 8.8   Negative AND and OR Logic Gates

Figure 8.9 shows DeMorgan's second law using a NAND gate. Note that the truth tables and the Boolean expression show the two circuits to be equivalent. Both forms of DeMorgan's law may be extended to more than two variables.

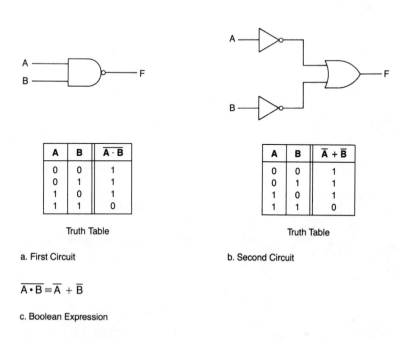

A	B	$\overline{A \cdot B}$
0	0	1
0	1	1
1	0	1
1	1	0

Truth Table

a. First Circuit

A	B	$\overline{A} + \overline{B}$
0	0	1
0	1	1
1	0	1
1	1	0

Truth Table

b. Second Circuit

$$\overline{A \cdot B} \equiv \overline{A} + \overline{B}$$

c. Boolean Expression

Figure 8.9 Equivalent Forms of DeMorgan's Second Law

EXCLUSIVE Logic

By far, the most widely-used exclusive logic operator is the exclusive-OR (XOR) function. The Boolean expression and its logic symbol and truth table are shown in *Figure 8.10*. In the Boolean expression, the plus sign designating the OR function has a circle drawn around it to indicate the exclusive-OR XOR function. The XOR describes the logic function of "either/or, but not both," but the inclusive OR (normally just called OR) that we have already discussed describes the logic function "either/or, or both." The XOR is used frequently in digital arithmetic circuits.

The exclusive-NOR (XNOR) gate is shown in *Figure 8.11*. This is sometimes called the equality comparator. The overbar on the expression indicates that the exclusive-NOR is the complement of the exclusive-OR function.

a. Symbol

$$F = A\bar{B} + \bar{A}B = A \oplus B$$

b. Boolean Expression

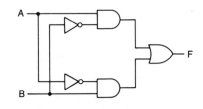

c. Equivalent Circuit

A	B	A $\oplus$ B
0	0	0
0	1	1
1	0	1
1	1	0

d. Truth Table

Figure 8.10   Exclusive-OR Logic Function

a. Symbol

$$F = \bar{A}\bar{B} + AB = \overline{A \oplus B}$$

b. Boolean Expression

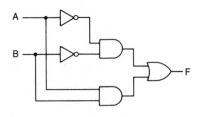

c. Equivalent Circuit

A	B	$\overline{A \oplus B}$
0	0	1
0	1	0
1	0	0
1	1	1

d. Truth Table

Figure 8.11   Exclusive-NOR Logic Function

LOGIC FAMILIES

In most circuit design and troubleshooting situations, the technician and engineer are more interested in the input/output characteristics, operating levels, and gate propagation times, than the internal structures of a discrete component or IC.

TTL

TTL logic (transistor-transistor logic) is the most widely used of the logic families. The two basic series of TTL logic are the military group (5400) and the commercial group (7400). Although there are several variations of the TTL family, they all have at least four properties in common:
1. Supply voltage
2. Noise immunity
3. Fan-in per gate input: 1/per unit
4. Fan-out limit per gate: 10/per unit

The input levels of TTL components typically range from an absolute minimum of 2.0 volts to a typical maximum of 3.5 volts. The input can tolerate up to 5 volts, but a reverse (or negative) voltage can damage the input to the gate and should not be allowed to occur. If the input of a TTL gate is left open (floating), it behaves as though there were from 2 to 5 volts positive potential being applied. Inputs should not be left open, because of the possibility of noise pickup and errors being induced in the logic.

The output levels typically range from 0.2 volt to 3.5 volts for a logic 0 output. The output of a TTL gate is designed to be directly connected to the input of another TTL gate. When the output of a TTL gate goes low, it receives current from the input of the gate to which it is connected. The output of the gate must be capable of receiving (sinking) a current of 1.6 milliamperes. The standard TTL gate can safely sink up to 16 milliamperes; therefore it can drive the inputs of 10 standard TTL gates. When the output of the TTL gate is at the high positive level for a logic 1, it supplies (sources) current to the inputs of the gates being driven. The gate must be able to source 400 milliamperes if its output drives 10 standard TTL gates. *Figure 8.12* shows the internal transistor circuitry of a TTL NAND gate.

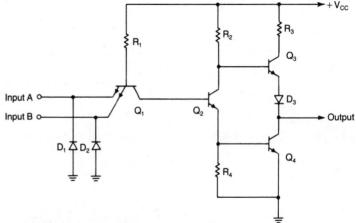

Figure 8.12 *Internal Circuitry of a TTL NAND Gate*

CMOS

A CMOS device is constructed using complementary MOS transistors The term complementary means that N-channel and P-channel MOS transistors are used. These are types of field-effect transistors with insulated gates to provide high input impedance. The CMOS equivalent of a TTL NAND gate in the 7400 Series would have a prefix of 74C00. Many of the parameters of equivalent TTL and CMOS gates are similar. The greatest differences between CMOS and TTL are that the V_{CC} voltage can be range from 3.0 volts to 15 volts (recall that TTL ranges from 0 to 5 volts), and the power consumption for TTL is much higher.

Figure 8.13 shows the internal circuit of a CMOS NAND gate. Because the insulating layer between the gate and the channel is of an extremely high resistance, the bias supply current is always very small for a CMOS device. This supply current is typically 50 nanoamperes. This compares to a typical value of 5.1 milliamperes of bias supply current per gate for TTL.

Because CMOS can be operated within the 0 to 5 volt level, it is compatible with TTL. A CMOS gate can drive any single low-power TTL gate, or if two CMOS gates are tied together, they can drive a single standard TTL gate. The quietest of the more common gates, the CMOS gate, generates almost no switching noise. When compared to TTL, the main disadvantage of the CMOS gate is its slower speed of operation. At the present time, bipolar TTL and CMOS dominate the small-scale and medium-scale integrated digital scene.

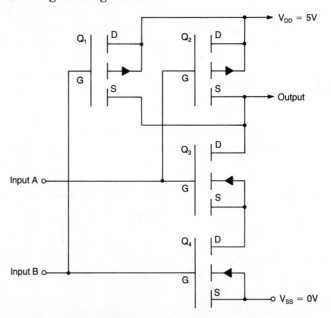

Figure 8.13   CMOS NAND Gate Internal Circuitry

MOS

MOS is made in one of two types: PMOS and NMOS. The original PMOS had a metal gate and required +12 volts and −12 volts from a power supply. Because it had a high threshold voltage, it was much more difficult to interface to TTL. It was also the slowest of the MOS devices — up to 300 nanoseconds switching time. Most recently, newer PMOS devices are constructed using a silicon gate in place of the earlier metal gate. The silicon gate reduces the threshold voltage and allows interfacing with TTL 5-volt logic. Also, the frequency is increased more than two times on the newer silicon gate PMOS devices.

ECL

The fastest logic family in use today is emitter-coupled logic (ECL). This logic system is widely used in industry today where cost is not the primary factor. Its main characteristic is its extremely high speed, making it very attractive for sophisticated high-speed computing systems. The main reason for its high-speed logic (typically 2 nanoseconds) is that the transistors that make up the ECL gate never operate in saturation; they operate in the active mode. The phenomenon that usually limits switching time for a bipolar transistor is the storage time, which is a result of the transistor junctions being saturated. The ECL family has eliminated storage time as a switching-speed limiting factor.

Figure 8.14 shows the internal structure of an ECL NOR/OR gate internal circuit along with its logic symbol. Note in the figure the power supply voltage requirements. This results in very different logic voltage levels for ECL, as compared to other logic types. A logical 1 voltage level is −0.9 volt and the logical 0 level is −1.75 volts. Notice that this gate has both OR and NOR outputs.

I^2L

Integrated Injection Logic (I^2L) is simple and inexpensive to produce. I^2L speed is comparable to TTL. I^2L technology is sometimes referred to as MTL (merged transistor logic) because of the way in which the transistors are merged within the substrate.

In designing a logic circuit, there is always a tradeoff between switching speed and power consumed. Each of the families discussed has its own speed/power characteristics. *Table 8.3* compares the logic families.

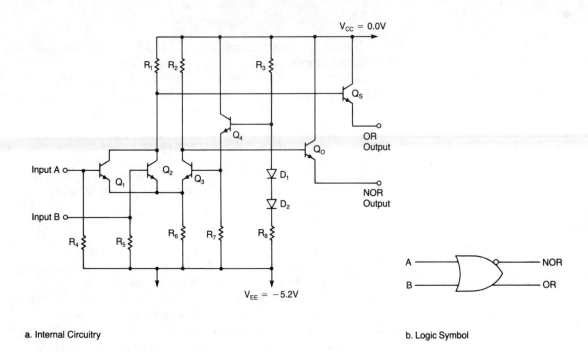

a. Internal Circuitry

b. Logic Symbol

Figure 8.14 ECL NOR/OR Gate Internal Circuitry and Its Logic Symbol

Family	Speed (nSec)	Power Dissipated (mW)	Voltages Required (V)	High Logical Level (V)	Low Logical Level
RTL	15	24	+3.6	+3.6	1.4
DTL	30	10	+5	+5	0.98
TTL	10	10	+5	+5	0.58
ECL	2	40	−5.2	−0.9	−1.75
CMOS	25	0.00001	+3 to +15	V_{CC}	1.17
Low Speed TTL	33	1	+5	+3	0.93
Schottky TTL	3	19	+5	+3	1.39
Low Power Schottky TTL	9	2	+5	+3	1.39

Table 8.3 A Comparison Between the Logic Families

FLIP-FLOPS

The primary emphasis so far in this chapter has been developing an understanding of combinational logic circuits. The outputs of these circuits are completely dependent upon the condition at the time the output is being observed; that is, combinational logic circuits do not possess memory.

In contrast, sequential logic circuits have an output that depends on not only the present input condition, but also on past input conditions. This capability of memory is the special feature that allows the sequential circuits to perform their function.

The term memory as used here should not be confused with the mass storage memory used in digital computers to store programs and data. Memory as used here refers to the immediate past, so that the basic sequential logic circuit may be analyzed based on information that is currently incoming.

Latch

Combinational logic circuits may be connected to perform sequential logic operations. One of the simplest is the flip-flop, or latch, as it is sometimes called. The term latch is used to describe a logic function that is similar to the action of mechanical latch. When the latch is moved to one position, it will stay there until a force is exerted to move it to the other position. Then the latch stays in that position until it is forced back to the original position.

The flip-flop latch functions similarly in that its output stays at one logic level until an input forces it to change to the opposite level. Thus, the flip-flop always remembers what its last input was, whether it was a microsecond ago or an hour ago.

$\overline{S}$-$\overline{R}$ Flip-Flops

As shown in *Figure 8.15a*, a basic NAND logic $\overline{S}$ (Set-NOT) $\overline{R}$ (Reset-NOT) flip-flop provides two outputs: Q and $\overline{Q}$. Whether the flip-flop is set or reset is determined by the state of Q. If Q is 1, it is set; if Q is 0, it is reset. Of course, the $\overline{Q}$ output is in the opposite state. As the truth table indicates, a logic 0 is required on the $\overline{S}$ input to set the flip-flop, and a logic 0 is required on the $\overline{R}$ input to reset it.

To explain the flip-flop operation, assume that it has been previously set, but the logic 0 has been removed from $\overline{S}$ and that logic 1 is on $\overline{S}$, $\overline{R}$, Q and the top input of gate 2. When a logic 0 is applied to $\overline{R}$, the output of gate 2 changes to logic 1 and is applied to the bottom input of gate 1 so it now has a 1 on both inputs and the Q output changes to 0. The 0 is coupled back to the top input of gate 2, which forces a 1 output. Because of this, the logic 0 applied to $\overline{R}$ can now be removed and the circuit will stay in this state, remembering that a 0 was applied to $\overline{R}$, until a 0 is applied to $\overline{S}$. When that happens, a similar sequence of events changes the state so that Q is again a logic 1.

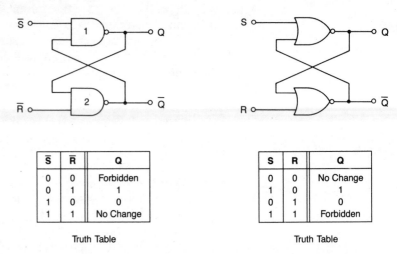

$\overline{S}$	$\overline{R}$	Q
0	0	Forbidden
0	1	1
1	0	0
1	1	No Change

Truth Table

S	R	Q
0	0	No Change
1	0	1
0	1	0
1	1	Forbidden

Truth Table

a. Basic $\overline{S}$-$\overline{R}$ Latch Using NAND Logic   b. Basic S-R Latch Using NOR Logic

Figure 8.15   Basic Latch Configurations Using NAND and NOR Logic

Latch circuits of this type are commonly called a flip-flop circuit because they flip from one logic state to the other, then flop back when appropriate logic levels are *momentarily* applied to the input. That word "momentarily" is important because the input signal is remembered even though it is present for only a fraction of a second. These circuits also are sometimes called bistable latches because the circuit will latch in either logic 1 or 0 state.

While the circuit described above was made with NAND gates, NOR gates also can be used to perform this function as illustrated in *Figure 8.15b*. As shown in the truth table, the active level for this circuit's inputs is logic 1 instead of logic 0.

Clocked S-R Flip-Flops

Figure 8.16a shows the addition of two more NAND gates to the S-R flip-flop which will prevent a signal on the S or R inputs from changing the state of the circuit unless the clock input is triggered. *Figure 8.16b* shows the truth table. This clocked S-R flip-flop is one of several types of triggered flip-flops with which counters, shift registers, and other synchronous circuits are built.

Figure 8.16c presents the symbol, which is recognized as a clocked S-R flip-flop by the input labels. When this symbol is used, it indicates that the flip-flop represented operates in accordance with the specific set of rules shown in the truth table in *Figure 8.16b*.

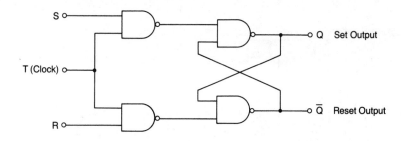

a. Circuit

Input			Command	Output	
S	**R**	**T**		**Q**	**Q̄**
L	L	L		NC	NC
L	L	H	Remember	NC	NC
L	H	L		NC	NC
L	H	H	Reset	L	H
H	L	L		NC	NC
H	L	H	Set	H	L
H	H	L		NC	NC
H	H	H	Invalid	H	H

Note: NC = No Change
     L = Low
     H = High

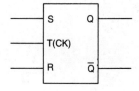

b. Truth Table   c. Symbol

Figure 8.16   Clocked S-R Flip-Flops Using TTL NAND Gates

D Flip-Flops

A modification to the clocked S-R flip-flop produces a gated flip-flop called a D-type flip-flop. *Figure 8.17a* shows the modification necessary to convert the clocked S-R flip-flop into a D-type flip-flop by adding an inverter. The logic symbol for the 7474 D flip-flop with the set and reset inputs is shown in *Figure 8.17b*. The set input for a D flip-flop is called PR (Preset) and the reset input is called CLR (Clear). These inputs are used for asynchronous operation. The equivalent circuit using an S-R flip flop is shown in *Figure 8.17c*, and the truth table for this 7474 D flip-flop is shown in *Figure 8.17d*.

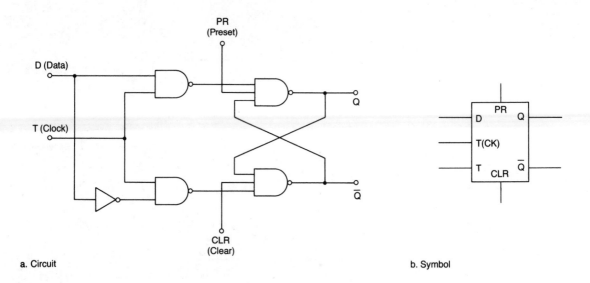

PR
(Preset)

D (Data)

T (Clock)

Q

Q̄

CLR
(Clear)

a. Circuit

b. Symbol

D   PR   Q

T(CK)

T   CLR   Q̄

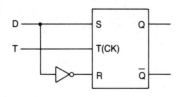

D   S   Q

T   T(CK)

R   Q̄

c. Type S-R Flip-Flop Wired to Form a Type-D

d. Truth Table

Input	Output	
D	Q	Q̄
H	H	L
L	L	H

Figure 8.17   D-Type Flip-Flop

If the D input is connected to the Q̄ output as shown in *Figure 8.18*, every clock pulse causes the output (both Q and Q̄) to change states. Each time the Q̄ output changes state, the new state (1 or 0) is applied to the D input. The Q̄ output will always program the D input to store the opposite state in the latch when the clock pulse arrives. Remember that for this device, a clock pulse is any logic transition from 1 to 0 from the clock input. Since the flip-flop circuit of *Figure 8.18a* changes output states with each clock pulse, two pulses are required to cycle the output from 1 to 0 and back to 1 again, thus, this circuit configuration is called a divide-by-two. In the waveforms shown in *Figure 8.18b*, notice that the output frequency (Q) is half the input frequency. Another important feature to notice is that this flip-flop can square a non-symmetrical waveform input at the T terminal since it is triggered by only the transistion. This is a very useful feature for certain devices, such as frequency counters.

J-K Flip-Flops

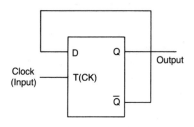

a. D-Type Connected to Form a Divide-By-Two

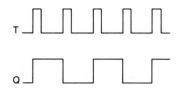

b. Input to Output Divide-By-Two Flip-Flop Waveforms

Figure 8.18 D-Type Flip-Flop Connected to Toggle with Each Clock Pulse

The most versatile flip-flop is the J-K flip-flop shown in *Figure 8.19a*. The J-K flip-flop will normally have PR (Preset) and CLR (Clear) inputs along with J-K and CK (clock) inputs. The PR and CLR inputs operate like set and reset inputs for asynchronous operation. These inputs operate with the clock line held low (logic 0). Its symbol and truth table appear in *Figure 8.19b* and *8.19c*. Since there are two input variables, there are four input conditions. If both J and K are low, the flip-flop is instructed to remain in its present state with the next clock pulse. If K is high (active) and J is low (inactive), the flip-flop is instructed to Reset (Q goes low at the next clock pulse). If J is high and K is low, the flip-flop is instructed to Set. The uniqueness of the J-K flip-flop is seen in the condition when both J and K are high (active), instructing the flip-flop to change (complement) with each clock pulse. The J-K flip-flop can be considered an S-R-T flip-flop (similar to an S-R type, with T used to force a change of state), but with two additional gates at the input. These two gates allow for input variables J and K.

To help understand the operation of the J-K flip-flop, as well as the active levels associated with them, a timing diagram is shown in *Figure 8.19d*. Trace through it for each time period.

Sequential Circuit Timing

The timing diagram shown in *Figure 8.19d* indicates a time dependence for sequential logic. It is these immediate memory and time dependency properties of sequential logic circuits that make them different from combinational logic circuits. Thus, in a sequential logic circuit, the outputs depend not only on the inputs immediately present, as in combinational logic, but also on the present state of the flip-flop which resulted from the immediate past condition of the inputs.

COUNTERS

In digital circuits, a counter is a device composed of properly connected sequential elements which count input pulses. Because they have the two important characteristics of timing and memory, they are sequential circuits, usually made with flip-flops. Digital computers and programmable controllers make extensive use of counters to control the sequence and the execution of their program steps. In industry, counters are used to determine the number of events that happen, such as steps in a machine operation or manufactured items placed in a packaging container.

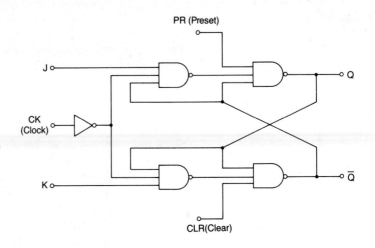

a. Circuit

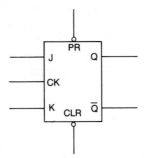

b. Symbol

Input		Command	Output	
J	**K**		Q	Q̄
L	L	Remember	NC	NC
L	H	Reset	L	H
H	L	Set	H	H
H	H	Complement	Toggle	Toggle

c. Truth Table

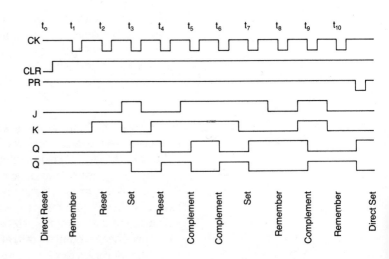

d. Timing Diagram

Figure 8.19   J-K Flip-Flop

BASIC ELECTRONICS TECHNOLOGY

All digital counters have four important characteristics:
1. A maximum number of counts.
2. The ability to count up or down or both.
3. Asynchronous or synchronous operation.
4. Free running or self-stopping.

Ripple Counter

All digital circuit counters count in binary or binary codes. The modulus of the counter is the number of counts through one pass. An example of a simple 4-bit ripple counter is shown in *Figure 8.20a*. The pattern is called a binary count because it is counting using only two numbers, 1 and 0. The first stage stores a count up to 2, the second stage up to 4, the third stage up to 8, and the fourth up to 16. In *Figure 8.20b*, notice how the output waveforms relate to the clock and to each other. Notice that 16 clock periods occur for one period of the Q_D output. Since this counter starts at 0 and counts up to 15, it is called a binary-up counter.

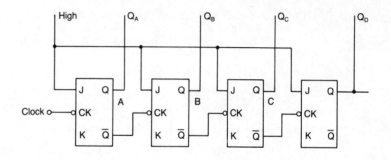

a. Circuit Using J-K Flip-Flops

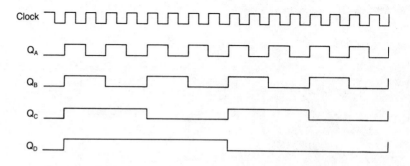

b. Input and Output Waveforms

Figure 8.20 4-Bit Ripple Counter

An up counter using D flip-flops is also easily constructed, as shown in *Figure 8.21a*. Both D and J-K flip-flops may also be wired as down counters. These are shown in *Figure 8.21b* and *8.21c*, respectively.

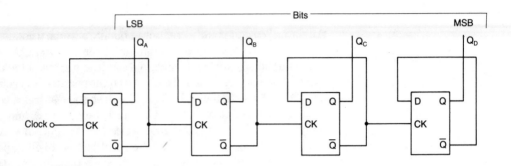

a. Ripple-Up Counter Using D Flip-Flops

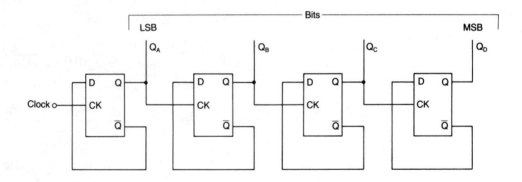

b. Ripple-Down Counter Using D Flip-Flops

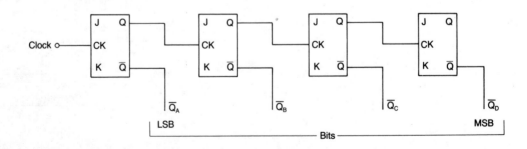

c. Ripple-Down Counter Using J-K Flip-Flops

Figure 8.21 Comparison Between Counters

The four counters considered thus far are asynchronous, where one stage triggers the next stage. The disadvantages of counters of this type are:

1. Slower operation than individual flip-flops.
2. The inability of the outputs to switch at precisely the same instant, due to propagation time through the flip-flop.

The slower operation results from a count of 1 having to ripple through the stages. Thus, in a 4-stage counter, the fourth stage must wait for the information (logic 1 or 0) to pass through from stages 1, 2, and 3. This propagation delay is very bothersome in an asynchronous or ripple counter that is designed to count to a high modulus. All logic devices have propagation delay, but this is a problem when stages are wired in series so that the delay times are cumulative; that is, the delay time of each device in series is added to the total circuit delay.

Synchronous Counter

In the synchronous or parallel counter, all the flip-flops are clocked (triggered) at the same time. Also, combinational logical elements (gates) are used to control flip-flop state changes. Thus, the stored count progresses only one unit each time a clock pulse is received.

Because the synchronous counter does not have the propagation delay of the asynchronous counter, it is better suited to high-speed operation. However, the combinational gates tend to slow down the operation of synchronous counters. Thus, some delay still exists in this type of counter and the real operational speed is less than the theoretical maximum speed.

A disadvantage is that the clock is used to drive all of the flip-flops simultaneously, requiring the clock circuit to supply more power than in a simple ripple counter. When the clock is heavily loaded by many flip-flops, the propagation delay is increased and the counter speed reduced. Despite these limitations, synchronous counters are usually superior to asynchronous counters.

Decoding Counters

By using a combination of logic gates and flip-flops arranged in a counter, a decoding circuit may be constructed to give an output indication at a predetermined count. The circuit in *Figure 8.22* is used to decode the counter and give an indication when the count reaches decimal 6. The output from the decoder could be used to initiate some stepping function in an assembly process after six operations, and to reset the counter and start over at 0. Since the counter has a 4-bit output, it can count up to decimal 15.

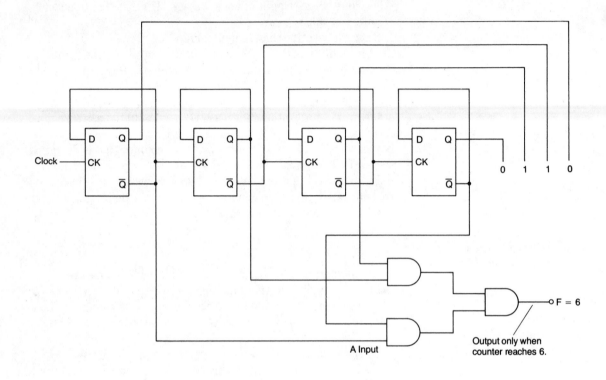

Figure 8.22   *Decoder Circuit for Decimal 6*

The binary number 0110 represents the decimal number 6, and the state of each digit provides an input to the logic gates that form the decoder. Since the Q outputs of the second and third flip-flops are high, these directly provide logic 1 inputs to the top AND gate so its output will be a logic 1. In order to get the lower AND gate to provide a logic 1 output, both its inputs must be high. Therefore, these inputs are obtained from the $\overline{Q}$ output on the first and fourth flip-flops. With a logic 1 output from both the upper and lower AND gates, the third AND gate produces a logic 1 output. No other combination of flip-flop states will produce a 1 output from the decoder.

Modulus Counter Techniques

The modulus of a counter is simply the number of counting states before it begins to repeat itself. A 4-stage counter has a natural modulus of 16. A 3-stage counter has a natural modulus of 8. The counters previously considered in *Figures 8.20* and *8.21* operate in their natural modulus; that is, they count to their full count range, then automatically start over.

A counter can be made to count to any desired modulus by selecting a counter with a natural modulus a step higher than the desired modulus, and then causing it to skip the proper number of steps. Counts can be skipped anywhere in the natural sequence. Some form of feedback is used to force the counter ahead for a determined number of counts, before it reaches its natural count sequence. Decoders like the one discussed in *Figure 8.22* can be used to make the counter operate at any modulus desired.

Figure 8.23a shows an asynchronous counter operating at modulus 3; thus the counter counts from 0 to 3 and then resets. *Figure 8.23b* shows a modulus 5 ripple counter. In general, the following procedure may be used to configure a counter to any modulus:

1. Find the number of flip-flops required by using the exponent of the nearest power of 2 larger than the modulus number (N). For a modulus 5:

$$2^2 = 4, 2^3 = 8$$

   therefore, three flip-flops are required.
2. Connect all the flip-flops as a ripple counter.
3. Convert the modulus number in decimal to a binary number. For modulus 5, it's 0101.
4. Find the flip-flops that have 1s on Q at the Nth count. In the example of *Figure 8.23b*, these would be flip-flops A and C.
5. Connect the Q outputs of these flip-flops to the inputs of a NAND gate. Connect the output of the NAND gate to the CLR (clear) or reset inputs on all flip-flops.

An analysis of this procedure shows that the circuit will count up to $(N - 1)$ and on the Nth count will go to the number N momentarily. The NAND gate detects the presence of N and then resets the counters to 0s.

Probably the most widely-used counter is the decade counter, also called a modulus 10 counter. *Figure 8.23c* shows a modulus 10 ripple counter using four J-K flip-flops, and one NAND gate. This circuit counts like a modulus 16 counter until it reaches 1001, which is the maximum count for this circuit. As soon as the counter advances to 1010, the logic 1 from each of flip-flops B and D activate the NAND gate, which resets the output to 0000.

IC Counters

IC packaging techniques have made available numerous inexpensive counter types. Designing appropriate configurations of synchronous, asynchronous, feedback, and inhibit circuits can provide any counter function required. For example, a modulus 2

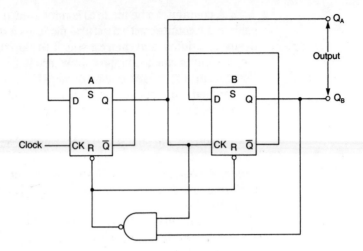

a. Modulus 3 Counter

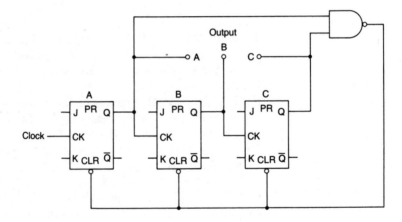

b. Modulus 5 Counter

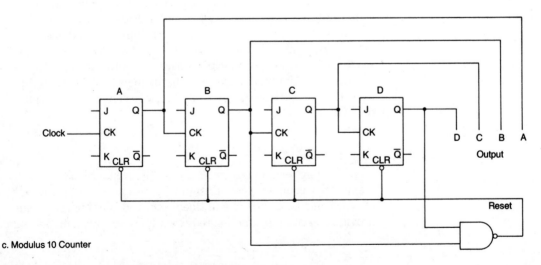

c. Modulus 10 Counter

Figure 8.23   Comparison Between Modulus Logic Diagrams

and a modulus 3 counter can be combined as a divide-by-three-by-two combination, providing a modulus 6 counter. A divide-by-three, divide-by-two pair can be combined with another divide-by-two, counter to obtain a modulus 12 counter.

When using a counter to indicate time, it is important to have divide-by-six and divide-by-twelve to fit the hours and minutes of our time measurement. A decimal counter can be formed by using a divide-by-two, divide-by-five. A counter can be made to count with any modulus by shortening the natural count.

Programmable counters are variable modulus devices. The modulus is determined by setting conditions on the programming inputs. The most popular type of programmable counter can be programmed to operate in any modulus by connecting each of the program inputs to either a high or low (+ 5 volts or ground).

REGISTERS

Flip-flops are commonly used as registers or data storage units. The shift register is a memory system consisting of flip-flops or MOS dynamic memory cells. The special feature of a shift register is that data can be moved from cell to adjacent cell upon command as many times as desired.

A good example of a shift register application is the pocket calculator, where the momentary depression of each key causes a continuous display to appear. Each subsequent depression shifts the previous displayed entry to the left. The example illustrates both the shifting and memory functions.

Shift registers are constructed from flip-flops, classifying them as sequential logic circuits. They are often used as temporary memories and for shifting data to the left or right. Another important use of shift registers is changing data from serial to parallel, or vice versa.

Storage Register

Each of the flip-flops that make up a register store one bit of binary information. A storage register is used whenever temporary storage of information is needed. Since the flip-flop inputs can be connected between a source of data and the circuit that uses that data, the flip-flops are considered to be storing the data (memory). Storage registers are used extensively in digital computers when data from the computer's memory is transferred temporarily to a storage register before it is sent to another functional part of the computer.

Shift Register

A shift register consists of a group of flip-flops connected so that each flip-flop transfers its bit of information to the next flip-flop of the register when the clock pulse occurs. Several types are common:

1. Serial-in, parallel-out (SIPO)
2. Parallel-in, serial-out (PISO)
3. Parallel-in, parallel-out (PIPO)
4. Serial-in, serial-out (SISO)

Table 8.4 summarizes the four basic shift register types.

Table 8.4   The Four Basic Shift Register Types

Register Type	Operation	Application
SIPO	Data clocked in a bit at a time. Entire output gated out at once.	Used to exchange data between computers and terminals.
PISO	Data bits input simultaneously to all stages. Output a bit at a time.	Used to exchange data between computers and terminals.
PIPO	All data bits input simultaneously. Data is output simultaneously.	Used to transfer data between subsections of computer-type equipment.
SISO	Data is clocked in a bit at a time. Data is clocked out a bit at a time.	Used to transfer data between subsections of computer-type equipment.

Serial-In, Parallel-Out Shift Register

Figure 8.24 shows a simple 4-bit, serial-in, parallel-out shift-right register. It uses four D flip-flops. Data bits are fed into the D input of flip-flop A. This input is labeled as the serial data input. The CLR (Clear) input will reset all four flip-flops to 0 when activated low. All the clock inputs are connected together, so a pulse at the clock input will shift the data from the serial data input, D_A, to the output Q_A, from D_B to Q_B, from D_C to Q_C, and from D_D to Q_D. The outputs at points A, B, C and D represent the contents of each cell (flip-flop) of the register.

Here's how to load the 4-bit number, 0101, into this shift register: First apply a 0 to the CLR input to clear the register so that the output is 0000. Return the CLR input to 1. Place the least significant 1 from the 4-bit number at the serial data input and clock the register. The output will be 1000 (A = 1; B, C, and D = 0).

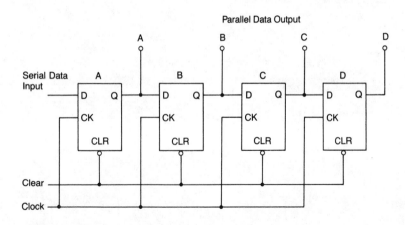

Figure 8.24   4-Bit Serial Loaded Shift Right Register

Place a 0 at the data input and clock the register a second time. The output is now 0100. Apply the next 1 to the serial data input, clock the register a third time and the output is 1010. Apply a zero at the input and clock the register for the fourth time. The output reads 0101 because the binary number has been loaded into the register one bit at a time. This is an example of serial loading with the data shifted from left to right through the register. An important point to note is that the entire number would not have to be loaded into the register if only a particular output was desired.

Parallel-In, Parallel-Out Shift Register

The serial-load shift register is for use when data is being received serially. If the data is already in parallel form, then the parallel-load shift register which loads all bits of information simultaneously, is the one to use. *Figure 8.25* shows a simple 4-bit, parallel-in, parallel-out shift register. It uses J-K flip-flops with both the CLR and PR inputs. Some parallel-load shift registers have preset-only capabilities. With this type, an individual 1 in any stage cannot be changed to 0. The entire register must be cleared to all 0s and reloaded with new data.

Universal Shift Register

Bidirectional shifting (right or left shifting) is accomplished by a circuit containing special gates to control shift direction. Generally, various combinations of parallel and serial inputs/outputs are available. The universal shift register's mode of operation is selected by control inputs.

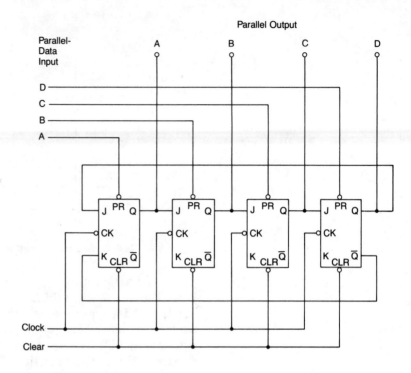

Figure 8.25 4-Bit Parallel-Load Shift Right Register

DIGITAL ARITHMETIC CIRCUITS

In addition to logic functions, digital computers also perform arithmetic operations. In fact, this ability is the fundamental requirement of digital computers. This function is performed in the computer's central processing unit (CPU), which contains the arithmetic logic unit (ALU). The ALU performs decision-making as well as arithmetic functions. Decision-making functions are primarily those of making comparisons to see if one number is greater than or less than another number, if two numbers are equal, or if a number is equal to zero. The arithmetic functions are essentially a process of addition and subtraction.

Adders

The basic adder stage accepts two inputs, generates a sum output, and a carry which it sends to the next more significant stage. The half-adder, which is much simpler than the full-adder, accepts only the input numbers to be added in binary, single bit form, and does not accept a carry-in. Thus, it is used as the least significant stage of a full-adder, where there is never a carry input.

The half-adder is shown in *Figure 8.26a* and its truth table in *Figure 8.26b*. Compare the "sum" portion of this circuit to the exclusive OR circuit and truth table shown in *Figure 8.10d* and note that they have the same function. If either of the inputs is a 1, then the sum is a 1. If both inputs are 1, it is adding $1 + 1$ and the result is 10. The sum output would be zero, and the carry output to the next stage would be 1.

A full-adder differs from the half-adder in that it accepts a carry input. One way of realizing a full-adder is by a combination of two half-adders and an OR gate as shown in *Figure 8.27a*. The truth table is shown in *Figure 8.27b*. Since the full-adder adds three bits — A, B and C_{input} — it can have a decimal output of 0, 1, 2, or 3 if both the sum and carry out digits are considered together. An output of 0 is represented as $S = 0$ and $C_{output} = 0$; an output of 3 is represented as $S = 1$ and $C_{output} = 1$. The symbols for a half-adder and full-adder are shown in *Figures 8.27c*.

Two's Complement Subtraction

Subtraction of binary numbers is most easily done by a method known as 2's complement. This is essentially subtraction by changing the sign and adding. In 2's complement notation, a positive number is represented as a simple binary number with the restriction that the most significant bit (MSB) is 0, so that it can be used as the sign bit (0 = negative, 1 = positive).

In working with 2's complement subtraction, it is important to remember that the MSB is the sign bit. Thus, to subtract a subtrahend from a minuend, first take the 2's complement of the subtrahend and add it to the minuend. The 2's complement of a number is obtained by first taking the 1's complement of the number (change all 1s to 0s and 0s to 1s) and then adding 1 to the least significant bit. These operations can be performed by an adder and logic inverter.

1. Represent the number as a positive binary number.
2. Complement it; that is, write 0s where there are 1s, and 1s where there are 0s in the positive number.
3. Add 1.
4. Ignore any carry out of the MSB.

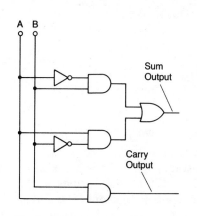

a. Circuit

Inputs		Outputs	
A	B	Sum	Carry
0	0	0	0
0	1	1	0
1	0	1	0
1	1	0	1

b. Truth Table

Figure 8.26   Half-Adder

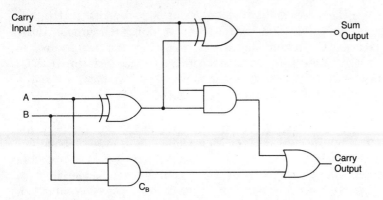

A	B	C_{IN}	Sum Output	C_O
0	0	0	0	0
0	0	1	1	0
0	1	0	1	0
0	1	1	0	1
1	0	0	1	0
1	0	1	0	1
1	1	0	0	1
1	1	1	1	1

a. Two Half-Adders Combined to Form Full-Adder Circuit

b. Truth Table

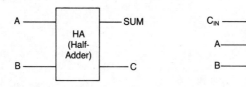

c. Symbols Compared

Figure 8.27   Full-Adder

Example 8-9: Subtract 30 from 53 using 8-bit numbers.

53 = 00110101 (minuend)
30 = 00011110 (subtrahend)
Remember, sign bit: 0 = neg. 1 = pos.
−30 = 11100001 Take one's complement of 30
+   1 Add 1 to get two's complement
11100010
00110101 Add 53 binary
00010111 Answer in binary

or

23 Answer in decimal

Multiplication by Successive Addition

Digital computers and microprocessor-based systems, which can perform addition extremely rapidly, can be programmed to multiply by a series of successive addition steps. The adder circuits may be clocked to add two numbers, storing the partial product for the next addition.

Figure 8.28 shows a binary multiplier circuit using the repeated addition method. In this figure, the multiplicand (1101) is loaded into the top register, and the multiplier (1100) is loaded in the down counter. The accumulator is cleared to 000000. The down counter is then decreased by 1 to 1011. The adder yields 1101 (decimal 13) because of the 1101 and the 0s being applied at Inputs A and B. This is the first partial product. The second clock pulse causes the down counter to decrement the multiplier to 1010. The adder adds the 1101 at Input A to the 1101 at Input B, yielding 011010 (decimal 26), which appears in the accumulator. This is the second partial product. The down counter decrements the multiplier to 1001 (decimal 9). The adder adds the 1101 at Input A, to 011010 at Input B. This yields the third partial product, the equivalent of decimal 39.

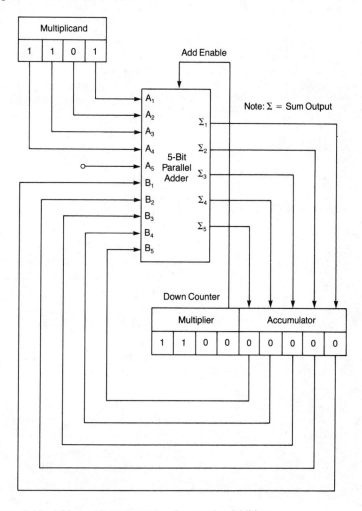

Figure 8.28   A Binary Multiplier Using Successive Addition

This procedure is continued until the last (12th) clock pulse causes the down counter to decrement the multiplier to 0000, and the adder adds the 1101 at Input A to the last partial product at Input B, yielding the final product 10011100 (decimal 156) at the accumulator. The down counter then stops at 0000 and the problem is completed.

An adder has been used here to do multiplication by the repeated addition method. This procedure is also easily adapted to digital computers and microprocessor-based systems.

Arithmetic Logic Unit

As we said earlier, the ALU section of the CPU performs the arithmetic and decision-making operations. As was shown above, the ALU can perform multiplication as a series of additions. Similarly, division can be performed as a series of subtractions. These same techniques can also be applied to the more complex operations, such as extracting roots and raising numbers to powers.

For decision-making operations, the ALU compares which of two numbers is larger or smaller, whether a number equals 0, and whether a number is positive or negative. An ALU may also perform basic logic functions such as AND, OR, and Exclusive OR.

The ALU works in conjunction with a number of registers which temporarily store data, on which logical or mathematical operations are performed. Current technology allows the combination of all of these functions on a single IC chip.

In the 7400 TTL series, the basic ALU is the 74181. A simplied functional layout of the 74181 is shown in *Figure 8.29a* and its operational table is given in *Figure 8.29b*. The inputs to the 74181 include two 4-bit words, A and B, as the data inputs, along with a carry-in, C_n. There are five control inputs which determine the operation that is performed on the data inputs. The M(mode) input determines whether the output is a logical or an arithmetic function of the inputs. The four select lines make it possible to choose one of sixteen logical or arithmetical operations.

The outputs of the 74181 include the 4-bit result (F outputs), a carry-out, an A = B output and the $\overline{G}$(generate) and $\overline{P}$(propagate) outputs. By carefully following the operational table in *Figure 8.29b*, the outputs for any given inputs may be determined. The obvious advantage of using a 74181 is its ability to perform a great diversity of operations simply by choosing the proper SL(select) and M(mode) inputs.

A simple calculator may be constructed using an ALU along with some registers, including an accumulator (which is used to store results of each arithmetic operation), a bus structure, some interfacing devices, and a display method for the output.

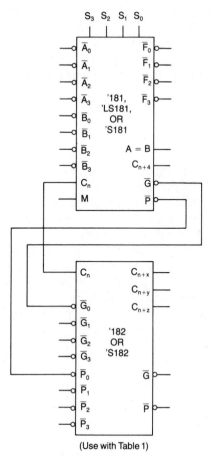
(Use with Table 1)

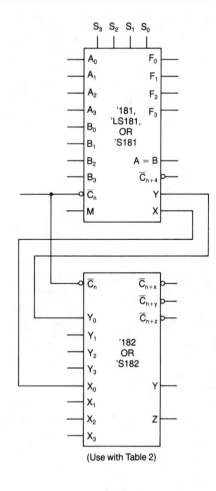
(Use with Table 2)

a. Functional Layout

TABLE 1

SELECTION	ACTIVE-LOW DATA		
	M = H	M = L; ARITHMETIC OPERATIONS	
S3 S2 S1 S0	LOGIC FUNCTIONS	C_n = L (no carry)	C_n = H (with carry)
L L L L	$F = \overline{A}$	F = A Minus 1	F = A
L L L H	$F = \overline{AB}$	F = AB Minus 1	F = AB
L L H L	$F = \overline{A} + B$	F = A$\overline{B}$ Minus 1	F = A$\overline{B}$
L L H H	F = 1	F = Minus 1 (2's Comp)	F = Zero
L H L L	$F = \overline{A} + \overline{B}$	F = A Plus (A + $\overline{B}$)	F = A Plus (A + $\overline{B}$) Plus 1
L H L H	$F = \overline{B}$	F = AB Plus (A + $\overline{B}$)	F = AB Plus (A + $\overline{B}$) Plus 1
L H H L	$F = \overline{A \oplus B}$	F = A Minus B Minus 1	F = A Minus B
L H H H	$F = A + \overline{B}$	F = A + $\overline{B}$	F = (A + $\overline{B}$) Plus 1
H L L L	$F = \overline{A}B$	F = A Plus (A + B)	F = A Plus (A + B) Plus 1
H L L H	$F = A \oplus B$	F = A Plus B	F = A Plus B Plus 1
H L H L	F = B	F = A$\overline{B}$ Plus (A + B)	F = A$\overline{B}$ Plus (A + B) Plus 1
H L H H	F = A + B	F = (A + B)	F = (A + B) Plus 1
H H L L	F = 0	F = A Plus A*	F = A Plus A Plus 1
H H L H	$F = A\overline{B}$	F = AB Plus A	F = AB Plus A Plus 1
H H H L	F = AB	F = A$\overline{B}$ Plus A	F = A$\overline{B}$ Plus A Plus 1
H H H H	F = A	F = A	F = A Plus 1

TABLE 2

SELECTION	ACTIVE-HIGH DATA		
	M = H	M = L; ARITHMETIC OPERATIONS	
S3 S2 S1 S0	LOGIC FUNCTIONS	$\overline{C}_n$ = H (no carry)	$\overline{C}_n$ = L (with carry)
L L L L	$F = \overline{A}$	F = A	F = A Plus 1
L L L H	$F = \overline{A + B}$	F = A + B	F = (A + B) Plus 1
L L H L	$F = \overline{A}B$	F = A + $\overline{B}$	F = (A + $\overline{B}$) Plus 1
L L H H	F = 0	F = Minus 1 (2's Compl)	F = Zero
L H L L	$F = \overline{AB}$	F = A Plus A$\overline{B}$	F = A Plus A$\overline{B}$ Plus 1
L H L H	$F = \overline{B}$	F = (A + B) Plus A$\overline{B}$	F = (A + B) Plus A$\overline{B}$ Plus 1
L H H L	$F = A \oplus B$	F = A Minus B Minus 1	F = A Minus B
L H H H	$F = A\overline{B}$	F = A$\overline{B}$ Minus 1	F = A$\overline{B}$
H L L L	$F = \overline{A} + B$	F = A Plus AB	F = A Plus AB Plus 1
H L L H	$F = \overline{A \oplus B}$	F = A Plus B	F = A Plus B Plus 1
H L H L	F = B	F = (A + $\overline{B}$) Plus AB	F = (A + $\overline{B}$) Plus AB Plus 1
H L H H	F = AB	F = AB Minus 1	F = AB
H H L L	F = 1	F = A Plus A*	F = A Plus A Plus 1
H H L H	$F = A + \overline{B}$	F = (A + B) Plus A	F = (A + B) Plus A Plus 1
H H H L	F = A + B	F = (A + $\overline{B}$) Plus A	F = (A + $\overline{B}$) Plus A Plus 1
H H H H	F = A	F = A Minus 1	F = A

b. Operational Table

Figure 8.29 Basic ALU

DATA HANDLING AND DISPLAY METHODS

Whether considering a large-scale digital computer, a microprocessor, or an industrial control system, five basic functions must be performed by an information processing device:

1. Input function, which interfaces between the device and the outside world.
2. Output function, which also interfaces between the device and the outside world.
3. Storage (memory) function, which stores information, and instructions on what to do with the information.
4. Arithmetic Logic Unit (ALU), which performs the mathematical and logical operations of the system or device.
5. Control function which sequences the device.

In almost every information processing device or computer, the flow of information must begin at the Input function. This information, as data, is sent to the ALU function for processing and is then sent back to storage to await further use. When called upon by the control function, the output function displays the results of the internal processing of information.

Bus Structures

The bus systems electrically tie together, via parallel structure, all the sections of the information-processing device. Each bus system, which consists of a separate conductor for each bit in the byte size used, is dedicated to a specific function. For example, memory addressing, data, and control each have their own bus.

Two important rules of bus operation are:

1. The bus must be dedicated to a particular source or destination at any given time.
2. There may be one or more destinations, but there can be only one source at a time.

Three-State Devices, Buffers and Drivers

The three-state inverter couples an input logic condition (1 or 0) to the bus line, while providing circuit isolation. An input, called $\overline{EN}$ (Enable), controls whether the inverter acts as a low impedance inverter or a high impedance open. This third or high impedance state provides isolation from the bus so that many drivers can be connected to a common bus. Only the single enabled inverter at any one time drives the bus. The symbol for a three-state inverter device is shown in *Figure 8.30*.

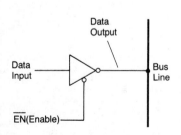

Figure 8.30　Symbol for a Three-State Device

A/D Conversion

Specially designed digital controllers called programmed controllers are often used to monitor and control processes in the industrial and commercial worlds, rather than solve problems as in the computer. The inputs and outputs to these systems are generally analog quantities. These input analog quantities must be converted to digital information before they can be processed by the digital circuitry. This requires an analog-to-digital (A/D) converter.

The two most common methods of achieving A/D conversion utilize comparators to match the input analog signal against a reference. (A comparator is a circuit which detects a small difference in the input voltage and produces a digital output.) These methods are:

1. Successive approximation
2. Ramp voltage

In the successive approximation method, a comparator controls the starting, stopping, and resetting of a counter by comparing an analog input with a digitally driven D/A converter output.

In the ramp voltage method, the linearily-rising ramp voltage takes a certain amount of time to reach the unknown analog voltage. Meanwhile, a clock-driven counter keeps incrementing until the comparator output stops the counter. Thus, the output count is proportional to the input amplitude.

D/A Conversion

A digital-to-analog converter (D/A or DAC) accepts digital information and delivers a voltage or current proportional to the numerical value applied to its input. The D/A converter examines each bit in the word that has a binary value 1, converts it to a current, and sums these currents directly or with the help of an operational amplifier.

Figure 8.31 shows a typical D/A converter. The D/A converter consists of two functional parts: a resistor network and a summing network. The resistor network weights the binary inputs represented by the switches A, B, C and D, while the summing amplifier scales the output voltage according to the weighted input values.

The voltage source for this D/A converter, as well as the values of the precision resistors, should be very accurate. The MSB resistor, R_4, is the lowest value resistor. The next significant bit resistor, R_3, is twice the resistance of R_4. The next significant bit resistor, R_2, is twice R_3, and so on to as many bits as are contained in the D/A converter. The D/A converter in *Figure 8.31* has a resolution of four bits. Example *8-9* shows how the digital input in binary form is converted to the analog output.

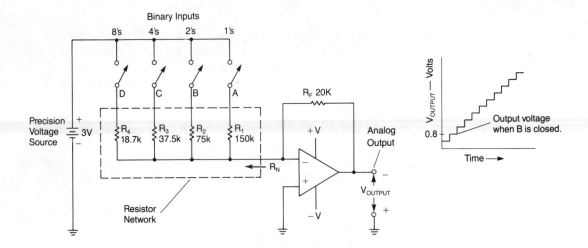

Figure 8.31 Digital to Analog Converter

Example 8-9: For binary input 0010 (Switch B only closed), calculate the analog output, V_{OUTPUT}.

The equation for determining the circuit gain is

$$A_V = \frac{R_F}{R_{IN}} \qquad (8\text{-}1)$$

Substituting into the equation (*8-1*),

$$A_V = \frac{20k\Omega}{75k\Omega}$$

$$A_V = 0.26667$$

The equation for determining the output voltage is

$$V_{OUTPUT} = V_{INPUT} \times A_V \qquad (8\text{-}2)$$

Substituting into equation *8-2*,

$$V_{OUTPUT} = 3V \times .26667$$

$$V_{OUTPUT} = 0.8V$$

Display Devices

One of the most popular display devices is the 7-segment light emitting diode (LED) shown in *Figure 8.32*. Illumination of the individual segments of the LED is accomplished in a number of ways. The 7-segment LED has eight PN junctions that emit light when forward biased. There are seven junctions for the numeral and one junction for the decimal point. Any desired numeral from 0 to 9 can be displayed by passing current through the appropriate segments. Typically, the forward voltage for the LED is 1.2 volts and safe forward current limit is 20 milliamperes.

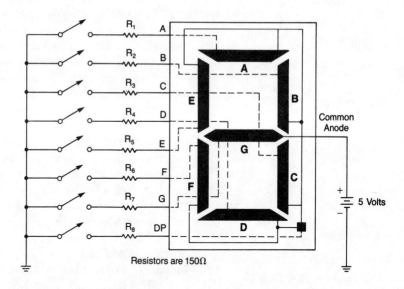

Figure 8.32   Standard LED Segmented Display and Circuitry

Interfacing Different Logic Families

The popular logic families each have a remarkably different set of characteristics. We saw some of these differences earlier in the chapter. Many times different families are used in different parts of a system to take advantage of a particular characteristic, such as power consumption or speed. Eventually, somewhere in the system, the different families must meet. Since they can't be directly connected together, additional circuitry is required to bridge this gap. This extra hardware is called interface circuitry. Sometimes the interface circuits are referred to as level shifters. Fortunately, interface circuits are available as self-contained integrated circuits.

SUMMARY

In this chapter, we have learned that digital circuits, using high and low voltage states to represent logic 1s and 0s, perform Boolean algebra. Although the circuits work at the binary number system level, the decimal, octal, and hexadecimal systems are useful conveniences for the human designer/operator.

Three basic logic gates, AND, OR, and NOT, are the building blocks of digital circuit design. Any of the other logic functions, including the inverse logic gates such as the NOR and NAND gates may be constructed using these three logic gates.

The main logic families are TTL, CMOS, MOS, ECL, and I²L. Each has its special combination of operating parameters, making it more useful in certain types of applications. For example, one family has faster switching speed, while another has extremely low current requirements.

Sequential logic circuits, such as flip-flops, counters, and registers, utilize the three logic elements of AND, OR or NOT in some form. Flip-flops consist of bistable circuits whose outputs are dependent upon the conditions prior to the time the output is being observed. Counters, which consist of flip-flop type circuits, may be designed to count only a certain number of pulses before producing an output. The modulus of a counter is the limit of the counting states before it begins to repeat itself. Registers are a type of temporary data storage device. Four basic types handle various combinations of serial and parallel data.

The heart of a computer system, the CPU, performs arithmetic and logic functions in its ALU. The basic circuit functions in the ALU are the half-adder and full-adder.

Most data handling and display designs involve certain common architectural structures. For example, all sections of an information processing device are tied together by a bus network. Since a great many individual devices are hard-wired to each bus, three-state devices are commonly used to isolate the devices from the bus when they are not active.

The outside world uses analog signals, therefore, they must be converted to digital form for processing. Conversely, the results in digital form must be converted to analog form when output to the outside world. Comparators, a type of differential amplifier, are used for this conversion. Display devices, such as the LED type, provide a visual output of the digital data without conversion.

CHAPTER 8 QUIZ

1. A way of representing decimal numbers using binary symbols in 4-bit groups is:
   a. hexadecimal.
   b. Gray code.
   c. BCD.
   d. octal.

2. The binary number 1101 is equivalent to the decimal number:
   a. 9.
   b. 13.
   c. 5.
   d. 17.

3. The number of variables that may exist in Boolean algebra is:
   a. any number.
   b. two.
   c. none, only constants exist.
   d. one.

4. The number of constants that may exist in Boolean algebra is:
   a. any number.
   b. two.
   c. none, only variables exist.
   d. one.

5. All possible logic switching functions can be realized by connecting the fundamental logic operators:
   a. NOR, NAND, NOT
   b. AND, OR, NOT
   c. NOT, XOR, XAND
   d. NAND, AND, NOR

6. According to DeMorgan's laws $\overline{A + B}$ equals:
   a. $\overline{A} \cdot \overline{B}$.
   b. $\overline{A} + \overline{B}$.
   c. $\overline{A \cdot B}$.
   d. none of the above — DeMorgan's law does not apply.

7. The most widely used family of logic gates is:
   a. ECL.
   b. CMOS.
   c. RTL.
   d. TTL.

8. The most common gate in use is the:
   a. NOT.
   b. AND.
   c. OR.
   d. NAND.

9. Which is a true statement?
   a. CMOS is faster than TTL.
   b. TTL consumes more power than CMOS.
   c. ECL is cheaper than TTL.
   d. CMOS is limited to lower voltages than TTL.

10. Combinational logic circuits:
    a. do not possess memory.
    b. are made from flip-flops.
    c. do not depend on inputs.
    d. are either in set or reset states.

11. With a high (1) on the D input, the flip-flop will have a _____ on its Q output after the clock pulse.
    a. low
    b. square wave
    c. high
    d. pulse

12. If both the J and K inputs are low (0), after the clock pulse the Q output will be:
    a. unchanged.
    b. toggled.
    c. definitely high.
    d. definitely low.

13. A major difference between combinational and sequential logic is that the latter is:
    a. binary.
    b. digital.
    c. time dependent.
    d. propagation delay limited.

14. If the flip-flops of a counter are all triggered (clocked) at the same time, then the counter is:
    a. synchronous.
    b. asynchronous.
    c. binary.
    d. a ripple type.

15. The number of counts that a counter goes through before repeating itself is called its:
    a. sequence.
    b. synchronization.
    c. ripple propagation.
    d. modulus.

16. A circuit that gives an output for a predetermined count is a _____ counter.
    a. memory
    b. decoder
    c. sequential
    d. register

17. _____ are commonly used as data storage units.
    a. AND gates
    b. OR gates
    c. XOR gates
    d. Flip-flops

18. A group of flip-flops connected so that each transfers its bit of information to the next when clocked is called a:
    a. shift register.
    b. half-adder.
    c. full-adder.
    d. one-shot.

19. A computer _____ performs arithmetic functions, as well as makes decisions.
    a. clock
    b. memory
    c. register
    d. ALU

20. Two inputs are common to an Exclusive-OR gate and an AND gate. Resulting outputs are _____ and _____ respectively.
    a. true, false
    b. sum, carry
    c. complement, NOT
    d. AND, OR

MICROPROCESSOR CONCEPTS

INTRODUCTION

The Central Processing Unit (CPU) which is the heart of the computer system has 3 major functional areas: (1) control of operations, (2) interpretation of data and (3) the execution of instructions. It is the nerve center of all activities.

When the CPU is made up of a small number of large scale integrated circuit (LSI) chips, it is called a microprocessor unit (MPU). If the MPU is implemented with one LSI chip, it is called a microprocessor, and if main memory is added to the microprocessor, either on the same chip or externally, or if an external memory is added to an MPU, a microcomputer is the end result. A majority of present day applications use microprocessors; however, in applications where memory is not a limitation, single chip microcomputers also are very popular.

There are two interrelated aspects of microprocessor operation — architecture and programming. This chapter will address both aspects, and thereby demonstrate how the program determines what operations the hardware, with its architecture, can perform and when they will occur.

Chapter subjects are covered in the following order. First, a discussion of the general functions of each major section of an MPU is presented. This is followed by a discussion of the methods and media of information exchange which occurs via the bus system within the MPU.

Next, how a MPU manipulates data, including computation, is covered. For data manipulation, special devices called registers are used as storage bins. They are used to convert a dynamic situation, that of data flow, into a static one, that of data storage, until it is needed. Also, recognize that the movement of data in and out of registers may itself be an act of data computation.

Every MPU needs instructions to tell it what to do. The techniques of getting the instructions to the MPU, called addressing modes, are discussed next. Explanations and examples of each type are provided. Finally, the MPU's internal instruction codes are examined.

CENTRAL PROCESSING UNIT

As shown in *Figure 9.1*, the Central Processing Unit (CPU) is made up of four major sections which will be discussed individually in the following paragraphs.

1. The Arithmetic Logic Unit (ALU)
2. The Control Unit (CU)
3. The Input/Output Unit (I/O U)
4. Clock

By adding memory to these sections, we can establish a basic computer system; therefore, the CPU with added external memory gives us a complete computer system.

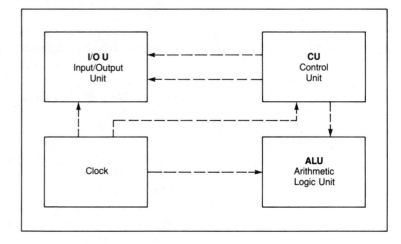

Figure 9.1   CPU Block Diagram

Arithmetic Logic Unit

The Arithmetic Logic Unit (ALU) is made up of an array of logic gates dedicated to the following functions:

1. Arithmetic (addition and subtraction)
2. Basic logic

Most ALUs can perform binary addition and subtraction, Boolean logic operations, shift right, shift left, branch, and comparisons. With the proper program the ALU, even though it only has addition and subtraction functions, can multiply and divide also.

Control Unit

The Control Unit (CU) is that portion of the CPU responsible for the following functions:
1. Fetching the program instruction codes from main memory.
2. Interpreting the instruction code for the operation required.
3. Executing the instruction once it has been interpreted.
4. Controlling the sequence in which the two other sections of the CPU, (the ALU and I/O U) interact with main memory, and the outside world.

Input/Output Unit

The I/O Unit is responsible for the transfer of data and/or control signals between the CPU and memory or any supporting circuits outside the CPU.

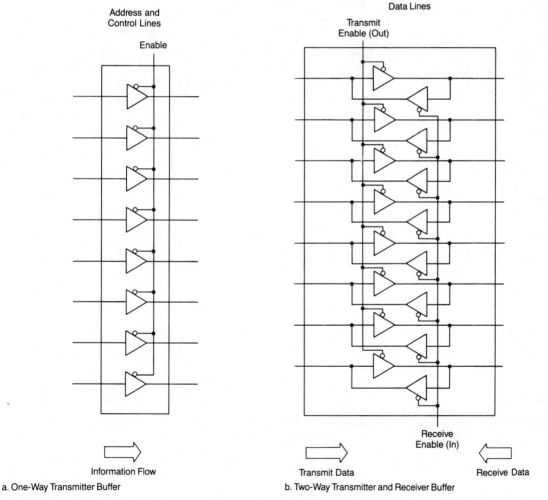

Figure 9.2 I/O Unit Buffer Control

The address and control lines use one-way buffers only *(Figure 9.2a)*, but data lines use two-way buffers to transfer data in and out of the CPU as shown in *Figure 9.2b*. Each of the buffers have an enable input that is controlled by the control unit to turn the buffers on or off.

Clock

The clock, which is the master time control of the microcomputer system, generates a single phase continuous square wave, or in some MPUs multiple waveforms which are displaced in phase. The timing output(s) is/are used to synchronize the MPU (microprocessor unit) with other support chips, such as memory, and I/O units. State-of-the-art MPUs each use an internal clock generator with one clock signal output.

The clock controls the timing of a sequence of events so that each event occurs in its proper order. An example is the typical instruction fetch cycle shown in *Figure 9.3*. An important part of a timing diagram is the cause and consequence relationship: cause is followed by consequence. In *Figure 9.3* cause is illustrated by a numbered circle, and consequence is illustrated by an arrow.

In this example, 1 the rising edge of clock cycle T_1, causes the MPU to place the desired address A_0 through A_{15} on the address bus. One-half cycle later, 2 causes the $\overline{\text{MEMREQ}}$ line to

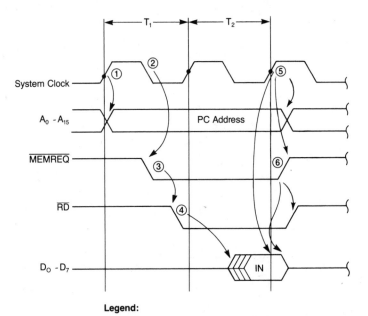

Legend:

A_0-A_{15}: 16-Bit Address Code
$\overline{\text{MEMREQ}}$: Memory Enable — Active low
$\overline{\text{RD}}$: Read Enable — Active low for read.
D_0-D_7: 8-Bit Data

Figure 9.3   Clock Signal Controlling a Typical Instruction Fetch Cycle

go active (low). The high-to-low logic level transition of the $\overline{\text{MEMREQ}}$ line 3, causes the high-to-low logic level transition of the $\overline{\text{RD}}$ line. The $\overline{\text{RD}}$ line going low at 4 results in the activation of the data bus buffers, allowing the desired data on the data bus. The clock transition at 5 samples the data bus during the time the data is stable, and 6 places the data in the instruction register. Edge 5 also triggers a sequence to disable memory and disable addresses. Edge 6 causes $\overline{\text{RD}}$ to return high and deactivate the data buffers.

Data Transfer Through the CPU

The Address Transfer Buffer (I/O A), shown in *Figure 9.4,* receives the 16-bit address code of the next instruction in memory from the program counter (a register). The data (in this case, an 8-bit instruction code) in that memory location is then moved into the CPU through the Data Transfer Buffers (I/O B). Once the data is in the CPU, it is transferred to the instruction register in the CU, where it is identified as a legal or illegal code by the instruction decoder. If it is a legal code, the timing and control circuits generate the proper timing and control outputs, while monitoring the control inputs, in order to carry out the operation dictated by the instruction.

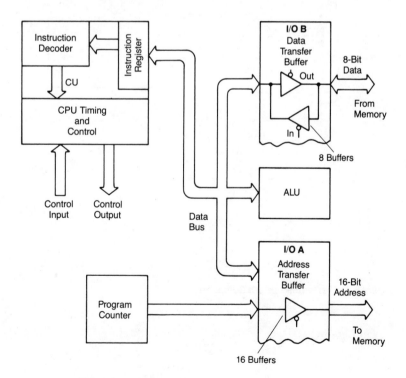

Figure 9.4   CPU Block Diagram

MICROPROCESSOR BUS STRUCTURE

Recall that the MPU + Main Memory = Microcomputer. The microcomputer is useless, however, unless it is able to interact with the outside world. As shown in *Figure 9.5*, the operator communicates with the computer via keyboard, with the use of a magnetic medium such as tape or disc, or possibly by voice commands. In return, the computer must be able to communicate with its human operator. This is done by outputting through a CRT Terminal (Monitor), a printer, or by electronically generated voice outputs. These communication devices are called peripherals.

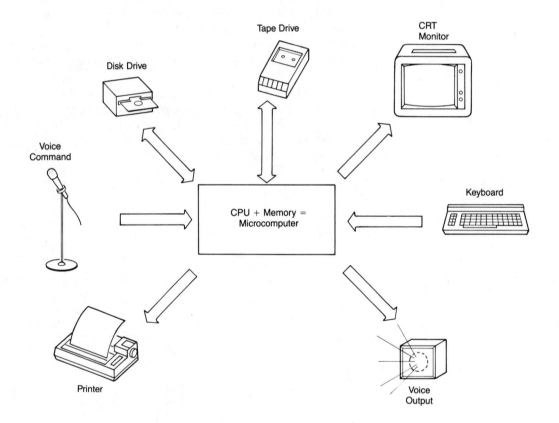

Figure 9.5 The Peripherals of a Computer

Peripherals and any other system units used to support the microcomputer system are connected to the MPU via a computer bus structure. A computer bus structure is similar to a highway system where each memory unit and each peripheral is connected to the MPU via a network of roads and highways. Some of the roads are one way (unidirectional), and others are two way (bidirectional). Some are eight lane (for 8 bits), while others are sixteen lane (for 16 bits) highways. The computer's bus system is made up of multiple conductors which carry information to and from the MPU and other elements of the computer system. It's just like placing data in a motor bus on the highway system and transfering it to or from the MPU to any memory location, peripheral device, or supporting unit.

The microcomputer has three main bus types:
1. Address bus
2. Data bus
3. Control bus

Address Bus

The address bus is unidirectional and is used to transmit a binary code that can represent a unique memory location. The memory location may be holding data to be processed, or it may be a memory location where data is to be stored. Or the binary code could represent the address of a port on an input or output unit. The MPU control section makes the distinction between a memory address and an I/O address, making it possible to use the same address for memory and I/O.

If each address bit has its own conductor, the number of conductors (address lines) used to make up the address bus dictates the maximum number of possible memory locations. For example, a sixteen line address bus can address 65,536 (2^{16}) individual memory locations. (The number 2 represents the base of the binary number system, and 16 represents the number of address lines).

Data Bus

The data bus is a bidirectional bus used to transfer data in binary code to and from the MPU. Although the data bus is bidirectional, data travels in only one direction at a time. A control line, called the read/write line, determines if the bus is reading out or writing into memory. The word size of the microcomputer system determines the number of data lines required. The more common word sizes today are 8-bit and 16-bit, with 32-bit being the latest entry into the computer market. The 8-bit word requires eight data lines, 16-bit requires sixteen data lines, etc.

Control Bus

The control bus is a unidirectional bus made up of a number of control lines. As previously mentioned, the signal on these lines are used to coordinate the timing sequence of system support units such as I/O units, memory, and other peripheral devices.

They control memory operation, control input and output transfers, determine ALU functions, and, in fact, control every operation within the system. Although the control bus is unidirectional, some of the control lines output control data, and others input control data to the MPU.

In this discussion of control signals, the typical signals for a NMOS single chip microprocessor will be used, that has an arithmetic unit that can operate on sixteen-bit words and on any eight-bit byte in memory.

Control signals are derived in two ways. They are produced by the control logic circuits, or they can be derived from the output of a read-only memory (ROM) where the control signals are programmed into the ROM. The control logic circuits respond to both internal and external CPU inputs to generate the required control signals. Some of these signals are available for use by the system designer to control various system operations or to control system states. For example, a common data bus signal is DBIN (Data Bus In). It controls the operation of a 16-bit data bus. When DBIN is at a high logic level, the CPU reads information from the data bus, that was put there by a memory read cycle. For writing information into memory, DBIN must be at a low logic level. In this state, the data bus is used to carry a 16-bit word from the CPU to memory.

Another example is a $\overline{\text{MEMEN}}$ (Memory Enable) active low logic level signal. $\overline{\text{MEMEN}}$ is used to enable memory when the address bus contains a valid memory address. It corresponds to the $\overline{\text{MEMREQ}}$ signal of *Figure 9.3*. Address code must be active and stable before $\overline{\text{MEMEN}}$ is active. The CPU issues the $\overline{\text{MEMEN}}$ (active low) signal at the beginning of all memory read and memory write machine cycles. In the discussions that follow, we will continue to refer to a logic low level as a low and a logic high level as a high.

Purpose

The purpose of a bus system is to have common conductors connecting common signals to a number of system circuits. As shown in *Figure 9.6*, common data bit lines of a data bus couple to two different RAM packages of 8K words by 8 bits. The problem with this arrangement is that many outputs will be connected together on one bus.

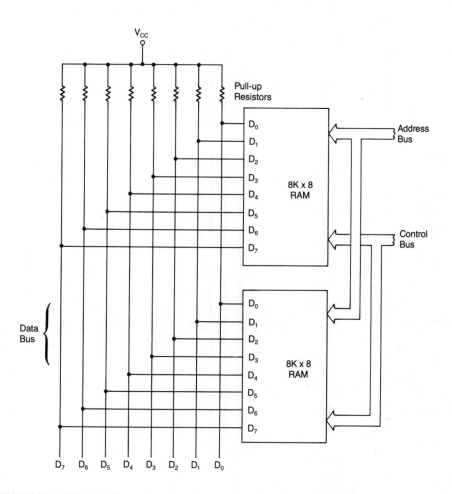

Figure 9.6   16K RAM Open Collector Bus

When more than one output is connected to a common bus line, such as the data bus, a problem arises. One gate could output a logic high while another is outputting a logic low. *Figure 9.7a* demonstrates this condition with equipment that has outputs feeding the bus with so-called "totem-pole gates", so named because of their component structure. One transistor Q_A is stacked on top of another transistor Q_B in Gate 1, and Q_C is stacked on Q_D in Gate 2. Each is represented as a switch in *Figure 9.7b*. If Gate 1 of *Figure 9.7b* is outputting a logic level 1 at the same time Gate 2 has Q_D on and is outputting a low logic level (0), a short circuit will result. There are two possible solutions to this predicament: the Open-Collector Bus and the Three-State Bus.

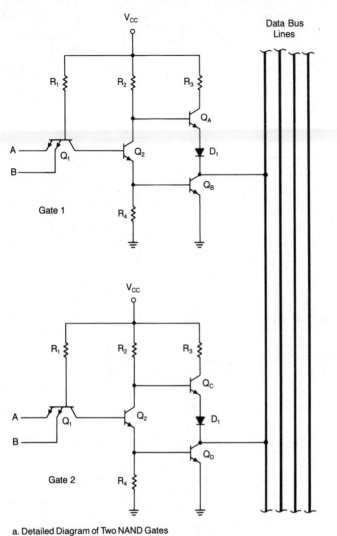

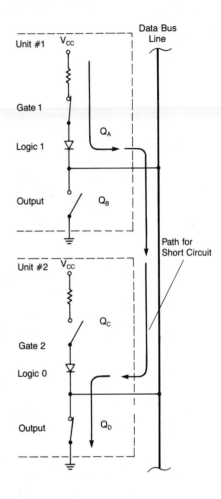

a. Detailed Diagram of Two NAND Gates

b. Symbolic Diagram Showing Short Circuit Path

Figure 9.7   Two Totem Pole Gates on One Bus Line

Open-Collector Bus

The open-collector bus takes advantage of the open-collector output gate shown in *Figure 9.8*. Notice the output transistor does not have a pull-up transistor. The open-collector gate can only output a low (0) by saturating the output transistor Q_1. In order to output a high (1), the bus would need an external pull-up resistor connected from the output to 5 volts. This arrangement is very convenient for an active low bus structure. One resistor connected to each of the bus lines will pull the entire bus high, but if any gate connected to the bus line goes low, that bus line is pulled low.

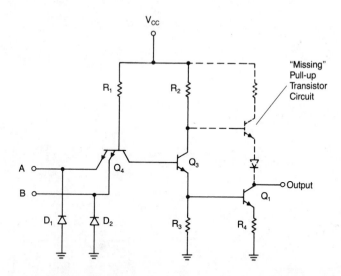

Figure 9.8   Open Collector NAND Gate

Figure 9.9a illustrates two identical circuits with a simple bus line using a pull-up resistor and three attached gates. This configuration is sometimes referred to as "wired AND" and other times referred to as "wired OR". Both references are correct and acceptable. The physical wiring of a "wired OR" and "wired AND" is exactly the same; the only difference is the way the truth table is interpreted. The truth table shown in *Figure 9.9b* is for a three-input wired AND gate. If the truth table is interpreted in terms of a logic 1, the only time the bus line can be a logic 1 is when gates A, B, and C are *all* outputting a high. This is the AND function. From another point-of-view, if the truth table is interpreted in terms of a logic 0, if *any* gate is outputting a logic 0, the bus line will be pulled low. This is the OR function. When this configuration is used in conjunction with an open collector bus structure, the bus is inactive when the line is high, and active when it is low. Therefore, an active low on any A or B or C will activate the bus line, and produce the "wired OR".

Two or more gates should not have their outputs tied together on a bus line unless an open collector gate is used. With an open collector gate, the value of the pull-up resistor must be selected so that the current on the line will not exceed the current that the lowest rated gate can conduct.

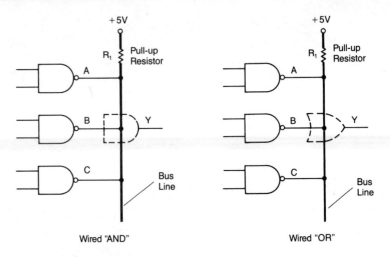

Wired "AND"   Wired "OR"

a. Equivalent Circuits

Inputs			Output
A	B	C	Y
0	0	0	0
0	0	1	0
0	1	0	0
0	1	1	0
1	0	0	0
1	0	1	0
1	1	0	0
1	1	1	1

b. Truth Table

Figure 9.9   *Two Perspectives on the Same Logic Bus*

Three-State Bus

Figure 9.7a illustrated the detailed circuitry of a standard "totem pole" gate. The advantage of a totem pole output is that the top transistor, resistor, and diode combination is a high resistance (Q_A and Q_C are cut-off) when the output of a logic low is desired; and the same transistor, resistor, and diode combination are a low resistance (Q_A and Q_C are on in saturation) when the output is a logic high. With the open collector output, the value of the pull-up resistor is fixed and must be selected so that it is not too high for a logic high, nor too low for a logic low. In the totem pole gate no current flows in Q_A or Q_C when the output is low; and full current flows when Q_A and Q_C are on (output high).

With the advent of the three-state buffer shown in *Figure 9.10*, the best of two worlds is available. The three-state buffer allows the totem pole output to be connected to a common bus line, and as long as the buffer is disabled, there is no concern of a possible short because one gate is high while another is low. It should be kept in mind, however, that only one three-state buffer may be enabled on the bus line at any one time.

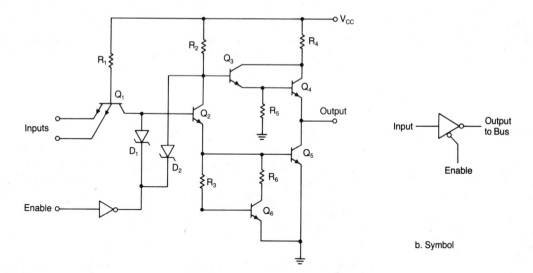

a. Schematic

Figure 9.10 Typical Three-State Buffer Circuit

The gate in *Figure 9.10* is a three-state buffer because its output has three possible states: high, low, and high impedance (electronically an open). When the buffer is enabled, the output can be a high or a low determined by the state of the input, but when it is disabled, the output is neither high nor low, but floating in the high impedance state. When the buffer is in the high impedance state (high Z), both transistors Q_1 and Q_2 are off at the same time; therefore, it is as if the buffer were not even attached to the bus.

The buffer in *Figure 9.10* is an inverting type which is enabled with a low. Three-state buffers can be non-inverting or inverting as well as being enabled with a high or a low. Today many LSI (large scale integration) ICs have three-state outputs built in, thus eliminating the extra buffer chip.

REGISTERS OF A MICROPROCESSOR

Every microprocessor has a limited number of internal temporary data storage locations called registers. For the 8-bit MPU, most of the registers are 8-bit registers, but there are 16-bit types also. Likewise most of the registers found in a 16-bit MPU are 16-bit registers with a few 8-bit registers. With some MPUs, the 8-bit registers can be paired together for handling 16 bits of information. In the 8-bit MPU, however, the 16 bits are handled eight bits at a time. The systems engineer chooses the unit best suited for the particular application.

BASIC ELECTRONICS TECHNOLOGY

Program Counter Register

The Program Counter (PC) register is charged with keeping track of the next memory location in a program. When software is developed, the programmer arranges the program to place the address of the first program instruction in the program counter register when the program is run.

The PC along with the CU keeps track of whether an 8-bit number is an instruction or data to be operated on. For example, *Figure 9.11a* is a simple program written in Motorola 6800 microprocessor assembly language. This program adds two 8-bit numbers. *Figure 9.11b* shows the same program in its Hex code form. First, the programmer writes the program in assembly language using mnemonics to represent Hex codes as in *Figure 9.11a*. Since the MPU only recognizes Hex numbers, as in *Figure 9.11b*, the mnemonic statements must be converted to the Hex numbers.

Memory Address (PC)	Mnemonic OP Code	Operand	Remarks	Number of Program Bytes
	ORG	$6000	Starting location in memory of first instruction Code	0
6000	LDAB	#$23	Load ACC B immediate with 23 Hex	2
6002	LDAA	#$10	Load ACC A immediate with 10 Hex	2
6004	ABA		Add contents of ACC B to contents of ACC A and store in ACC A	1
6005			PC 6005 is the next memory location in Program memory in which an instruction code should be located.	?

a. Simple Program Written in Assembly Level Language

Memory Address (PC)	Memory Contents (Hex)	Remarks	Bytes
6000	C6	Instruction Code	2
6001	23	Data	
6002	86	Instruction Code	2
6003	10	Data	
6004	1B	Instruction Code	1
6005			

b. Program in *Figure 9.11a* Written In Hex Code

Figure 9.11   Comparison Between Same Program Written in Two Formats

The Hex program is created from the mnemonic statements by a program called an assembler program. The assembler translates the people-oriented mnemonic program into a computer oriented Hex program. In *Figure 9.11a* and *b*, the column labeled Memory Address (PC) shows the address in the program counter. When the PC register contains a number such as 6000, it is said to be pointing to the next address of the program.

In the *Figure 9.11b* example, location 6000 is the first location of the program, and its contents C6 will be considered to be an op (operation) code. The Hex number C6 could just as easily be data, but because it is the first location of the program, it will be treated as an op code. C6 is the code for the mnemonic LDAB (load accumulator B immediately with Hex 23, the contents of the next memory location). The CU will decode C6 and find that it is a two byte instruction, the first is the operation to be performed, the second the data or operand to be operated on. The CU also determines that the contents of location 6002 should be the next op code, and it will be treated as such.

Instruction Register

The instruction register is a temporary one byte (8-bit) memory register. When the CU fetches an op code instruction, it is temporarily stored in the instruction register. The PC is then incremented to the next memory location in the program while the CU samples (looks at) the op code to see if it is a valid instruction. This is referred to as the decoding process. If it is a valid instruction, the CU then carries out the instruction.

Memory Address Register

The Memory Address Register (MAR) is a register used to hold the address of a memory location where data is to be deposited (written to), or retrieved (read from). This register is connected directly to the address lines and is a vital part of the I/O unit. Most MPUs today, especially 8-bit MPUs, have sixteen address lines, allowing access to 65,536 individual memory locations.

The size of the MAR is dependent on the number of individual memory locations which the MPU is required to address. If the maximum number of address locations to be accessed is 256, only an 8-bit MAR would be required. ($2^8 = 256$). The MAR is sometimes referred to as the memory address buffer because it is often attached to the address lines through a three-state buffer which can be disabled when needed. *Figure 9.12* is a block diagram of an MPU showing the MAR and its companion register, the Memory Data Register (MDR).

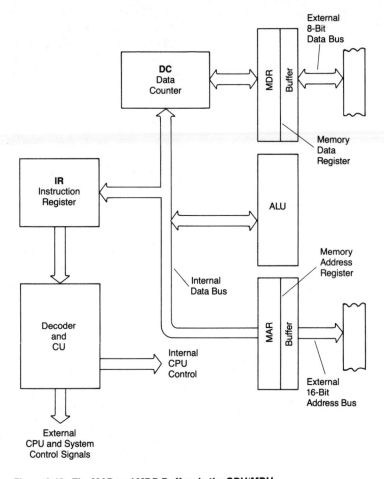

Figure 9.12   The MAR and MDR Buffers in the CPU/MPU

Memory Data Register

Working in connection with the Memory Address Register is the Memory Data Register (MDR). The size of the MDR is equal to the number of data lines. An 8-bit microprocessor would have an 8-bit MDR, and a 16-bit microprocessor would have a 16-bit MDR. To transfer data into or out of the MPU, the Memory Address Register and the Memory Data Register must work together.

The MDR must handle the contents of the memory location pointed to by the MAR. In other words, the MAR address selects the memory location, and the MDR stores the contents of the selected location when the memory is read. All data transferred to or from memory or the I/O ports must pass through the MDR. In many cases, the MDR is attached to the data lines through a three-state buffers so the data bus can be electrically detached from the MPU. Electronically detaching the address and data buses from the MPU is called floating the bus.

Data Counter

There is one more register that plays an important part in the transfer of data and that is the Data Pointer or Data Counter.

The Data Counter (DC), sometimes called the Data Register, is a 16-bit register or, occasionally, two 8-bit registers used together as a 16-bit pair. The Data Counter is similar to the Program Counter with the exception that the PC points to the next address inside the program, whereas the DC points to the next address outside the program.

Example 9-1: The Intel 8085 microprocessor uses the register pair technique. The H — L registers (which individually can be used as scratch pad registers) are 8 bits each, but together they represent a 16-bit register called the M (Memory) register. The M register is the 8085's data counter register. *Figure 9.13* shows an assembly language program which converts ASCII code (American Standard Code for Information Interchange) to Hex codes. *Figure 9.14* shows the Hex numbers which represent both data and op-codes as they appear in the memory locations assigned to the program memory and the data memory. It is important to understand that these two memory areas are each a part of the system's overall main memory. Notice that the PC points to data in the program, while the H — L register, the Data Counter (M), holds the address of the data in the section of memory set aside for 'data' that is to interact with the program. The MOV A,M instruction of *Figure 9.13* moves the data (42H) in the memory location pointed to by the H — L (M) register (6070H) into the accumulator. As a result, the accumulator (Acc) contains the Hex) number 42 which is an ASCII B.

This program converts the ASCII code in memory location 6070H into Hex and stores it in location 6071H.

Label	OP Code	Operand	Remarks
	ORG	6000H	
	LXI	H, 6070H	; Place address in M register
	MOV	A,M	; Move contents of 6070 in ACC.
	ANI	1111 0000 B	; Mask off bits 0,1,2, and 3
	CPI	40 H	; Compare ACC to 40H
	MOV	A,M	; Retrieve original data
	JNZ	NUMBR	; If data < 40 jump to number
	SUI	07H	; If data > 40 subtract 07H
NUMBR:	ANI	0000 1111 B	; Mask off bits 4 - 7
	INX	H	; H&L = H & L + 1
	MOV	M,A	; Store Hex in location 6071H

Figure 9.13 Program for Converting ASCII into Hexadecimal Code

Program Memory	
PC (Address)	Contents
6000	21
6001	70
6002	60
6003	7E
6004	E6
6005	F0
6006	FE
6007	40

Data Memory		ASCII
DC (Address)	Contents	
6070	42	
6071	0B	(B)
6072	00	
6073	00	

a. Program in Memory

b. Data in Memory

Figure 9.14 Chart Showing Data and Op Codes in Hex Form as They Exist in Memory Locations

General Purpose Registers

General Purpose (GP) registers are registers which are not assigned a specific task by the designer. Some MPUs have very few GP registers while others have as many as fifty. The GP registers are used to hold data temporarily and are therefore referred to as scratch pad registers. They are commonly used as counters. If a number such as 10 is placed in the register, that register is then decremented by (reduced by) 1 each time an event occurs, thereby counting the number of events.

Accumulator Register
The Accumulator register stores data used during arithmetic and logical operations. It often contains the results of an operation which must be temporarily stored in a GP register while the Accumulator is used for the next operation. After the Accumulator completes its task, the data can be returned to the Accumulator. Moving data about inside the MPU requires fewer instructions than moving it in and out of memory. If necessary, memory locations can be used as GP registers when few or no GP registers are available.

The Accumulator (Acc) is the register the system programmer uses most often. This register is a very powerful and flexible register that can be found in almost every MPU built today. Most MPUs will use the Accumulator in conjunction with the ALU (Arithmetic Logic Unit) as the source and destination register. As you recall the ALU is used for all arithmetic operations and all logic operations such as AND or OR.

Example 9-2: *Figure 9.15* illustrates an MC 6809 program that is used to mask off (clear) the most significant 4 bits of the contents of memory location 0040H. The program will then store the results in memory location 0041H.

This program is written in MC6809 Assembly Language, and is used to mask off (do away with) the most significant 4 bits of address location 0040H contents and store masked data in location 0041H.

PC	OP Code	Mnemonic	Operand	Remarks
6000	96 40	LDA	$40	Load cont of LOC 40 into A
6002	94 0F	ANDA	#$0F	AND 0F with ACC
6004	97 41	STA	$41	store cont of ACC in LOC 41 HEX

Note: $ = Hex Number
\# = Immediate Instruction

Figure 9.15 Simple Program for Clearing Bits of Memory Location

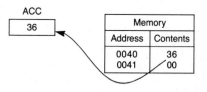

a. Load Accumulator with Contents of Location 0040 HEX

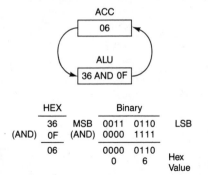

b. AND 0F with 36 and Place Results in Accumulator

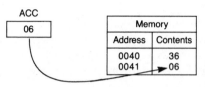

c. Store Results In Location 0041

Note: LSB = Least Significant Bit
MSB = Most Significant Bit

Figure 9.16 Converting Hex 36 to Decimal 6 Using the Masking Process

Let us assume that memory location 0040H contains an ASCII code that represents a number input from the keyboard. If, for example, we had pressed the number 6 key, an earlier portion of our program would store the ASCII code in location 0040H. The ASCII code for number 6 in Hex is 36_{16}. If we wish to use this number input from keyboard as a count, we must convert it from 36_{16} to decimal 06. This can be done by ANDing 36_{16} with $0F_{16}$. Recall that any binary number ANDed with zero is zero, and any number ANDed with one is that number, or unchanged.

Figure 9.16 demonstrates this process. *Figure 9.16a* shows the Acc loaded with the contents of 0040H. *Figure 9.16b* shows the logical AND operation. The number 0011 0110 (36_{16}) is ANDed with 0000 1111 ($0F_{16}$). Looking at the least significant column first and moving left for four bits gives: one AND zero is zero; one AND one is one; one AND one is one; and one AND zero is zero. Anything ANDed with zero is zero, so the most significant four bits are all zero. The result is 0000 0110. This procedure strips the 30_{16} from 36_{16} leaving 06.

This small portion of a larger program shows how much the Acc is used. Look at *Figure 9.16* as we discuss what is happening. The mnemonic LDA $40 *(Figure 9.15)* says to load Acc with the contents of memory location 0040. The number 36_{16} *(Figure 9-16a)* is therefore moved to the Acc. Next 36_{16} is ANDed with $0F_{16}$ to mask off the most significant four bits *(Figure 9.16b)*. Notice how the Acc is used as the source (36_{16}) of the ALU and how it is also used for the destination (06_{16}). Finally, the Acc is used to store the results (06_{16}) in memory location 0041_{16} *(Figure 9.16c)*.

The Acc is used in most MPUs as the main register for all input and output I/O operations. The Acc is so useful and powerful that many MPUs now have more than two accumulators.

Status Flag Register (SFR)

A flag is a bit whose status indicates that some condition is either true or false. For example the Z80 uses six of the eight available bits in the status flag register (SFR). The SFR and the symbol for each flag is shown in *Figure 9.17*. The SFR, sometimes called the condition code register (CCR), can be an 8-bit register or a 16-bit register with each bit being used as a flag.

When a flag is set, it represents a high (1), the condition is true. The following is a listing of the meaning of each status flag bit of a typical status flag register.

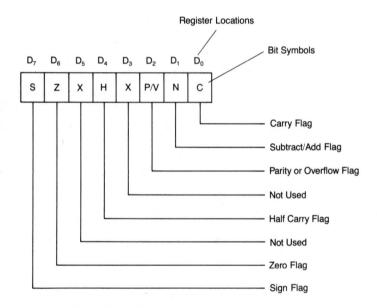

Figure 9.17 Typical Status Flag Register

The C Bit

The C Bit or carry bit is used to indicate one of five following possible conditions:

1. The most common use of the carry bit is to indicate that an addition problem has a carry. In an 8-bit MPU, any register selected to receive the sum cannot accommodate the ninth carry bit. Rather than throwing it away, it is represented by setting the carry bit of the SFR.

2. The carry flag may be set when a subtraction or a comparison instruction is used. Under this condition, the set carry flag indicates a borrow was required. The compare instruction internally subtracts a number from the Acc and does not change the contents of Acc. If the number to be compared to Acc is larger than the Acc contents, the carry flag will be set. (Borrow.)

3. The shift and rotate instructions may also affect the carry flag if it is included in the rotation sequence.
4. Logical operation will reset the carry flag. Reset means that the carry flag is cleared to a low (0).
5. The Set Carry Flag (SCF) instruction will set the carry flag to one.

The N Bit
The N Bit is the subtract flag. This bit is set if the previous operation was a subtract.

The P/V Bit
The P/V flag is the parity (P) or the overflow (V) indicator. This bit is shared by parity and overflow. A logical operation will set this bit if there is even parity, and reset it if there is odd parity. An overflow will set this bit for an overflow indicator.

The H Bit
The half-carry bit is set when a carry or a borrow was required of the fourth bit of the Acc.

The Z Bit
The zero flag is set when the result of an operation is equal to zero. A very common use of the zero flag is to compare two 8-bit numbers. You will recall from the discussion of the carry bit that compare is an internal subtraction in which the only register affected is the SFR.

Example 9-3: An example compare instruction is CPI 3CH. This instruction compares immediately the Hex number 3C to the contents of the Accumulator. If the Acc contains 3CH also, the results of the compare would be 0, and the zero flag will be set to 1. Often the zero flag is used with the jump and call instructions. For example following the CPI 3CH instruction one might find the JZ (label) instruction or the JNZ (label) instruction. Instruction JZ (label) would cause the program sequence to jump to the address represented by the label, if after the CPI instruction the zero flag was set to 1 (zero result). The JNZ (label) instruction would cause the program sequence to jump to the address represented by the label if after the CPI instruction the zero flag was at 0 or reset to 0. This would indicate that the comparison was not equal, thus the result was not zero.

The S Bit
The sign flag is set if the MSB (most significant bit) of a number is equal to 1. This usually indicates that the sign of the number is negative.

DESIRABLE FEATURES

So far we have discussed the basic registers one would find in almost any microprocessor. Most MPUs today also contain additional registers we will call desirable features. These desirable features include the Stack Pointer, Index Register, and Interrupts.

Stack Pointer

In order to understand what a Stack Pointer (SP) is or how it works, we must first discuss what is a stack. A stack is a number of consecutive memory locations allocated for temporary storage of data in a sequential, stacked arrangement. Initial data are placed on the bottom of the stack and each new data are stacked on top. Data are said to be "pushed" onto the stack and "popped off" the stack. This concept may best be understood by comparing the stack to a box in which you wish to store a number of books. You would stack the books one on top of the other in the box. The first book would be on the bottom of the stack, and the last book would be on the top. If you want the first book, you must first pop off (take off) the top books until you reach the first book at the bottom of the stack. This is a last in first out (LIFO) arrangement.

There are two common ways of implementing a stack. One way is to use a number of registers inside the CPU or MPU. The second way is to use consecutive memory locations somewhere in the main memory area. This second method is the more common method.

Recall that a microcomputer system using a microprocessor with a 16-bit address bus has 65,536 memory locations available, which is called main memory. The system programmer can use different areas of main memory for different applications. We have already discussed the first two areas of main memory: the program area and the data area. The program area is accessible to the programmer by using the program counter. The data area is accessible to the programmer by using the data counter. The third area, the stack, is accessible to the programmer by using the stack pointer.

The SP holds the address of the next vacant location on the stack. It is said to be pointing to the top of the stack. If for example the stack area was defined by the system programmer to be from 0400H to 04FFH (256 stack locations), the first data pushed on to the stack would reside in memory location 04FFH. The SP would immediately be decremented to point to the next available location, 04FEH, currently the top of the stack.

The system programmer would use an instruction like LD SP, 04FFH to set the stack pointer to the first location of the stack. This instruction loads the stack pointer immediately with the Hex address of the first stack location (04FFH).

Index Register

The index register (XR), usually referred to as the X register, is a 16-bit register used for addressing. The contents of the XR (an address itself) can be added to a number such as 0CH to create an offset address or a new effective address. 0CH in this example is called the offset. Assume the X register contains the Hex address $6040. The instruction LDA $0C,X would add the Hex number $0C to $6040 for a new (effective) Hex address of 604C. The contents of 604C would then be loaded into register A. (The $ sign in this instruction indicates the number is in Hex.)

Interrupts

The interrupt is similar to the subroutine call instruction except that interrupts are usually generated outside the program. Some are program initiated, however. Another major difference is that a subroutine call generally pushes the PC (program counter) containing the address of the next instruction in the main program onto the stack. This allows the program to return from the jump to the subroutine to the next instruction in the main program as if the subroutine call hadn't occurred, by popping the PC off the stack. The interrupt saves not only the PC, but other pertinent information as well.

Some MPUs push onto the stack the contents of the PC, the condition code or status flag register (sometimes referred to as the program status word or PSW), and the contents of all processor registers. Other MPUs save only the PC, and PSW on the stack, and it is up to the programmer to save the other pertinent data by using the interrupt service routine to push the processor registers onto the stack.

An interrupt request can be thought of as an unexpected interruption of the main program. For example, assume you are washing your car and the telephone rings unexpectedly. The ringing phone is an interrupt request. Quickly you toss your sponge into the pail and turn off the running water, before dashing to answer the phone. We will call these housekeeping chores. After servicing the interrupt request by answering the phone and talking to the caller, you hang up the phone so that it can ring again (interrupt enable). You would then return to your car, turn on the water again, pick up your sponge, and continue washing where you left off.

The interrupt request for microprocessor service is similar. Assume you know there is a possibility of an interrupt. You would enable the interrupt with the interrupt enable instruction (EI) early in your program and then start your main program. At some time in the process of the program an interrupt request is received. First the MPU finishes its current instruction, then does a few housekeeping chores, such as pushing the PC, PSW, and registers onto the stack. Then it inserts a predetermined address, called a vector, into the PC and proceeds to that vectored address. At this address the programmer would have inserted, as the contents of the address location, a jump instruction to the starting address of the interrupt service routine. After the service routine is completed, the last few instructions are interrupt enable and return from interrupt. Following the return from interrupt instruction, the MPU pops the PC, PSW, and processor registers off the stack and continues with the main program just where it left off, as if there was no interrupt at all.

ADDRESSING MODES

An assembly language program is made up of numerous instructions. Each instruction performs an operation, and many instructions require data to perform the required operation. Sometimes the required data is already located in a register, or perhaps it must be inserted by the programmer. This data must be addressed in some manner, and as a result, the MPU designer creates addressing techniques known as addressing modes. Addressing modes refer to the operand field and how the address of data is determined.

An assembly language instruction, for example, is divided into four parts, called fields: label field, operation field (mnemonics), operand field, and the comment field. *Figure 9.18* illustrates these four fields.

Label Field	Operation Code or Mnemonic Field	Operand or Address Field	Comment Field
Start	MVI	A, 07	; Move 07 into Reg. A
	MVI	B,03	; Move 03 into Reg. B
	ADD	B	: Add B to A (sum in a)
	STA	SUM	; Store sum in memory

Figure 9.18   Four Fields of Assembly Language

Immediate Addressing

The immediate addressing mode is perhaps the easiest addressing mode to understand. In this mode the actual data is placed in the operand field and is immediately transferred. Assume you want the data 45H in the accumulator. An immediate mode instruction might be LD A,45H. This instruction for the Zilog Z80 microprocessor loads (LD) the data 45H immediately into the accumulator (A). This mode is extremely valuable when loading a register to be used as a counter.

Direct Addressing

The direct addressing mode requires three bytes of data and the following three fetches: first the op code, next the low order byte of the address, and last the high order byte of the address. An example of direct addressing is LD (6040H),A. This instruction loads the contents of the accumulator into memory location 6040H. *Figure 9.19a* illustrates this operation.

Another form of direct addressing is paged addressing. In paged addressing the high order byte of the address is maintained in a page register, if provided. Then the CPU will be required to make two fetches instead of three. Not all MPUs have a page register. An example of direct page addressing is illustrated in *Figure 9.19b.* The instruction STAA (03) instructs the MPU to store the contents of accumulator A into memory location PP03, in this case PP represents the contents of the page register. Since PP is 40H, the combination 4003H is the address in which the accumulator data will be stored.

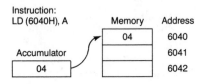

a. Example of Direct Addressing

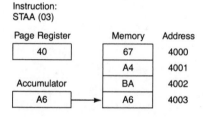

b. Example of Direct Paged Addressing

Figure 9.19   Using Direct Addressing Mode to Load the Accumulator Contents Into Memory

Indirect Addressing

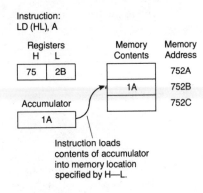

Instruction:
LD (HL), A

Figure 9.20 Indirect Addressing

As previously mentioned, in direct addressing the actual memory address is contained in the instruction, whereas in indirect addressing, the location of the address is contained in the instruction. Follow the example shown in *Figure 9.20*. The instruction LD (HL), A loads or moves data in the A register into the memory location pointed to by the H — L register pair. The instruction LD (HL), A is illustrated in *Figure 9.20*.

The contents of the accumulator (1AH) is loaded into the memory location whose address is found in the H — L register pair. Assume your boss instructed you to deliver a message to the VP of Marketing. When you inquire about the phone number, he tells you to look it up in the phone book. The phone number is obtained indirectly by way of the phone book. The H — L register pair represents the phone book. The address used for the instruction LD(HL)A, 752B is obtained indirectly from the H — L register pair.

Register Addressing

This mode is used to move data from register to register inside the MPU. An example is LD B,C where the contents of register C is copied into register B. If register B contains A7H and register C contains 2BH, after the instruction LD B,C both registers B and C will contain 2BH.

Implied Addressing

The implied addressing mode is a one byte instruction requiring only one fetch cycle. An example of implied addressing using Motorola's 6800 MPU is the instruction DEX. DEX means to Decrement the Index Register by reducing its contents by one. If the index register contains the Hex number $1A74, after executing DEX the index register will contain the Hex number $1A73. (Recall that the symbol $ in the 6800 programming language indicates that the number following it is a hexadecimal number).

Another example of Implied Addressing is the return from interrupt instruction RTI. This instruction is implemented at the end of an interrupt service routine. It pops the program counter off the stack and returns to the same point in the main program where it was before the interrupt.

Extended or Absolute Addressing

The Motorola 6800 MPU uses the extended addressing mode to distinguish between zero page addressing, which for the 6800 is direct addressing.

Extended addressing is like direct addressing, discussed earlier. Extended addressing refers to a three byte instruction which can address 65,536 locations. *Figure 9.21a* shows how the instruction LDAB $876F loads accumulator B with the contents of memory location 876F. For the 6800 MPU, however, direct addressing refers to a two byte instruction such as LDAB $6A. This instruction loads the contents of address PP6A into accumulator B, where PP equals 00 (zero page). *Figure 9.21b* illustrates zero page (direct) addressing.

Indexed Addressing

Indexed addressing is closely related to indirect addressing shown in *Figure 9.20*. Recall that when using indirect addressing, the destination or source memory address was obtained from a register whose identity was found in the operand field. Indexed addressing is indirect addressing with a twist. The index register is loaded with an address using the instruction LDX #$6040. The symbol # indicates immediate addressing. Assume 6040 is an indirect address which is maintained in the X (index) register. To implement the indexed mode, an instruction such as ANDA 3,X is used. The 3,X means that 3 is added to the contents of the index register (6040) to create an effective indirect address of 6043.

Example 9-4: *Figure 9.22a* illustrates the indexed addressing mode. The contents of Accumulator A (47H) is ANDed with the contents of the memory location pointed to by index register plus the offset (03H), sometimes called displacement. The net effective address is 6043H. *Figure 9.22b* shows the binary arithmetic of the AND operation. The results are then placed in Accumulator A.

If the offset was zero, (ANDA 0,X), the addressing mode would be indirect, and the contents of 6040H would be ANDed with Accumulator A.

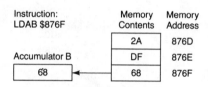

a. Extended Addressing Mode

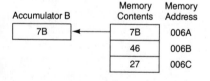

b. Zero Page Addressing

Figure 9.21 Extended Addressing Mode Compared to Zero Page Addressing

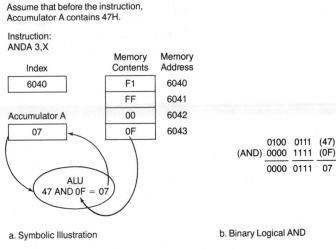

Assume that before the instruction,
Accumulator A contains 47H.

Instruction:
ANDA 3,X

a. Symbolic Illustration

b. Binary Logical AND

Figure 9.22　Indexed Addressing Mode

INSTRUCTIONS

Every MPU has its own set of instruction codes called the instruction set. The size of the instruction set does not necessarily indicate the power nor desirability of the MPU. Rather, the power of the processor lies in the individual instructions and addressing modes available. If one processor requires only half as many instructions to do the same job, it might be considered a more powerful microprocessor.

There are a number of ways to categorize instructions. We will use the following four categories. The four categories are memory referenced, non-memory referenced, program management, and input/output.

Memory Referenced

Memory referenced instructions are those that affect at least one memory location outside the program memory area. *Figure 9.23* illustrates the programming model for three MPUs. Each of these MPUs have multiple accumulators and index registers. *Figure 9.24a* illustrates three such commands using the Zilog Z80, Motorola 6809, and Intel 8086/88 MPUs. The 8086 and 8088 have the same instruction set so a single reference of 8086/88 will be used. The three examples of memory referenced instructions are:

1. Add accumulator with the contents of the address represented by the label "count".
2. Compare accumulator with contents of memory location 6040 Hex.
3. Load or move the contents of an index register with an offset of 4 into an accumulator.

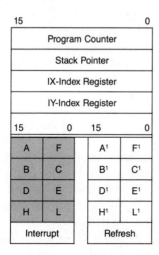

a. Zilog Z80

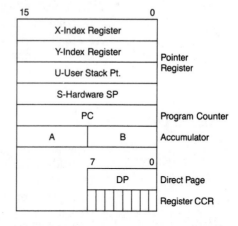

b. Motorola 6809

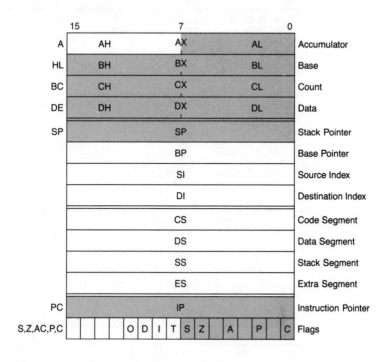

c. INTEL 8086/88

Figure 9.23 Programming Models for Three Microprocessors
(8080/85 Register Subset Shaded)

Non-Memory Referenced Instructions

Non-Memory Referenced Instructions are those instructions that do not affect memory locations outside the program area. Instructions that fit into this category are illustrated in *Figure 9.24b*. The first example is the add accumulator immediately with the Hex number 64. Another example is rotate accumulator left one bit. Last is the increment accumulator instruction. Increment means to increase by one or add one to a register.

Program Management

Program Management Instructions usually affect the program counter. Recall that the PC points to the next sequential instruction address in the program memory area. This instruction category alters the PC's sequential flow. *Figure 9.24c* shows three such instructions. The jump instruction replaces the PC address with the address represented by the label "NEXT". As a result the program's sequential flow is altered.

Z 80		MC6809		iAPX 8086/88	
ADD	A,COUNT	ADDA	COUNT	ADD	AL,COUNT
CP	(6040H)	CMPA	$6040	CMP	AL,6040H
LDA	,(1X+4)	LDA	4,Y	MOV	AL,[SI+4]

a. Memory Referenced Instructions

Z 80		MC6809		iAPX 8086/88	
ADD	A,64H	ADDA	#$64	ADD	AL,64H
RLA		ROLA		ROL	AL,1
INC	A	INCA		INC	AL

b. Non-Memory Referenced Instructions

Z 80		MC6809		iAPX 8086/88	
JP	NEXT	JMP	NEXT	JMP	NEXT
CALL	SUB	LBSR	SUB	CALL	SUB
RET		RTS		RET	

c. Program Management Instructions

Z 80		MC6809		iAPX 8086/88	
IN	A,1CH	Memory Mapped		In	AL,1Ch
OUT	B,A	I/O		Out	1CH,AX

d. Input/Output Instructions

Figure 9.24   *Four Ways of Categorizing Instructions*

The call or branch to subroutine instruction is similar to jump, with the exception that a subroutine call or branch saves the PC on the stack before replacing it with the address "SUB". The last example is the return from subroutine instruction. This instruction is the last instruction of a subroutine program. It pops the PC from the stack and then returns control of the program to the instruction following a subroutine call or branch.

Input/Output

The last category is Input/Output instructions as shown in *Figure 9.24d*. There are two common ways of handling I/O operations. One way is called memory mapped I/O and the other is called I/O mapped.

Memory mapped I/O usually indicates that the MPU has no I/O control lines, so some memory addresses are set aside for I/O operations only. MPUs having I/O control lines do not have to set aside memory locations for I/O. Rather, they can use all addressable memory locations for memory. Additional addresses are used for I/O. Input and output instructions are usually limited to load accumulator from I/O bus and move contents of accumulator onto the I/O bus.

SINGLE CHIP COMPUTERS

As mentioned earlier CPU + Memory = Computer System. With the advent of large scale integration (LSI), microcomputers can now be integrated on a single 40-pin chip. The Texas Instruments TMS7000 series 8-bit microcomputers are a good example of the technology. The TMS7000 series includes the TMS7000, TMS7020, and the TMS7040 microcomputers. The computers contain a single integrated circuit, a CPU, ROM, RAM, and I/O. *Figure 9.25* is a block diagram illustrating the functions available.

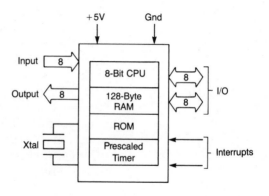

Figure 9.25   TMS7000 Series Functions

Each of the three devices has a 128 byte RAM, and 2K and 4K bytes of on chip ROM for the TMS7020 and TMS7040 respectively. This series also includes an instruction set of 61 commands.

An example of the versatility of the microcomputer series is configuration options available for memory expansion. These modes are summarized in *Figure 9.26* and include: Single Chip, Peripheral Expansion, Full Expansion, Microprocessor, and System Emulator.

Mode	On-Chip RAM Bytes*	On-Chip ROM Bytes*	On-Chip I/O Lines*	Off-Chip Memory Bytes*
Single-Chip	na/128/128	na/2048/4096	na/32/32	na/0/0
Peripheral Expansion	na/128/128	na/2048/4096	na/20/20	na/246/246
Full Expansion	na/128/128	na/2048/4096	na/12/12	na/63224/61176**
Microprocessor	128	0	12	65272 +
System Emulator	128	0	0	65280 +

* Information is structured in the columns in the following order: TMS7000/TMS7020/TMS7040 (when necessary).
** Address 0080 to 00FF are additionally available off-chip when using extended addressing modes.
na TMS7000 cannot be configured in the single chip, peripheral expansion, or full expansion mode.

Figure 9.26 Memory Expansion Configuration Options

Single-Chip mode provides for all 32 lines of the general purpose input/outputs to be used with no off-chip memory bus being implemented. The on-chip ROM and RAM contain all program and data.

Peripheral Expansion mode allows for an 8-bit address bus to external memory, and 20 lines are used for I/O. The 8-bit address bus allows for an additional 246 external addresses for RAM, ROM, or peripheral devices.

Full Expansion mode allows for a 16-bit address bus as well as a multiplexed (timeshare) 8-bit data bus to external memory. The on-chip ROM can be used in conjunction with additional off-chip memory. This mode also provides for twelve I/O lines.

Microprocessor mode provides the same advantages as the full expansion mode with the exception that the addresses for the on chip ROM are available off chip. This allows the use of an EPROM for prototype programming.

System Emulator mode facilitates development and emulation of future TMS7000 family systems. In this mode the interrupts, on-chip timer, and on-chip I/O are disabled.

The TMS7000 series has many additional features not mentioned here.

SUMMARY

In this chapter we have learned that the MPU consists of four major functional sections: the ALU, which performs arithmetic and logic operations, the CU which performs fetching, interpreting, executing, and controlling, and the I/O unit, which performs the task of interfacing to the world outside the chip. The fourth section is the master clock, which closely synchronizes every operation.

The exchange of information occurs over the system bus lines, of which there are 3 types — address, data, and control. Each of the sources and destinations are hardwired to their appropriate buses through interfacing three-state buffers that allow inactive elements on the bus to "float". Nearly all buses are either 8 or 16 conductors.

Registers are temporary data storage bins, and are also usually either 8 or 16 bits wide. There are many kinds of functions they perform, and are appropriately named according to their purpose. For example, the Program Counter is used to keep track of the next memory location in a program. The other types include the Instruction Register, Memory Address Register, Memory Data Register, Data Counter Register, General Purpose Register, Accumulator Register, and the Status Flag Register. In addition, there are those special purpose registers in the more sophisticated microprocessors providing some unique features. The Stack Pointer Register, the Index Register and the Interrupt Register each provide special operating capabilities.

Addressing modes are the techniques used to locate instructions and the data required to perform desired functions. The common addressing modes are Immediate, Direct, Indirect, Register, Implied, Extended, and Indexed. Each mode has its own applications, rules, and format.

The instruction set is a menu of instructions a MPU can execute. Separate MPU's must have identical instruction sets to run the same programs. The categories of instructions are as follows: memory referenced, non-memory referenced, program management, and I/O.

CHAPTER 9 QUIZ

1. The CU is that portion of the CPU responsible for:
   a. fetching the instruction.
   b. interpreting and executing the instruction code.
   c. controlling the sequence in which the ALU and I/O unit interact with the memory.
   d. all of the above.

2. The microcomputer has three main buses:
   a. control bus, register bus, and address bus.
   b. right bus, center bus, left bus.
   c. address bus, data bus, and control bus.
   d. none of the above.

3. The Z-80 is an 8-bit MPU. How many address lines does it have?
   a. 16
   b. 8
   c. 32
   d. 4

4. Why is a three-state buffer called three-state?
   a. It has three possible output states.
   b. It takes three chips to implement the bus state.
   c. It requires a three-state power supply.
   d. None of the above

5. The program counter is charged with:
   a. keeping track (counting) of the number of subroutines in a program.
   b. keeping track of the next memory location used to store data.
   c. keeping track of the next memory location in a program.
   d. b and c above.

6. General purpose registers are registers:
   a. used as auxiliary stack pointers.
   b. used as scratch pads for temporary storage.
   c. used for decoding general purpose op codes.
   d. all of the above.

7. The stack is:
   a. an output port.
   b. consecutive memory locations in which data are stored temporarily.
   c. an area of consecutive memory in which a program is stored.
   d. a register that points to the next op code in memory.

8. The direct addressing mode:
   a. places the address directly on the data bus for transfer.
   b. uses the direct address pointer register to point to the data.
   c. uses the index register to direct the control logic unit.
   d. places the memory address directly in the operand field.

9. An interrupt request signal will:
   a. interrupt the MPU and clear the stack.
   b. interrupt the MPU and save the program counter contents.
   c. automatically halt the MPU and clear all data in memory.
   d. all of the above.

10. The C bit of the status flag register:
    a. indicates that the count register is full.
    b. indicates if the crossover bit is high or low.
    c. sets the count high.
    d. indicates if a carry was generated.

SOLID-STATE COMPUTER MEMORIES

INTRODUCTION

The history of computer memories includes such devices as electromechanical relays, vacuum tubes, magnetic cores, transistors and integrated circuits. Each of these devices meets the fundamental specification for digital computer memory elements: they have two distinct states of operation which can be used to represent the two unique states of binary information. In the evolutionary steps from relays to ICs, arrays of such elements have been used to construct computer memory systems for thirty or more years.

In this chapter, we will survey the various types of solid-state memory devices and circuits. Tape and disk systems, because they are external to the basic computer, will be covered in the next chapter, which discusses I/O devices. All memory systems have certain physical and electrical parameters in common, which are described in terms of the specifications.

The two major categories are read/write-memory and read-only memory. Each has several variations of a main component so that a family of components is available. These components are here described both in terms of discrete operating principles and in terms of practical circuitry.

Figure 10.1 shows the evolution of the most common type of memory devices.

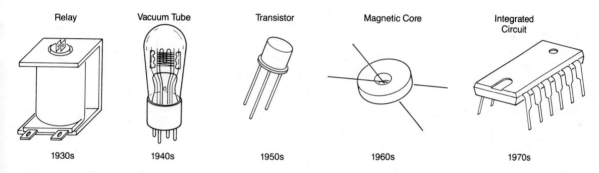

Relay	Vacuum Tube	Transistor	Magnetic Core	Integrated Circuit
1930s	1940s	1950s	1960s	1970s

Figure 10.1 Evolution of Memory Devices

OVERVIEW OF SEMICONDUCTOR MEMORIES

Memory Size and Organization

In more recent times, arrays of transistors in integrated circuit form have been used to reduce the volume, weight, and power consumption of computer memories. Typical microcomputer systems use memory ICs capable of storing anywhere from 1024 to 262,144 bits each. Arrays of these integrated circuits form both sections of the main memory for the system, the program memory and the data memory. Some program memory is designed using read-only memory devices (ROMs), but most main memory which includes program and data memory uses read/write memory devices, called RAM. Although RAM is an acronym for random-access memory, (which describes a means of memory addressing), the term is used to identify read/write memories almost exclusively.

On the memory chip, the storage elements are organized into words which, for microcomputers, consist of from one to 32 bits. Main frame computers may use words with 64 bits. A memory IC capable of storing 256 four-bit words, which is described as a 256×4 memory, has a bit storage capacity of 256×4, or 1024. Other ICs might also store 1024 bits, but may be organized differently. A 1024×1 memory, for example, stores the same number of bits, but they are arranged differently. Instead of 256 four-bit words, it stores 1024 one-bit words.

Storage size is frequently specified by the number of groups of 1024 bits that can be stored. Each group is called 1K. A so-called 4K memory actually stores 4×1024, or 4096 bits. A memory that stores 16K bits actually stores 16×1024, or 16,384 bits. Individual memory integrated circuits, as stated previously, have 8K, 16K, 64K or 256K sizes that are used widely.

A 4K memory IC which is organized into 4-bit words is called a $1K \times 4$ memory. It stores 4096 bits, stored in 1024 4-bit words. An $8K \times 8$ memory organizes its 64K bits into 8192 8-bit words. The major manufacturers of semiconductor memory offer an extensive variety of memory sizes and organizations in standard integrated circuit packages. Continuous improvements have been made in the density and performance of memory ICs since the introduction of the first 1K memory circuit. In fact, in many cases, IC memory innovations have paced and made possible the design of innovative microcomputer systems.

Device Characteristics

To understand how such memory ICs are specified, let's look at a very popular 16K memory IC. There are units that are higher density, but we use this one as a typical example. *Figure 10.2* is a specification sheet for the Texas Instruments TMS4016 static random-access memory. This is a static read/write memory IC as opposed to a dynamic read/write memory IC. The first entry in the list of features for this device is its organization, $2K \times 8$. Thus, the memory holds 16K bits, organized into 2048 8-bit words. The amount of storage and the organization of the bits is a primary specification of all integrated circuit memory devices.

A second major specification is called access time, which indicates the speed at which information can be retrieved from the memory, starting from the instant the CPU presents its request. When a computer's central processing unit (CPU) requests a piece of data or a program instruction from memory, the memory must respond by sending the requested information to the CPU. For the TMS4016, the maximum access time is given as 150 nanoseconds. Factors that influence access time include the semiconductor technology (bipolar or MOS), and the information storage format (serial or parallel) of the device.

One other major memory specification is the power dissipation. Like all electronic components, memory ICs also dissipate power during operation. Since memory systems often consist of arrays of ICs, the total power required for the memory system can present a significant load for the system power supply. Power dissipation for the TMS4016 is no more than 495 milliwatts. Power dissipation is determined mainly by the semiconductor technology, with MOS memories having the lowest power consumption and bipolar memories the highest.

It is important to note that the TMS4016 is a static random access memory. Static means that the information stored in the memory cells will remain and maintain itself as long as power is supplied to the memory IC. If power were to be removed, the information would be lost. To maintain information in static memories during long idle periods and reduce power consumption, voltage supplies are reduced to a standby level.

- **2K x 8 Organization**
- **Single +5 volt Supply (± 10% Tolerance)**
- **Fully Static Operation (No Clocks, No Refresh)**
- **JEDEC Proposed Standard Pinout**
- **24-Pin 600 Mil Package Configuration**
- **Plug-in Compatible with 16K 5 volts EPROMs**
- **8-Bit Output for Use in Microprocessor-Based Systems**
- **Max Access/Min Cycle Times Down to 150ns**
- **Three State Outputs with $\overline{CS}$ for Or-ties**
- **$\overline{OE}$ Eliminates Need for External Bus Buffers**
- **Common I/O Capability**
- **All Inputs and Outputs Fully TTL Compatible**
- **Fanout to Series 74, Series 74S, or Series 74LS TTL Loads**
- **N-Channel Silicon-gate Technology**
- **Power Dissipation under 495mW Maximum**
- **Guaranteed dc Noise Immunity of 400mV with Standard TTL Loads**

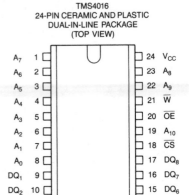

TMS4016
24-PIN CERAMIC AND PLASTIC
DUAL-IN-LINE PACKAGE
(TOP VIEW)

Pin Nomenclature	
A_0-A_{10}	Addresses
DQ_1-DQ_8	Data In/Data Out
$\overline{CS}$	Chip Select
$\overline{OE}$	Output Enable
$\overline{W}$	Write Enable
V_{SS}	Ground
V_{CC}	+5V Supply

description

The TMS4016 static random-access memory is organized as 2048 words of 8 bits each. Fabricated using proven N-channel, silicon-gate MOS technology, the TMS4016 operates at high speeds and draws less power per bit than 4K static RAMs. It is fully compatible with Series 74, 74S, or 74LS TTL. Its static design means that no refresh clocking circuitry is needed and timing requirements are simplified. Access time is equal to cycle time. A chip select control is provided for controlling the flow of data-in and data-out and an output enable function is included in order to eliminate the need for external bus buffers.

Of special importance is that the TMS4016 static RAM has the same standardized pinout as TI's compatible EPROM family. This, along with other compatible features, makes the TMS4016 directly plug-in compatible with the TMS2516 (or other 16K 5 volts EPROMs). No modifications are needed. This allows the microprocessor system designer complete flexibility in partitioning his memory board between read/write and non-volatile storage.

Figure 10.2   Static RAM Specifications for TMS4016

Trends in Semiconductor Memory Technology

Memory technology advances are most often demonstrated by increased storage densities (more bits within a given IC), lower access times, and lower power dissipation. Lately most of these advances have been achieved by using MOS technologies. While early semiconductor memories used bipolar transistors in flip-flop structures to form static memories, greater densities and lower power consumption can be realized by using MOS transistors in capacitive dynamic designs. The main disadvantage of dynamic memories is that the capacitive elements exhibit leakage characteristics like all discrete capacitors, and therefore must be refreshed periodically. That is, the memory cells would lose their information even though full power was maintained across the memory IC. The charge leaks off the capacitor storing the information, destroying the information. The circuitry to provide the refreshing, and the time required to refresh, increase the complexity of dynamic memory designs. However, the current trend is to integrate the refresh circuitry into the microprocessor chip or into the memory itself. As a result, the refreshing process is transparent to the designer or user of the dynamic memory. It makes the dynamic memory IC look more like a static memory IC to the user.

Other memory technologies, like charge-coupled devices and magnetic bubble memories, are recent developments which find application in special environments. These will be discussed in more detail later in this chapter.

All semiconductor RAM is volatile, which means that it is unable to retain information when power is removed. Back-up power, usually in the form of batteries, must be provided in systems where retention of information is critical, which increases system complexity, weight, and cost. Current memory research will likely produce non-volatile RAM, but at the moment, true non-volatility is available only in magnetic memories, like core memory. Core memory is seldom used in microprocessor-based systems.

READ-WRITE MEMORY DEVICES

Read-write memory, or RAM, is used for the data section of the main memory in computer systems, and it may also be used for scratch-pad memory in many other types of equipment. No matter what the application, the devices are essentially the same.

General Requirements for RAM Devices

Because this chapter is concerned primarily with computer memories, the discussion here is oriented toward RAMs used in main memory sections of microcomputers. In this application, RAM must accept address and control inputs from the microprocessor. Then, depending on the state of the control inputs, the RAM must either accept and store input data or it must output previously stored information for use by the microprocessor. The random-access feature means that all storage locations may be accessible with equal speeds. Said another way, the information from any addressed location in a RAM will arrive at the output in a certain access time (within specified limits). RAM ICs include address decoders, which select the storage location indicated by the address inputs. They also include read/write buffers, which prepare the selected storage location for the memory operation (read or write) indicated by the control inputs. *Figure 10.3* shows a block diagram of a general RAM device.

The number of address input lines is determined by the number of words stored on the IC. A memory storing 2^N words requires N address lines.

Example 10-1: The TMS4050 dynamic RAM has twelve address inputs, labeled A_0 through A_{11}. How many word storage locations can be addressed?

Twelve address inputs allow for 2^{12}, or 4096, addressable locations. Notice that the address inputs in no way affect the number of bits in each word.

Figure 10.4 is the specification sheet for the TMS4116 dynamic RAM. Notice that although the organization indicates that the memory stores 16K words, the device has only seven address inputs. According to the rule just stated, seven address lines allow for only 2^7, or 128, addressable locations. In order to address all 16K locations, the TMS4116 arranges the storage cells into rows and columns. A 7-bit address is latched into the address decoder by the $\overline{\text{RAS}}$ strobe input to select the row. Then, another seven-bit address is applied to the inputs and is latched by the $\overline{\text{CAS}}$ strobe to select the column address. The 14 bits are then decoded to select the desired location. This approach, called multiplexed addressing, saves seven pin connections for the address signals, and allows the device to be housed in a 16-pin package.

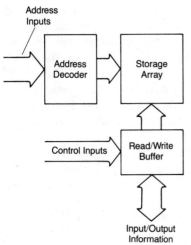

Figure 10.3 General Block Diagram of RAM

- **16,384 x 1 Organization**
- **10% Tolerance on All Supplies**
- **All Inputs Including Clocks TTL Compatible**
- **Unlatched Three-State Fully TTL-Compatible Output**
- **3 Performance Ranges:**

	Access Time Row Address (MAX)	Access Time Column Address (MAX)	Read or Write Cycle (MIN)	Read Modify-Write† Cycle (MIN)
TMS4116-15	150ns	100ns	375ns	375ns
TMS4116-20	200ns	135ns	375ns	375ns
TMS4116-25	250ns	165ns	410ns	515ns

- **Page-Mode Operation for Faster Access Time**
- **Common I/O Capability with "Early Write" Feature**
- **Low-Power Dissipation**
  - **— Operating   462mW (max)**
  - **— Standby   20mW (max)**
- **1-T Cell Design, N-Channel Silicon-Gate Technology**
- **16-Pin 300-Mil Package Configuration**
- **Refresh time: 2ms or less**

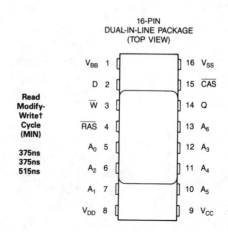

16-PIN
DUAL-IN-LINE PACKAGE
(TOP VIEW)

Pin Nomenclature			
A_0-A_6	Address Inputs	$\overline{W}$	Write Enable
$\overline{CAS}$	Column Address Strobe	V_{BB}	−5V Power Supply
D	Data Input	V_{CC}	+5V Power Supply
Q	Data Output	V_{DD}	+12V Power Supply
$\overline{RAS}$	Row Address Strobe	V_{SS}	0 V Ground

Figure 10.4   Dynamic RAM Specifications for the TMS4116

The control input required on all RAM devices is a read/write select input. Obviously, the state of this input line determines whether the memory is to output or input information. Many RAMs also include a $\overline{CS}$ (Chip Select) or $\overline{CE}$ (Chip Enable) control input. This input allows sections of a memory array, for a system made up of many memory ICs, to be accessed while all other sections are disabled. This feature is detailed later in this chapter.

The number of data inputs and outputs on a RAM device equals the number of bits stored at each location. The 2K × 8 organization of the TMS4016 indicates that 8-bit words must be transferred into or out of the device at one time. Referring back to *Figure 10.2*, notice that the eight input/output lines are labeled DQ_1 through DQ_8. The same lines are used for both input and output.

The TMS4116 of *Figure 10.4* is a 16K × 1 dynamic RAM organized to have 16K 1-bit words. Only one bit is transferred at any time. Two different lines are used, one for input, labeled D, and one for output, labeled Q. The only other connections to the IC are the power supply connections.

Static RAM Devices

Static RAMs may be constructed with either bipolar or MOS transistors. *Figure 10.5* shows the circuit of a bipolar RAM cell. The two transistors and their associated load resistors form a flip-flop circuit capable of storing one bit. When this cell is selected by the address-decoding circuitry, ROW LINE is raised to the logic 1 level. If the memory cell is to be read, a sense amplifier connected to BIT LINE detects current, or no current in that line, depending on the state of the cell. For example, if the flip-flop has Q_1 latched ON, then current flows in BIT LINE and the sense amplifier reads this current as a logic 1.

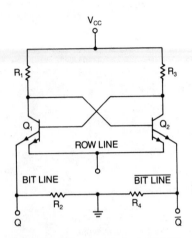

Figure 10.5   Bipolar Static RAM Cell

If a bit is to be written into the cell, ROW LINE is again set to logic 1. Then, the input data bit is applied to $\overline{\text{BIT LINE}}$, and its complement is placed on BIT LINE. For example, to store logic 0, 0 is placed on $\overline{\text{BIT LINE}}$ and 1 is placed on BIT LINE. Q_2 conducts and Q_1 is cut off, thereby storing logic 0.

Any time the cell is not selected by the address-decoding logic, ROW LINE is at the logic 0 level. The emitter connected to ROW LINE becomes the active element of the transistors, and the BIT LINE/$\overline{\text{BIT LINE}}$ emitters do not function. The sense amplifier connected to BIT LINE, therefore, detects no data.

Bipolar RAM cells are very fast, and bipolar RAM memories typically have access times of less than 50 nanoseconds. Their chief disadvantage is that they dissipate relatively large amounts of power, typically about 0.5 milliwatt per bit. This is because of the flip-flop circuit, where one transistor is always saturated, conducting current through its load resistor.

The circuit of an MOS static RAM cell is shown in *Figure 10.6*. MOSFETs Q_1 and Q_2 correspond to the bipolar transistors in *Figure 10.5*, and MOSFETs Q_3 and Q_4 correspond to the load resistors. The other four MOSFETs are used to select or to isolate the cell. Q_5 and Q_6 are controlled by the row decoder, and Q_7 and Q_8 are controlled by the column decoder. They are driven by the address-decoding logic. When they are enabled, the cell may be read or written into in much the same manner as the bipolar cell.

The advantage of the MOS cell over the bipolar cell is its lower power dissipation. Typical power dissipated is about 0.15 milliwatt per bit. MOS transistors switch more slowly than bipolar transistors, and the access time for a MOS static RAM is typically in the range of 50 to 100 nanoseconds.

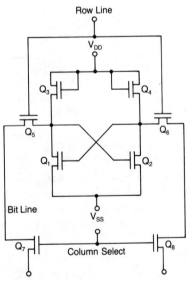

Figure 10.6   MOS Static RAM Cell

Static RAM Operation

The operation of static RAM systems is best understood by examining timing waveforms. The timing waveforms for a memory read operation are given in *Figure 10.7*. The cycle begins when the CPU outputs a valid address onto the address bus. For a read, the R/$\overline{\text{W}}$ control line is held at the 1 logic level. The memory interface circuitry selects the particular RAM IC (or ICs) by decoding a chip select ($\overline{\text{CS}}$) signal from the address signal on the address bus. After the access time delay, which starts when the address is valid, the memory device outputs the data bit(s). The output data remain valid until the CPU removes the address from the bus, plus a short switching delay time required to disable the memory output drivers. The read operation is straightforward; the CPU generates the request for data by outputting address and a read control signal by holding R/$\overline{\text{W}}$ at a 1 logic level, and the memory responds by outputting the stored data.

Figure 10.8 is the timing diagram for a memory write operation. The most obvious difference between write timing and read timing is the read/write control signal (R/$\overline{\text{W}}$). During the write cycle, the CPU outputs an address on the address bus and data on the data bus. Time is allowed for the memory interface to select the memory ICs involved, and the CPU activates the write control signal by holding the R/$\overline{\text{W}}$ line at logic 0. The data on the bus are latched into the memory at that time.

When static RAM devices are not selected, they operate in a standby mode. MOS devices dissipate considerably less power during standby than during active mode. When they are selected, static RAMs, even though they are MOS devices in most cases, output and input data at standard TTL levels.

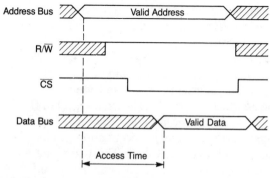

Figure 10.7 Memory-READ Timing

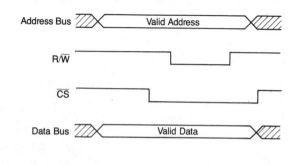

Figure 10.8 Memory-WRITE Timing

Dynamic RAM Devices

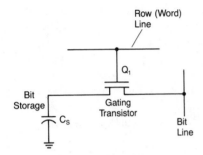

Figure 10.9 shown with labels:
Row (Word) Line, Q₁, Bit Storage, Gating Transistor, Cₛ, Bit Line

Figure 10.9   One-Transistor DRAM Cell

As mentioned previously, static RAMs dissipate significantly more power than dynamic RAMs. In addition, they take up much more space on an integrated circuit chip. Dynamic RAM (DRAM) cells were developed to overcome these drawbacks. Three MOS transistors were used initially in the most popular DRAM cells, but current designs use a one-transistor cell. This one-transistor cell design has made the 64K DRAM a practical integrated circuit memory. *Figure 10.9* shows the circuitry of the one-transistor cell.

In the cell, the data bit is stored as a charge on the capacitor C_S. The MOSFET gating transistor Q_1 is used to connect the capacitor to the bit line when the cell is selected. If the cell is not selected, the transistor isolates the capacitor from the line. The cell is selected when the signal on the row (word) line turns ON the MOSFET gate (sometimes called a transmission gate). A sense amplifier attached to the bit line detects current generated by the charge on the capacitor. After the cell is read in this manner, the capacitor must be recharged. Additional circuitry is contained within the memory IC to accomplish the recharging.

To write data into the cell, the data bit is placed on the bit line and the cell is selected. The capacitor is charged to the proper level through Q_1. When the address decoding turns off Q_1, the capacitor retains the charge, thereby storing the data bit. Normal capacitor leakage requires that the cell be refreshed periodically, typically every 2 milliseconds. Essentially, refreshing is done by rewriting the data into the cell to recharge the capacitor.

The refresh cycle, of course, must be accomplished independently of the normal computer operations. One way this is done is by providing dedicated refresh circuitry consisting of a row address generator, a multiplexer to switch between the system address bus and the refresh address generator, and logic to isolate the memory from the data bus during the refresh operation. Originally the refresh circuitry was implemented on the memory printed wiring board with special integrated circuits and support components. This was cumbersome because it required additional design, additional space, and added complexity to the system. One possible solution integrated the refresh circuitry into the microprocessor, but this used valuable space on the microprocessor IC. A more recent approach has the refresh circuitry designed into the RAM IC. This technique is likely to become more popular because of the simplicity it offers for memory designers.

Dynamic RAM Operation

A block diagram of a dynamic RAM (DRAM) system is shown in *Figure 10.10*. The obvious difference between static RAM and dynamic RAM systems is the refresh circuitry. The control logic block disables the RAM outputs during the refresh operation. It also generates the read/write signal as a part of the refresh. The refresh counter is a binary counter which generates the row addresses for cell selection. Each row line and all the cells on the line must be energized so they can be refreshed by circuitry in the DRAM at least every 2 milliseconds. A burst of refresh would quickly sweep across all the rows in sequence to accomplish the refresh. In 2 milliseconds this would happen again. A "cycle stealing" refresh would pick out a DRAM cycle periodically to refresh a row. Each row is selected in sequence and a cycle stolen until the full refresh is completed within the 2 millisecond period. The multiplexer is used to select system address inputs for normal operations or refresh addresses for refresh operations.

From the computer system's point of view, the only difference between static RAM and dynamic RAM operation is that DRAM sections must be given time to be refreshed. During refreshing, normal read/write operations must be suspended. When refresh is completed, read/write cycles may be accomplished normally.

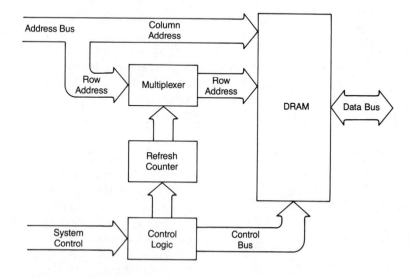

Figure 10.10   DRAM System

Three-State Outputs

Most modern memory devices, both static and dynamic, use three-state circuitry to isolate their inputs and outputs from the system data bus. Usually these three-state circuits are activated by the $\overline{CS}$ (Chip Select) or $\overline{CE}$ (Chip Enable) control input(s) one the device. These built-in three-state buffers eliminate the requirement for external data bus buffers, which were integral parts of early semiconductor memory systems.

READ-ONLY MEMORY DEVICES

Read-only memory elements, called ROM, are used for all or part of the program memory of computer memories. They also have a number of other special applications which will be covered later. As program memory, ROMs store the instructions which determine a computer system's functional operation. ROMs are non-volatile so that the program is always available as soon as power is applied to the system. Several different types of read-only devices are available, and each will be described briefly in the sections to follow. Essentially, they represent different levels of flexibility for the user of read-only memories.

ROM

The lowest-cost devices are the mask-programmable ROMs usually referred to by the straight acronym ROM. They are also the least flexible because they are programmed during the manufacturing process, and the program, once stored, cannot be changed. As the term mask-programmable implies, these ROMs are programmed during one of the masking steps in the manufacture of the ICs. ROMs are used for high volume production after a design has been proven to be correct and no changes are expected.

PROM

PROMs, or programmable read-only memories, are more flexible than ROMs because they are programmed after manufacture. They can be programmed using special equipment by the memory user rather than the manufacturer. They are somewhat more expensive than ROMs because they use more chip space. PROMs cannot be reprogrammed (in the strictest sense, a bit or two might be changed if they had not been programmed the first time; however, the likelyhood of a second use is somewhat remote).

EPROM

Erasable, programmable read-only memory is much more flexible than either ROM or PROM, because it can be reprogrammed by the user. EPROM devices are constructed with a quartz window over the silicon chip. An ultraviolet light beamed through this window erases the stored information and leaves the device ready for reprogramming. However, because it is erasable, EPROM costs more to manufacture than ROM or PROM.

EPROM is often used during the development of system software to store intermediate versions of a program before the final design is achieved. The typical sequence is to develop the program initially in static RAM and then to transfer it to EPROM. As the development progresses, modifications and improvements are stored in EPROM until the system design stabilizes. Finally, when the system is proven and is in volume production, masked ROM is substituted.

EEROM

EEROM, or electrically erasable-programmable read-only memory, might better be classified as read-mostly memory, because it can be erased and reprogrammed in a relatively short time. Whereas EPROM changes are timed in minutes, EEROMs can be erased and reprogrammed in a matter of microseconds. In terms of access times, currently available EEROMs are slower than other read-only devices. In fact, EEROMs are still not practical for most designs. They represent a class of devices which hold significant promise for the future.

For a comparison of these read-only memory devices, refer to *Figure 10.11a*. To a great extent, the choice of a ROM device depends not only on the parameters compared in this figure, but also on the current stage of a system's design. As has already been pointed out, the EPROM used during the prototyping stages is likely to be replaced with PROM once the design is proven. Even later, masked ROM may be chosen when design changes are no longer probable. Such a progression allows designers to take advantage of the trade-off between flexibility and cost as the *Figure 10.11b* indicates. In addition, EPROMs are used extensively to adapt programmable systems to specific application areas. By the change of an EPROM, a microcomputer can be adapted to a specific program for real estate, farmers, lawyers, etc.

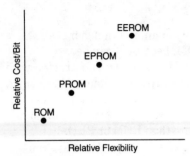

	ROM	PROM	EPROM	EEROM
Cost (Rank)	1	2	3	4
Program Time	Weeks	Minutes	Minutes	Minutes
Set-Up Charge	Yes	No	No	No
Reusability	No	No	Yes	Yes
Speed	Fast	Very Fast	Medium	Slow

a. Characteristics

b. Cost/Bit Versus Flexibility

Figure 10.11 Comparison of Read-Only Memory Devices

ROM Applications

Non-volatile memory finds a number of applications in digital systems. The use of ROM for storing system programs has already been mentioned. All computers require some form of control software. It may be as simple as a machine language monitor or as complicated as a multi-tasking operating system. In either case, this control software is unchanging and must be a permanent part of the system configuration. Storing such software in ROM is one way to be sure it is always present in the system memory.

Storing System Constants or Fixed Tables

Another possible use for ROM is the storage of fixed data tables. For example, sines or cosines of angles (or any other function) could be stored in a read-only memory. To make a table of sines, the sine of 30 degrees would be stored at ROM address 30, the sine of 45 degrees would be stored at address 45, and so on. To look up the sine of an angle, say 30 degrees, the address code for the address 30 is applied to the address bus. The sine of 30 degrees, 0.500, is output by the ROM device. Since information of this nature never changes, ROM is an ideal way to store such tables for a computer system.

Code Converters

Code converter ROMs are a variation of the look-up table application. The commonly used BCD-to-7 segment code converter, for example, is a 16 × 7 ROM. The 4-bit BCD input addresses a memory location which stores a 7-bit word. The output word causes a 7-segment display to form the decimal equivalent of the BCD input. This process is illustrated in *Figure 10.12*.

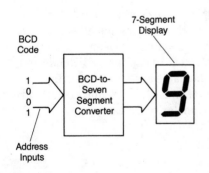

Figure 10.12 BCD to 7-Segment Converter

Character Generators

An extension of this idea is used to construct character generators. *Figure 10.13* is a partial specification sheet for the TMS4710 ASCII Character Generator ROM. When ASCII codes are input as addresses to this device, the outputs correspond to the elements of a character to be displayed on a CRT terminal using a 5×7 character size in an 8×8 matrix. Operation of the character generator is seen more clearly in *Figure 10.14*.

The address inputs A_0 through A_6 are used to input the 7-bit ASCII code. In this figure, the ASCII input is 1010101, the code for upper case U. The other three address inputs, A_9, A_8 and A_7 are used to select which row outputs of the eight block rows are to be activated at any point in time. This is necessary because each scan line of the CRT can trace only one row of the character per horizontal sweep. For example, when the row address is 000, outputs Q_1 through Q_8 are all low, representing the blank line at the top of the letter. This provides the space between consecutive rows of characters. Row address 001 causes the eight outputs to change to 10001000, where the 1s activate the display and the 0s blank it. Row addresses 010 through 110 also cause the outputs to produce 10001000. Row address 111 causes the outputs to change to 01110000. The pattern of 1s in the outputs corresponds to the pattern of illuminated dots in the display.

- **TMS4710 (Standard TMS4700 8K ROM)**
- **Full Upper and Lower Case ASCII Character Generator**
- **Ideal for Video Terminal Applications**
- **Fully Static Operation**
- **Block Size 8 x 8**
- **Character Size 5 x 7**
- **1024 x 8 Organization**
- **All Inputs and Outputs TTL-Compatible**
- **Maximum Access Time ... 450ns**
- **Minimum Cycle Time ... 450ns**
- **Typical Power Dissipation ... 310mW**
- **3-State Outputs for OR-Ties**
- **Output Enable Control**
- **Silicon-Gate Technology**
- **8-Bit Output for Use in Microprocessor Based System**

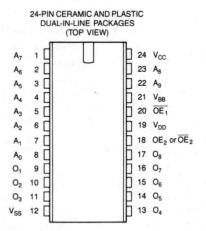

24-PIN CERAMIC AND PLASTIC
DUAL-IN-LINE PACKAGES
(TOP VIEW)

A_7	1	24	V_{CC}
A_6	2	23	A_8
A_5	3	22	A_9
A_4	4	21	V_{BB}
A_3	5	20	$\overline{OE_1}$
A_2	6	19	V_{DD}
A_1	7	18	OE_2 or $\overline{OE_2}$
A_0	8	17	O_8
O_1	9	16	O_7
O_2	10	15	O_6
O_3	11	14	O_5
V_{SS}	12	13	O_4

Figure 10.13 *Character Generator Specifications for the TMS4710*

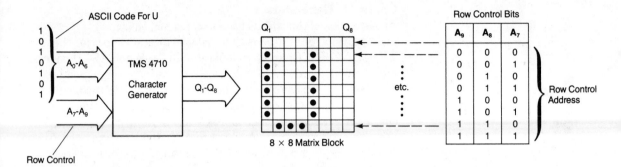

Figure 10.14   Character Generator with ASCII Code Input

Combinational and Sequential Logic

ROMs can also be used to implement combinational and sequential logic functions. In the case of combinational logic, input variables are combined by logic gates to produce one or more outputs. If the input variables are used as ROM addresses, each combination of input variables addresses a different ROM location which stores the corresponding output(s).

Example 10-2: *Figure 10.15a* shows a simple gate circuit and *Figure 10.15b* the truth table of the function it implements. In *Figure 10.15c*, an 8 × 1 ROM is shown which replaces the gate circuit. Variables R, S, and T are used to address the memory locations. Each location stores the output bit Q, which corresponds to the combination of R, S, and T. For example, if the code for RST is 100, respectively, the ROM outputs a 1, but if RST is 101, respectively, the output is 0.

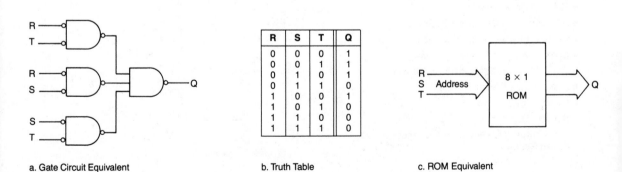

a. Gate Circuit Equivalent

b. Truth Table

c. ROM Equivalent

Figure 10.15   Using ROM to Implement Combinational Logic

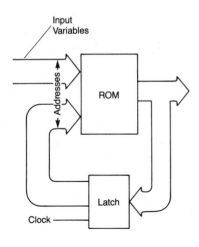

Figure 10.16   Using ROM to Implement Sequential Logic

ROMs may also be used to implement sequential logic functions. In sequential logic, the current output depends not only on the current inputs, but also on the previous output. *Figure 10.16* shows how the previous output is used to determine the current output in a ROM circuit. The previous output is latched and is used along with the current input to address the ROM. Using ROM to implement sequential or combinational logic is not really practical for circuits as simple as the ones shown in these two examples. However, if the logic circuit is complex and requires many more gates and/or flip-flops, a ROM may often be a practical alternative to discrete logic circuitry.

Plug-In Software

One other application for ROMs is in plug-in cartridge programs used with personal and professional computers. Applications programs are stored in ROMs and the ROMs are attached to small printed wiring boards which are packaged in plastic cartridges. By inserting the cartridge into a special memory-expansion port on the computer, the system configuration can be easily changed to meet the needs of the user. Typical cartridge-based programs include word processors, programming aids, educational programs, games, and various utilities. In fact, almost any type of consumer-level program can be stored in ROM and packaged in a cartridge.

SIMPLE RANDOM ACCESS MEMORY SYSTEMS

Computer systems require both RAM and ROM sections to complete the main memory component. In modern computers, the semiconductor RAM and ROM devices already discussed in this chapter are often combined to form a complete semiconductor main memory. This memory unit is then interfaced to the system buses using standard logic products.

Memory Interface Features

The memory interface in a computer system performs three primary functions, each of which is related to one of the system buses:
1. The interface decodes address bus information to determine which memory device(s) must be enabled.
2. The memory interface gates the appropriate control signals (R/$\overline{\text{W}}$, $\overline{\text{MEMEN}}$, etc.) to the memory device(s).
3. The interface controls the buffer enable signals so that information is loaded to or from the data bus without interfering with other system elements.

The discussion that follows details how these functions are implemented in the simple memory systems.

Simple RAM Section

The TMS4016 static RAM specification sheet was shown in *Figure 10.2*. The IC is a 16K RAM organized as 2K × 8. For small memories, like the one to be considered here, word-wide memory organizations are often used. Word-wide organization means that the memory device stores words having the same length as the computer system word length. The TMS4016 would be a word-wide memory for an 8-bit computer. Larger memories are more likely to be designed with bit-wide memory ICs. A bit-wide memory IC stores only one bit at each location, and several identical ICs must be cascaded to provide storage for an entire word. A memory of this design will be examined later in this chapter.

Figure 10.17 shows a 2K × 8 RAM portion of a much larger memory using a TMS4016. The memory is designed so that its 2048 addresses range from 0800H through 0FFFH. This is accomplished by connecting the CPU's 16 address lines as shown in the figure. Address bus lines $A_0 - A_{10}$ are used to select storage locations within the TMS4016. Address lines $A_{11} - A_{15}$ are decoded by the NAND gate to select the RAM chip when an address in the 0800H to 0FFFH range appears on the address bus. The NAND gate's output drives the TMS4016 $\overline{CS}$ (Chip Select) input. Only when A_{11} is high and A_{12} through A_{15} are low will this RAM be selected. For all other combinations of A_{11} through A_{15}, the TMS4016 is disabled and it operates in the reduced-power standby state.

The data bus connections, DQ_1 through DQ_8, are used for both input and output. These eight lines are fully TTL compatible and, when $\overline{CS}$ is high, they are switched to a high impedance mode by built-in three-state buffers to prevent the RAM from interfering with other system operations which involve the data bus.

Two control inputs determine the exact function of the RAM whenever it is selected. The $\overline{W}$ input is high for read operations, and low for write operations. In effect, it controls the data direction on the eight input/output lines. Internally, it controls the read and write circuitry for the memory cells.

The other control input, $\overline{OE}$, is used to disable the output buffers during write operations. The CPU's R/$\overline{W}$ control line drives the $\overline{W}$ input directly and the $\overline{OE}$ input through an inverter. The inverter ensures that $\overline{OE}$ is active (low) during memory-read operations. The only other requirements for this memory section are the +5V and ground connections for operating power.

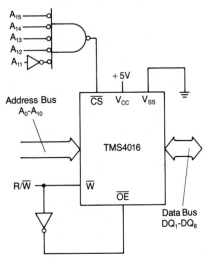

Figure 10.17 2K X 8 RAM Section

Simple ROM Section

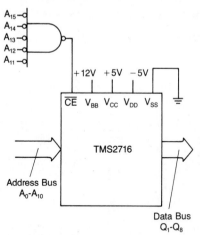

Figure 10.18 2K X 8 ROM Section

A similar 2K × 8 ROM portion of a computer system's main memory, is diagrammed in *Figure 10.18*. The ROM IC used is the TMS2716 EPROM, a 16K memory organized as 2K × 8. This ROM portion has been designed to complement the RAM portion just described. Used together, these two memories could comprise the main memory for a small computer system.

The 2048 addresses for this ROM section must be in the range 0000H through 07FFH. This range is determined by the NAND gate, which combines A_{11} through A_{15} to drive the $\overline{CE}$ input. When $\overline{CE}$ is active (low), the eight output lines, Q_1 through Q_8, are all connected to the data bus. When $\overline{CE}$ is high (not enabled), Q_1 through Q_8 float in a high impedance state due to the three-state buffers built on the ROM IC.

Because data is not written to ROMs during system operation, the data bus connections are unidirectional. There is no need for an input/output control since there are no data inputs. The TMS2716 outputs are fully TTL compatible.

No other control signals are needed for the TMS2716. Whenever the TMS2716 is selected by the address bus signals, a read operation occurs. Otherwise, the outputs are disabled. The four power supply connections (+12V, +5V, −5V, ground) required by the TMS2716 are shown.

Total Memory System Operation

The combination memory is shown diagrammed in *Figure 10.19*. There are no addressing conflicts because the NAND gate decoders select a memory device only when an address in the proper range appears on the address bus. Three-state outputs prevent data bus interference.

Suppose, for example, that the CPU enters a memory-read cycle and places address 0100H on the address bus. Since address lines A_{11} through A_{15} are all low, the TMS2716 ROM is enabled and, after the access time delay, the contents of address 0100H appear on the data bus. Since the TMS4016 RAM is not selected, its inputs and outputs are all disabled.

Bit-Wide ICs

As memory capacity is increased, it becomes more efficient to use bit-wide devices. In *Figure 10.20a*, a 4K × 8 RAM portion of a main memory is illustrated. The RAM is a TMS4044 static RAM which is organized as 4096 × 1. Eight ICs are interconnected in parallel to form the 4K × 8 memory. Notice that a common input, $\overline{S}$ enables all eight of the chips at once. The address bus is connected so that the same location on every IC is addressed. (Notice that one more address line is required to address 4K locations than 2K). The input pins D_1 through D_8 are connected to the data bus line. The same is true for the output pins (Q_1 through Q_8). In this way, each IC stores only one bit of the 8-bit word, but all eight bits are accessed simultaneously. Of course, the read/write control lines ($R/\overline{W}$) from all the ICs must be connected together. Other factors related to increasing memory size are examined in the next section.

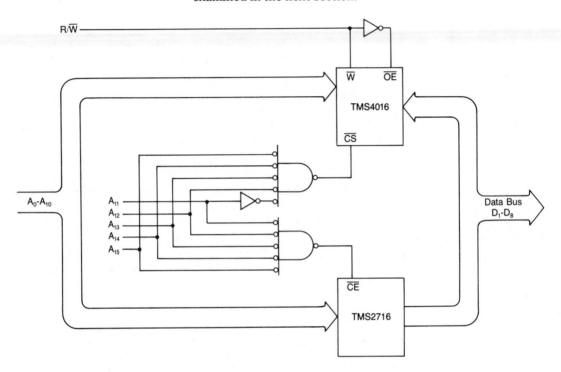

Figure 10.19 Main Memory for a Small Computer System

EXPANDING MEMORY CAPACITY

General purpose computer systems typically have 48K or more 8-bit words of read/write storage. Newer designs even use longer words, usually 16 bits, instead of the 8-bit word common in most early microcomputers. In the future, 32-bit words may become common.

Memories for these computer systems are straightforward extensions of the RAM of *Figure 10.20a*. As an example, the 4K × 8 RAM of *Figure 10.20a* will be used to illustrate the principles. To make the diagrams more clear, the memory in *Figure 10.20a* will be redrawn as in *Figure 10.20b*. Although the individual ICs are not shown in this diagram, it should be understood that they are combined for clarity into a single block in the figure. Most large memories use dynamic RAM devices, but as has already been indicated, operation of DRAM and static RAM is identical except for the refresh requirement for DRAM.

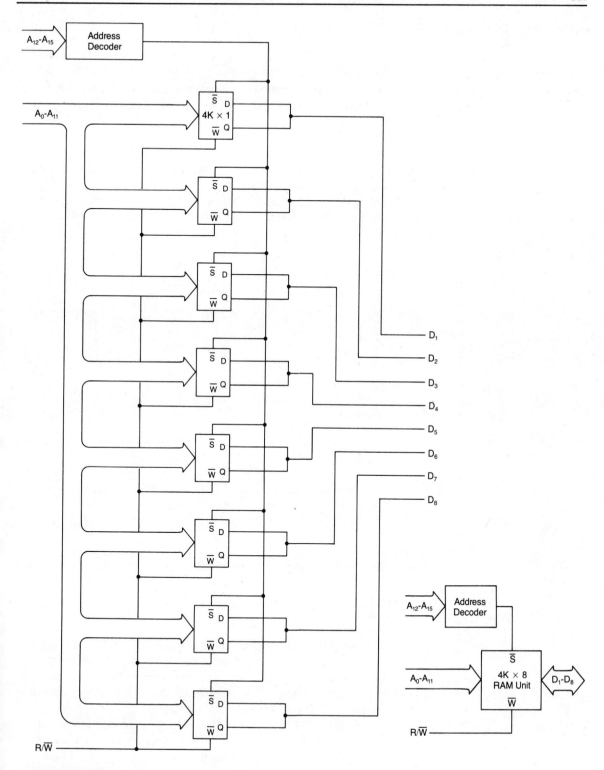

a. Interconnection of RAMs for 4K × 8

b. Equivalent Simplified Diagram

Figure 10.20 Bit-Wide Memory Devices (TMS4044)

Increasing Word Length

A RAM section for a 16-bit computer system may be designed as illustrated in *Figure 10.21*. Two 4K × 8 memories like the one in *Figure 10.20b* are combined to provide 16 input/output lines. In the top section, these lines are connected to data bus lines $D_1 - D_8$, and in the bottom section they are tied to $D_9 - D_{16}$. All other inputs to the two memory blocks are common. The 16-bit address from the CPU selects both units and it addresses the same location within each unit. The read/write control line causes both units to perform the same operation. Word length can be increased to 32 bits by adding two more 4K × 8 units, and so on. Word length can be increased indefinitely by this scheme.

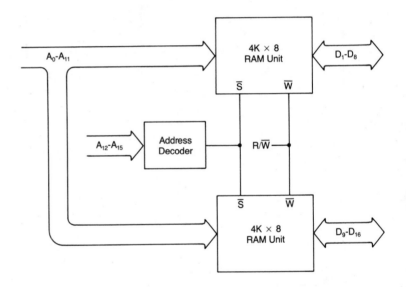

Figure 10.21   Forming a 16-Bit Memory From an 8-Bit Memory

Increasing Word Capacity

Word length for a given computer is fixed by the CPU design; however, more word storage locations can always be used if the address bus has the capacity to address them. Once again, we can use the 4K × 8 unit to illustrate this process. A 16-bit address bus will be used. It could handle 64K words.

Figure 10.22 shows two 4K × 8 units combined to form an 8K × 8 memory. Address bus lines $A_0 - A_{11}$ are used to select one of the 4096 storage locations on one of the two 4K units. Lines $A_{12} - A_{15}$ are decoded to determine which of the two units is to be selected. The data lines of the selected unit are enabled and connected to the data bus, but are disabled and in a high impedance state for the unselected unit. The R/$\overline{\text{W}}$ control is common, since it affects only the selected unit. Using this approach, the memory can be expanded in 4K increments by connecting additional 4K × 8 units and decoding $A_{12} - A_{15}$ to drive the $\overline{\text{S}}$ input(s).

It should be noted that the amount of additional memory provided by each unit is determined by the RAM device used to construct the units. In these examples, the TMS4044 4K × 1 RAM was used as the basis for each memory unit. If the original unit had been constructed using eight TMS4116 16K × 1 DRAM ICs, for example, each unit would add 16K 8-bit locations. The wide variety of available memory organizations makes it possible to design and construct memories of almost any desired size.

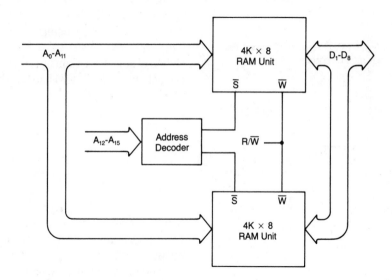

Figure 10.22   Increasing Word-Storage Capacity

Interfacing Larger Memories

In the discussion of *Figure 10.22*, it was noted that address bus lines $A_{12} - A_{15}$ were decoded to select one of the two memory units. Except for the simple connection of $A_0 - A_{11}$, $D_1 - D_8$, and the R/$\overline{\text{W}}$ control line, this decoding is the only interfacing required for the RAM section. All other interfacing functions (address latching, line buffering, etc.) have been incorporated into the memory IC. Modern semiconductor memories, therefore, are quite simple to use.

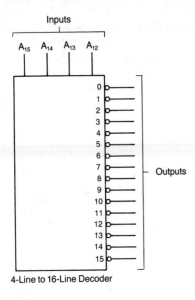

Inputs

A₁₅ A₁₄ A₁₃ A₁₂

0
1
2
3
4
5
6
7
8 — Outputs
9
10
11
12
13
14
15

4-Line to 16-Line Decoder

Figure 10.23 Four-to-Sixteen Line Address Decoder

The purpose of the address-decoding part of the interface is to determine which RAM section to select for a given address input. In the simple memory of *Figure 10.19*, two NAND gates were used to decode the high-order address bits. In larger memories, however, the decoding logic is often more complex. Still, it is most-often implemented using combinational logic circuitry. The address decoder in *Figure 10.22*, for example, could be implemented using a 4-line-to-16-line decoder as shown in *Figure 10.23*. The binary number from 0 through 15 represented by the four inputs, $A_{12} - A_{15}$, causes the corresponding normally-high output line to go low. For example, if $A_{15} - A_{12}$ equal 1100, output line 12 is driven low, but all other outputs remain high. In this way, up to 16 different memory units can be individually selected. If only a portion of the 16 units are used in a given system, the decoder outputs used can be chosen to locate the memory sections at desired addresses. For example, addresses for the 8K RAM of *Figure 10.22* could be set to the range E000H through FFFFH by using decoder outputs 14 and 15 to drive the $\overline{S}$ inputs of the two RAM units. Addresses from E000H through EFFFH select locations in the lower 4K unit, while addresses F000H through FFFFH select the upper 4K.

SERIAL ACCESS MEMORY

Shift Registers

So far in this chapter, all the memories described have been random access memories, where access time essentially is the same for information stored at all locations. The next three devices covered are serial access systems. Data are circulated through the memory until the desired information reaches the output point, at which time it can be read. Access time for the desired data depends on its position in the circulation loop at the time it is requested.

Serial access memories are designed primarily for auxiliary storage systems, not for main memory. In fact, they are expected to compete with magnetic disk in some applications. The flip-flop shift register is the oldest version of the serial access memory. A simple shift register is diagrammed in *Figure 10.24*. A practical shift register memory requires many more flip-flops, since the memory requires one flip-flop per bit stored.

The speed of the shift register is determined by the clock rate, and is limited by the switching speeds of the gates and flip-flops. Each clock pulse causes the data to shift right one stage.

The bit stored in the rightmost stage is returned to the first stage. The NAND gate network at the input allows a new data bit to be substituted for the old. This is done by placing the new data bit on the DATA IN line and activating the $\overline{\text{REPLACE}}$ control input by pulling it low. Data is read out one bit at a time on the DATA OUT line.

Example 10-3: In *Figure 10.24*, the data stored in the three flip-flops is 110. When the clock is energized and $\overline{\text{REPLACE}}$ is held high, the output will be a string of bits that come out in the sequence 011011011 as shown. If the middle flip-flop were changed to a 0, the output would come out in the sequence 001001001.

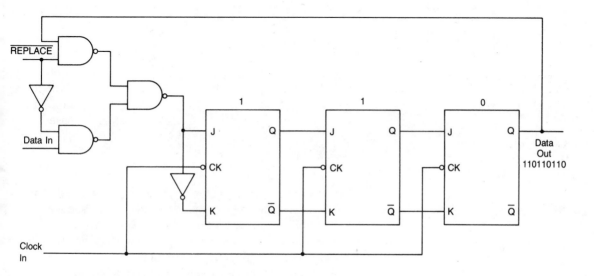

Figure 10.24   Flip-Flop 3-Bit Shift Register

Magnetic Bubble Memory

Bubble memory is a magnetic version of the flip-flop shift register which uses magnetized domains to represent logic 1s in a magnetic film deposited on a non-magnetic substrate. Chevron-shaped metallic patterns are deposited on the magnetic film to control the direction of bubble travel around a circulating loop, called a major loop. The complete substrate is operated in a permanent magnetic field perpendicular to the substrate surface. *Figure 10.25* shows the basic structure.

Bubbles are formed at the input by sending a current pulse through a special bubble generator structure. They are then propagated around the loop until the desired sequence of bits has been entered. Then, the sequence is transferred to one of the minor loops for storage. Special transfer gates connect the minor loops to the major loops.

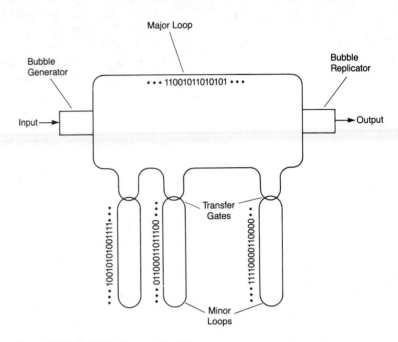

Figure 10.25   Bubble Memory Structure

To read information, a bubble sequence is transferred from a minor loop back to the major loop. When the bubble sequence reaches the bubble replicator, each bubble is split into two bubbles, one of which continues around the loop and the other is output to special detectors and sense amplifiers.

Bubble memories are non-volatile. This is achieved by including a large external permanent magnet to maintain the magnetic field even when power is removed. The size and speed of available bubble memory systems have limited their application to only a few applications so far. Still, their potential for storing millions of bits in a non-volatile environment makes them viable alternatives to other mass storage devices.

Charge-Coupled Device Memory

One other serial access memory, the charge-coupled device, was originally developed as a semiconductor alternative to magnetic bubbles. Charge-coupled device (CCD) memories store bits in channels of capacitors integrated on a common substrate, as indicated in *Figure 10.26*. Bits are stored as a "bucket" of charge or no charge on the capacitors, and are circulated through the channel by a multiphase clock driver. In addition to the clock circuitry, a CCD system also includes address latches, input/output buffers, and recirculation counters to control the system operation.

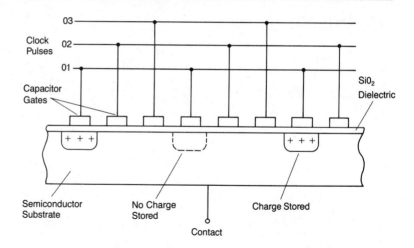

Figure 10.26 *Charge-Coupled Device Structure*

Because the CCD storage cell is a single capacitor, extremely dense memories can be integrated onto a single chip making them competitive with bubble memories. Also, like the DRAM, the CCD must be refreshed by recirculating the data when it is not being written or read.

CCD memory devices are cascaded to form large serial access memories. In terms of density and speed they are comparable to other popular auxiliary storage media. However, their volatility is a distinct disadvantage and probably accounts for their lack of application in many memory systems.

OTHER MEMORY DEVICES

Although semiconductor memory devices are used in most microcomputer systems for main memory, magnetic tape and disk are commonly used for auxiliary mass storage. In addition, larger systems may use some other type of storage devices. A few of these are described briefly in the following paragraphs.

Magnetic Core Memory

Magnetic cores are tiny doughnut-shaped beads which can be magnetized by the field surrounding the current-carrying wire through the center of the bead. The magnetic polarity is determined by the direction of current in the wire. One polarity represents a logic 0, and the opposite polarity represents a logic 1.

Core memory is non-volatile. It was widely used for main memory for many years, and it is still used in certain applications. However, its relatively large size and weight, and its requirement for high drive currents generally prohibit its use in microprocessor-based systems.

Programmable Logic Arrays

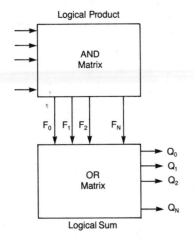

Logical Product

Figure 10.27   Block Diagram for a PLA

A programmable logic array (PLA) is a circuit which, like a ROM, can function as a memory, a code converter, or a logic function generator. However, a PLA is more efficient than a ROM in many applications because it can be implemented in a much smaller area on an integrated circuit chip.

A ROM is organized such that if it has five inputs, it will have 2^5, or 32, storage locations and can output 32 different words. Space is required in the ROM for each of the 32 words, even though some of them may not be needed. A PLA, on the other hand, may have five inputs, but it will not necessarily have 32 outputs.

A PLA consists of two gate matrices. The inputs are applied to the AND gate matrix and the outputs are taken from the OR gate matrix as shown in *Figure 10.27*.

For simplicity, assume that a PLA is to be used to generate two logic functions: $Q_0 = (\overline{A} \cdot B) + (A \cdot \overline{B})$, and $Q_1 = (A \cdot \overline{B})$. The PLA would require two inputs, one for variable A and one for B. The inverted form of these inputs would be generated in the PLA so that a total of four lines, A, $\overline{A}$, B, and $\overline{B}$, provide inputs to the gates in the AND matrix.

The AND matrix requires two gates because Q_0 and Q_1 contain a total of two different terms (the term $(A \cdot \overline{B})$ appears in both functions). Each gate requires two inputs because two variables are involved. As *Figure 10.28* shows, inputs are connected to generate only the terms needed for the two functions Q_0 and Q_1. In this example, only the terms $(\overline{A} \cdot B)$ and $(A \cdot B)$ are needed.

The outputs of the gates in the AND matrix provide inputs for the OR matrix. The required logic functions are generated as indicated in *Figure 10.28* by ORing the terms $(\overline{A} \cdot B)$ and $(A \cdot \overline{B})$. Note that only NAND gates are used to provide the AND or OR. This makes it easy to implement the circuitry in integrated circuit form because all gates are the same.

An example of a simplified diagram to represent the Logic Array (LA) is shown in *Figure 10.29*. Each circle in the diagram represents a MOSFET, which selects a gate input to a matrix term. The top matrix represents the ANDed terms, and the bottom matrix the ORed terms.

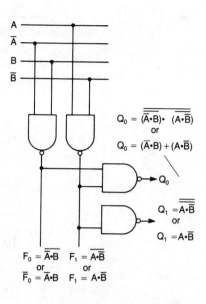

$Q_0 = \overline{(\overline{A}\cdot B)\cdot \ (A\cdot \overline{B})}$
or
$Q_0 = (\overline{A}\cdot B) + (A\cdot \overline{B})$

$Q_1 = \overline{A\cdot \overline{B}}$
or
$Q_1 = A\cdot \overline{B}$

$F_0 = \overline{\overline{A}\cdot B}$ $F_1 = \overline{A\cdot \overline{B}}$
or   or
$\overline{F}_0 = \overline{A}\cdot B$ $F_1 = A\cdot \overline{B}$

**Figure 10.28   Circuit Schematic for a
Standard Logic PLA**

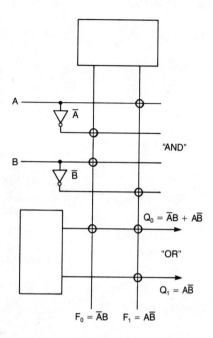

"AND"

$Q_0 = \overline{A}B + A\overline{B}$

"OR"

$Q_1 = A\overline{B}$

$F_0 = \overline{A}B$ $F_1 = A\overline{B}$

**Figure 10.29   Equivalent Schematic of
Array Logic**

SUMMARY

Memory is an integral part of any computer system. Both permanent and temporary storage is required for main memory, and some form of non-volatile mass storage is usually desirable.

The emphasis in this chapter has been on the semiconductor devices used to form main memory for microcomputer systems. In many ways, semiconductor RAM and ROM improvements have been responsible for the proliferation of microprocessor-based systems. Generally, these improvements have made the memories more efficient and easier to interface with the rest of the system. This chapter has examined and demonstrated the operational characteristics and the basics of interfacing RAM and ROM devices in computer systems, and has given a brief survey of serial access memory components.

CHAPTER 10 QUIZ

1. The total number of bits stored in a 4K × 8 RAM is:
   a. 8.
   b. 4,000.
   c. 4,096.
   d. 32,768.

2. A memory device with ten address inputs has how many word storage locations?
   a. 10
   b. 1,024
   c. 4,096
   d. 10K

3. A statement which is not true about dynamic RAM is that:
   a. cells are smaller than static RAM cells.
   b. it dissipates less power than static RAM.
   c. it must be refreshed during operation.
   d. cells are constructed with MOS flip-flops.

4. How many RAM ICs are needed to construct a 16K × 8 memory if each IC is organized as 16K × 1?
   a. 16
   b. 8
   c. 4
   d. 1

5. To say that a memory is volatile means that:
   a. storage cells are erased by reading.
   b. storage cells must be refreshed.
   c. it dissipates relatively large amounts of power.
   d. removing power erases the memory.

6. Which of the following is a type of non-volatile memory?
   a. MOS RAM
   b. Bipolar RAM
   c. EPROM
   d. SRAM

7. From a user's point of view, the most inflexible read-only memory is:
   a. EPROM.
   b. EAROM.
   c. PROM.
   d. ROM.

8. A word-wide memory device for a 16-bit computer might be organized as:
   a. 16K × 1.
   b. 4K × 16.
   c. 4K × 4.
   d. 2K × 8.

9. Two word-wide memory devices organized as 4K × 8 could be used to implement what size memory?
   a. 32K × 2
   b. 8K × 16
   c. 8K × 8
   d. 4K × 4

10. Which of the following is not a random access device?
   a. DRAM
   b. Bubble memory
   c. PROM
   d. Core memory

COMPUTER INTERFACE AND COMMUNICATIONS

INTRODUCTION

The major parts of a computer system were previously identified in Chapter 9 as the Central Processing Unit (CPU), memory and the input/output units. As we learned, the CPU in a microcomputer system is a microprocessor or microprocessor unit (MPU). Input and output units are the units that interface the computer system to the outside world. The input unit senses inputs from the outside world that the computer system must react to. The output units provide output action to the outside world as a result of the instruction in the computer system's program and its reaction to the inputs.

Input units and output units (commonly called I/O) are not necessarily made up of pieces of equipment that are self-contained within the computer system. Many of the units are separated from the main body of the computer system. They are peripheral to the system; as a result, they are called peripheral units. Keyboards, CRT terminals, disk drives, and printers are common input/output peripheral units.

Peripheral input/output units must be coupled to the computer system with special circuits called interfacing circuits. Many of these circuits are contained in specially designed integrated circuits called interfacing ICs. There are many types of interfacing chips available, so many that discussing each of them is beyond the scope of this chapter; however, we will discuss some of the most common types. The interconnecting point for the interface IC to the computer system is called a port, either input or output, but more commonly just I/O port.

The chapter begins with a discussion of parallel and serial I/O ports including discrete IC examples, typically addressed using memory mapping or I/O mapping.

As just mentioned, the I/O port is made active by connecting the peripheral unit to it with an interfacing IC. The interfacing IC translates between signals the computer uses and signals the peripheral unit uses. As a result, when an I/O port is provided in a computer system, it is assumed that the interface IC is included.

Complete interface ICs are discussed next — parallel peripheral, peripheral interface adapters, and programmable peripheral interfaces.

Next, the three basic I/O control methods — polling, interrupt control, and direct memory access — are discussed, followed by examples of typical hardware-based interfacing ICs — the ACIA, the UART and USART.

After a discussion of standard codes, signal characteristics and interconnections, the chapter concludes with a discussion of common peripheral I/O hardware: auxilary memory, video terminals and keyboards are covered.

PARALLEL and SERIAL I/O PORTS

Two types of I/O ports are in widespread use — parallel and serial. A parallel port allows output or input of a given number of data bits at the same time. Data words of 8 bits and 16 bits are common. A serial port allows only one bit to be input or output at a time.

A Parallel Port from Individual ICs

One of the simplest parallel ports for eight bits can be constructed using two SN7474 D-type flip-flops used as latches, two SN74126 bus buffers with three-state outputs, and one-third of a SN7404 inverter for the control circuit. The circuit is shown in *Figure 11.1*. This discrete port requires five 14-pin ICs. Texas Instruments offers this same combination of circuits in a single 20-pin IC package as illustrated in *Figure 11.2*. It is a SN74S374 octal D-type edge-triggered flip-flop that can be used easily as a simple input or output port with built-in three-state outputs.

Figure 11.3 is an example of the SN74S374 used as an output port. Only one bit is shown along with the control gates. The output control (pin 1) is connected to the address bus with a two-input NAND gate G_1. Address lines A_0 and A_1 are connected to the NAND gate, thereby identifying the port address as being any address combination including A_0 and A_1 with both high. The clock (pin 11) is connected to a two-input AND gate G_2 with inverters on the inputs. The address of the port is selected first, and when the output instruction is executed, the latch is clocked to latch the data on the data bus into the flip-flops. Let's assume that we want to output an ASCII "A" (41H) to the port. The D_0 line of the data bus will be a 1.

The sequence begins when the MPU sends an address (e.g., 03H) to the address bus to cause address lines A_0 and A_1 to both go high. G_1 will output a low to gate G_3, which outputs a high to enable the three-state outputs of all bits (pin 2 of bit line D_0).

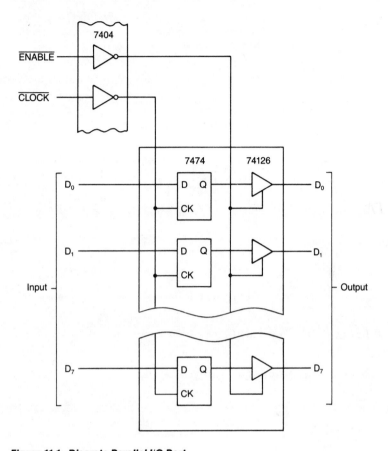

Figure 11.1   Discrete Parallel I/O Port

Next, the MPU will place the contents of the accumulator (41H) onto the data bus. As a result, the data is ready at the input and the outputs are enabled when the MPU activates the $\overline{\text{IOREQ}}$ and the $\overline{\text{WR}}$ signal. Both $\overline{\text{IOREQ}}$ and $\overline{\text{WR}}$ are active low. Placing two lows on the input of G_2 will output a high. As a result, G_4 will output a low, clocking the data from the data bus (pin 3 for D_0) into the latches and through the enabled three-state output (pin 2 for D_0) to the data output. Keep in mind that *Figure 11.3* is simply a partial diagram of *Figure 11.2*, and the data (41H) is placed on data lines D_0 through D_7.

A Serial Port from Individual ICs

A simple serial port can be constructed using S-R flip-flops, AND gates, NOR gates, and inverters. IC manufacturers, including Texas Instruments, offer the circuit illustrated in *Figure 11.4* in a single 14-pin package. The SN74S95B is a 4-bit parallel-access shift register that can be used either as a serial transmitter (parallel in, serial out) or a serial receiver (serial in, parallel out).

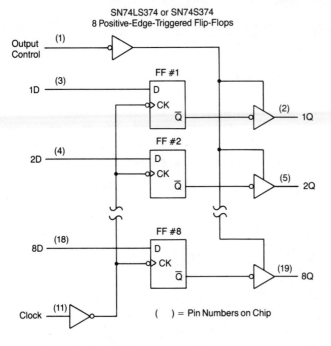

The eight flip-flops of the SN74LS374 and SN74S374 are edge-triggered D-type flip-flops. On the positive transition of the clock, the Q outputs will be set to the logic states that were setup at the D inputs.

Schmitt-trigger buffered inputs at the enable/clock lines simplify system design as ac and dc noise rejection is improved by typically 400 millivolts due to the input hysteresis. A buffered output control input can be used to place the eight outputs in either a normal logic state (high or low logic levels) or a high-impedance state. In the high-impedance state the outputs neither load nor drive the bus lines significantly.

The output control does not affect the internal operation of the latches of flip-flops. That is, the old data can be retained or new data can be entered even while the outputs are off.

Figure 11.2 Octal D-Type Edge-Triggered Flip-Flops

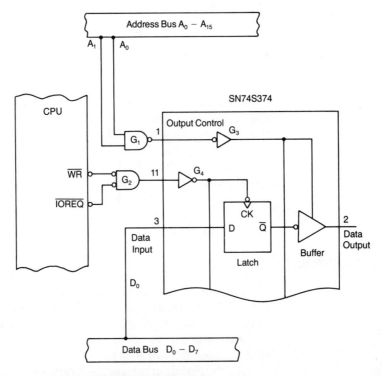

Figure 11.3 SN74S374 Chip Used as an I/O Mapped Paralled Port

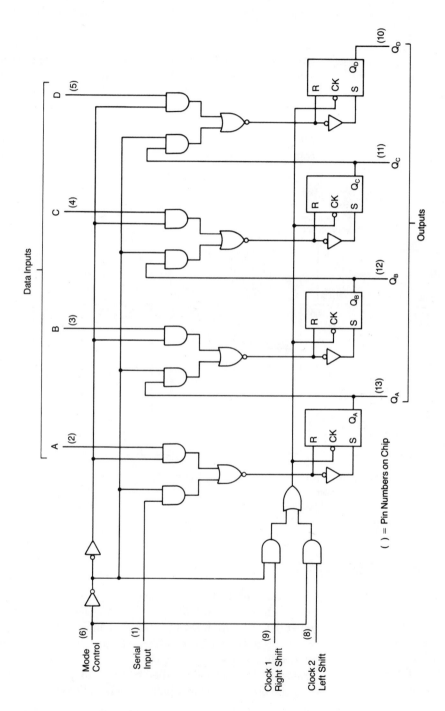

Figure 11.4 SN74S95B 4-Bit Parallel Access Shift Register

Figure 11.5 shows one possible way to use the SN74S95 shift register for serial data communication. Parallel data from a computer is input to the transmitter. The parallel data is converted to serial data by the SN74S95 shift register and transmitted to a distant receiver one bit following another in sequence along the line. At the receiver, the serial data is converted back to parallel data by the SN74S95 and coupled to the receiving computer. Serial data transmission is preferred for long distances because fewer wires are required. Ordinary telephone lines are used regularly for long distance serial communications.

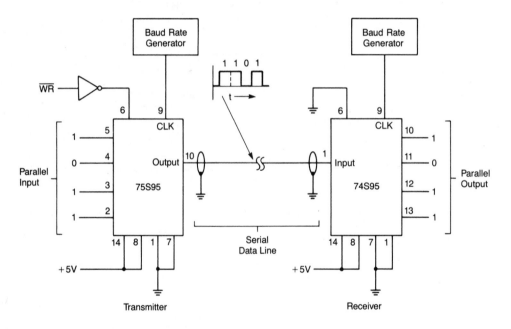

Figure 11.5   Discrete Serial Port

I/O MAPPING vs. MEMORY-MAPPED I/O

Whenever information is brought into a computer system by an input unit or output from the system by the output unit, the I/O must use the data bus to transfer the information to/from registers in the CPU or to/from memory locations. Two methods are available to control the I/O in order to accomplish the transfer. One method is called memory-mapped I/O; the other method is called I/O mapped control. Let's look at memory-mapped I/O first.

Memory-Mapped I/O

In memory-mapped control of I/O, the I/O is considered just like any other memory location, and I/O is addressed just as if memory were being addressed. In fact, the memory addresses used to locate I/O are reserved for I/O and are not to be used for the normal memory function.

One of the simplest ways of implementing memory-mapped control is shown in *Figure 11.6a*. The I/O port requires that both chip select signals CS_1 and CS_2 be high in order to activate the I/O. The $R/\overline{W}$ control line is high to read data to the CPU and active low to write data from the CPU. The I/O will be selected when any memory address is presented on the address bus that has A_{15} high. This means that all addresses from 8000H to FFFFH will activate the I/O unit. As a result, these memory locations (from 32,768 to 65,535) cannot be used for memory, only for I/O. If there is no need for a 64K memory, then using 32K locations for I/O is no problem; however, if memory locations are at a premium, then more address decoding or I/O mapped control is required.

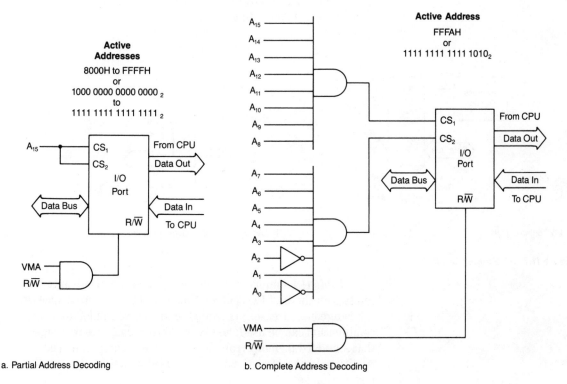

a. Partial Address Decoding

b. Complete Address Decoding

Figure 11.6 Memory Mapped I/O

More address decoding can be added to the I/O unit to restrict the amount of memory allocated for I/O. In *Figure 11.6b*, a complete decode of all 16 bits of a 64K memory address bus is shown. Only one address, FFFAH, will enable the I/O unit in this application. For the use of the additional memory, additional decode circuitry had to be added to the I/O unit.

I/O-Mapped Control

For I/O mapped control, essentially the I/O is given priority to use the data bus over memory. As shown in *Figure 11.7a*, an I/O request control signal is brought into the I/O unit. This is a control signal from the CPU that says that the I/O unit is activated and any addresses on the memory address bus can be used to select the I/O unit or port or even the particular I/O bit, if that is desirable.

As shown in *Figure 11.7b*, there is a corresponding memory request signal ($\overline{\text{MEMREQ}}$) that is sent to memory to keep the memory inactive during the time the I/O request signal ($\overline{\text{IOREQ}}$) is active. This figure also shows a control logic circuit that generates the four signals for the four modes: memory read, memory write, I/O read, I/O write. Some microprocessors do not generate the I/O request control. In that case, the I/O request signal must be generated with further logic circuitry.

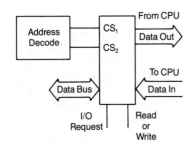

a. I/O Control Signals

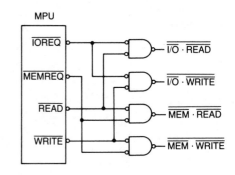

b. Generating I/O and Memory Control Signals

Figure 11.7   I/O Mapped Control

Table 11.1 summarizes the advantages and disadvantages of the two methods of I/O control. Since in I/O mapping control the full-range of addresses are available to control the I/O unit, any combination can be used; however, there usually are restrictions that standard memory transfer instructions cannot be used. Additional I/O instructions must be used which add to the instruction set.

Table 11.1 Memory Mapping vs I/O Mapping

Type of Mapping	Advantages	Disadvantages
Memory Mapping	1. Standard memory transfer instructions can be used. 2. Full instruction set available to manipulate data in I/O. 3. High speed parallel data transfer in most cases.	1. Takes up memory locations. 2. Requires three fetch instructions requiring longer execution time. 3. More address decoding required. 4. For maximum flexibility and productivity, the full address code must be decoded. 5. Data transfer usually in 8 or 16 bits. Wasteful of hardware, if only one bit is required.
I/O Mapping	1. Full decode of address code not necessary. Any combination can be used. 2. Individual bit control and transfer if desired. 3. I/O in and out instructions are easily distinguished as an I/O operation. 4. Usually less decoding hardware is required, because of shorter addressing. 5. Some instructions can be more direct and shorter.	1. Lose the power and flexibility of memory transfer instructions. 2. Lose the efficiency of the full instruction set for transferring data. 3. Additional control pins are required on an already crowded MPU package. 4. Information transfer can be much slower because of special circuitry and special instructions.

PARALLEL PERIPHERAL DEVICES

A unit especially designed to interface between a peripheral unit and a microprocessor of a microcomputer system is a parallel peripheral device, commonly called a PPD. As shown in *Figure 11.8,* the PPD interfaces between the microcomputer system data bus and peripheral devices either through one port or through multiple ports. The ports may handle 8 bits, 16 bits or individual bits; and they may be unidirectional or bidirectional. The PPD can have an input register, an output register, a control register, and/or a status register. The input and output registers are used to latch in data that is received from or transmitted to the peripheral. The control register is used to control or route the data through the PPD. Many times it is called a data direction register. A status register, if it is available, indicates whether certain conditions within the PPD are true or not. A common use is to detect interrupt inputs from a peripheral that wants to be serviced by the microcomputer system. All registers are multiple-bit registers, usually 8 or 16 bits wide for microcomputer systems.

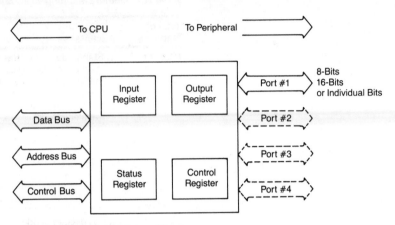

Figure 11.8 Parallel Peripheral Device

Programmable PPD

If a PPD is not hardwired, but can be altered in its function using software commands, it is called a programmable PPD. The control register is the main register changed to provide the programmable feature. To demonstrate the programmability, let's look at *Figure 11.9*.

Figure 11.9 shows a 3-bit portion of a PPD's 8-bit output register and 8-bit data direction register (control register) and the logic gates used for control. The data path of the output register is bidirectional and controlled by the condition of the three-state buffers, T_1 and T_2. If T_1 is enabled, the port is an input port and data flow is from peripheral to the microcomputer. If T_2 is enabled, the port is an output port, and data flow is from the microcomputer system to the peripheral. T_1 and T_2 are never enabled at the same time; however, they can be disabled at the same time, in which case their outputs are in a high impedance state.

To enable T_1 to provide an input port, the output of the AND gate, G_4, must be high; therefore, both of its inputs must be high. One input is from the control gate, G_3, and the other the output of the data direction register. The output of the data direction register, Q_0, Q_1, Q_2, ... Q_7, can be set by a software command, by applying a control word of 8 bits of data, via the data bus, to the D inputs of the data direction register (identified as C_0, C_1, C_2, ... C_7 on *Figure 11.9*). If C_0, C_1, C_2, ... C_7 is a 1 and this data is clocked into the register, Q_0, Q_1, Q_2, ... Q_7, would be a 1 or high. If the output of G_3 is high, then the output of G_4 will be high, T_1 will be enabled and the port will be an input port.

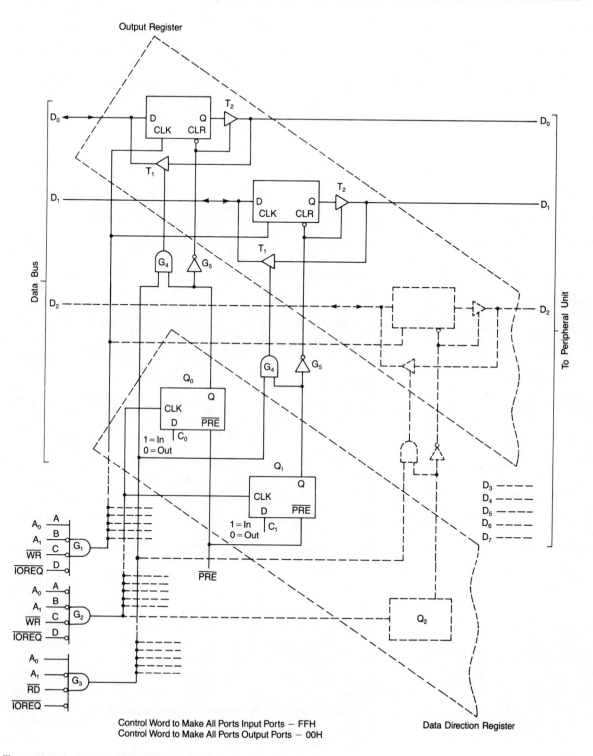

Figure 11.9   An Example PPD Chip (3 of 8 bits)

If C_0 through C_7 are set to 0 by the control word and clocked into the register, Q_0 through Q_7 will be a 0 or low. T_1 is disabled because of a low on the output of AND gate G_4, but T_2 is enabled due to the high at the output of the inverter G_5. With T_2 enabled, the port is an output port and data that is latched into the output register will be sent to the peripheral.

Thus, it should be clear that the port is programmed to be an input port or an output port by the control word that is programmed into the data direction register. Also, it should be clear that this control can be determined bit-by-bit by the state of the bits in the control word.

The timing signal to clock the control word into the data direction register is provided by gate G_2. In like fashion, the output of gate G_1 provides the timing signal to clock the data into the output register. The output of gate G_3 determines the timing of when T_1 is enabled to make the port an input port. Each output of gates G_1, G_2 and G_3 is dependent on the state of address signals A_0 and A_1 and control signals $\overline{IOREQ}$, $\overline{WR}$, and $\overline{RD}$ from the microprocessor.

Table 11.2 shows the conditions needed to provide a high output from each gate. As a result, the ports can be selected using the state of address bits A_0 and A_1, and can be selected and timed by the signals $\overline{IOREQ}$, $\overline{WR}$, and $\overline{RD}$. For example, when an 8-bit address of 01H is applied to the address bus, gates G_1 and G_3 will have their outputs active high when the microprocessor outputs the low active signals $\overline{IOREQ}$ and $\overline{WR}$ or $\overline{IOREQ}$ and $\overline{RD}$. $\overline{IOREQ}$ means that an I/O signal is requested, $\overline{WR}$ means that the data should be written, depending upon how the data direction register is programmed, to the I/O peripheral, and $\overline{RD}$ means read. Other I/O PPDs would be selected using other address bits in addition to A_0 or A_1.

Table 11.2   **Signals Required on G_1, G_2, G_3**

A_1	A_0	$\overline{IOREQ}$	$\overline{WR}$	$\overline{RD}$	OUTPUT		
					G_1	G_2	G_3
0	1	0	0	1	1		
0	0	0	0	1		1	
0	1	0	1	0			1

Selecting Data Direction

The sequence of events to input data from a peripheral using the PPD of *Figure 11.9* is as follows:

1. Choose the control word, 1111 1111 (FFH), to make all 8-bits input ports.
2. Load FFH into the microprocessor accumulator.
3. Place the address 00H on the address bus, selecting the data direction register.
4. Place the contents of the accumulator (FFH) onto the data bus.

5. When the microprocessor outputs $\overline{\text{IOREQ}}$ and $\overline{\text{WR}}$, the data bus contents (FFH) will be latched into the data direction register to set conditions that all ports are to be inputs.
6. Give the microprocessor an instruction to input data from the I/O (a fetch instruction).
7. Place address 00000001 (01H) on the address bus to select the I/O and set conditions to enable the input buffer.
8. When the microprocessor outputs $\overline{\text{IOREQ}}$ and $\overline{\text{RD}}$, the data on the input lines from the peripheral will be placed on the data bus and latched into the accumulator.

The sequence of events to output data from a microprocessor to a peripheral using the PPD of *Figure 11.9* is as follows:
1. Choose the control word, 0000 0000 (00H), to make all 8 bit output ports.
2. Load 00H into the microprocessor accumulator.
3. Place the address 00H on the address bus to select the data direction register.
4. Place the contents of the accumulator (00H) onto the data bus.
5. Conditions are set for all ports to be outputs when microprocessor control signals $\overline{\text{IOREQ}}$ and $\overline{\text{WR}}$ are sent to gate G_2, which latches 00H into the data direction register.
6. Load the accumulator with data that is to be sent to the I/O peripheral (e.g., AAH).
7. Place the address of the output register 0000 0001 (01H) on the address bus.
8. Place accumulator data (AAH) on the data bus.
9. When the microprocessor is given an output instruction to output data, it sends out the control signals $\overline{\text{IOREQ}}$ and $\overline{\text{WR}}$. The data will be latched in the output register and sent out on the data lines to the peripheral.

PERIPHERAL INTERFACE ADAPTER

Another type of I/O interface integrated circuit is the peripheral interface adapter (PIA) shown in *Figure 11.10*. It is manufactured by Motorola as the MC6821. It has two 8-bit parallel interfaces, Port A and Port B. Each port has two control registers and an output register, all of which are addressable. There is a seventh bus input register which is not addressable. As with the PPD, the data direction register can be programmed to determine which of the port lines will be inputs and which will be outputs. The control register is just what the name implies. It controls the data port. The output register latches data before it is coupled to the peripheral I/O unit. There are two interrupt channels per A and B section that interrupt the microprocessor using the signals $\overline{\text{IRQA}}$ and $\overline{\text{IRQB}}$.

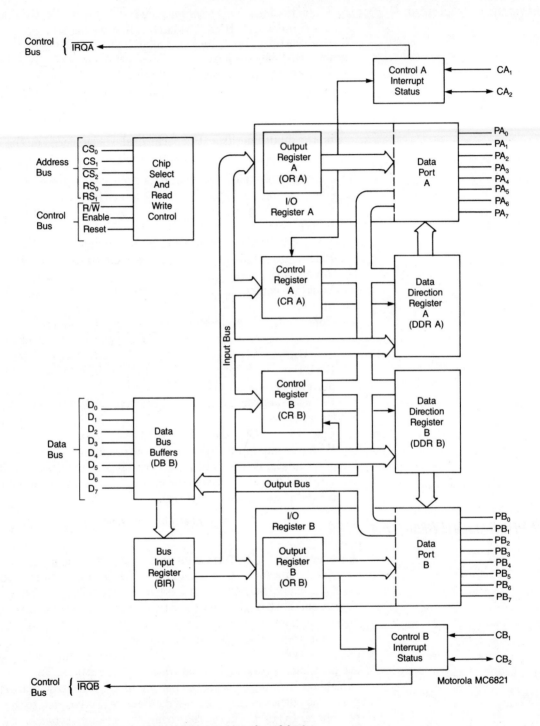

Figure 11.10   Block Diagram of a Typical Peripheral Interface Adapter
(Source: Courtesy of Motorola, Inc.)

Addressing the Various Registers

The addressing of the various registers occurs by using the five signals identified as address bus signals in *Figure 11.10*. CS_0, CS_1, and $\overline{CS_2}$ are chip select signals that are ANDed together inside the MC6821; therefore, CS_0 and CS_1 must be active high and $\overline{CS_2}$ active low before the PIA is selected. This is a means of addressing various PIAs that may be available for the microcomputer system. RS_0 and RS_1 are the main signals for addressing the registers inside the PIA. Because there are six registers to address, another bit must be used to provide the full address coding. Bit 2 of the control register (either CR A or CR B) is used for this purpose.

Control Word Format
Figure 11.11 shows the control word format that is loaded into the control register of each section to control the interrupt channels CA_1, CA_2, CB_1 and CB_2 and bit 2 which completes the address code for the register selection inside the PIA. Setting the state of bits 0, 1, 3, 4, 5, 6 and 7 provides various modes of interrupt control.

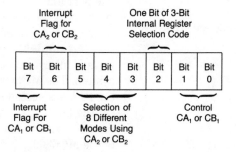

Figure 11.11 *Control Register Format (Common Notation for Either A or B)*

Register Addressing
Figure 11.12 shows how bit 2 of the control word from control register A or B is used in conjunction with RS_0 and RS_1 to form the 3-bit code to address the various PIA registers. Access to the control register for Port A (CR A) is obtained by setting RS_0 to a 1 and RS_1 to a 0. Access to control register for Port B (CR B) is obtained by setting RS_0 to 1 and RS_1 to 1. Bit 2 of CR A or CR B makes no difference in either case. The control word can be loaded into the control register when access is obtained.

With RS_0 at 0 and RS_1 at 0 and control register A bit 2 at 1, the output register for Port A (OR A) is selected to transfer the data to Port A. If control register A bit 2 had been a 0, the data direction register A (DDR A) would have been selected.

RS₁	RS₀	CR A Bit 2	CR B Bit 2	Register Selected
0	0	1		I/O Register A (Port A)
0	0	0		Data Direction Register A
0	1	X		Control Register A
1	0		1	I/O Register B (Port B)
1	0		0	Data Direction Register B
1	1		X	Control Register B

X = Don't Care

Figure 11.12   Register Addressing

P₇	P₆	P₅	P₄	P₃	P₂	P₁	P₀
1	1	0	1	1	1	0	1

1 = Output Data Line
0 = Input Data Line

Figure 11.13   Data Direction Register Format

The output register of Port B (OR B) is selected if the control register bit 2 of CR B is a 1 and RS_0 is a 0 and RS_1 is a 1. When bit 2 of CR B is a 0 under the same states for RS_0 and RS_1, the DDR B is selected.

Data Direction Register Contents

When Port A or Port B is selected, the individual port lines are programmed by the state of the bits in the DDR. The format of the DDR register is shown in *Figure 11.13*. A bit in the 1 state sets the port line as an output data line; a bit in the 0 state sets the port line as an input data line. *Figure 11.13* sets P_1 and P_5 as input lines and the rest of the lines as output lines.

Example 11-1: *Figure 11.14* illustrates one of many possible ways of interfacing the MC6821 to a MC6800 microcomptuer system. The MC6800 does not provide an I/O request signal, so the PIA is selected by memory-mapped addresses. We wish to set the DDR A so that only Port A bits P_1 and P_5 are input data lines and also to read the inputs from Port A into the accumulator of the MC6800.

There are several additional control signals that need to be clarified in *Figure 11.14*. These are:

1. R/$\overline{\text{W}}$ is a signal supplied by the microprocessor to control if data is to be read or written to the PIA. Data is written to the PIA by the MPU when the signal is active low, and is read from the PIA to the MPU when the signal is active high.
2. E is a phase 2 (φ2) timing signal that determines the time of all PIA operations.
3. $\overline{\text{RESET}}$ is a system signal to set the system to initial conditions.
4. $\overline{\text{IRQA}}$ and $\overline{\text{IRQB}}$ come from peripheral I/O to interrupt the MPU.
5. VMA (valid memory address) is a signal to indicate that a valid address is on the address bus. Data should not be written to or read from a PIA unless the address is valid.

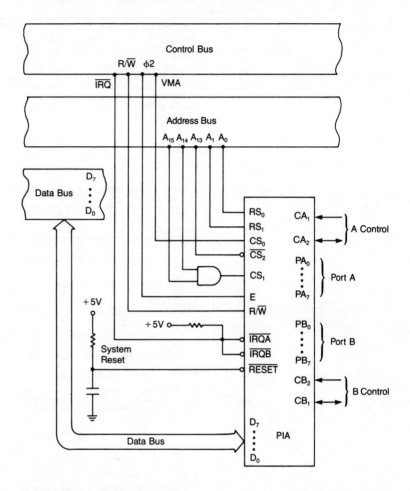

Figure 11.14   Interfacing the Peripheral Interface Adapter to the System Bus

Recall that CS_0, CS_1, and $\overline{CS_2}$ must all be activated at the same time to select the particular PIA.

The first step in the problem solution is to determine the addresses required for the program instructions. *Table 11.3* shows the memory-mapped address range that selects the PIA. *Table 11.4* shows the specific port addresses and control register bit conditions that are required to address the specific PIA registers.

Table 11.3   Address Code Range

Address Lines	15 14 13 12	11 10 9 8	7 6 5 4	3 2 1 0	Hex
Decoded Address Lines	1 1 0 X	X X X X	X X X X	X X X X	CXXX
Minimum Address	1 1 0 0	0 0 0 0	0 0 0 0	0 0 0 0	C000
Maximum Address	1 1 0 1	1 1 1 1	1 1 1 1	1 1 1 1	DFFF

X = Don't care

Table 11.4   PIA Addressing

Address	CR A Bit 2	CR B Bit 2	Selection
C000H	1		Port A
C000H	0		DDR A
C001H	X		CR A
C002H		1	Port B
C002H		0	DDR B
C003H		X	CR B

With the addresses in *Table 11.4*, the subprogram using MC6800 instructions to set PA$_1$ and PA$_5$ as input lines and read data to the accumulator is as follows:

Instruction		Comment
LDAA	#$DD	Set control word of P$_1$ and P$_5$ as inputs
STAA	$C000	Store control word in DDR A
LDAA	#$00	Set control word for 0 in bit 2
STAA	$C001	Store control word in CR A
LDAA	#$04	Set control word for 1 in bit 2
STAA	$C001	Store control word in CR A
LDAA	$C000	Input bits 1 and 5 data through Port A to Acc

Notes:
LDAA   #$XX   = Load Accumulator A with Hex Number XX
STAA $XXXX   = Store Accumulator A in Hex Address XXXX

The Rockwell 6520 PIA is pin-compatible with the 6820 and the 6821 PIA by Motorola. The 6520 was designed to work with the R6500 family of microprocessors. The PIA is a cost effective way of implementing I/O interfaces in very complex systems.

PROGRAMMABLE PERIPHERAL INTERFACE (PPI)

The Intel 8255 is a general purpose programmable input/output device designed to be used with the Intel microprocessor family. As shown in *Figure 11.15*, it has three 8-bit I/O ports (Ports A, B, C) which can be divided into two groups of 12 bits each (Groups A and B). It also has three modes of operation (modes 0, 1, 2).

The 8255 is a parallel interface similar to the 6821 PIA. The 8255 has four addressable registers. They are Port A, Port B, Port C and a control register. The MPU can write to all four registers, but can read from only the three port registers. It has a data bus buffer that is a three-state 8-bit bidirectional buffer used to connect the 8255 PPI to the system data bus. Control words, data, and status information can be passed to and from the PPI over the system data bus by use of In and Out MPU instructions.

The read/write control logic block is used to select the PPI through the $\overline{\text{CS}}$ signal which must be active low, determine if the PPI is to be read from or written to with an active low on either $\overline{\text{WR}}$ or $\overline{\text{RD}}$, address the internal registers using A_0, A_1 and $\overline{\text{CS}}$, and reset the system initially with RESET. A high on RESET clears the control register and sets all ports as inputs.

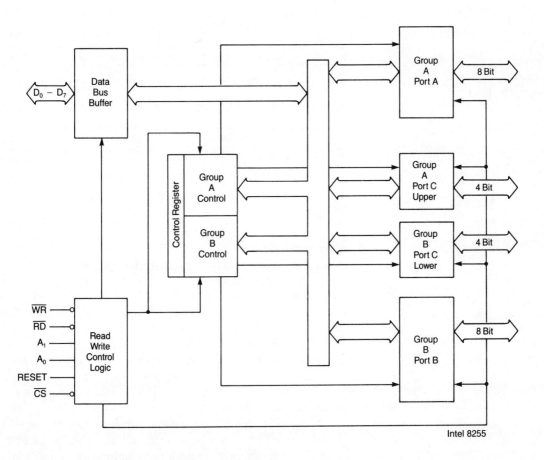

Figure 11.15   Block Diagram Showing Architecture of a Typical PPI

Control Register

The control register is an addressable register which, depending upon the bit selection, will dictate the operation of the 8255 PPI. *Table 11.5* lists the operations of the PPI that are controlled by the bits of the control word. Bits D_6 and D_5 control the mode of operation for Group A (Port A and upper four bits of Port C), and bit D_2 controls the mode of operation for Group B (Port B and the lower four bits of Port C). The state of bits D_4, D_3, D_1 and D_0 determine whether Port A, upper Port C, Port B, and lower Port C will be inputs or outputs. D_7 determines if the mode selection is active. A control word of 10011011 would have the PPI in mode 0 with all ports as inputs.

Table 11.5   Control Bit Format for 8255 PPI

Control Bit	Operation		
D_7	Mode Set Flag	1 = Active 0 = Inactive	
D_6 D_5	Mode Selection	D_6 D_5 0 0 = Mode 0 0 1 = Mode 1 1 X = Mode 2	G R O U P
D_4	Port A	1 = Input 0 = Output	A
D_3	Port C (upper)	1 = Input 0 = Output	
D_2	Mode Selection	0 = Mode 0 1 = Mode 1	G R
D_1	Port B	1 = Input 0 = Output	O U P
D_0	Port C (lower)	1 = Input 0 = Output	B

X = don't care

Operating Modes

Mode 0 is a basic input/output operation requiring no signals to assure proper connection to the I/O, commonly called handshaking signals. Unlike the 6821 PIA, the 8255 PPI cannot select the data direction of each bit separately. Each port of the 8255 PPI must be programmed as an output port or an input port. Because Port C is divided into two 4-bit ports, the upper and lower four bits can be programmed separately. In essence, the 8255 really has four I/O ports, two 8-bit ports and two 4-bit ports. In mode 0, the output data is latched into registers, but the inputs are not latched.

Mode 1 is used when handshaking signals are required. It uses Groups A and B for input or output and uses the four bits of Port C in each group for handshaking signals. Both the input data and output data are latched into registers in mode 1.

Mode 2 can be used in Group A only. This mode allows bidirectional I/O bus operation (Port A) with Port C used for handshaking signals. Interrupt generation with enable and disable is also available with this mode.

Addressing Registers Within 8255

Figure 11.16a shows how A_0, A_1 and $\overline{CS}$ are combined to provide the address code to select the various registers within the 8255. $\overline{CS}$ must be low to address Port A, B, C, and the control register.

Example 11-2: To illustrate a practical use of the Intel 8255 PPI with an 8085 MPU, let's interface a printer to the microcomputer system. *Figure 11.17* shows the system. Since the 8085 MPU provides an $IO/\overline{M}$ (I/O or Memory) select line, the PPI will be I/O mapped. When $IO/\overline{M}$ is low, the addresses are for memory; when $IO/\overline{M}$ is high the MPU is addressing I/O. Note that $IO/\overline{M}$ is NANDed with address bit A_2 to produce $\overline{CS}$, the chip select signal. As a result, the addressing for the system is as shown in *Figure 11.16b* and given in Hex in *Figure 11.17*.

A_1	A_0	$\overline{CS}$	Register Selected
0	0	0	Port A
0	1	0	Port B
1	0	0	Port C
1	1	0	Control
0	0	1	Data Bus (Three-State)

a. Register Addressing for 8255

A_7	A_6	A_5	A_4	A_3	A_2	A_1	A_0	Register Selected
X	X	X	X	X	1	0	0	Port A
X	X	X	X	X	1	0	1	Port B
X	X	X	X	X	1	1	0	Port C
X	X	X	X	X	1	1	1	Control
X	X	X	X	X	1	X	X	PPI Enabled

Note: Requires $IO/\overline{M}$ to be at high logic level.
X means don't care.

b. Addresses for System of *Figure 11.17*

Figure 11.16   Register Addressing for Intel 8255

Let's demonstrate how to:
1. Select the ports needed to connect the printer to the 8255.
2. Set up the ports for output and handshaking control.
3. Write a simple status driven print routine.

First we will want to connect the eight data lines from the printer to one of the two 8-bit ports. We will use Port A in this example. Next, we will choose our control (handshaking) data lines. Looking at *Figure 11.17*, we can see that the printer outputs two control signals, BUSY (Busy) and $\overline{ACK}$ (Acknowledge), and requires a data strobe ($\overline{STROBE}$) to strobe the data into the printer buffer. This means we need two input port lines and one output port line. Because Port C can be split and programmed so that half is output and half is input, we will use the upper four bits for the input control and the lower four bits for the output port. Port B will not be used in this example.

With the port assignments defined, the control word can be set to program the ports so that Port A is an output port, upper Port C is an input, and lower Port C is an output. Examining *Table 11.5* the control word is 10001010 or 8AH. D_4 is a 0 to make

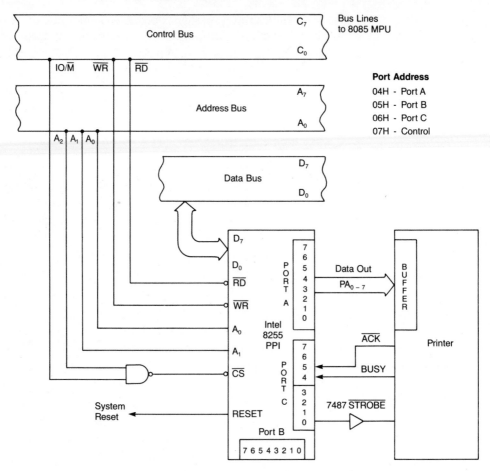

Figure 11.17   Interfacing a Printer to Intel 8085 MPU Using Intel 8255 PPI

Port A an output, D_3 is a 1 to make upper Port C an input, D_0 is a 0 to make lower Port C an output, D_6, D_5 and D_2 are 0 to select mode 0, D_7 is a 1 to activate the mode, and even though Port B is not used it is made an input by setting D_1 to a 1.

The program for the MPU to implement the above takes the following two instructions:

```
MVI    A,8AH      ; load control word 8AH into accumulator
OUT    07H        ; output control word to control register.
```

The move immediate instruction (MVI) loads the accumulator with the control word and the Out instruction addresses the control register of the PPI and transfers the control word to the control register to set up the ports.

Figure 11.18 is a flow chart for a status driven print subroutine. This subroutine prints the contents of the accumulator. Each time an ASCII code in the accumulator is to be printed, the subroutine PRINT is called. The assembly language program implementing the flow chart follows.

In this program the following are equal:

CPORT	EQU	06H
APORT	EQU	04H
STROB	EQU	00H
CONTROL	EQU	07H

Label	Instruction		Comment
PRINT:	PUSH	PSW	; Save ASCII data
	MVI	0FH	; Set Strobe line high
	OUT	CPORT	; Output Strobe line high
CKBSY:	IN	CPORT	; Looking for Busy
	ANI	10H	; Set mask to input Port C bit 4 only
	CMP	10H	; Check for Busy low
	JZ	CKBSY	; If Busy is high, continue to check for low
	POP	PSW	; Retrieve data to output
	OUT	APORT	; Outputs data to data lines Port A
	MVI	A, STROB	; Set up for Strobe (00H)
	OUT	CPORT	; Output Strobe
CKACK:	IN	CPORT	; Looking for $\overline{ACK}$
	ANI	20H	; Set mask to input Port C bit 5 only
	CMP	20H	; Check for $\overline{ACK}$
	JZ	CKACK	; If $\overline{ACK}$ is high, continue to check for low
	RET		; Return

The program will save the ASCII data found in the accumulator by pushing it to a temporary storage part of memory called the stack. This is done because the accumulator will be needed in the subroutine. The program then checks to see if BUSY (bit 4 of upper Port C) is high, indicating a full printer buffer. If the buffer is full, the software routine will continue to check until BUSY is low. When BUSY goes low, the program continues and fetches the ASCII character code to be printed by popping it off the stack, and outputting the ASCII data through Port A onto the data bus. While the data to be printed is on the data bus, the program will output a strobe, which will clock the data into the printer buffer.

After the strobe, the software looks for an acknowledgement ($\overline{ACK}$) from the printer that the data was received. Once the acknowledge signal goes low, the subroutine will return to the main program for the next character to be printed. The detail of each step is left to the reader.

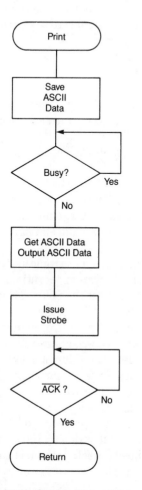

Figure 11.18   Sample Status Driven Software Flow Chart

INPUT/OUTPUT CONTROL METHODS

There are three basic input/output control methods:
1. Polling or program control
2. Interrupt control
3. Direct memory address control
and two basic serial I/O control methods:
1. Software
2. Hardware

Polling

Polling, sometimes referred to as program control, depends totally upon executing a program to control when data is read from or written to I/O. The basic concept is similar to a program which samples data. Each I/O unit is assigned a position in a sequence. The MPU under program control in a set time sequence scans the I/O ports looking for a flag bit that may be set on particular handshaking signal lines. If the flag bit is set, the MPU stops and services the I/O unit. If the flag bit is set, the MPU goes on and looks at (polls) the next I/O port in sequence. The same polling sequence is always followed. If the MPU stops and services an I/O, after it is finished it polls the next I/O port in the sequence.

As is apparent, polling is a very inefficient use of the microcomputer system, because it can do computation only during the non-polling intervals. If there are a large number of I/O ports, the MPU could spend its full time polling and have little or no time left for computation.

Example 11-3: Modern automobiles with electronic systems may incorporate a polling program in their system operation. Some may even have a dedicated MPU for just the polling. Such systems check the vital operating characteristics of the automobile system. Engine temperature, oil pressure, fluid levels (such as fuel, brake, power steering, and water), alternator output and battery voltage, and the safety condition of doors, lights, and brakes are all checked. If any of these characteristics exceed set limits, a warning flag bit is set. The MPU detects it and initiates a service routine, which may be a light, audio warning, or it may be a specific action such as providing oil or water from a reserve tank. It is some output action by the system to alert the user that something has been detected which is not normal.

Interrupt Control

I/O control using interrupts is a much faster method of servicing a peripheral than the polling technique. The disadvantages of polling control are the advantages of interrupt control. Interrupts are much faster and require little of the MPU's time searching for flags. The interrupt control method allows the MPU to perform other tasks without concerning itself with an I/O peripheral unless the system needs it.

There are two basic interrupt types, the non-maskable interrupt (NMI) and the maskable interrupt (INT). The term non-maskable means that the interrupt cannot be disabled, whereas the maskable interrupt can be disabled or given a priority over other interrupt signals. The non-maskable interrupt is reserved for the highest priority interrupt condition which, in most systems, is a signal which tells the system that power has failed. As an example of how such an interrupt works, suppose a power failure is detected, but several milliseconds remain before the voltage falls to a level which will result in loss of data in the RAM and MPU registers. This is plenty of time to receive the interrupt, place the vital register information in memory, and switch to battery backup. Other interrupts work in a similar way, but they can be program-controlled by incorporating a mask in the program which allows them to be recognized or not by the system. Or, the software can prioritize the interrupts so that the receipt of a particular interrupt will be serviced before another if both are received at the same time.

There are three basic ways to service an interrupt request. They are:

1. Hardware only.
2. Software only.
3. A combination of the two.

The hardware method (1) is the fastest. This method requires the peripheral's interrupt controller to provide the interrupt request and an address, called a vector address, where the service routine is found.

The software method (2) is a polling routine. After an interrupt request is received, the polling routine polls all I/O signal lines that can provide an interrupt looking for a flag indicating which I/O unit requested the interrupt. The polling routine will poll the highest priority device first, the next highest next, and so on. Once the requesting device is found, the routine will jump to a service routine, make the correction, then return to poll the remaining devices.

The combination method (3) is a hardware polling technique called daisy chaining. *Figure 11.19* shows how a daisy chain works. When a MPU receives any interrupt, it must stop what it is doing in its main program and save vital data such as the program counter contents (address of next instruction) and the content of vital registers so it can return to the main program where it left off after the interrupt is serviced. When completed, it issues an interrupt acknowledge to the first port of the daisy chain. If it is not the interrupting port, it will propagate the acknowledge signal to the next port in the chain. The propagation will continue until the interrupting port is detected. Once the proper port and I/O is detected, the I/O will place its identification number on the data bus and the MPU will jump to the proper service routine.

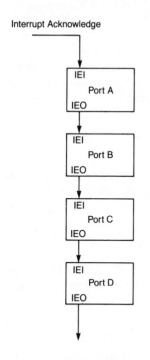

Figure 11.19 Daisy Chain Interrupt Servicing

Direct Memory Address Control

Although the interrupt request is a fast and efficient method of detecting a request for service, it relies on software to transfer data. In some cases, the software transfer of data may be too slow. For example, the transfer of data from a disk to memory or vice versa should be achieved as rapidly as possible.

The Direct Memory Address Control (DMAC) is a dedicated processor of data used for fast and efficient transfer of blocks of data. The DMAC will require the use of the data bus and address bus. This is achieved by a variety of methods, such as stopping the MPU, stealing memory cycles, or MPU suspension. The suspension of the MPU is a common bus access method.

If the DMAC is to be used by an I/O unit, the I/O unit would send its interrupt request to the DMAC, and the DMAC would request the use of the address and data buses by sending the MPU a hold signal. As a result, the MPU would complete its current instruction and place its bus drivers in a high impedance state to release the buses. Once the MPU releases control of the buses, it provides a hold acknowledge to the DMAC indicating that the DMAC now has control of the buses. The DMAC places an address on the address bus and proceeds to transfer data. Usually a DMAC has an 8-bit counter which is used for 1 to 256-word transfers. Once the counter is decremented to zero, the block transfer is completed. The tradeoff for speed and efficiency of a DMAC is its complexity and high cost.

Serial I/O

Software Generated I/O

The transfer of data serially to an I/O by the software-generated method is an inexpensive method using the accumulator to shift the parallel data out serially one bit at a time. The data is output at a predetermined clock rate called the baud rate. A baud rate of 110 is the rate used by the teletypewriter (TTY). Ten characters per second with eleven bits per character equals a baud rate of 110. The 11 bits per character illustrated by *Figure 11.20* are the start bit, seven character bits, one parity bit, and two stop bits.

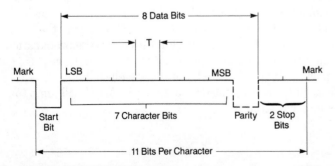

Transmission Rate: 10 Characters per Second
Bits Per Character: 11
Baud Rate: $10 \times 11 = 110$ Baud
Time Period per Baud $= \dfrac{1}{110} = 9.09$ Milliseconds

Figure 11.20 Serial TTY Bit Pattern

The time period (t) per baud is 9.09 milliseconds. As shown in the figure, each bit that is transmitted will be on the serial transmission line for 9.09 milliseconds when the baud rate is 110. The transfer program will set the bit into the accumulator, shift it to the output and hold it for 9.09 milliseconds. *Figure 11.21* is a flow chart for transferring data serially at 110 baud using an 8080 MPU.

The assembly language program that follows couples the 8-bit accumulator data out to the data bus, but the only active bit is D_0 for the serial transmission. D_0 is coupled through an Intel 8255 to the I/O unit on PA_0. The number of times through the time delay loop (1210) is based upon 7.5 microseconds to complete one loop when the clock is 2MHz. The carry bit register is used to generate the start and stop bits. First, the carry is set to 0 for the start bit and then is set to 1 for the stop bits.

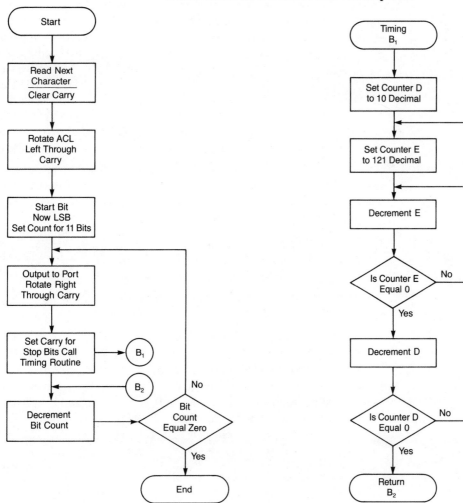

a. Main Program

b. Time Delay Subroutine

Figure 11.21   Flow Chart for 110 Baud Serial Transfer of Data

This program will send ASCII characters to data line D_0:

Label	Instruction		Comments
BDOS	EQU	5H	
CONIN	EQU	1H	
	ORG	6000H	;Starting point
	MVI	A,80H	;Data control word to Acc
	OUT	3H	;Set 8255 Port PA$_0$
NEXTC:	MVI	C,CONIN	;Read next character
	CALL	BDOS	;Place character to Acc
	STC		;Set Carry to 1
	CMC		;Change Carry to 0 for start bit
	RAL		;Rotate start bit to LSB
	MVI	B,11	;Count off 11 bits
BITOUT:	OUT	00H	;Output data to port
	RAR		;Rotate next bit for output
	STC		;Set Carry for stop bit of 1
	CALL	TIMING	;Time delay subroutine
	DCR	B	;Reduce B by one
	JNZ	BITOUT	;Countdown 11-0
	END		
; ***	TIMING ***		
;			
;			
TIMING:	MVI	D,10	;Count of 10
TIME1:	MVI	E,121	
TIME2:	DCR	E	
	JNZ	TIME2	;Countdown 121 - 0
	DCR	D	
	JNZ	TIME1	;Countdown 10 - 0
	RET		;Return from sub.

The first step sets the PA port of an 8255 to output data. The next steps load the accumulator with the desired character to be output and set the carry bit to a 0. Rotate the carry bit (start bit) clockwise into the LSB for output. Set counter for eleven bits, then output the start bit and rotate the accumulator to next output bit. The next stop is to set carry to a 1 for the stop bits, and call the time delay subroutine for a 9.09 millisecond delay. After the delay routine, the bit counter is decremented and if not zero, the program will output the next bit. The program continues until all 11 bits are transferred.

Hardware Generated I/O
Hardware-generated transfer of serial input/output data is usually achieved with an LSI (large scale integrated circuit) device. An early LSI serial interface for I/O is the universal asynchronous receiver-transmitter (UART). Two UART type devices are: the Motorola MC6850 Asynchronous Communications Interface Adaptor (ACIA) and the Intel 8251 Universal Synchronous Asynchronous Receiver-Transmitter (USART).

TYPICAL COMPONENTS

ACIA

Figure 11.22 shows typical interconnections of an Asynchronous Communications Interface Adapter (ACIA) to a 6800 MPU system bus. The typical UART, as demonstrated by the ACIA, has a data bus buffer, a control section, a control and status register, a transmitter, and a receiver. The ACIA is memory mapped using address lines A_{15}, A_{14} and A_{13}, which means the ACIA occupies the address block location from C000H to DFFFH. The registers in the ACIA are addressable, and in the interconnecton of *Figure 11.22*, C000H is the address of the control/status register and C001H is the address for the transmit or receive data registers. Control signals VMA, φ2, and R/$\overline{W}$ are the same as previously discussed.

Example 11-4: Assume we want to program the ACIA port to transmit data to an I/O peripheral such as a modem or a printer at 110 baud. In order to set the ACIA into the correct operating conditions, the control register is programmed with specific control words determined by the format shown in *Figure 11.23*.

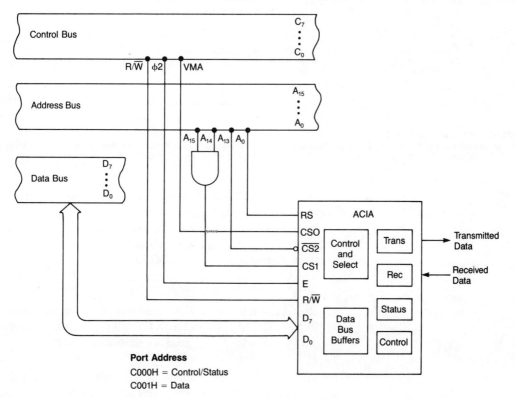

Port Address
C000H = Control/Status
C001H = Data

Figure 11.22   System Interconnection for an ACIA

Control Register

CR$_7$	CR$_6$	CR$_5$	CR$_4$	CR$_3$	CR$_2$	CR$_1$	CR$_0$

CR$_1$	CR$_0$	Function
0	0	Divide by 1
0	1	Divide by 16
1	0	Divide by 64
1	1	Master Reset

CR$_4$	CR$_3$	CR$_2$	Function
0	0	0	7 Bit — Even Parity — 2 Stop Bits
0	0	1	7 Bit — Odd Parity — 2 Stop Bits
0	1	0	7 Bit — Even Parity — 1 Stop Bit
0	1	1	7 Bit — Odd Parity — 1 Stop Bit
1	0	0	8 Bit — No Parity — 2 Stop Bits
1	0	1	8 Bit — No Parity — 1 Stop Bit
1	1	0	8 Bit — Even Parity — 1 Stop Bit
1	1	1	8 Bit — Odd Parity — 1 Stop Bit

CR$_6$	CR$_5$	Function
0	0	$\overline{RTS}$ = 0, Trans Interrupt Disabled
0	1	$\overline{RTS}$ = 0, Trans Interrupt Enabled
1	0	$\overline{RTS}$ = 1, Trans Interrupt Disabled
1	1	$\overline{RTS}$ = 0, Transmit a Break Level on the Transmit Data Out. Trans Interrupt Disabled

CR$_7$	Function
0	Disable: Receive Data Register Full, Overrun, and $\overline{DCD}$ Interrupts
1	Enable: Receive Data Register Full, Overrun, and $\overline{DCD}$ Interrupts

Figure 11.23   ACIA Control Register Format
(Source: *The Versatile Microcomputer: The Motorola Family,* by Roy W. Goody, Copyright® Science Research Associates, Inc. 1982, 1984. Reprinted by permission of the publisher. 2. Hitachi American, Ltd. Semiconductor and IC Sales and Service Division.)

When the ACIA is reset initially when power is turned on, it locks into a given state. Examining *Figure 11.23* shows that the ACIA can be reset by making CR$_0$ and CR$_1$ a 1. It is best to make this the first step in the program. The reset is accomplished with the following instructions (6800 MPU):

```
LDAA    #$03    Load Acc with 03H (XXXXXX11₂) to reset
STAA    $C000   Write Acc to port control register
```

To set the port to do what is desired, the control word 0000 0100$_2$ (04H) will be used with the following instructions:

```
LDAA    #$04    Load Acc with 04H (0000 0100₂)
STAA    $C000   Write Acc to port control register
```

The ACIA is now set to: transmit at a clock rate equal to the baud rate 110, output 7 bits plus odd parity and two stop bits, disable transmitting interrupts, and disable receive interrupts.

To receive data or to transmit data, the data register must be written to or read from. In this example, we will want to write data to the port, using the following instructions:

```
LDAA    $A720        Get data to transmit
STAA    $C001        Output data to port
```

With the instruction:

```
LDAA    $C000        Read status register
```

the status register can be read to monitor the status of the transmit data register, the receive data register, framing or parity errors, and the signals which indicate the peripheral status.

USART

The Universal Synchronous Asynchronous Receiver Transmitter (USART) is similar to the ACIA with the exception that the ACIA is asynchronous only, and the USART can operate in either the synchronous or asynchronous mode. *Figure 11.24* illustrates one possible method of interconnecting a USART (Intel 8251) to a system bus. The resulting port register addresses are given. Because the Intel system provides an I/O request line, IO/$\overline{\text{M}}$, I/O mapping is made possible, resulting in an 8-bit port address as compared to a 16-bit port address for Motorola's ACIA. The $\overline{\text{CS}}$, $\overline{\text{WR}}$ and $\overline{\text{RD}}$ signals are used as previously discussed for the PPI interface. However, C/$\overline{\text{D}}$ is a new signal. C/$\overline{\text{D}}$ is an input used to select the command register when high, and the data register when low. It is controlled by the state of the least significant address line A_0 as shown in *Figure 11.24*.

Because the USART can operate in either the synchronous or asynchronous mode, the control register word must be programmed to put the USART into the mode required. *Figure 11.25* identifies the control register format. It shows that if D_0 and D_1 are 0, then the 8251 is in the synchronous mode and in the asynchronous mode for other bit combinations.

Example 11-5: Let's program the 8251 to operate in the asynchronous mode to transmit eight bits at an x1 clock rate with no parity and two stop bits. The first control word will set the mode. All other control words to the control register will be command register instructions. If the system is reset, the USART will require a mode selection again.

The following instructions will set the USART in the asynchronous mode with an x1 clock rate, 8 bits, no parity and two stop bits (8085 MPU):

```
MVI     A, CDH       ; Control word 11001101₂ to Acc
OUT     03H          ; Mode control word to control reg
```

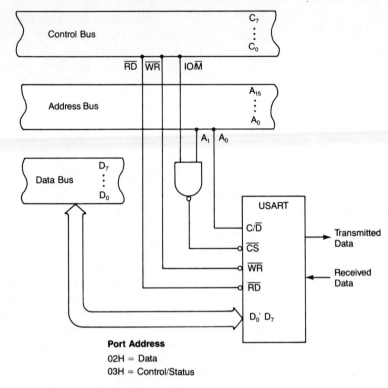

Port Address
02H = Data
03H = Control/Status

Figure 11.24 Interfacing the USART to the System Bus

D₇	D₆	D₅	D₄	D₃	D₂	D₁	D₀
S₂	S₁	EP	PEN	L₂	L₁	B₂	B₁

S₂	S₁		EP	PEN	L₂	L₁		B₁	B₂	
0	0	Invalid	0 = Odd	0 = Parity	0	0	5 Bit	0	0	Sync Mode
0	1	1 Bit	Parity	Disable	0	1	6 Bit	0	1	1X
1	0	1.5 Bits	1 = Even	1 = Parity	1	0	7 Bit	1	0	16X
1	1	2 Bits	Parity	Enable	1	1	8 Bit	1	1	64X

a. Asynchronous Mode for Intel 8251A

D₇	D₆	D₅	D₄	D₃	D₂	D₁	D₀
SCS	ESC	EP	PEN	L₂	L₁	0	0

Single Character Sync	External Sync Detect	EP	PEN	L₂	L₁	
0 = Double Sync Character	0 = Sync Detect is an Output	0 = Odd Parity	0 = Parity Disable	0	0	5 Bit
1 = Single Sync Character	1 = Sync Detect is an Input	1 = Even Parity	1 = Parity Enable	0	1	6 Bit
				1	0	7 Bit
				1	1	8 Bit

b. Synchronous Mode for Intel 8251A

Figure 11.25 Mode Instruction Formats for Typical USART

Next, we will write the command word to the control register to enable transmit and disable receive according to *Figure 11.26*.

```
MVI     A, 01H          ; Control word 00000001₂ to Acc
OUT     03H             ; Command word to control reg
```

Once the port is configured, data can be written to the port as follows:

```
MOV     A,A716          ; Get data from address A716
OUT     02H             ; Output data to data port
```

The following instructions will read the status register to monitor the status of the port.

```
IN      03H             ; Read status register
```

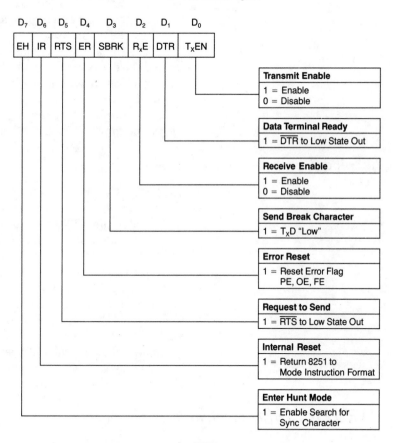

Intel 8251

Figure 11.26 Command Instruction Format for Typical USART
(Reprinted by permission of Intel Corporation)

STANDARDS AND PROTOCOLS

Standards in the young microcomputer industry are not widespread; however, there are a few I/O interface standards that have been established. These are concerned with system buses, signal characteristics and interconnections, and character codes.

S-100 Bus

The S-100 bus is thought of as a standard even though it was not originally meant to be one. In 1975, MITS, Inc. developed a bus system for their 8080-based Altair computer. The S-100 is a 100-line bus system of address lines, data lines, control lines (many control lines), and power lines laid out in a particular arrangement. It was well accepted by industry and became a virtual industry standard. Hundreds of 10 x 5.5 inch cards from memory to I/O boards were designed around the S-100 bus layout. With such widespread application, it was discovered the S-100 had some flaws. The S-100 was designed around the 8080 MPU and adapting to other microprocessors was often difficult. It appeared the layout had not been planned as well as it could have been. The signal line assignment seemed aimless. Clock signals ran too close to control signals. The bus also required that each card provide its own voltage regulation. With the advent of 16-bit microprocessors and megabyte memory, the S-100 began to lose appeal. Other buses were designed which became standards correcting for the S-100's disadvantages.

IEEE-488 (GPIB)

The GPIB (General Purpose Interface Bus) was developed by Hewlett-Packard to interface instrumentation equipment, as compared to the S-100 that was designed to interface memory, I/O and such. (Hewlett-Packard refers to this bus as the HPIB.) Unlike the 100 bus lines, the GPIB has eight data lines, three data byte transfer control lines, and five interface lines. This bus system has no address lines so the control lines available are used to control how the eight data lines are used. The instrumentation connected to this bus must become a controller, a listener, or a talker. The three data byte transfer control lines are used to fulfill the handshaking signals between the talker and the listener. This handshaking technique is patented by HP, and companies using it must purchase a license from HP.

EIA RS-232C Serial Communications Standard

EIA RS-232C is the title of the Electronic Industries Association's popular standard for serial data communications. The standard defines the electrical characteristics of an interface which links a transmitter of serial data to a receiver. The transmitter might be a computer output unit whose receiver is a CRT terminal, a serial printer, or some similar output device. Another possible transmitter is a keyboard which sends serially encoded characters to a computer's input unit.

The receiver, in this example, is the input unit. Because of the wide variety of transmitter-receiver configurations, the RS-232C standard was written to help ensure compatibility between serial data transmission devices.

The two types of signals communicated with an RS-232C interface are data signals and control signals. The data signals are negative logic digital signals. Logic 1 is represented by a voltage level in the range -3 to -25 volts. In its idle state (no information being transmitted or received), the data line goes to the logic 1 level. When a character is to be sent, the data line switches to the logic 0 level for one bit time, and then the character is transmitted, beginning with the LSB. The logic 0 before the character is called the *start bit*, and it marks the beginning of each new character. The start bit is used to alert the receiver that a character is about to be transmitted on the data line. The sequence of events on the data line as an 8-bit character code is transmitted are the same as the TTY bit pattern of *Figure 11.20*.

At the end of the character code an optional parity bit may be generated, and then one or two stop bits are transmitted. The parity bit is used in some systems to detect single-bit transmission errors in the character code. Parity, if it is used, may be odd or even. The stop bit(s) mark the end of the character and allow the receiver to prepare for the next character.

Beside the data signals of the RS-232C interface that have been described, there are other signals defined in the standard called control signals. They are used to supervise the communications process, making it possible to establish a handshaking exchange between transmitter and receiver. However, the exact description of the handshake is not included in the RS-232C standard, and different equipment manufacturers implement it in different ways. The interconnection pattern and the 25-pin connector, however, are specified as shown in *Figure 11.27*. Not all the defined control signals are used by all systems.

The RS-232C standard also requires that the data signal line be terminated in an impedance within the range from 3 kilohms to 7 kilohms. Line length is limited to about 50 feet, and the maximum baud rate is less than 20 kilobits per second. However, by using line drivers to amplify the signal and compatible line receivers, the maximum distance for transmission can be extended to several miles.

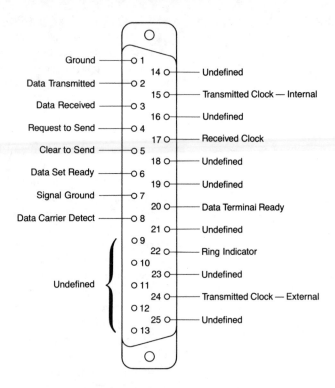

Figure 11.27   Hardware Line Assignments for RS-232C

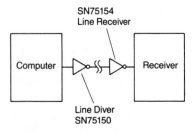

Figure 11.28   RS232C Voltage Level Translators

Standard Codes

When RS-232C equipment is to be connected to +5 volt computer systems, signal voltage levels must be translated to properly couple the data between the two devices. Special line drivers and line receivers are available to facilitate this translation. The Texas Instruments SN75150 line driver converts the +5V computer output to RS-232C levels and the Texas Instruments SN75154 line receiver translates RS-232C voltage levels to input TTL compatible levels. *Figure 11.28* illustrates a typical application of an RS-232C line driver and line receiver.

The American Standard Code for Information Interchange (ASCII) is an industry standard for microcomputers and data communication. ASCII is a 7-bit code which allows 128 different letters, numbers and symbols. When used in data communications, the eighth bit can be used for parity.

Another popular code used in many larger computers manufactured by IBM, is the Extended Binary Coded Decimal Interchange Code (EBCDIC). EBCDIC is an 8-bit code providing for a possible 256 characters. Both of these codes are listed at the end of the chapter.

COMMON I/O PERIPHERALS

Common I/O peripherals are printers which have been mentioned. Others that will be discussed in this section are auxiliary memory, video displays, keyboards and modems. D-to-A and A-to-D converters were discussed in Chapter 8.

Auxiliary Memory

One of the first requirements of a microcomputer system is additional memory that can be used to store completed programs, files which provide data for programs, or results of specific tasks performed by a program or programs. Such memory, separate from the main internal working memory of the microcomputer system, is called auxiliary memory. The auxiliary memory may be a separate peripheral unit to the main computer system or it may be self-contained within the computer system.

The two common types of auxiliary memory used with computer systems are magnetic tape and magnetic disk. These memories are non-volatile, so that stored information is not subject to being lost due to power failure, but remains until electrically erased. Access is not random access as in the main internal memory; therefore, the time it takes to read one data word or byte will be different than for another, and much slower than the access to data in the main internal memory. Even so, the auxiliary memories are very useful because the storage is long-term and the information does not take up valuable memory space in the computer system until it is needed and loaded.

Common formats for magnetic tape are reels or cassettes. Common formats for magnetic disks are flexible plastic diskettes called floppy disks and hard rigid disks. Let's very briefly look at each of these.

Reel-to-Reel Magnetic Tape

This was the first widely used auxiliary memory for large computer systems and is still used today; however, it is used very little in microcomputer systems. Information is recorded in a multiple-track format (seven to nine tracks), shown in *Figure 11.29*. The magnetic tape is pulled by a multiple record head assembly by a capstan from a supply reel to a takeup reel. The information is recorded linearly on the tape in sequence. Playing back the tape past a multiple read head assembly recovers the stored information. Using the 9-track format of *Figure 11.29*, data is stored that has been ASCII or EBCDIC coded and one or two bits are available as error correcting parity bits. Storage density is from 256 to 1600 frames per inch, allowing a 2400-foot reel of tape to store millions of bits of data.

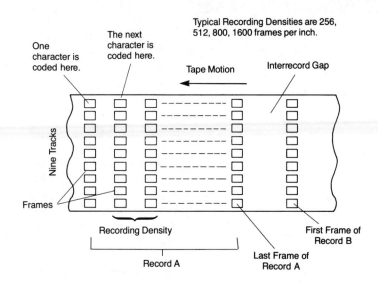

Figure 11.29 Magnetic Tape Format

Cassette Magnetic Tape

A very popular auxiliary memory for home computer systems is cassette magnetic tape, because it is an inexpensive non-volatile storage medium. The cassette is the same size as the standard audio cassette for music and speech, but the formatting technique is different.

Binary computer output data is converted to analog tones before it is recorded on the magnetic tape. One frequency or tone is used for a binary 0 and a second for a binary 1. A conversion circuit is contained within the computer system to perform the conversion so the analog tones can be applied to a standard cassette recorder/player. Special high quality tape for digital recording is required to minimize dropout (loss of bits). The data is recorded bit by bit linearly along the tape. Playback of the tones is converted by the computer system to the internal digital codes required. A blank cassette tape is much less expensive than a blank disk and a cassette tape recorder/player is much less expensive than a disk drive. However, programs on cassette tape are harder to load than programs on disk and take a much longer time to locate.

Floppy Disks

An auxiliary memory that has become a standard for microcomputer systems is a thin flexible plastic disk commonly called a floppy disk because of its flexibility. The thin plastic base disk is coated with a thin layer of iron oxide used for the recording medium, and the disk is sealed in a plastic envelope. A slot in the envelope permits the read/write head(s) of the disk drive to contact the surface of the disk.

The magnetic disk must be inserted into a disk drive unit, which rotates the disk and moves the read/write head(s). A disk drive controller, either contained with the microcomputer system or as a peripheral unit, is required to control the operation of the disk drive. As the disk rotates at a constant speed, information is written on the disk when electrical signals in the write head magnetize very small areas on the iron oxide coating. When the disk is read (played back), the small magnetized areas reproduce the original signals in the read head. Floppy disk storage provides long-term non-volatile storage of information with faster access and much better reliability than cassette tape. As mentioned previously, the disks, the drive and controller are much more expensive than a cassette recorder.

As shown in *Figure 11.30*, the information is placed serially upon the disk in concentric circles called tracks. Each track contains blocks of information called sectors that are separated by gaps. The gaps delineate the beginning and ending of blocks of data on the disk. As the disk rotates, the read/write head(s) are moved linearly back and forth across the disk one track at a time by a stepper motor. Some disk drives have permanent heads for each track. In that case, the disk drive controller is programmed to select the correct track.

Floppy disks are normally 3.50, 5.25 or 8 inches in diameter. They can store thousands of bytes of data. The exact amount depends on whether the disk can record on one side (single-sided) or on both sides (double-sided), or whether it can record in single-density or double-density (double the bits per inch in each sector). A 5.25-inch double-sided, double-density disk can store from 300 to 400 kilobytes of data (about 100 pages of single-spaced text) or more.

Magnetic disks are either soft-sectored disks or hard-sectored disks. A hard-sector disk has a reference hole in the disk for each sector. A soft-sectored disk has only one hole *(Figure 11.30)*. The hole is used as a timing reference so the disk controller can locate the sector boundaries.

Magnetic disk storage systems have the following advantages:
1. The media can be used over and over.
2. A large amount of information can be stored in a small volume.
3. The cost of equipment is very reasonable for the speed of access of data and storage capacity.
4. The standardization of disk formats has contributed to the use of the stored information on different computer systems.

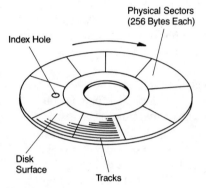

Physical Sectors
(256 Bytes Each)

Index Hole

Disk
Surface

Tracks

Figure 11.30   Floppy Disk Format

Hard Disk

The hard magnetic disk auxiliary memory systems are essentially the same as the floppy disk systems, except the recording medium is one or more rigid disks that are usually not removable. These disks are capable of storing from 5 to 20 million or more bytes of data and programs on a single disk. The access time and transfer rate of stored information are much faster than those for the floppy disk system. However, the disadvantage is the much higher cost of the hard disk system.

Video Display

Video display is the most common method of displaying computer system data. The home television set has become a widely used video device for microcomputer systems. A wide variety of displays have been produced for computer use. The higher quality cathode-ray tube display devices are used where high resolution is required.

There are two basic methods of interfacing the microcomputer with the home television set. The first method is RF modulation, which requires no connection to the inside of the television. Much like a broadcast signal, the RF modulated signal is coupled to the television at its antenna and is processed accordingly. The television is tuned to whatever channel frequency the computer RF modulator is producing. The screen shows what is being sent by the computer. The disadvantage of RF modulation is its limited bandwidth, allowing fewer characters to be shown without losing legibility. A broad bandwidth is required to produce graphics with the degree of detail (resolution) demanded by present day computer systems. Still, the RF modulation method is perhaps the most popular for home computer systems, because of its low cost.

The second method of interfacing the computer to a television set is the direct video connection. By eliminating the tuning and detection stages of the TV set, a wider bandwith is possible and better resolution of characters can be attained. This is the normal connection for a computer system that has a dedicated monitor. The monitor normally has higher resolution than a standard TV set CRT. To make a direct video connection to a TV set, plug the computer's video output into a television's video input jack. Many recently manufactured TV sets have these jacks. If a television has no video input jack, a TV serviceman should be able to install one.

Keyboards

Keyboards are classified into encoded and non-encoded types. The encoded keyboard has the on-board hardware necessary to detect which key is depressed and store the data until a second key is depressed. The non-encoded keyboard requires a software routine to detect, first, if any key has been depressed, and then which specific key was depressed. An 8×8 keyboard matrix is shown in *Figure 11.31*. The ASCII codes representing the upper case and lower case alphabet are shown at the intersection. Data is clocked into the row line register by placing data on the data bus and sending an address 01H. The information on the column lines is obtained on the data bus by enabling the data bus buffers by sending address 00H.

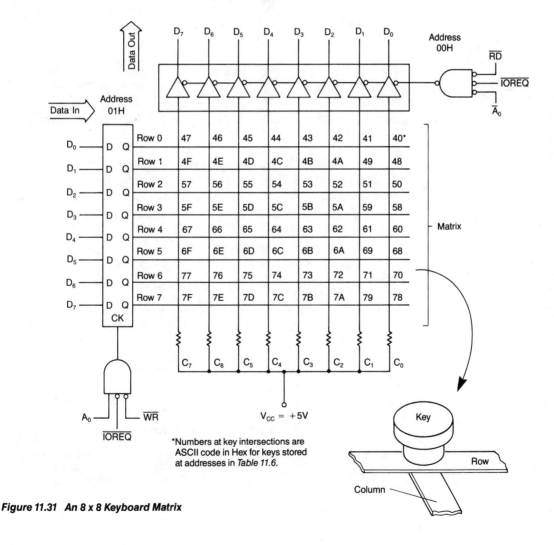

Figure 11.31 An 8 x 8 Keyboard Matrix

The following program identifies the depressed key in the 8×8 matrix of *Figure 11.31* and places the corresponding ASCII code in the accumulator (8085 MPU).

```
ROW     EQU     ;01H
COL     EQU     ;00H
```

Label	Instruction		Comments
	ORG	6000H	
LOOK:	MVI	A, 00H	;Acc = 0000 0000$_2$ (Clear ;Acc)
	OUT	ROW	;Ground all rows
	IN	COL	;Read COL into A
	CPI	OFFH	;Compare A to 1111 1111$_2$
	JZ	LOOK	;Keep looking for key
	STC		;Set Carry to 1
	MVI	B, FEH	;B holds ROW D$_0$ low
	MOV	A, B	;A holds 111 1110$_2$
	MVI	D, 27H	;Set Count for 8 row scan
SCAN:	OUT	ROW	;Set ROW D$_0$ low
	MOV	B, Acc	;Save Acc
	IN	COL	;Read COL
	CPI	OFFH	;Compare A to 1111 1111$_2$
	CNZ	TABLE	;Sub to find key address
	MOV	A, B	;Load A for next scan
	RLC		;Rotate to scan next row
	DCR	D	;Reduce row count
	JNZ	SCAN	;Scan next row if D is not zero
	JMP	LOOK	;Return to look for key press

This subprogram determines table address for key pressed and places ASCII code in accumulator from address location.

Label	Instruction		Comments
TABLE:	MOV	C, A	;A holds COL, move A to C
	STC		;Set Carry to 1
	MVI	E, OFFH	;Set count of COL rotates
ROTCOL:	RAR		;Rotate COL to next bit position
	INR	E	;Increase COL count
	JC	ROTCOL	;Rotates until Carry is 0
	MOV	A, B	;Get ROW in A
	STC		;Set Carry to 1
	MVI	D, OFFH	;Set count of row rotates
ROTROW:	RAR		;Rotates ROW to next bit position
	INR	D	;Count rotates from FF to 0, 1, 2
	JC	ROTROW	;Rotates until Carry is 0
	MOV	A, D	;Get ROW count for rotate
	RLC		;
	RLC		; Move MS Nibble to LS Nibble (4 bits)
	RLC		;
	RLC		;
	ANI	OFOH	;Mask LS Nibble
	ADD	E	;E holds LSB add to A
	MOV	L, A	;Address of table in L (low order byte)
	MVI	H, 01H	;High order address of table (high order byte)
	MOV	A, M	;A holds ASCII of key pushed
	RET		;Return from sub
	END		

The program grounds all rows, then reads the columns looking for a low resulting from a depressed switch which would ground one of the columns. Once a ground is detected, indicating a depressed key exists, the MPU places a low on row D_0 and scans all the columns. If no low is detected, that means the depressed key is located on some other row. Next, the MPU rotates the low on row D_0 left to row D_1, and once again scans all columns looking for a low. This continues until the coordinates of the row and column of the depressed switch are detected. When the coordinates are detected, the coordinate address is placed in the low byte (L) address register and 01 placed in the high byte (H) register of the look-up table and the corresponding ASCII code at that address is placed in the accumulator for output to the screen. The look-up table is shown in *Table 11.6*.

Table 11.6   Addresses of ASCII Codes For Keyboard

MSB	LSB	Addresses 0100H through 0177H							
01	00	10	20	30	40	50	60	70	R_0
	01	11	21	31	41	51	61	71	R_1
	02	12	22	32	42	52	62	72	R_2
	03	13	23	33	43	53	63	73	R_3
	04	14	24	34	44	54	64	74	R_4
	05	15	25	35	45	55	65	75	R_5
	06	16	26	36	46	56	66	76	R_6
	07	17	27	37	47	57	67	77	R_7
	08	X	X	X	X	X	X	X	
	09	X	X	X	X	X	X	X	
	0A	X	X	X	X	X	X	X	
	0B	X	X	X	X	X	X	X	
	0C	X	X	X	X	X	X	X	
	0D	X	X	X	X	X	X	X	
	0E	X	X	X	X	X	X	X	
	0F	X	X	X	X	X	X	X	
		C_0	C_1	C_2	C_3	C_4	C_5	C_6	C_7

X = Don't Care

MODEM

A modem (<u>mo</u>dulator/<u>dem</u>odulator) makes possible the reliable transfer of digital data over telephone lines. The composition of a digital pulse waveform includes frequencies beyond the bandwidth of a telephone line. To overcome the limitations of the telephone line, the modem that is sending converts the computer's 1s and 0s into two preset frequencies (one for each state). The receiving modem demodulates these two frequencies, thereby recovering the digital data.

The modem detects the ones and zeros output in serial form from a USART and converts them to two different frequencies, called frequency shift keying (FSK). The low is a space, and a high is a mark. The space and mark are dc voltage levels, (zero and five volts). A voltage-controlled oscillator (VCO) is used to convert voltage to frequency. The VCO outputs 2.4kHz for a mark, and 1.2kHz for a space. The receiving modem detects the incoming frequencies and converts them back to dc voltages representing the logic levels. *Figure 11.32* shows an example of FSK.

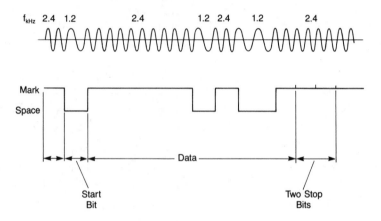

Figure 11.32   Frequency Shift Keying Modulation

SUMMARY

In this chapter, we have covered the various hardware and software methods used when the computer communicates with the outside world. Most communication takes place with I/O peripherals such as a keyboard, printer, CRT monitor, disk drive and modem.

Most communication takes place through integrated circuits which provide parallel or serial ports for the interface between the computer system and the peripherals. I/O mapping and memory mapping are control techniques used to address the I/O units. Common interface integrated circuits were described, their architecture examined, and the methods used to control and program the interface were covered in detail. Examples illustrated how port control is accomplished. Some common standard codes, buses, and signal characteristics were described, followed by a discussion of auxiliary memory, keyboards, CRT monitors and modem signals. With this information, one has a rather broad overview of how to interface to I/O units from a computer system.

Here are two commonly used digital data codes included for your reference.

EXTENDED BINARY CODED DECIMAL INTERCHANGE CODE (EBCDIC)

Bits xxxx 4567	00				01				10				11				Bits x0,x1
	00	01	10	11	00	01	10	11	00	01	10	11	00	01	10	11	Bits x2,x3
0000	NUL	DLE			SP	&							{	}		0	
0001	SOH	DC1					/		a	j			A	J		1	
0010	STX	DC2	SYN						b	k	s		B	K	S	2	
0011	ETX	DC3							c	l	t		C	L	T	3	
0100									d	m	u		D	M	U	4	
0101	HT		LF						e	n	v		E	N	V	5	
0110		BS	ETB						f	o	w		F	O	W	6	
0111	DEL		ESC	EOT					g	p	x		G	P	X	7	
1000		CAN							h	q	y		H	Q	Y	8	
1001		EM							i	r	z		I	R	Z	9	
1010					[	]	|	:									
1011	VT				.	$	,	#									
1100	FF	FS		DC4	<	•	%	@									
1101	CF	GS	ENQ	NAK	(	)	—	'									
1110	SO	RS	ACK		+	;	>	=									
1111	SI	US	BEL	SUB	!	∧	?	"									

AMERICAN STANDARD CODE FOR INFORMATION INTERCHANGE (ASCII)

BIT POSITIONS:

6				0	0	0	0	1	1	1	1
5				0	0	1	1	0	0	1	1
4				0	1	0	1	0	1	0	1
3	2	1	0								
0	0	0	0	NUL	DLE	SP	0	@	P		p
0	0	0	1	SOH	DC1	!	1	A	Q	a	q
0	0	1	0	STX	DC2	"	2	B	R	b	r
0	0	1	1	ETX	DC3	#	3	C	S	c	s
0	1	0	0	EOT	DC4	$	4	D	T	d	t
0	1	0	1	ENQ	NAK	%	5	E	U	e	u
0	1	1	0	ACK	SYN	&	6	F	V	f	v
0	1	1	1	BEL	ETB	'	7	G	W	g	w
1	0	0	0	BS	CAN	(	8	H	X	h	x
1	0	0	1	HT	EM	)	9	I	Y	i	y
1	0	1	0	LF	SUB	*	:	J	Z	j	z
1	0	1	1	VT	ESC	+	;	K	[	k	{
1	1	0	0	FF	FS	,	<	L		l	|
1	1	0	1	CR	GS	–	=	M	]	m	}
1	1	1	0	SO	RS	.	>	N	∧	n	~
1	1	1	1	SI	US	/	?	O	—	o	DEL

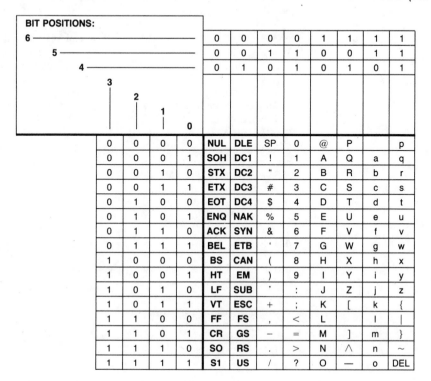

CHAPTER 11 QUIZ

1. The two basic types of I/O ports are:
   a. input and output ports.
   b. peripheral and non-peripheral ports.
   c. serial and parallel ports.
   d. printer and cassette ports.

2. The major difference in I/O mapping and memory mapping of I/O ports is:
   a. memory mapping is more expensive.
   b. memory mapping will not work for an I/O port.
   c. I/O mapping does not waste memory space.
   d. there is no difference.

3. Considering the control register in *Figure 11.9*, what control word would be required to set data bits D_0, D_1, D_5, D_6, and D_7 as input and all other data lines as output?
   a. 37H
   b. 32H
   c. D3H
   d. E3H

4. What type of I/O addressing does the Intel microprocessor family use?
   a. ROM mapping
   b. Memory mapping
   c. Bus mapping
   d. I/O mapping

5. Select the control word required to program the Intel 8255 PPI so that: Port A and Port C (lower) are input ports; mode selection is mode 0; and Port B and Port C (upper) are output ports:
   a. C2H
   b. 91H
   c. 11H
   d. EAH

6. The MC6821 PIA has how many addressable registers?
   a. 2
   b. 4
   c. 6
   d. 8

7. Notice that each additional address line used in the decoding of an I/O port will reduce the size of the memory block used by the I/O port. If four address lines are ANDed to select a PIA, how many memory locations are restricted to I/O?
   a. 4K
   b. 8K
   c. 16K
   d. 32K

8. What is another word for program control of I/O?
   a. I/O request
   b. Interrupt
   c. ASCII
   d. Polling

9. The interrupted control input and output is a much faster method of servicing a peripheral than the polling technique.
   a. True
   b. False

10. A DMAC is a dedicated processor of data used for fast and efficient transfer of blocks of data.
    a. True
    b. False

TROUBLESHOOTING MICROCOMPUTER SYSTEMS

INTRODUCTION

Troubleshooting a microcomputer system is like troubleshooting any digital circuit. The basic approach is to isolate the problem to a smaller and smaller part of the circuit or system. Basic troubleshooting skills and methods required for troubleshooting a simple digital circuit or system are used in like fashion to isolate problems in a much more complex system or subsystem. Basic combinational and sequential circuit theory, timing fundamentals, signal levels and signal characteristics are in many cases, the same in the complex circuit as they are in the simple circuit. It's just that they are packed much closer together and not as accessible in the complex circuitry.

The procedures and instruments used to troubleshoot microcomputers are similar to those used to troubleshoot other digital systems. Logic probes, logic pulsers, and integrated circuit test clips are as helpful when testing certain portions of a microcomputer system, as they are in troubleshooting simpler systems. Therefore, even though microcomputers are the main subject of this chapter's troubleshooting discussion, the information is applicable to digital troubleshooting in general.

Since microcomputer systems include some relatively simple digital circuitry as well, some fundamental troubleshooting procedures will be explored also. On the other hand, even though microcomputer systems have much in common with systems containing simpler logic circuits, they have unique features which require special troubleshooting skills, special measuring instruments, and different procedures.

SPECIAL FEATURES OF MICROCOMPUTER SYSTEMS

Microcomputer systems differ from simple digital circuits in at least four ways.
1. Computer system signal paths are usually multiconductor buses as compared to the single-wire signal path of a simple circuit.

2. Microcomputer systems are constructed from integrated circuit devices which are more complex than the gates, flip-flops etc. found in simpler circuits.
3. Many of these complex devices are capable of two or more different functions. They operate in one mode under one set of inputs, but in a completely different mode under other inputs.
4. The computer system itself may function differently at different times, depending on the software used to program it. Simple digital circuits are hardware driven and always perform the same function.

How do these four differences impact microcomputer troubleshooting? In the next few paragraphs we explore the answers to that question.

Bus Structure

The main system components of a microcomputer are interconnected by three buses as shown in *Figure 12.1* — the data bus, the address bus, and the control bus. Symptom diagnosis may require that the signals on one or more of these buses be analyzed, requiring that all lines in the bus be observed simultaneously. For example, to test the signals on the data bus in an 8-bit microcomputer system, some type of 8-channel measuring instrument must be used, as shown in *Figure 12.2*.

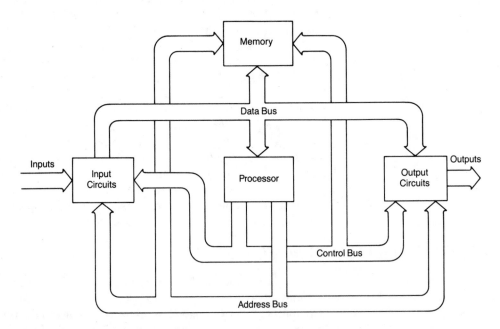

Figure 12.1 Block Diagram of a Computer System

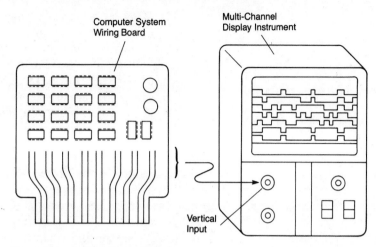

Figure 12.2 *Monitoring an 8-Bit Bus*

Computer systems may be unique in this respect because few other electronic systems require the simultaneous observation of so many signals. To satisfy this requirement, specially designed test instruments must be mastered by the computer system troubleshooter. One such instrument, the logic analyzer, will be described later in this chapter.

Device Complexity

Special purpose test equipment also is necessary in the testing of complex integrated circuits, such as microprocessors used in microcomputer systems. As *Figure 12.3* shows, the number of transistors integrated onto a single silicon chip has increased steadily.

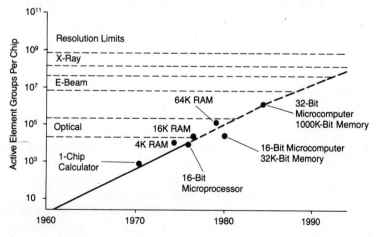

Figure 12.3 *Semiconductor Chip Complexity*
(Source: Courtesy M. Sheppard, 1977 NCC)

The very large scale integrated circuits (VLSI) used in microcomputer systems are so complex that simple voltage measurements usually provide very little information. Some other method must be employed to verify the satisfactory operation of these devices or to detect malfunctions. Logic clips and logic probes are useful in some situations, but in many cases, special techniques must be applied.

Dynamic Logic

Integrated circuits like microprocessors perform so many different functions that problems which occur during one mode of operation may not even appear during another mode. *Figure 12.4* shows how the ALU section of the CPU may function as an adder, a shift register, and a comparator within a period of only a few microseconds. Two of these three operations may be performed correctly, but the one incorrect result may "crash" the system. Failures of this nature can be isolated only by an in-circuit test of the microprocessor while it is operating, using special techniques.

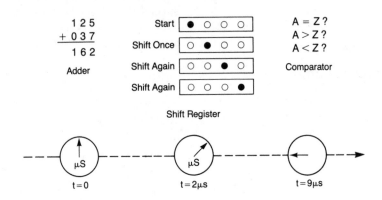

Figure 12.4   Rapidly Changing Functions of the ALU Section

Software Control

Microcomputer systems are unique as compared to other digital systems in that they are controlled by the software stored in their memories. For example, in one application, a microcomputer may operate as a word processor, in another as a spreadsheet, and in another as an arcade-style game. Each application uses the same hardware. Only the software changes. In many cases, this makes it difficult to diagnose the problem. The troubleshooter must determine whether a system malfunction is due to a hardware or a software failure. While hardware failures may be isolated by using test equipment, software problems can be verified only if the troubleshooter understands the programming language.

Only after the functions of the machine instructions are understood in detail can the troubleshooter use an approach such as single stepping through the program to detect the microcomputer system's problems.

We have seen some specific differences and some general similarities in microcomputer systems and simpler logic circuits. As we proceed, keep these comparisons in mind. They can help you determine appropriate steps in your own troubleshooting procedures. We will begin by describing some of the more important test instruments used for digital troubleshooting.

TEST EQUIPMENT

Much of the general-purpose test equipment described in previous chapters is also useful in digital troubleshooting. Voltmeters, for example, whether digital or analog types, can be used for measuring voltage levels in digital systems to determine signal levels and functional states just as in other equipment. The following paragraphs will concentrate on instruments designed specifically for digital troubleshooting or on procedures unique to troubleshooting logic circuits.

Conventional Oscilloscopes

When troubleshooting microcomputer systems, a general purpose oscilloscope is one of the most useful pieces of test equipment. Simple dc voltage measurements can verify logic levels and steady-state states, and can indicate marginal conditions. *Figure 12.5* shows an oscilloscope displaying the clock waveform for a microcomputer. It is the best instrument for making this important measurement because it permits analysis of both amplitude and time-related parameters. If the time relationship of one or more signals must be tested, multiple trace oscilloscopes are required to check if a particular control signal is present at a particular point in time during a system's operation.

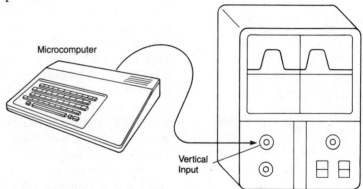

Figure 12.5 Using an Oscilloscope to Check Clock Waveforms

The primary limitations of general purpose oscillscopes in digital troubleshooting are:

1. Even though it has multiple traces, it is difficult to display glitches that are occurring at random or intermittently.
2. The inability to display all the information on a bus at a particular instant.
3. The bandwidth may be too limited. It should have a bandwidth of at least 35MHz.

The first of these limitations can be overcome to a certain extent by using a sophisticated storage-type oscilloscope. Such an instrument is able to trigger on a specific event and to store the signal that follows it for more detailed analysis.

Logic Probes and Pulsers

Most logic probes are simple voltage level indicators. Instead of indicating just 0 and 1 logic levels, they also may indicate intermediate levels and even pulse trains. They may be battery powered, but usually they have leads with alligator clips to allow them to be connected to the power suppy of the system under test. Some include controls to select the type logic levels to be measured — CMOS or TTL. A typical probe is illustrated in *Figure 12.6*.

Figure 12.6 Typical Logic Probe
(Source: Courtesy of Hewlett-Packard Company)

Logic Probe Use

To use a logic probe, the tip is connected to a point in the circuit. A light emitting diode (LED) indicator or indicators display the status of the point. The point may be a steady level at a high, low, intermediate, or floating (high Z) logic state, or the point may be pulsating or alternating between a high and low logic level. Probes made by different manufacturers have different ways to indicate these conditions. Some use different colored LEDs, while others use varying brilliance of a single LED. Some more expensive models also may include a memory feature which allows the probe to detect and indicate the logic level of a single pulse on a line. Others may indicate the duty cycle of a pulse train by varying the time an LED remains on. Also, various other special features are available.

Because logic probes can monitor only a single line in a circuit, they are most useful in simple logic or interface circuits. However, the usefulness of a logic probe may be extended by using it in combination with a logic pulser.

Logic Pulser Use

Logic pulsers are basically signal injectors. Like logic probes, they usually draw power from the system under test. Logic pulsers detect the level of the point to which they are connected. When the pushbutton switch is activated, the pulser injects a signal that drives the logic level to the opposite state. That is, if the point is at a low logic level, the pulser generates a transition to a high logic level; but if the point is already at a high logic level, the pulser generates a transition to a low logic level. By applying these signals to the inputs of gate circuits, the gates may be tested by monitoring their outputs with a logic probe. Usually pulsers will not have enough drive power to override short circuits or other such extreme load conditions.

Some pulsers can be set to generate a series of negative-going or positive-going pulses. These pulses can be used for a variety of purposes, but a common one is to use them to provide clock drive for sequential circuits. Like logic probes, most pulsers affect only one line at a time, although some are available which allow stimulation of up to four points at once by using a special kit to add multiple tips.

Logic Analyzers

Logic analyzers were designed specifically for troubleshooting computer systems. Essentially, a logic analyzer is a multitrace (usually from 8 to 16 traces) oscilloscope which allows the logic states of all the lines of a bus to be displayed on a CRT screen simultaneously. A common application is a timing display like the one in *Figure 12.7a*, which show the time relationship between various signals in a system.

Not all logic analyzers offer the timing display feature. Most do, however, offer the data domain display shown in *Figure 12.7b*. The bus information is converted directly to 1s and 0s and displayed in tabular format. *Figure 12.7c* shows a third display format that is offered by some logic analyzers. It is called a mapping display. The mapping display consists of an array of dots. The MSBs of a bus drive the vertical deflection circuits and the LSB's drive the horizontal deflection circuits. The resulting display is a unique pattern which may be recognized as proper or improper for a particular computer operation. There is some disagreement about the value of mapped displays. Some computer system troubleshooters find them valuable, while others find them difficult to use.

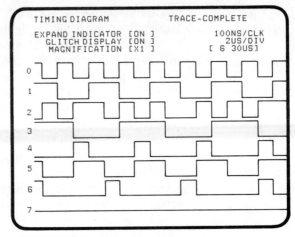

a. Timing Diagram

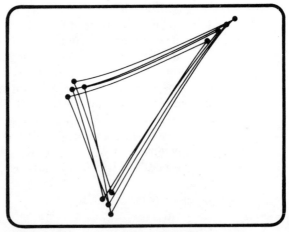

b. Data Domain

c. Mapping

Figure 12.7   Three Logic Analyzer Displays
(Source: Courtesy of Hewlett-Packard Company)

To help understand how a logic analyzer is used, an example will be described using the data domain display, the most commonly used display format. Typically, troubleshooting with a logic analyzer begins by connecting the instrument's inputs to the bus to be monitored, usually the data bus. A piece of information (usually an instruction or a data code) is entered into the logic analyzer to be used as a key. This is done with switches or from a keyboard, depending on the logic analyzer model. The key information is chosen to be near the point of malfunction in the computer system operation.

Next, the computer system is operated. When the information on the bus matches the key information stored in the logic analyzer, the information on the bus will be displayed. The amount of information that can be displayed at any time depends on the characteristics of the logic analyzer. Sixteen words is a typical display size. Also, most logic analyzers allow the key information (usually called the trigger) to be either the first word or the last word displayed. That is, the display shows either the trigger word followed by the next fifteen words on the bus (assuming a sixteen word display), or the fifteen words preceding the trigger word followed by the trigger word itself. By comparing the displayed information with the expected information, the troubleshooter can determine the point at which the system fails to function properly.

Logic analyzers are useful for isolating both software and hardware problems, but some types of hardware failures may not be manifest directly in a data domain display. Timing problems caused by noise spikes and glitches caused by hardware problems are identified by using the timing diagram display. Of course, logic analyzers are of little value if the microcomputer system will not function at all.

Other Types of Test Instruments

Logic Clip

A number of other instruments have been designed especially for digital troubleshooting. Logic clips, for example, are devices which clamp onto a dual inline IC package (DIP), contact all the pins simultaneously, and display the state on each pin via a set of LEDs along the top of the clip. At this time clips are available for ICs with up to sixteen pins. Logic clips are useful for static checks only; when data changes rapidly the states cannot be read from the clip. *Figure 12.8* shows a typical logic clip.

Figure 12.8   Logic Clip
(Source: Courtesy of Hewlett-Packard Company)

Current Tracer

Another digital troubleshooting instrument is the current tracer
shown in *Figure 12.9*. It is used to locate low impedance faults
such as short circuits in logic circuits. The magnetic field
surrounding a current pulse causes the current tracer's indicator
to light. When conventional troubleshooting procedures indicate
a short circuit, the current tracer is used to locate the precise
point of the short by sensing the current in specific conductors on
the printed wiring board.

Signature Analyzer

Still another test instrument, the signature analyzer, is used to
monitor specific test points in the digital system. When the
equipment operates properly, a known sequence of data bits
appears at each test point. The signature analyzer samples and
captures these bits, displaying an alphanumeric code that
represents a signature unique to that test point. Improper
operation results in a bad signature. Obviously, signature
analysis requires that the digital system be designed to generate
the expected signature during normal operation.

   As new computer systems become more complex, test
equipment designers are developing new test equipment to try
and find better ways to assist the troubleshooter.

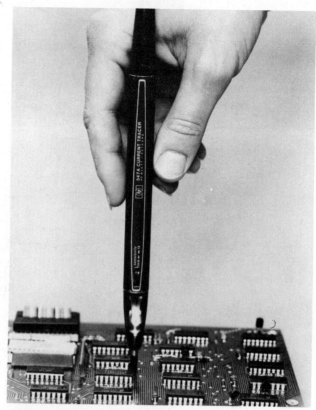

Figure 12.9   Current Tracer Probe
(Source: Courtesy of Hewlett-Packard Company)

Documentation

An indispensable troubleshooting tool is the set of documents
which describe the microcomputer system. They include system
block diagrams, logic schematic diagrams, and timing diagrams.
Program listings, especially those in the system ROM, also can be
quite helpful. Most of these documents accompany the
microcomputer system, but if not available, they can also be
obtained from independent publishers or from the microcomputer
manufacturer.

TYPICAL MICROCOMPUTER FAULTS

What can go wrong with a microcomputer? A detailed block
diagram of a typical microcomputer system is shown in *Figure
12.10*. Troubleshooting a complex system like this requires that
the technician understand the basics of microcomputer system
operation. The system operating manual is a good source of
technical data. Sometimes this manual will even provide a
troubleshooting chart which suggests remedies for particular
problems.

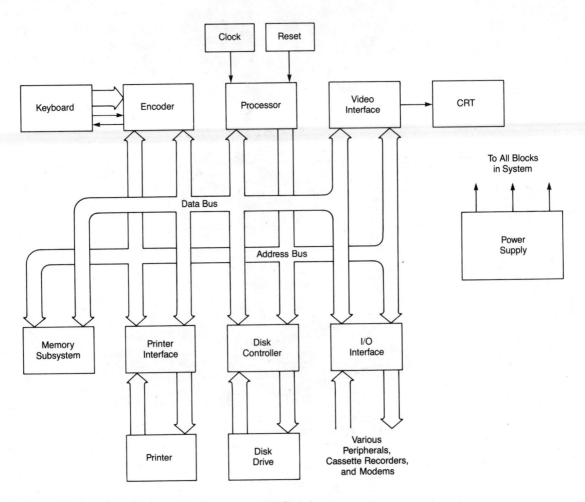

Figure 12.10 Block Diagram of a Typical Microcomputer System

In general, microcomputer system problems can be grouped into one of four major categories. We will consider each of these four categories and suggest ways to isolate the source of the problem. We will concentrate on hardware problems that occur regardless of the software that is used.

Computer Is Dead

The first category is a computer system which does not respond when power is applied. Troubleshooting a dead computer system is often easier than troubleshooting one which works partially or intermittently. As *Figure 12.10* indicates, the system power supply is the only part of the microcomputer which connects directly to all other parts of the system. It should be tested to make certain that it is operating properly. If it is, the next step is to disconnect the peripherals one by one. If disconnecting one of the peripherals suddenly seems to fix the problem, the fault probably is in that peripheral. If none of the peripherals seems to be causing the problem, the fault is likely in the CPU. More details on CPU troubleshooting are given later.

Random Output When Power Is Applied

The second category occurs when the computer screen fills with illegible material (commonly referred to by the slang term, garbage). A screen filled with garbage is usually the result of the microcomputer executing an illogical sequence of instructions. This can be caused by transients during the power up sequence. However, if it occurs every time the computer is turned on, or if it cannot be cleared by resetting the system, the fault is probably in the hardware.

Many microcomputers require two or more voltage levels from the power supply. If only one section of a multi-section power supply fails, screen garbage is often the result. If testing the power supply reveals no problems, a faulty peripheral may be causing the problem. As before, disconnecting the peripherals one at a time will isolate the culprit. If the problem persists, however, the fault is most likely in the CRT interface circuitry, in the CPU, or in the system memory.

Computer Fails During Normal Operation

A computer which operates normally when power is first applied, but which fails some time later, is a third category we will discuss. This category may be much harder to troubleshoot, especially if this same sequence of events occurs every time the system is used. The technician should first make certain that the fault is with the computer system and not the result of a power line transient. Usually this can be determined by resetting the system. If the problem remains, the fault is with the computer. Systematically unplugging peripheral devices will either eliminate units as problem sources or isolate the fault to one of them.

Failures of this type are often caused by heat, the common enemy of any electronic system. After a system has operated for a period of time, the ambient temperature inside the case may cause a marginal component to fail. Isolating the marginal component may be very difficult because the temperature drops rapidly when the case is removed. In the cooler environment the component may suddenly return to normal operation. There are two ways that possibly can be of assistance in isolating the problem. Sometimes it is possible to rapidly cool a specific component by spraying it with an aerosol refrigerant while the temperature of all other components remains at the elevated level. To go in the other temperature direction, a hair dryer or other concentrated source of heat can be used with some success to heat isolated components to see if the failure can be induced.

Computer Fails Intermittently

The fourth category is intermittent failures. Intermittent failures are the most difficult to troubleshoot. Often there is no apparent pattern of failure, and the problem may not exist when the troubleshooting effort begins.

A logic analyzer or a storage oscilloscope can be of great value when troubleshooting intermittent failures. Both these instruments can be set to trigger on the abnormal event and display the information. Since intermittent failures are often the result of spikes or other timing glitches, the test instrument's display might pinpoint the source of the problem.

Bad memory components may cause apparently intermittent failures. Diagnostic programs to test memory are available for most microcomputer systems. If a memory IC is the culprit, the diagnostic program should reveal the faulty chip.

Categorizing the failure and making the preliminary checks just described are the first steps in locating and repairing a microcomputer fault. Isolating a problem to a specific component requires more detailed testing and a more detailed understanding of how components fail. Let's look at some of these failure modes and the tests used to isolate them.

CPU TESTING

The CPU is the brain of the system. It may be a single microprocessor or it may be a microprocessor and several supporting ICs used with it. If the CPU is suspected of causing a fault, the first test performed when checking the CPU is to measure the power supply inputs. Only when these are correct are any other tests meaningful.

Clock Circuitry

After power supplies have been verified, the system clock should be checked. The microcomputer schematic diagram will show one or more inputs to the microprocessor IC labelled CLK or $\phi1$, $\phi2$, etc. The clock generator is internal to some newer microprocessor ICs, so the clock pins are actually outputs. In either case, the signals on the clock pin(s) should resemble the square wave shown in *Figure 12.11*.

Of course, the exact voltages, frequencies, and phases vary from system to system. In general, the amplitude A will be either −12 to +12 volts or 0 to +5 volts. The frequency will be at least 2MHz.

The CPU and the entire microcomputer system depend on these clock pulses for synchronization and overall timing. If the clock is not operating properly, consult the CPU schematic to locate the clock generator circuitry. It will include a crystal oscillator and, usually, one or more counters used to divide the oscillator frequency down to the rate required by the microprocessor. The outputs of each of these circuit elements should be checked. It may be necessary to disconnect the clock from the rest of the system to verify proper operation. Some other component may be loading the clock to cause a malfunction in the clock circuit.

If a microprocessor includes the clock generator circuitry within the same package internally, lack of a clock signal usually indicates a faulty microprocessor IC. Substituting a new microprocessor should solve the problem.

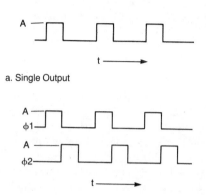

a. Single Output

b. Two-Phase

Figure 12.11   Typical Clock Signals

Reset Circuitry

If the clock circuitry is operating properly, proceed to the reset circuits. The reset input is usually an initial signal to the CPU that is generated automatically when power is first applied to the microcomputer system so that the CPU always starts from the same point. It may also be generated from the keyboard of most systems by pressing the Reset key. Reset causes the microcomputer system to begin operation under a known set of conditions. It is usually an active-low signal; i.e., it is normally high, but it switches low momentarily to reset the system. *Figure 12.12a* illustrates a typical reset signal.

Check the reset signal at the microprocessor input using an oscilloscope or a logic probe. Press the Reset key or switch the power off and back on. A short, negative-going pulse should be indicated. If it does not appear, check the reset circuitry. A typical reset circuit is diagrammed in *Figure 12.12b*. When power is applied, the one-shot multivibrator produces a single short pulse to reset the system. The pushbutton switch represents the Reset key which allows manual resetting at any time.

If the reset system does not function, the computer has no known starting point. The usual result is garbage on the display. It is a simple but critical part of the CPU.

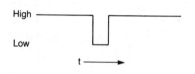

a. Reset Signal

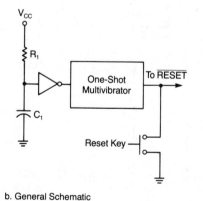

b. General Schematic

Figure 12.12   CPU Reset Circuit Operation

Control Signals

After the microcomputer system is reset, the first thing it should do is to read an instruction from ROM. *Figure 12.13* shows the input and output signals of a TMS9900 microprocessor. Several control signals, labeled $\overline{\text{MEMEN}}$, DBIN, and $\overline{\text{WE}}$, are shown at the lower right of the diagram. Other similar control signals were discussed in Chapter 9. The CPU generates these control signals as indicators to the rest of the system that particular operations are in progress.

If the microprocessor IC is functioning properly, activity can be observed on these control lines immediately after system reset. In the TMS9900 case, the $\overline{\text{MEMEN}}$ should go low to enable the memory subsystem to read an initial instruction into the CPU. To determine exactly what should happen in other systems, refer to a memory read timing diagram.

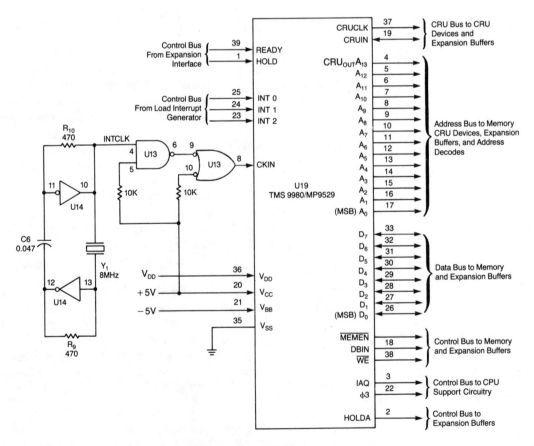

Figure 12.13 Microprocessor Output Signal Lines for the TMS9900

The activity can be tested with an oscilloscope or with a logic probe. The microprocessor IC is probably faulty if it fails to generate the correct control signals. However, because these lines connect to other system components, faults in other system components or bad connections on the printed wiring board(s) may produce improper results. Substituting a known good microprocessor IC is the best way to check for a faulty microprocessor.

Address and Data Buses

If all previous tests indicate nothing abnormal, it is possible that a problem exists on the address or data bus. Diagnostic software can be used to exercise these buses so that some quick tests can be made. With the diagnostic program running, check each bus line with an oscilloscope or a logic probe. Under normal conditions, the check should indicate a lot of activity, with frequent switching between high and low logic levels. A bus line that measures a constant high or a constant low or one that is continuously in between, indicates a problem. The problem may be in the microprocessor, the memory, or on the printed wiring board.

Check the printed wiring board for cracked or broken conducting paths and for bits of solder or other conductors which could short circuit a bus line. Substituting a good microprocessor IC will determine if that IC is at fault. Also, a logic analyzer could have been used to quickly locate a bus problem. However, if none of these tests produce results, the fault probably resides in the memory.

Memory

Basically, memory subsystems consist of combinational circuits for address decoding and memory ICs for data storage. When a gate in the address decoding circuitry fails, an entire section of memory usually becomes inaccessible. If it is a part of ROM which is inaccessible, the computer may appear to be dead, certain system functions may fail to work, or the system may lock up in a particular condition. When RAM is disabled, the system may still function properly for some programs, but may crash for others. Obviously, if the program never accesses the disabled portion of RAM, no problem will occur. In any event, gate failures in the address decoding circuitry disable large blocks of memory, not single addresses.

Troubleshooting address decoding circuitry is a matter of stimulating gate inputs and testing outputs for appropriate responses. A logic pulser is useful for stimulating the inputs, and an oscilloscope or a logic probe can be used to monitor the outputs. Of course, memory test diagnostics also test the address decoding circuitry, but the diagnostics only locate decode problems at particular addresses. Troubleshooting the circuits is required to locate the faulty components. Of course, an enabling signal may not be activating certain memory ICs. This would also cause blocks of memory to be inaccessible. Enabling signals can be detected with an oscilloscope.

The effects of a failure in a specific memory IC depend on the memory configuration. Consider first a memory comprised of bit-wide chips (16K $\times$ 1 RAM chips, for example). Failure of an entire chip of this type will cause every word in its address range to be incorrect. On the other hand, failure of a single storage location will cause a single bit error at one specific location. The exact effect of these failures on system operation depends on the type information stored in the faulty memory. An incorrectly stored instruction code may cause the system to crash, while an error in a data code might cause the system to behave erratically or to produce obviously incorrect results.

Word-wide memory devices (2K $\times$ 8 in an 8-bit system, for example) are more likely to produce system crashes when they fail. This is because word-wide devices are used almost exclusively in ROM, and ROM contains the system control program. Also, most ROM locations are accessed every time the system is used, while some RAM locations may be used intermittently depending on the program that is being executed.

Memory diagnostic software is the fastest method for locating memory faults. Such software tests RAM by writing a known code into every storage location and then reading the locations to see whether the code was stored properly. Errors are reported on the monitor screen.

ROM testing requires that the stored information be available for comparison. As each location is read, the data bus is monitored and compared to the correct information. A logic analyzer or other special memory test equipment is required for these comparisons.

It is clear that testing memory chips is a difficult task. Without using diagnostic routines, it is virtually impossible to test every memory location. With the exception of specially designed memory testers, logic analyzers are the most useful test instruments for memory troubleshooting because they allow simultaneous observation of all the bits in a stored word.

COMMON I/O DEVICES

The majority of hardware problems in microcomputer systems occur not in the CPU or in memory, but in the input/output devices — keyboards, disk drives, printers, monitors, cassette recorders, etc. With the exception of the monitor, all these I/O devices are electromechanical; that is, they contain moving parts. Mechanical failures account for the majority of microcomputer system hardware problems.

Keyboards

The most common problem associated with keyboards is dirty keyswitch contacts. When a dirty key is pressed, it may produce no character on the monitor or it may produce multiple characters. In either event, the solution is the same. The key switch must either be cleaned or replaced.

Some keyboards have individually removable key switches, while others are assembled as a unit and sealed. If the keys are individually accessible the keytops may be removed and the contacts cleaned with a contact burnisher and/or a chemical solvent. If the keyboard is a sealed unit, the entire unit may have to be replaced.

Sometimes keyboards are damaged when liquids are spilled on them. If such is the case, unless the liquid dries and leaves no residue, most of the keys will be affected. It is a good idea to replace the entire keyboard when this happens because it is practically impossible to completely clean every dirty contact. Besides, such liquids usually cause corrosion which will eventually produce additional failures.

Monitors

Troubleshooting monitors is very much like troubleshooting television systems. If screens are unstable and rolling, or if deflections are not linear, similar troubleshooting techniques must be used as are used on TV receivers. Consult the manufacturer's documentation to determine the coupling of the signals from computer to the monitor, and then use the same techniques as used for finding faults in TV receivers.

Other I/O Devices

The troubleshooting of electromechanical devices like printers and disk drives will not be covered here. In many cases, diagnostic routines are recommended by the manufacturer, and if a fault is located, service depots or servicemen usually have to perform the maintenance. The operating manuals for devices like these typically contain troubleshooting sections. These should always be consulted for the specific brand of peripheral unit.

I/O Interfaces

Finally, it should be noted that all these I/O devices are interfaced to the microcomputer system by relatively simple circuits. Gates are used to decode addresses and to generate selection signals. Registers may be used to store input or output data as it passes between the peripheral and the system data bus. In some instances special encoders are used to convert electromechanical actions to binary codes. Troubleshooting the interface circuits, therefore, requires only an understanding of the logic elements and the test equipment (logic probes, pulsers, oscilloscopes, etc.) already described in the previous chapter.

IC FAILURE MODES

There are some common types of failures for digital IC's. Understanding these failures and the symptoms they produce can make the troubleshooting procedure more efficient. Let's look at several of these. They apply to simple SSI circuits as well as to VLSI chips. The failures that are described occur internal to the IC.

Open Input Bond

It is possible that an input pin may lose its connection to the silicon chip inside the package. This is called an open input bond. When this occurs, a normal signal is applied to the pin, but the IC does not respond. In the case of a TTL IC, the input will always be interpreted by the gate IC as a high input, although the input to the gate is actually floating. The output of the IC responds as if the input were a high, regardless of the level applied to the pin.

Open Output Bond

When an output bond opens, the output level floats. An oscilloscope or a logic probe will indicate a constant floating level regardless of the input(s) applied to the circuit.

Input Bond Shorted to V_{cc} or Ground

An input bond shorted to a power supply connection causes that input to always be at that level (V_{cc} or ground). Changes in the signal at the input pin will have no effect on the circuit's operation. Instead, the internal circuitry of the IC reacts as though a constant high or low is applied.

Output Bond Shorted to V_{CC} or Ground

An output bond shorted to a power supply line causes that output to remain at a constant level. Stimulating the input(s) has no effect whatever on the output level.

Short Between Two Inputs or Outputs

When two pins are shorted internally, but no power supply line is involved, the levels on the two pins are always the same. Even if one connection is driven high while the other is driven low, the short circuit forces both connections low, because low dominates. Of course, if both connections are driven to the same level no conflict occurs and the circuit may appear to operate properly.

Internal Circuitry Failures

Finally, it is possible for the IC's circuitry simply to fail. The cause of such failure and the results it produces cannot be defined because there are too many possibilities, especially in complex circuits like microprocessors. Internal failures are the most difficult to acertain, since the problems they cause may be the same as those caused by external shorts, opens, etc. If such a failure is expected, substitute a new IC for the package to see if the IC is the problem.

TROUBLESHOOTING EXAMPLES

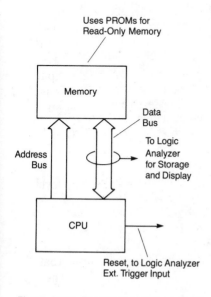

Uses PROMs for Read-Only Memory

Memory

Data Bus

To Logic Analyzer for Storage and Display

Address Bus

CPU

Reset, to Logic Analyzer Ext. Trigger Input

Figure 12.14 Troubleshooting an Erratic Reset Sequence

We conclude this chapter with a few examples of troubleshooting microcomputer systems using a logic analyzer. The examples are chosen to illustrate typical faults and to show how the logic analyzer is used to pinpoint the faults.

Example 12-1: After power up or after reset most general purpose microcomputer systems enter a "wait for interrupt" mode. In this mode the system idles, waiting for the operator to press a key on the keyboard. *Figure 12.14*, our first example, is a block diagram for a microcomputer which operates erratically when Reset is pressed. To locate the source of the problem, the data bus is monitored with a logic analyzer. The reset signal is used to trigger the logic analyzer.

When the system works properly, pressing Reset should cause a short program sequence to be executed by fetching instructions from a known PROM location. When that sequence is completed, the "wait for interrupt" mode is entered. With the set up shown here, pressing Reset allows the instruction sequence to be stored and displayed on the logic analyzer. In this case, the logic analyzer display would show that a storage location in PROM has changed a bit in an instruction word.

Instead of entering the "wait for interrupt" mode, the CPU was directed to an incorrect location in memory. The information at this location was interpreted as instructions and the computer attempted to execute them, causing the erratic operation. The troubleshooter was able to solve this problem quickly by comparing the logic analyzer display to the correct listing of the PROM program. A data domain display was used in this instance.

Example 12-2: In the second example, assume that CPU troubleshooting has reached the point of testing the address bus. The question is, does the program counter in the microprocessor generate the correct sequence of addresses as the system steps through the execution of programs?

Figure 12.15 illustrates the test setup. The system data bus is hardwired to the NOP (No Operation) instruction. After reset this will cause the program counter to step through the entire range of addresses, causing the NOP to be fetched and executed each time. By monitoring the address bus with a logic analyzer, faulty address generation can be spotted. Most logic analyzers are able to display the states of all sixteen address bus lines simultaneously.

A timing diagram is the most useful type of logic analyzer display for this operation. Sequentially counting through the addresses should cause each address line to carry a square wave signal, with the highest frequency on the least significant line, usually called A_0. The frequency on A_1 should be half that of A_0, the frequency on A_2 should be half that of A_1, and so on. *Figure 12.16* shows the correct timing diagram display for the first four address bus lines. If the program counter is not functioning properly, the display might indicate no signal or a signal with the wrong frequency on one or more of these address lines. Of course, an oscilloscope could have been used to test each address bus line one at a time, but the logic analyzer speeds the process by checking all sixteen at once.

Example 12-3: A final example illustrates a method for testing the control signals generated by a microprocessor during memory read operations. To make the test, an unconditional jump instruction, jump to location 0, is stored in memory location 0. Running this "program" causes the system to enter an endless loop, generating an endless cycle of read control signals. The logic analyzer can be used to display these signals using a timing diagram display for study by the technician. Memory enable and read/write control lines can be checked to make sure the proper signal levels are available at the right time. In this case, the oscilloscope would be just as useful as the logic analyzer since only a few signals are involved.

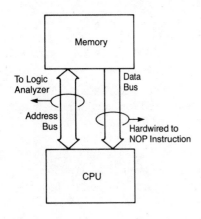

Figure 12.15   Testing the Address Bus

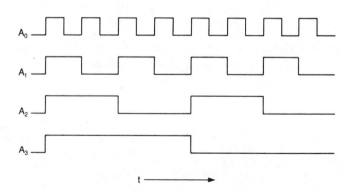

Figure 12.16   Correct Display of A_0 - A_3

SUMMARY

In this chapter we have considered the problem of troubleshooting faults in microcomputer systems. The examples dealt with hardware faults because they are easier to describe. Software faults, even though they are the majority of computer system problems, are difficult to describe because they are unique to the software being used.

Similarities and differences between microcomputers and simpler digital systems were investigated, and special digital troubleshooting tools were described. Four categories of microcomputer system failures were analyzed: the "dead" computer, the computer which displays random, useless data (garbage) when power is applied, the computer which operates properly for a period of time and then fails, and the computer which behaves erratically. Possible causes for each of these types of failures were explored and procedures for isolating the problem were suggested. CPU, memory, and I/O testing were outlined, and some examples of troubleshooting and testing procedures were given in conclusion.

It is important to realize that the success of all troubleshooting depends heavily on how well the technician understands the basic operation of the system under test and the equipment used for the testing. It is also necessary to understand that digital systems may fail in a virtually infinite number of ways, and that no textbook can predict all the possibilities. Hopefully, this book (and this chapter) can serve as a springboard for learning about troubleshooting, but nothing can take the place of experience. So dive in, and good luck.

CHAPTER 12 QUIZ

1. A factor which complicates computer system troubleshooting as compared to troubleshooting simple digital circuits is that computers:
   a. include sequential circuit elements.
   b. are software-controlled.
   c. process pulsating timing signals.
   d. are likely to include MOS devices.

2. A logic pulser is used to drive the input of a TTL inverter to the high level. A logic probe on the output should indicate what level if the device works properly?
   a. Low
   b. High
   c. Floating
   d. Intermediate

3. If the inverter in the previous question has its output bond shorted to V_{cc} the logic probe will indicate:
   a. low.
   b. high.
   c. floating.
   d. intermediate.

4. Primary advantage of logic analyzers is their ability to:
   a. stimulate and monitor gate circuits.
   b. store and execute diagnostic programs.
   c. calculate checksums.
   d. monitor many data lines simultaneously.

5. A test instrument designed to locate low impedance faults, such as a short circuit is a:
   a. current tracer.
   b. signature analyzer.
   c. logic pulser.
   d. logic clip.

6. When troubleshooting a "dead" computer, the first step is to:
   a. disconnect the peripherals.
   b. check system clock operation.
   c. reduce the ambient temperature.
   d. check the power supply.

7. Overheating may cause a computer system to:
   a. display garbage when power is applied.
   b. fail after a time of normal operation.
   c. appear dead when power is applied.
   d. operate at a higher-than-normal speed.

8. A single-bit error at a specific memory location would most likely be caused by a failure in:
   a. the address decoding circuitry.
   b. a bit-wide memory chip.
   c. a word-wide memory chip.
   d. the CPU.

9. The majority of problems in microcomputer systems occur in:
   a. the CPU.
   b. the reset circuitry.
   c. memory devices.
   d. I/O devices.

10. A TTL gate will always interpret an input as a high if:
   a. the output bond is shorted to V_{cc}.
   b. the input is shorted to another input.
   c. the input bond is open.
   d. the input bond is shorted to ground.

GLOSSARY

Accumulator: The basic working register of a computer. It stores the operands for and the results of an arithmetic logic unit operation.

Adder: A building block which provides a sum and a carry when adding two numbers.

Amplification: Increasing the voltage current or power level of an input signal to a circuit, by a predetermined ratio, before it reaches the output.

Amplitude Distortion: In an amplifier, a change in the relative output waveshape compared to the input waveshape.

Anode: 1. In a CRT, those (positive) electrodes used to concentrate and accelerate the electron beam. 2. Name for any positive electrode.

Aquadag: A conductive graphite coating on the inner side walls of CRTs. It is generally used as a post-deflection and acceleration anode.

Architecture: Operational structure of a CPU or microprocessor system.

Arithmetic and Logic Unit (ALU): A portion of the Central Processor Unit which performs mathematical operations for calculations and logical operations to make decisions.

Assembly Language: An abbreviated computer language using mnemonics which humans can use to program computers. It is converted to machine language code by a program called an assembler.

Asynchronous Device: A device in which the speed of operation is not related to any frequency in the system to which it is connected. There is an irregular time interval between successive bits, characters, or events (opposite of *synchronous*).

Auxiliary Storage Systems (auxiliary memory): Extra computer memory storage capacity besides main memory, such as magnetic tape, disk, or drum.

Avalanche voltage: In a semiconductor, the voltage that produces the non-destructive breakdown of PN junction resistance.

Bandwidth: The band of frequencies over which an amplifier's gain remains within specified limits. In the case of resonant circuits, it is the band of frequencies over which the resonant effect exists.

Barrier Potential: In a semiconductor, the electric field between the acceptor ions and the donor ions at a junction.

Baud: A unit of signaling speed equal to the number of discrete conditions or signal events per second.

Bias: A fixed voltage or current level applied to a circuit to establish its operating conditions.

Bias Oscillator: The oscillator that produces a 60-100kHz or higher signal used to supply the record head with magnetic biasing to obtain a linear recording characteristic, and supply the erase head signal in a tape recorder.

Binary Code: A code in which each allowable position has one of two possible states (0 and 1).

Binary Coded Decimal (BCD): A binary numbering system for coding decimal numbers in groups of 4 bits.

Bit: 1. An acronym for binary digit. 2. The smallest piece of binary information. 3. Specification of one of two possible alternatives, often designated as 0 and 1.

Blocking (Coupling) Capacitor: Capacitor used to couple one stage to the next by allowing only the ac signal to pass, while blocking the dc bias.

Boost Voltage: The voltage resulting from the combination of the B+ voltage from the power supply and the average value of the voltage pulses from the horizontal sweep circuit in TV receivers.

Branch Instruction: An instruction to a computer to follow one of several courses of action, depending on the nature of control events that occur later.

Branch (Program): A program is said to branch when an instruction other than the next instruction in the program sequence is executed.

Breakdown Voltage: That minimum voltage which will ionize the atoms of an insulator, resulting in conduction.

Bus (Address, Data, Control): In a computer, one or more conductors used as a path over which information is transmitted from any of several sources to any of several destinations.

Bypass Capacitor: A capacitor in a circuit used to shunt certain frequencies around something, or to ground.

Byte: A sequence of usually eight adjacent binary digits operated upon as a unit.

Cathode: 1. In a CRT, the element that produces electrons in the electron gun. 2. General name for any negative electrode.

Central Processor Unit (CPU): Part of a computer system which contains the arithmetic and logic unit, the control unit and special register groups. It performs arithmetic operations, controls instruction processing, and provides timing signals.

Chip Enable Input: A control input that when active permits operation of the integrated circuit for input, internal transfer, manipulation, refreshing, and/or output of data.

Chroma: The quality that characterizes color (hue and saturation) without reference to brightness in color TV.

Clear: To remove data and return all circuitry to an initial condition, usually 0.

Clock Generator: An electronic circuit that generates periodic clock (timing) signals for synchronization of a system.

Closed-Loop System: A control system in which information from the output is fed back and compared to the input to generate an error signal. This error signal is then used to generate the new output signal.

Color Burst: In a color receiver, approximately nine cycles of chrominance subcarrier added to the horizontal blanking pedestal, used as a phase reference.

Color Subcarrier: A monochrome signal to which modulation sidebands have been added to convey color information.

Combinational Logic: Logic circuits whose outputs depends only on the present logic inputs.

Command: An operation the computer performs in the immediate mode.

Comment Field: In a computer, an area located in a record assigned for entry of explanatory comments about a program.

Comparator: A circuit that compares two signals and provides a digital output that indicates which signal is larger, or if they are equal.

Compiler: A master program that translates high-level program statements into machine language, allocates storage, and produces a program for the job.

Complement: A number that can be derived from a specified number by subtracting it from a second specified number. The negative of a number is often represented by its complement.

Conditional Jump: A jump that occurs if specified criteria are met.

Convergence: The precise intersection of the three electron beams at the correct point, so they strike only the appropriate color dot of a TV's CRT.

Cross Assembler: A program which converts symbolic machine instructions to the actual machine instructions. However, the machine language generated is for a different machine than the one on which the assembler was executed.

Crossover Distortion: The distortion produced by two amplifiers operating in class B and AB, in a push-pull configuration.

Crossover Network: An electrical filter that separates the output signal from the audio amplifier into two or more frequency bands for a multispeaker system.

Crosstalk: The undesired transferring of signals between two adjacent magnetic tape tracks or channels during playback.

Current Transfer Ratio (β): The current gain of a transistor, where the collector current change is compared to the base current change.

Cutoff Frequency: Specified end frequency points that define bandwidth. In the case of resonance, the frequency at which the effects of resonance fall outside specified limits.

Cycle: An interval of space or time in which one set of events or phenomena is completed.

DC Offset: A bias voltage added to an ac signal.

Daisy Chaining: In a computer, a bus line interconnected so that the signal passes serially from one unit to the next.

Damping: Absorption of electrical or mechanical energy to suppress oscillations or vibrations.

Data Base: A large collection of information.

Decoder: 1. A circuit that delivers a pulse to one of 2^n lines as selected by an n-bit binary code. 2. A combinational building-block receiving several parallel inputs, which "recognizes" one or more combinations of input bits and outputs a unique signal for each combination. 3. A conversion circuit that accepts digital input information that appears on a small number of lines and selects and activates one line of a large number of output lines.

De-emphasis: For recording and/or FM transmission, reduction in the higher audio frequency levels during reception or playback, to compensate for the original pre-emphasis inserted during transmission or recording. This technique improves S/N.

Degenerative Feedback: The combining of output with the input of an amplifier in an out-of-phase relationship, partially canceling the output.

Delayed Sweep: In an oscilloscope, a type of sweep system that doesn't begin until a preset time has elapsed after triggering.

Differential Amplifier: A circuit that amplifies the difference between two input signals.

Direct Access: Pertaining to the process of obtaining data from, or placing data into, storage where the time required for such access is independent of the location of the data most recently obtained or placed in storage.

Direct Addressing: 1. A basic addressing procedure designed to reach any point in main storage directly. 2. Method of programming that has the address of data contained in the instruction that is to be used.

Direct Memory Access Channel (DMA): A method of input/output for a system that uses a small processor whose sole task is that of controlling input/output, transfers to/from memory.

Distortion: The altering of the output waveform as compared to the input, by an amplifier in an unacceptable way.

Distributed Capacitance: In a circuit, component, or transmission line, the capacitance that is caused by the relative proximity of all conductors to each other.

Doping: In semiconductor fabrication, the addition of controlled minute amounts of impurities to create free electrons or free holes.

Dump: To copy the contents of all or part of a storage, usually from an internal storage into an external storage.

Duplex: In communications, pertaining to a simultaneous two-way independent transmission. Contrast with half duplex. Synonymous with full duplex.

Duty Cycle: The average amount of time a circuit or component is active.

Dynamic Memory: Read/write memory that must be read or written into periodically to maintain the storage of information.

Eddy Current: In a transformer, a loss caused by tiny short-circuit current loops induced into the iron core by the varying magnetic field.

Effective Address: The address that is derived by applying any specified indexing or indirect addressing results to the specified address and that is actually used to identify the location of the current operand.

Electron Gun: The subassembly in the neck of a CRT that emits a narrow beam of electrons.

Electrostatic Deflection: A method of controlling the electron beam in a CRT by applying a varying charge to the pairs of elements through which the beam passes.

Encoder: A circuit that delivers an n-bit binary code that corresponds to the one of the 2^n lines that has an input signal on it.

Execute: That portion of a computer cycle during which a selected instruction is performed.

Extended Addressing: An addressing procedure designed as an operation that can reach practically any place in memory.

Fall Time: The time duration during which the trailing edge of a pulse is decreasing from 90 percent to 10 percent of its maximum amplitude.

Feedback: The return of a sampling of an amplifier's output into its input, to affect the output.

Fetch: The act of the CPU when it obtains the next instruction from memory.

Flag Bit: A single bit, whose status is used to indicate that a certain condition had occurred, such as the end of a word.

Flywheel Effect: In a resonant circuit, the tendency of the circuit to keep oscillating once it is pulsed. This principle is used for transmitter output stages.

Form Factor: A figure of merit which indicates how much the current or voltage departs from a continuous, non-pulsating current.

Forward Current: In a P-N junction device, the current that flows in the low-resistance direction.

Frequency-Shift Keying (FSK): A method of transmitting digital information that utilizes two tones, one representing a 1 level, the other a 0 level.

Front End: The complete tuner assembly of a receiver, with an antenna input and IF output.

Gain: 1. The increase (or decrease) of a signal level. 2. The ratio of a system's output magnitude to its input magnitude.

Glitch: Term given to a random signal which causes data or addressing errors.

Half-Duplex: A circuit that carries information in both directions, but only in one direction at a time.

Half-Power Points: The upper and lower frequency points of a frequency response curve at which the real power dissipation in the circuit is exactly one-half of what it is at the mid-band frequency.

Handshaking Signals: A colloquial expression describing a process whereby a predetermined arrangement of characters is exchanged by the receiving and transmitting equipment to establish synchronization.

Hardware: Physical equipment, as opposed to the computer program or method of use, e.g., mechanical, magnetic, electrical, or electronic devices.

Hard-Wired: An expression meaning permanently wired or having dc continuity.

Hexadecimal: A system of numbers whose base is 16.

Hole: In the valence structure of a semiconductor, a mobile vacancy which acts like a positive mass.

Immediate Address: 1. Pertaining to an instruction which contains the value of an operand. 2. Pertaining to an instruction in which an address part contains the value of an operand rather than its address. Synonymous with zero-level address.

Impedance: The combined dc and ac opposition to the flow of current.

Impurity: A material added to a semiconductor material to produce either a P- or N-type material.

Indexed Address: An address that is added to the contents of an index register prior to or during the execution of a computer instruction.

Indexing: In a computer, a method of address modification that is implemented by means of index registers.

Indirect Addressing: A form of computer mass-referencing where one memory location stores the correct address of the data sought.

Instruction: 1. A statement that specifies an operation and the values or locations of its operands. 2. A step in a microprocessor program.

Instruction Code: Digital information that represents an instruction to be performed by a computer.

Instruction Cycle: The period of time during which a programmed system obeys an instruction.

Instruction Register: A register that stores an instruction for execution.

Instruction Set: Description of a computer capability through listing of all the instructions the computer can execute.

Interface: Term given to the circuitry which performs I/O signal-conditioning between the processor and a peripheral device.

Interrupts: An efficient method of quickly requesting a computer's attention to a particular external event.

Intrinsic Material: A semiconductor material with an equal number of holes and electrons.

Inverter: A binary digital building-block with one input and one output. The output state is the inverse (opposite) of the input state.

Inverting Amplifier: An amplifying device whose output is 180 degrees out of phase with its input.

Ion: An atom or molecule with an electrostatic charge.

I-signal: See Q-Signal.

Jump: A departure from the normal sequence of executing instructions in a computer.

Jump Instruction: An instruction which causes deviation from the normal sequence of execution.

Kirchhoff's Current Law: A circuit analysis law which states that the sum of the currents arriving at any point in a circuit must equal the sum of the currents leaving that point.

Kirchhoff's Voltage Law: A circuit analysis law which states that the algebraic sum of all the voltages encountered in any loop equals zero.

Label: One or more characters used to identify a statement or an item of data in a program.

Leakage Current: The undesirable flow of current through insulators, dielectric materials, or P-N junctions.

Leakage Resistance: The normally high resistance of an insulator such as a dielectric between the plates of a capacitor.

Level Shifter: An interfacing device that allows one family of logic devices to connect to another.

Lissajous Pattern: Patterns produced on an oscilloscope when two different sine waves are input to the horizontal and vertical system simultaneously; useful for phase and frequency comparison.

Load: Any device that receives energy from another circuit.

Load Line: A graph showing the operating characteristics of an amplifying device for a given fixed load value.

Local Oscillator: The oscillator that provides the signal for the mixer stage in a receiver.

Loop: Term used to describe an operation in a computer program which is performed many times in succession. Exit may be after the loop has been performed a specified number of times or after specific conditions have been satisfied.

Low Pass Filter: An L-C network that allows only the frequencies below a specified cutoff point to pass.

Luminance Signal: The signal that provides the picture detail information in a color TV receiver.

Machine Language: The lowest level programming language. The coded instructions consist of a string of binary digits, which can be recognized by a machine.

Magnetic Deflection: For a CRT, the deflection method that uses a yoke to provide electron beam bending.

Main Storage: The general-purpose storage of a computer. Usually, main storage can be accessed directly by the operating registers. Contrast with *auxiliary storage*.

Majority Carrier: The predominant carrier in a semiconductor type.

Mask: A pattern of characters that is used to control the retention or elimination of portions of another pattern of characters.

Memory Refresh: The periodic renewing of data or data-carrying electrical charge in a semiconductor memory, such as the MOS type.

Menu: A display on the screen which lists the choices available to the user. Also called a directory or catalog.

Microwave: The range of frequencies around and above 1000MHz.

Mixer: In a receiver, the stage that combines the RF signal from the preselector with the output of the local oscillator to produce the beat frequencies.

Mnemonic: Term given to a phrase which defines an assembly language step in easy-to-remember symbols.

Modulus: A number designating the number of states through which a counter sequences during each cycle.

Multiplexing: The division of a transmission facility into two or more channels.

N-Type Material: Pure semiconductor material that has been doped with an electron donor.

Negative Temperature Coefficient: The characteristic of a PN junction that causes electron conduction to increase as temperature is increased.

Negative Ion: An atom which has gained one or more electrons.

Negative Resistance: The characteristic of PN junctions that causes electron conduction to decrease as voltage is increased.

Nest: To imbed subroutines or data in other subroutines or data at a different hierarchical level such that the different levels of routines or data can be executed or accessed recursively.

Non-Volatile Memory: Any memory which can hold information even if the operating power is removed.

Null: In a bridge circuit potentiometer, the condition where the bridge is balanced and no current flows through the microammeter.

Object Code: Output from a compiler or assembler which is itself executable machine code or is suitable for processing to produce executable machine code.

Octal: A system of numbers whose base is 8.

Ohm's Law: Circuit current varies directly with the applied voltage and varies inversely with the resistance of the circuit. Stated in equation form as: $I = E/R$, $E = IR$, $R = E/I$.

Operand: The quantity that is affected, manipulated, or operated upon.

Operating System: 1. A brief program that is a type of management function which oversees the information stored in the computer and directs the activities of its various components such as disk drives, keyboard, peripherals, etc. 2. A set of programs which monitors and controls the execution of various user programs.

Operational Amplifier: A standard analog building block with two inputs, one output and capable of very high voltage gain.

Operator: A symbol which represents an operation to be performed on one or more operands.

Output Enable: A signal applied to three-state devices to connect internal outputs to external bus lines.

P-Type Material: Pure semiconductor material that has been doped with an electron acceptor.

Page Addressing: A procedure of memory addressing where memory is divided into segments, each of which can be addressed by the available addressing capability.

Parallax Error: When reading a meter, the reading error caused by reading the meter from an angle.

Parity Bit: An additional bit used with a binary character code or electronic channel data processor to provide a check for accuracy.

Phase Angle: In color TV encoding/decoding, the method of transmitting hue information, where the time relationship between the 3.58MHz burst signal and the I-Q vector is the reference.

Piezoelectric Effect: The phenomena exhibited by certain materials, that when a voltage is applied to them, they expand or contract contrast. Also, when they are subjected to stress, they generate a tiny voltage.

Point-of-Use Regulation: A circuit design technique where the regulator device is at the load instead of within the power supply.

Polling: Periodic interrogation of each of the terminals to share a communication line to determine whether it requires attention.

Positional Weighting Factor: The relative value of digits occupying each location in a complete number.

Positive Ion: An atom that has lost one or more electrons.

Positive Logic: In electronic binary digital circuits, the higher, more positive of the two voltage levels represents an enabled condition, and the lower, more negative level represents a disabled condition.

Pre-emphasis: See *de-emphasis*.

Priority Interrupt: A method of providing commands that have precedence over others.

Processor: The portion of a computer which performs all decision-making, arithmetic, timing, control, and routing functions.

Program: A series of actions proposed in order to achieve a desired result.

Program Counter: A register that holds the address of the memory location containing the instruction word to be executed next in the time sequence, following the current operation.

Propagation Delay Time: The time between the application of a digital input waveform and the resulting output.

Push-Pull Operation: A type of output stage where the negative and positive alternations of the input signal are divided between two amplifying devices, allowing Class B or AB operation and improving efficiency.

Q-Signal: In a color TV, one of the 2 signals used to modulate the chrominance subcarrier. The other is the I-signal. The two signals which are 90 degrees out of phase, are each a combination of the B-Y and R-Y signals.

Quality Factor (Q): The ratio of the reactive power in an inductance to the real power dissipated by its internal resistance. In a coil or capacitor, the figure of merit, where the reactance to resistance ratio indicates internal losses.

Ramp Voltage: In an oscilloscope, the rising portion of the sawtooth wave, which sweeps the beam from left to right.

Random Access Memory (RAM): Storage arrangement in which each byte of information may be retrieved within the same amount of time as any other byte.

Raster: On a CRT screen, the illumination of the screen by the scanning beam, regardless of the presence of an actual image.

Reactance: The opposition to the flow of ac by inductive and capacitive circuit elements.

Read-Only Memory (ROM): A type of memory whose locations can be accessed directly and read, but cannot be written into.

Rejection Filter: A filter which offers a very high impedance to a band of frequencies.

Relative Address: The number that specifies the difference between the absolute address and the base address.

Reset: An input used to cause all binary elements to assume a predetermined state.

Resonance: A circuit whose inductive and capacitive reactances are the same at a particular frequency.

Retrace: Referring to the raster on a CRT, the return of the beam to the point where it must begin the next scan.

Reverse Breakdown Voltage: The voltage that produces a sudden increase in reverse current in a semiconductor.

Ringing: In a steep wavefront waveform, the damped oscillation caused by excitation of circuit LC resonance.

Rise Time: The time required for the leading edge of a pulse to rise from 10 percent to 90 percent of its fixed value.

Rotary Transformer: On a VCR, a device used to couple, through a micromagnetic gap, the rotating tape heads to the circuitry; one set of windings rotates with the head assembly, the other is stationary.

Routine or Programmed Routine: A series of instructions followed by a programmed system in doing a particular job; usually contained within a main program.

Saturation: 1. The absence of white light in a given color. 2. The operating condition of a transistor where an increase in base current produces no further increase in collector current.

Serial: The sequential processing of the individual parts of a whole such as the bits of a character or the characters of a word.

Set: To set a stored bit means to make it a 1.

Shunt: A precision, low value resistor placed across a current reading meter, to increase its range.

Simplex: A circuit which can carry information in only one direction; for example, broadcasting.

Sink: In a digital circuit, a device which drains off current from a source.

Skin Effect: The tendency of high frequency current to flow near the surface of a conductor.

Software: Programs, routines, codes, and other written information for use with digital computers.

Source Code Program: A computer program written in a high-level or in assembly language, which must be converted to an object code for execution.

Source Current: Supply of current from a device upstream from the sink source.

Stack: A block of successive memory locations that are accessible from one end of a last-in/first-out basis.

Static Memory: Memory that maintains information storage as long as power is on, and does not require refreshing.

Stored Program: A set of instructions in memory specifying the operations to be performed.

Subroutine: A small portion of a routine which performs a specific function as part of a larger task.

Synchronous: A term applied to a computer in which the performance of a sequence of operations is controlled by an equally-spaced clock signal. See *asynchronous*.

Tank Circuit: A parallel combination of an inductor and capacitor which resonate at a certain frequency.

Temporary Storage: In programming, storage locations reserved for intermediate results; synonymnous with working storage.

Thermal Runaway: In a semiconductor, the self-destructive effect of overheating, where heating at the collector junction causes collector current to increase, causing more heating, etc., until the device is destroyed.

Three-State Output: An output from an electronic circuit that has three possible states — active high, active low, and high impedance.

Time Constant: 1. A number characterizing the time required for the output of a device, subsystem or circuit to reach 63 percent of the final value following a step change of its input. 2. Equal to the product of R (in ohms) times C (in farads) in a resistive-capacitive circuit.

Transducer: A device that converts between two forms of energy, such as a loudspeaker, microphone or an LED.

Transient Response: The immediate response of a system to a change of input.

Tweeter: A middle-to-high frequency speaker.

Two's Complement: A form of computer binary arithmetic used to perform subtraction using addition techniques.

Volatile Memory: Any memory which can store information only as long as power is applied.

Voltage Amplifier: A circuit that is designed to enhance the output voltage level of an input signal.

Voltage-Controlled Oscillator: An oscillator whose frequency is varied by an applied bias voltage.

Winchester Disk Drive: A disk drive which uses a rigid (hard) disk which normally is not user-accessible; the read/write head does not make physical contact with the disk surface.

Woofer: A low-to-middle frequency speaker.

Word: A computer word is composed of one or more bytes which must be treated by the computer as a whole.

Write: To record data in a storage device or a data medium.

Zener Voltage (Breakdown Voltage): The reverse bias voltage applied to a PN junction for which large currents are drawn for relatively small voltage increases.

INDEX

QUIZ ANSWERS

Chapter 1
1. b
2. a
3. b
4. d
5. c
6. a
7. d
8. b
9. c
10. d
11. c
12. b
13. d
14. a
15. b
16. b
17. c
18. a
19. b
20. a

Chapter 2
1. c
2. b
3. a
4. b
5. c
6. b
7. c
8. d
9. b
10. b

Chapter 3
1. c
2. d
3. a
4. b
5. b
6. d
7. c
8. d
9. a
10. b

Chapter 4
1. c
2. d
3. c
4. b
5. a
6. c
7. b
8. d
9. b
10. a
11. a
12. d
13. d
14. b
15. b
16. a
17. c
18. d
19. a
20. a

Chapter 5
1. b
2. b
3. a
4. d
5. c
6. a
7. c
8. b
9. d
10. c
11. a
12. b
13. b
14. a
15. d
16. a
17. a
18. c
19. c
20. b

Chapter 6
1. b
2. d
3. a
4. a
5. b
6. c
7. a
8. a
9. a
10. b
11. d
12. d
13. b
14. d
15. a
16. c
17. a
18. a
19. b
20. d

Chapter 7
1. c
2. a
3. b
4. c
5. a
6. a
7. d
8. b
9. a
10. b
11. d
12. c
13. a
14. b
15. c
16. b
17. d
18. a
19. c
20. c

Chapter 8
1. c
2. b
3. a
4. b
5. b
6. a
7. d
8. d
9. b
10. a
11. c
12. a
13. c
14. a
15. d
16. b
17. d
18. a
19. d
20. b

Chapter 9
1. d
2. c
3. a
4. a
5. c
6. b
7. b
8. d
9. b
10. d

Chapter 10
1. d
2. b
3. d
4. b
5. d
6. c
7. d
8. b
9. c
10. b

Chapter 11
1. c
2. c
3. d
4. d
5. b
6. c
7. a
8. d
9. a
10. a

Chapter 12
1. b
2. a
3. b
4. d
5. a
6. d
7. b
8. b
9. d
10. a